A CIVIL WAR SOLDIER'S DIARY

A Civil War
SOLDIER'S DIARY

★ ★ ★

Valentine C. Randolph, 39th Illinois Regiment

Edited by David D. Roe

With commentary and annotations

by Stephen R. Wise

NORTHERN ILLINOIS UNIVERSITY PRESS

DeKalb

Published by the Northern Illinois University Press, DeKalb, Illinois 60115

Manufactured in the United States using acid-free paper

Frontispiece courtesty of—Ohio Wesleyan University Historical Collection.

Library of Congress Cataloging-in-Publication Data

Randolph, Valentine C. (Valentine Cartright), 1838–1895.

A Civil War soldier's diary / Valentine C. Randolph, 39th Illinois Regiment ; edited by David D. Roe ; with commentary and annotations by Stephen R. Wise.—1st ed.

p. cm.

Includes bibliographical references and index.

ISBN-13: 978-0-87580-343-2 (clothbound : alk. paper)

ISBN-10: 0-87580-343-1 (clothbound : alk. paper)

1. Randolph, Valentine C. (Valentine Cartright), 1838-1895—Diaries. 2. United States. Army. Illinois Infantry Regiment, 39th (1861–1865). 3. Illinois—History—Civil War, 1861–1865—Personal narratives. 4. United States—History—Civil War, 1861–1865—Personal narratives. 5. Illinois—History—Civil War, 1861–1865—Regimental histories. 6. United States—History—Civil War, 1861–1865—Regimental histories. 7. Soldiers—Illinois—Diaries. I. Roe, David D. II. Wise, Stephen R., 1952- III. Title.

E505.539th .R36 2006

973.7473092—dc22

2005029203

Contents

Maps

Preface

David D. Roe

I received the diary of Valentine C. Randolph as a gift from Deborah Gay, a longtime family friend. Deborah decided to move from Ohio to California, sometime around 1970, and my mother and I found ourselves helping her to pack her belongings for the long move. As we were finishing, she looked at me and said, "I understand you like things from the Civil War."

"Well, yes," I responded.

"Wait right here. I've got something that I think you will appreciate." When she returned, she handed me a brown paper bag with writing across the front, which read: "Valentine Cartwright Randolph was my mother's uncle. I have been told many times that he was visiting cousins in Tennessee when the war broke out and went home to Illinois to enlist. He was a theological student and carried Greek and Hebrew testaments with him all during his army service." I opened the bag and found six bound essay notebooks and one envelope with loose pages from a seventh notebook, filled with handwritten daily entries that started on the day Randolph enlisted and ended the evening before he arrived home after being mustered out of the army.

After I recovered from the shock of learning that such a treasure belonged to someone I knew personally, I told Deborah I would read the diary as quickly as possible and then ship it to her in California. She smiled. "No, you don't understand. I want you to have it. I know you'll appreciate it for what it is and will take good care of it. It's yours now."

When I finished reading the diary, I knew I was in possession of an important piece of history. I knew I must get it into print so as to share it with other people who could enjoy Randolph's story and its historical significance. I had a problem, though. I am not a typist, and I did not want to lend the diary long enough to have it typed by a professional. I have allowed several people to look at the diary over the years; they all agreed that it should be published.

In 2000 I obtained a voice recognition program for my computer, which can convert speech into print. It took me about six months to read the diary aloud to the computer, and another year of editing and reediting to correct misinterpreted words and phrases and to check the transcript against the original. I wanted the transcript to reflect the original diary entries exactly. If Randolph misspelled a word or proper name, I copied it just the way he wrote it. If a particular spelling was so terrible that it might cause confusion, I corrected it in brackets. When Randolph dropped a word, I tried to figure out from the context what he meant to say and inserted the missing word in brackets. I did not have to make very many such corrections—this is the most well-written diary I have had occasion to read. Throughout, I have tried to keep this transcription as true to the original as possible so that readers will experience Randolph's evocative way of writing.

I would like to warn the impatient reader that Randolph's diary starts slowly. Please keep reading! Halfway through the second volume, Randolph will draw you into the world of an infantry soldier and you will relive every step of his tour in the army through his words. You will tour the ruins of Fort Frederick, join the siege of Charleston and Fort Sumter, and witness the parading and execution of two deserters. Randolph's words paint an unusually clear picture of the day-to-day activities of Company I of the Thirty-ninth Illinois Infantry. Some of the events he describes are not found in any other known diary or history for this regiment. Here, then, is a fascinating eyewitness account of the Civil War, kept by a soldier with a unique flair for detail.

A CIVIL WAR SOLDIER'S DIARY

Introduction

Stephen R. Wise

In many ways, the Civil War regiment served as an extended family for its soldiers, reflecting both their community and their home. The regiment functioned as heart and soul of the Civil War military. It was the building block for all larger formations: brigade, division, corps, and army. Soldiers experienced the war through their regiments while serving with their comrades.

The Thirty-ninth Illinois was a typical U.S. regiment, with 806 men from nearly every conceivable background and profession in its ranks. Private Valentine Cartwright Randolph, from the town of Lincoln in Logan County, Illinois, was one of these men. On September 16, 1861, Randolph joined Company I, recruited primarily from the hamlet of LeRoy, in McLean County, Illinois. Well-educated, he had attended both Illinois College and Dickinson College. He was trained in the classics and knew Greek, Latin, and Hebrew and was learning Spanish at the time of his enlistment. Randolph was a devout Christian and a keen observer of people and geography. From his first association with the Thirty-ninth Illinois, Randolph kept a journal to chronicle both his adventures and the regiment's career. In a sense, the journal became a personal travelogue full of fascinating descriptions and candid comments.

THE DIARY OF

Valentine Cartwright Randolph

Preface

What things I have seen, what things I have experienced and what things I have heard, since enlisting in the service of the United States, are, in part, herein written. My object in keeping this diary was to remind me, in my old days, what occurred while I was a soldier. The greater part of this book has been written amidst great confusion. That there are many mistakes in grammar and orthography I am aware. These and all other errors I trust will not be criticised too severely. This was not intended for any body to read excepting myself and those whom I permit.

V. C. Randolph

Bath, Va.

Volume 1

LINCOLN, ILLINOIS, SEPTEMBER–DECEMBER 1861

The Thirty-ninth Illinois Regiment of Infantry was born in the law office of Moore and Osborn, in the Tremont Building on Dearborn Street, Chicago, Illinois. Fort Sumter had been fired on, and a group of patriotic businessmen led by Thomas O. Osborn decided to raise a company of volunteers for immediate service. Soon the men expanded their goal and began enlisting a regiment. In fewer than six weeks, some thirteen hundred men had volunteered. Named the Yates Phalanx after Illinois governor Richard Yates, the regiment anxiously waited to be mustered into Federal service. Unfortunately, the Illinois quota for President Lincoln's initial call for seventy-five thousand volunteers had already been filled. Discouraged, some men joined other units that had been accepted for Federal service, but the regiment's core remained, and in the wake of the Northern disaster at First Bull Run, Lincoln issued a new call for volunteers and the regiment was accepted for government service.

The regiment's initial camp was at the Wigwam, the site of the 1860 Republican presidential convention in Chicago. In late July 1861, a veteran of the Mexican War, Austin Light, took over the volunteers and began organizing the regiment. In early August, the regiment moved to the Illinois training depot at Camp Mather, and the monotony of drill became a daily routine as the men evolved from citizens to soldiers. Toward the end of September, when the men elected their officers, Austin Light officially became the regiment's colonel and Thomas Osborn its lieutenant colonel. The Thirty-ninth Illinois was mustered into the service of the United States on the morning of October 11, 1861.

Randolph and the Thirty-ninth Illinois were then shipped to the Camp of Instruction at Benton Barracks, St. Louis, where the regiment remained for a few weeks and underwent additional training. In late October, orders were received for the unit to proceed to Williamsport, Maryland, to join Colonel Ward H. Lamon's brigade, Banks's division, Army of the Potomac. A thirty-six-hour train trip carried the men to their new home along the Potomac River. There they received their permanent arms and equipment. Colonel Light was dismissed from service because of an incident that had occurred previously, while he was a corporal in the regular army. The regiment's historian—Charles M. Clark, the regiment's surgeon—refused to comment on the reasons for the dismissal but did observe that some felt the removal to be unjust and commented that "our 'Light' had gone out."[1] Light's replacement, Thomas Osborn, was well received and enjoyed the regiment's confidence.

In early December 1861, the Thirty-ninth was moved across the Potomac River to Alpine Station, Virginia, and distributed to guard the Baltimore and Ohio Railroad. A small earthwork, Fort Osborn, was built at Alpine Station. For the rest of the month the men skirmished with enemy cavalry, but the year ended with no major engagement. —*S.R.W.*

★ ★ ★ ★ ★

—Dulce pro patria est mori [sweet it is to die for one's country].[2]

If I should fall in battle please write below, "He died like a man," and send this book to Mrs. N. M. Randolph, Lincoln, Illinois.

September 16, 1861—Lieutenant Waller, who stayed all night with us last night, Bid goodbye to the family this morning, when he came to me, I said to him, "Do you think that I would make a good soldier?" "Yes sir," said he, "first rate." After a few moments thought, I determined to enlist. We have but few days to live; one had as well die fighting for his country as not. "To die for one's country is sweet." Farewell to home and friends dear. If the Lord will, I shall see you again; but if I should fall fighting for our country, for truth, for justice and for God, weep not for me. We will soon be together where sorrow is a stranger, "where the weary are at rest and the wicked cease from troubling." In God is my trust. I hate war. O that peace might again smile on our country! Duty only calls me away from the usual vocations of life. May the temple of Janus soon be closed is my wish. I would never treat with Traitors. If the Union cannot be maintained one and inseperable let it be forever blotted out of existence. I am very fearful for the perpituity of our country.[3]

After enlisting, I was greatly hurried to get off in time. Took the train at eleven o'clock and twenty minutes for Atlanta. From Atlanta we went to Waynesville. The men in whose wagons we rode charged us 25 cts apiece. Shame on them for their stingyness. We stayed all night at Waynesville.

Sept. 17—Rose early this morning and took a walk in a beautiful grove. In the forenoon we endeavored to get some new recruits but did not succeed. We left Waynesville in a hack in the afternoon. Reached Clinton about night, where we taried till morning. Spirits rather low.

Sept. 18—Started from Clinton early in the morning. There were two passengers in the hack, besides Lieutenant Waller and myself, the most interesting of whom was a fair young lady. I tried to ingratiate myself into her feelings. To my sorrow I learned, when I got to Mt. Pleasant, that she was married. Nothing very serious. All right. Next time I will be more cautious.

Sept. 19—This morning Henry Poff and I visited a friend. Henry was requested, by the lady of the house where we went, to kill a chicken for dinner. Hen took a shot gun and went out into the poultry yard; when he got a flock just to his notion he fired away and killed three fat young chickens. We had chicken at dinner as plentiful as the Israelites had quails in the wilderness. In the afternoon I went to see a young lady. I became so interested in her company that I determined to stay all night with her. My visit was countermanded; news came that we must go to Chicago on Saturday and on Monday to St. Louis. Hen and I went on down to Point Isabel and tarried there all night.[4]

Sept. 20—Walked to Mt. Pleasant this morning distant 8 miles. Time drug heavily today till in the afternoon when Hen and I went to see some of the fair sex. I sat up late at night writing and reflecting on the dangers to which I would soon be exposed. I fear not the enemy so much as the temptations that I will have to contend with in camp.

Sept. 21—This morning bid farewell to friends in Mt. Pleasant. We started to Urbana, at half past nine o'clock, where we took the train for Chicago. Went to Urbana in a two horse wagon. When we got out of Mt. Pleasant some of the boys commenced singing that beautiful song "I belong to the band." We reached Urbana in the afternoon. Nothing strange occured on the way. We did not start for Chicago till about two o'clock in the night consequently we got but little sleep.

Sept. 22—Had rather a tedious journey from Urbana to Chicago. There nothing to relieve the monotony of the scenery. All the towns that we passed through, excepting Kankakee, are small. Kankakee, on a river of the same name, is a large business place. Passed over a great deal of swampy prairie. We arrived at camp, about ten o'clock A.M. Eat dinner, took a nap of sleep and was sworn in. In the evening, at dress parade, there was a wedding in camp. One of the privates thought best to take to himself a wife. May good luck attend him. We had a lecture this afternoon on temperance. At night I attended church at the Clark Street Chapel. The sermon was not at all suited to the times.

Sept. 23—This is Monday. I am now a soldier of the United States; I desire also to be "a soldier of the cross." The name of our camp is, "Camp Mather." It is located in the southern suburbs of Chicago, near the lake shore. The day passed off without anything extraordinary occuring. At some other time I will record the regular routine of the day.[5]

Sept. 24—Myself and five other boys got excused from duty that we might go to the city. Our camp is about four miles from the main business part of the city. We therefore had quite a long walk. Chicago, like most, if not all, other large cities, abounds in wickedness. The finest residences in the city are on Michigan Avenue fronting the lake. We had a fine view of the city, lake and surrounding country. Lake Michigan is a fine body of water. The ground, on which the city of Chicago is built, is very low, but a few feet above the level of the lake. Chicago River, on both sides of which the city is built, is a small stream having little or no current. We took the Lake Street and Cottage Grove City railway car and returned to camp in the afternoon. We got our knapsacks and haversacks this afternoon. The boys were glad to get them. They strapped them on their backs and went about through the camp bidding one another "goodbye" pretending as if they were going on a long journey. Nothing more uncommon occured today.

Sept. 25—Nothing remarkable took place today. The reveille beats at sun up. The boys get up, dress and wash themselves. Next the Captain cries out "Company I fall into ranks for roll call." The company falls into ranks and when the roll is called it is dismissed. For about half an hour the soldiers amuse themselves as they wish. Some engage in conversation, some read, others wash their faces and hands & comb their heads. Next, when breakfast is ready, one of the cooks cries out, "Company I fall into ranks for breakfast." The order is soon obeyed and the boys march and take their places at the table. The breakfast consists of light bread, beef or pork, coffee, sugar, molasses, potatoes boiled with the rind on, pepper and salt. Dinner and supper the same with the addition, sometimes, of rice and beans. Our table is made of rough pine boards. The dishes are tin plates, knives and forks, iron spoons and tin cups. After breakfast is over there is nothing to do till nine o'clock when company drill commences; this lasts about two hours. We are then dismissed. The next thing on the programme is dinner. We are called out again at 2 o'clock P.M. battalion drill. We are drilled for two or three hours and then dismissed. Next is dress parade at five o'clock. Then at six o'clock we take supper. We have nothing more to do till roll call which takes place at seven o'clock. This finishes up the duty of the day. We are now at liberty to do what we please. The time is spent in reading, writing, swearing, praying, singing and whatsoever else is concordant to the taste of the soldiers. At nine o'clock, when the "tattoo" is beaten, all lights should be extinguished, this is not strictly observed in our camp.

Sept. 26—This is the day appointed by the President for humiliation and prayer to Almighty God. The Yates Phalanx had an invitation by the young men's christian association to attend services at Bryan Hall. We accepted the invitation. As we marched down into the city, fair ladies, little girls, men and women greeted us by the waving of handkerchiefs and hats. The windows and doors were crowded with ladies and gentlemen. We noticed one beautiful young lady displaying the Stars and Stripes. We all took off our caps. On Michigan Avenue, I noticed a strange sight; in front of one of the fine houses, for which Michigan Avenue is noted, stood a little girl poorly dressed with a dejected countenance, evidently having seen hard times. Passing down the same avenue were well dressed persons with bibles and hymn books in their hands. Had they have given heed to the teachings of their bibles, how could this poor girl have stood there in want? "Let no man seek his own but every man an others wealth." The harshness of the sight was somewhat molified by what I saw when we were marching back to camp; viz a large comfortable looking house with this sign, "Home for the friendless." In the afternoon we were drawn up into a hollow square and a flag was presented to the regiment. At the same time a sword was presented to Captain Slaughter. Rather cool today. "Tempus fugit" [time flies].[6]

Sept. 27—Early this morning, I took a walk to the lake. In the evening I attended a prayer meeting in a tent of Company G. Two soldiers desired to be prayed for. Today it was decided to remain at our present encampment, for some weeks instead of moving. Slept very cold tonight. One of our company, known by the name of "Pony" got drunk and was taken to the guard house for misbehavior.

Sept. 28—Henry and I went to the "Myrick House" and got our breakfast. Two girls, of the isle of "Emerald," sympathised with us greatly on account of our hardships. We walked to the lake; it was very rough. I like camp life equally as well as I expected that I would. I did not expect to like it. I am not disappointed. I do not, here in camp, find society congenial to my feelings. The state of the morals of the soldiers is very low. All sorts of profanity, low and vulgar slang may be heard. It can hardly be said that the English language is spoken in this camp by the privates. The most of the soldiers are very illiterate. There are many privations here which, one that has any taste, must endure. I am willing to endure all the hardships & privations incident to camp life, not that I like them, but for the good of my country and for the cause of humanity. Today there was a fight in Company K of this camp. At Dinner one of the company accused an other of stealing his bread. From this they gave each other the lie. Next came the "Tug of war." They did not do much damage. This evening I took a bath in the lake; the water was very cold. There was a meeting tonight in camp.

Sept. 29—This is a rainy day. We had to be reviewed this morning. There was class meeting this afternoon in one of Company G's tents. Camp life is very monotonous. Today we are excused from the usual drill. I have spent the day very poorly. We hear not the accustomed church bell. I long to see the time when law and order shall triumph, when peace may take up her abode in this our distracted country and when we all shall be restored to our friends. I have now been in camp one week. I had engaged to teach school. Had I have complyed with my engagement I would now, perhaps, be in the enjoyment of society more suited to my taste than that by which I am surrounded. Society, friendship and love, at my country's call, I bid you all adieu. This is certainly the time when we should "Beat your plowshares into swords, and your pruning hooks into spears." Joel 3,10. This has been a rainy day.

Sept. 30—There was a complaint in Company I this morning on account of not having enough to eat. Some of "the boys" went down into the city to get their breakfasts, consequently we were not called out on company drill. Myself and two of my fellow soldiers visited Cottage Grove. This is a beautiful grove about four miles from the chief business part of Chicago. The trees are mostly scrubby oaks. Cottage Grove is noted as being the seat of the late Stephen A. Douglas, it is also the place where Chicago University is situated. The University is a fine stone building, five stories high. The location is most excellent, about four miles from the public square of Chicago. It is easy of access from all parts of the city by means of the city railways. The Cottage Grove and Lake Street railway passes within a few rods of the building. The University is under the care of the Baptist Church. S.A. Douglas donated ten acres of land to the institution, a magnificent gift. On the whole Chicago University presents many inducements to those wishing to secure the advantages of a collegiate education. We visited the grave of the Honorable S. A. Douglas. While gazing on it I exclaimed, *"Hic jacet magnus et bonus vir"* [Here lies a great and good man]. The grave is near the lake shore. There shall rest the remains of one who loved his country, till "the grave shall give up its dead." The waves of Lake Michigan shall sing his requiem till "time shall be no more." The grave is railed in with a neat wooden fence. There is no monument yet erected. Near to the grave is the residence of the honored Senator. It is a small one story frame building. This was a clear day. The Captain & 2nd Lieut went home.[7]

October 1—Lieutenant Waller marched the company to Cottage Grove. We visited two camps. This afternoon there was some difficulty with some of the boys of our company. Six of them put into the guard house for refusing to go on extra duty. They went out of camp without permission. The penalty for so doing is that the person offending shall go on extra duty. Two deserters were brought into camp, tried by courtmartial and condemned, the one to be confined in the guard house for three days, the other to be confined for five days and to be fed on bread and water.

Oct. 2—I am detailed for guard today. The tedium of camp life is intolerable. I am anxious to see active service. My convictions, now, are that I will be spared to return home. I was not put on guard today. Nothing extraordinary occured today.

Oct. 3—I was detailed for guard. The guard is divided into three divisions called the first relief, the second relief and third. The first relief is put on guard at 9 o'clock A.M. One set of guards stands on duty two hours at a time. They are then relieved for four hours, at the expiration of which time they are placed on guard again. I was on the third relief. I was therefore put on guard at one o'clock P.M. Nothing remarkable occured during the day. At night, when we were placed on guard, we were instructed not to let any body pass without the countersign. When any body would come and want to pass, the sentinel would challenge him thus "Halt, who comes there?" He answers who he is. "Advance and give the countersign," says the sentinel. The countersign tonight was "Yates." If the person wishing to pass can give the countersign he is allowed to pass, if not he is stopped. This was a clear day.

Oct. 4—Two soldiers of Company B were tried by courtmartial for stealing and selling a blanket. They were found guilty. The blanket belonged to the United States. At dress parade this evening the sentence of the court was read. They were condemned to confinement all night and to stand on a barrel head from six o'clock A.M. till twelve o'clock M. This was a rainy day. It rained nearly all night. Our tent was very wet on the inside, the water stood in it.

Oct. 5—It rained and was wet and muddy. Tomorrow will be Sunday. I look forward to it not with anticipations of wanted pleasure. There is a rumor in camp that we will leave here next week and go to Missouri. As soon as we are sufficiently drilled we expect to see active service.

Oct. 6, Sunday—We, the regiment, went out on review at half past nine o'clock with our overcoats on, knapsacks, haversacks, canteens and belts. We looked somewhat like soldiers. There was preaching, in camp, in the afternoon. The sermon was not all suited to soldiers. The theme was the love of God to man. The text was John 3:16 "For God so loved the world" etc. The preacher began thus; "A good man, who baptized me, in Plymouth, that cradle of liberty, once asked me, 'What is the peculiar doctrine of Christianity?'" The sum toto of the sermon was that Love to our fellow men is a doctrine taught by Christianity only. This was a beautiful day. In the evening I attended church in the city at Trinity Church. This is a magnificent building. The services were very pompous. The performance on the organ was excellent.

Oct. 7—This is a beautiful day. We can dry our hay which has been quite damp for several days. Nothing unusual occured. The tedium continues oppressive.

Oct. 8—There was preaching tonight in camp. The sermon, from the text, "Quit ye like men," was more of a patriotic address than a sermon.

Oct. 9—Our uniforms, which arrived yesterday, are now being distributed among the soldiers. Some of the soldiers had worn out their pants and were going with their [shirts] on without any pants. They presented an odd appearance wearing their heavy overcoats furnished by the government without pants on. None of "Company I," to which I belong, were so poorly clad. We are expecting momentarily to receive orders to march. We do not know where we will go. We went out today on battalion drill in full uniform. We, the regiment, marched in front of the Mosley School. The scholars, who are all small, cheered us to the utmost of their capacity.

Oct. 10—This has truly been a pleasant day. The sun shone brightly. All is peace in my mind. Early in the morning, in company with several others, I went into the city. From the top of the Court House I had an excellent view of the city, lake and surrounding country. The city looked like a mammouth beehive. Wagons, drays, carriages and all sorts of wheeled vehicles were passing to and fro. The streets appeared alive with human beings. All was bustle and business. Far away stretches the prairie towards the south and west. In the far distance are seen skirts of timber appearing like a blue cloud in the horizon. To the north and east lies Lake Michigan, on whose bosom is carried the commerce of the different parts of the United States and Canada. The lake was very placid. It was whitened by the sails of many ships. "The black ships of the Greeks" is an expression often used by Homer. The ships, which sail on Lake Michigan, appear white. As I passed down Clark Street I beheld a building with this inscription, "Union prayer meeting here every day at 12 o'-clock M. Our Saviour calls." I attended this noon prayer meeting. It was good to be there. How pleasant it is to turn aside from the bustle, confusion and wickedness of camp and meet, in the house of God, persons who are accustomed to say, in sincerity, "Our Father which art in heaven"! The meeting was opened by singing and prayer. A young man then read a chapter from James. The rest of the time, three quarters of an hour, was occupied in singing, praying and speaking. Each person is requested not to take up more time than three minutes. Many men and women shook hands with me at the close of the meeting. We have received orders to go to Missouri tomorrow. This perhaps is the last day that I will spend in Chicago, if so it is the most pleasant that I have spent here.[8]

Oct. 11—We arose at the sound of the reveille and called roll as usual. After breakfast we were mustered into the services of the United States. This being done, then commenced the bustle and busy scene of preparing to move. Here a man is packing a knapsack; there a squad of men are taking down a tent. Some are filling their canteens with water. All things being ready, with our knapsacks on our backs, we fell into ranks. We took one day's scanty rations in our haversacks. After much delay, the order "march" was given. With alacrity we took up the line of march for the land of "Secessia." This was about 10 o'clock A.M. The sun had gone down before we were being borne to "Dixie's land" by steam velocity. Many of the soldiers were drunk. There was no sleep for us tonight. We were tired, hungry and sleepy.

Oct. 12—We reached Bloomington this morning at sun up. Lincoln, my residence, is on the road over which we passed. The cars did not stop here. I saw my sister and brother-in-law but I could not speak to them. At Springfield breakfast was provided for us; it consisted of crackers, cheese, dried beef and sugar cakes. At Alton we took a steamer for St. Louis. Our way from Bloomington to Alton was one continued ovation. Men, women and children manifested their enthusiasm by waving hats, handkerchiefs, aprons, table cloths and many other such things. We had a very pleasant trip down the river. The night was clear and serene. The new moon shone brightly. As we sailed down the "Father of waters," the shores and trees, on either side of the river, seen by the pale light of the moon, appeared to fine effect. We disembarked at St. Louis about 8 o'-clock in the night. Several hours were occupied, by detachments from each company of the regiment, in unloading the baggage. I was so unfortunate as to be detailed for this service. A very poor supper was prepared for us in St. Louis. After the boat was unloaded and we had partaken, not of a supper, but only, an apology for a supper, we took our line of march for Benton Barracks distant about four miles from the main part of the city. We arrived at the barracks about 3 o'clock A.M.[9]

Oct. 13—Sunday. Fatigued, sleepy and hungry were we this morning when we came into the barracks. For a few hours we lay down, in dirty quarters, to rest our weary limbs. We arose from our beds of filth, with nothing to satiate our hunger but hard crackers, hams, not very decently cooked, and coffee without sugar. As I had been awake for two nights nearly, I slept the most of the forenoon. In the afternoon I attended preaching at the fairground. There was a vast concourse of people in attendance both soldiers and citizens. The sermon was from the text "All things work together for good to them that love God."

Oct. 14—The 8th Wisconsin Regiment [came] into camp today. This is a camp of instruction. We are quite comfortably quartered here since we have done considerable cleaning up.

Oct. 15—The weather is much more pleasant here than in Chicago. The rules are more strict here than they were in Camp Mather. Everything has to be done promptly at the appointed time. This evening one wing of the 8th Wisconsin Regiment left here; the rest are to leave in the morning. Their destination is unknown. The Colonel drew us up in battle array to witness them leave. They had a live eagle. When they got opposite us Colonel Light commanded "Attention, battalion, three cheers for the eagle." We gave three rousing cheers. Tonight news was received in camp that General Fremont had taken Gen. Price and twenty thousand prisoners. This caused great joy in camp. I do not believe this news is true.[10]

Oct. 16—It rained this morning so we did not drill by company. My health is excellent. We were drilled this afternoon by company.

Oct. 17—Arms for part of the regiment have arrived. They are old United States muskets. They are very indignant on account of the inferior quality of thc arms. They expected to get rifles. The Colonel drew the regiment up in close column. Lieutenant Colonel Osborn then made a short speech. "Soldiers of the Yates Phalanx," said he, "you are indignant on account of the kind of arms which you are about to receive. Before we enlisted you we had the assurance, by the Governor and our superior officers, that arms of the best quality would be furnished us; when you enlisted we promised you such. When these arms arrived your Colonel called on the General commanding, Curtis, and entered your protest. The General told him that it was the best that could be done and that these arms are intended only for temporary use. He also informed the Colonel that Governor Yates was now in Washington City raising heaven and earth from the Atlantic Ocean to the Mississippi River trying to get good arms for the volunteers of Illinois and the West. The General promised that, as soon as they could be procured, we would get better arms. These are not to be your arms to take into the field. You are not to make an attack with them; they are simply for your defense. The Rebels are near. Jeff Thompson is 30 or 40 miles with a large army marching towards St. Louis. Had you not better have these arms than none?" "Yes, yes," cried the regiment. Captain Slaughter asked if there had been any writing between the General and the Colonel with regard to the regiment getting better arms. The Colonel told him that there had not but that the General pledged his word and honor in the presence of twelve honorable witnesses. Captain Phillips spoke briefly expressing the wish that Company I and all the regiment might take the arms. Colonel Light said that he wanted to have good arms. Captain Slaughter proposed three cheers for Colonel Light. We gave him three hearty cheers. The regiment was then dismissed and the companies were marched out on their regular company drill. The arms were distributed in the afternoon. Tonight we expected an attack. The boys were greatly excited. Some of them were terrified. After the tattoo had sounded and all should have been still in the barracks the boys were very noisy speculating on the probability of a surprise. Some made sport, others seemed timid. Lieutenant Fellows came in, while the boys were thus excited, and told them that the best thing they could do would be to go to sleep for he knew not how long we would be permitted to lie. For a while the boys calmed down but they were soon in as great confusion as ever. Next the Captain came in and ordered us to have our clothes ready to put on in a minute's warning; he also ordered us to have our knapsacks ready to strap on our backs. Notwithstanding the anticipated attack, I slept soundly.[11]

Oct. 18—All is quiet this morning. No "rebelers," as some of the boys call them, came last night. The guards report that they heard heavy firing last night. There is prospect of hot time here soon. The troops are poorly armed; many of them have no arms at all. If Thompson succeeds in taking Pilot Knob we may soon expect him here.[12]

Oct. 19—I was detailed for guard today. Myself and another sentinel were stationed at a gate, in front of the hospital, to guard it. My fellow sentinel had an altercation, at night, with a Lieutenant. The Lieutenant wanted to pass into the hospital without a pass. He had the countersign; it had not been given to us. According to our instructions we could not let him pass; he became enraged and threatened to arrest my co-sentinel for using contemptuous language to an officer. He got the Corporal of the guard to pass him in. There was no further difficulty. This was a cold and frosty night. I got but little sleep. One year ago I did not expect such hard times.

Oct. 20, Sunday—I felt sad this morning when I heard the church bells in the city. I am shut up in camp and am not permitted to go out, not even to the house of God. "How amiable are thy tabernacles, O Lord God Almighty!" It seems but little like Sunday, here in camp. Today there was little less card playing than common. At 1 o'clock P.M. there was class meeting in Mr. Parkhurst's room, at 4 P.M. preaching in the amphitheatre of the fair ground.[13]

Oct. 21—There was nothing took place in camp today but the regular routine. The weather is fine. The news today is encouraging. Seward says that the war will not last more than 3 months.[14]

Oct. 22—This has been a cool chilly day. There was a light shower of rain in the afternoon. Today there was a scandalous fuss in our company; no blood shed.

Oct. 23—I was detailed today for fatigue duty. The duty to be performed was sweeping out the barracks. It was very disagreeable but not very fatigueing work.

Oct. 24—Our regiment is to join Gen. Sigel as soon as it is armed and equiped. This Gen. Fremont has ordered. The orders were published to us this evening at dress parade by the Adjutant. Thus our hopes of forming a part of the grand army on the Potomac, are frustrated. The feverish excitement, as to when we shall take the field and where we shall go, is allayed. Our chaplain has arrived.[15]

Oct. 25—Nothing uncommon occured today. Part of the 1st Iowa Cavalry left for the seat of war. It rained this afternoon. It pains me to see so much frivolity amoung my fellow soldiers. I fear that they will not "quit themselves like men." Dancing and card playing are common pastimes. They seem to care more for the gratification of the animal appetite and their morbid tastes than for anything else. Intellectual enjoyment is almost if not an entire stranger here. Yet amid all the wickedness and vanity here manifest, I believe there is some serious thought. The New Testament is read by nearly if not quite all the soldiers of this regiment. It appears like seed sown on stony ground; At least I know not that it has brought forth any fruit. One would think that a person exposed to dangers, like a soldier is, would be sober-minded. Such is not the case. The soldiers give loose reins to their passions. Tonight a Temperance Society was organized in Colonel Burgess' 1st Regiment of Sharpshooters.[16] Several interesting speeches were made and beautiful songs were sung. After which 67 soldiers signed the pledge not to drink any intoxicating liquor during the war. A President, Vice-President and Secretary were appointed. The reason why I make so many mistakes is because of the exciting news just received. Good news! Good good!

Oct. 26—General Lemman is here.[17] The report is that we are to go under his command. We are to form a part of the "grand army of the Potomac." A few hours will demonstrate the truth or falsity of this rumor. If we go east we will start tonight or in the morning. The boys are wild with excitement. Witherso-ever we go preserve us, O Lord God of hosts. Restrain us from doing violence to anyone. Protect us from danger and restore us to our homes free from crime. In thee do we put our trust. We know that thou art able to save. Thou hast ever heard those that cry unto thee in sincerity. For the sake of Christ forgive our sins and be merciful to us. I fear not to go to meet the enemy. I, today, received some clothes per express. I also received a letter from a good lady in the East. It cheers my weary soul to hear from dear friends. This has been a good day to me. Together with the clothes, which I got today, I received a new, or rather my old companion in whose society I expect to enjoy much. I refer to my Greek Testament. Tonight a meeting was held in Company G's quarters, 39th Reg Ill Vol, to organize a regimental temperance society. The meeting was opened by prayer by Rev. McReading, Chaplain of the regiment. He prayed that "Peace might spread its silken wings over our distracted country." Next that beautiful song The Cottage Home was sung by two of the sharp shooters. The time was then taken up by speeches from gentlemen of this and other regiments, interspersed with singing. At the close of the meeting near sixty soldiers signed the pledge not to drink any intoxicating liquor, unless prescribed by the regular regimental surgeon, during the war. Before signing the pledge officers were elected. Lieutenant Savage of Company G was elected President, Lieutenant Waller of Company I Vice-President, Plinton was elected Secretary. Captain Munn was elected Treasurer. The meeting was closed by singing the Doxology. This society promises to exert a good influence in the Yates Phalanx.[18]

Oct. 27, Sunday—There was a general review, this morning, of all the troops here by General Curtis. There was an appointment for Dr. Post of St. Louis to preach at the fair grounds in the afternoon. He failed to be there; consequently there was no preaching today for the soldiers to attend. At night our Chaplain held a prayer meeting in Company G's quarters.[19]

Oct. 28—Today the cooks are providing three days rations for each soldier. There has been no drill today. In the morning we expect to start to Maryland. Our sojourn in Missouri has been short. We have been so closely confined that we have seen but little of the surrounding country. Many are the evils that follow in the train of war. Yesterday I received letters from Kentucky. From them I learned that several of my cousins, in Virginia, are in the rebel army. Only a few months have elapsed since I visited them. I had a very pleasant visit. Now I am going to meet my friend, my blood relations, those whom I love dearly in mortal conflict. It is a painful duty, one in which I take no delight, that I am now called to perform. There are duties, which a person may be willing to perform but in which he can take no pleasure. Abraham must have been grieved at having to offer up his son Isaac a sacrifice. Isaac was the child of promise the son of his beloved Sarah. High had been the hopes which

Abraham entertained of his son becoming the progenitor of a peculiar people. But the word of God had gone forth, he must offer up his son a sacrifice. See him toiling up Mount Moriah. How his heart must have melted within him when his son spake unto him, "My father; Behold the fire and the wood; but where is the lamb for a burnt offering?" There was so much filial affection in this address, "My Father," that his heart must have yearned with love towards his son. It was Abraham's duty to obey the word of God. It was doubtless a painful duty to him, one in which he could take no delight. His arm must have been paralyzed when he stretched it forth to strike the fatal blow. He trusted God and he averted the fatal stroke.[20] This evening the order to march was published to the regiment. We are to start in the morning to Williamsport, Maryland, via Chicago. We will be in the military department of Western Virginia and in General Lammon's division. I suppose that we would be in the Potomac department. I was also mistaken in the name of the General; its Lamon, instead of Lemmon. I spelt it as I had heard it pronounced.

Oct. 29—We arose early this morning and began to prepare for the long journey which we were about to start on. The older soldiers busied themselves by instructing the younger ones in the mysteries of rolling their blankets and overcoats, adjusting their knapsacks to their backs and putting on their belts, cartridge boxes, haversacks and canteens. About 7 o'clock A.M., all things were ready to march. We went down through the city of St. Louis to the river, distant four miles. We crossed the river in a steam ferryboat to Illinois Town; here we were delayed till late in the afternoon. We did not go via Chicago as we expected. At Illinois Town some of the boys disgraced themselves by breaking into a car and stealing sugar. Such conduct is scandalous, mean, low-lived and unbecoming a man in any situation. Being a soldier is no palliation whatever for such pilfering. We traveled all night. About Midnight I witnessed a grand scene, one which was formerly more common in the West than at the present time, the "prairie on fire." For miles the whole earth seemed to be a blaze of fire. This was to most of us a sleepless night.

Oct. 30—We reached Terra Haute, Indiana about day light. The Hoosiers along our route seemed very patriotic but none more so than a lass who threw kisses with both hands at the soldiers as the cars passed by where she stood. The citizens of Indianapolis prepared breakfast for us. We got off the cars and marched through the city. About noon breakfast was ready! Some, by acting the hog, which animal they more resemble in their manners, than a man, got as much as they wanted to eat and waste, others got but little. The breakfast was in the market house. Indianapolis is a beautiful little city. The streets are remarkably clean. Here we changed cars. The 36 Reg Ia Vol left the city about the same time that we did for Louisville, Kentucky. We traveled all night again.

Oct. 31—The first town of any size that we passed this morning was Mansfield, Ohio. The country was subject to a great deal of ridicule; the suckers thought it was very poor.[21] At Wooster some of the boys got off the cars to forage. The cars started leaving two or three behind. One of their comrades, on the train, seeing that they were not about to succeed in getting aboard, drew out the coupling pin and put on the brakes thus stopping part of the train. This was done the second time, when the villain or rather senseless boy was arrested. It is no light thing to play with human life in such a way. The cars detached might have been left several miles behind and run into by an other train causing a great destruction of life. My fellow "Suckers" beheld the hills of Eastern Ohio with wonder and admiration. They thought that it was a poor place for a man to make a living but that the hills were beautiful to look at. We arrived at Pittsburg a few hours before night. Here we changed cars again. When we got off the cars we were formed in regular order for drill in companies, platoons and sections. We were then marched into a hall over the market house. I was surprised and delighted to find there an excellent supper prepared for us. We were marched up to the tables in regular order. Some of the hogs commenced eating as soon as they got to the table. When they all got their places at the table, the Colonel commanded, "Attention," the chaplain then returned thanks and invoked the blessing of God. "Now eat," said the Colonel, and eat we did. The hall was beautifully adorned with flags. Pious ladies distributed religious papers and tracts among the soldiers. After supper was finished Colonel Light proposed three cheers for the ladies of Pittsburg; we gave them three hearty cheers. I do not believe much in cheering but this time I could cheer with a good will. One brute in human form had the impudence to insult a lady who was waiting on the table. He had no sooner uttered the foul language of his rotten heart than the floor was polluted by the touch of his filthy carcass. He was knocked down. He ought to have been kicked into the middle of the Ohio River. We left Pittsburg about an hour after dark. Tonight we passed over the most interesting part of our route. The night was so dark that we could not see any thing. This was a sleepless night again to us.

November 1—When the "rosey fingered morn" appeared we found ourselves on the banks of the Juniata River. For a great many miles the rail road runs near the river. We passed through several towns. The Pennsylvania Canal is also near the rail road for many miles. There is but little business done on the canal. It is owned by the same company that owns [the] rail road. At the towns where the cars stopped "the boys" rushed out in pursuit of something to eat. Many ridiculous remarks were made about the hills and mountains. Some said that they would not live here for all the state; others again liked it better than the West. One of our boys said, (speaking of a certain mountain) that he could pick up a stone there the darkest night he ever saw. An other said that he saw a

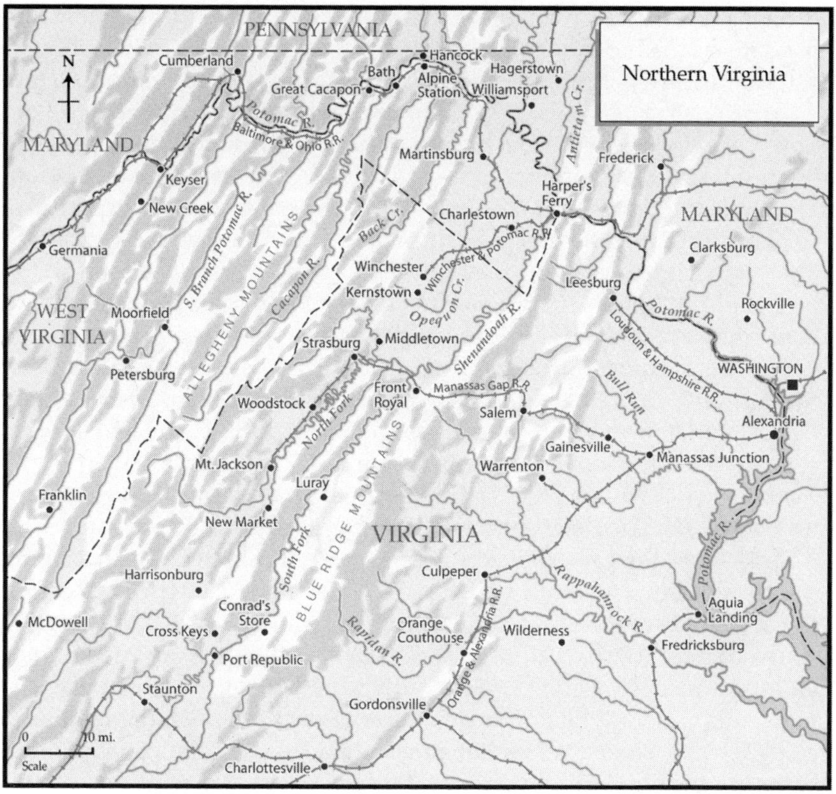

mountain up which his mules could not pull thirty bushels of wheat. The scenery today was very grand and sublime. The road follows the course of the river, Juniata, to its mouth. This river empties into the Susquehanna River. The road then runs along the banks of the river for several miles. Susquehanna is said to mean in the Indian dialect "River of many islands." The river is wide but very shallow and islands are very numerous so it is not navigable. In the Spring vast quantities of timber is rafted down this stream. Some of the islands are cultivated. We made only a short stop in Harrisburg. We did not change cars here although we went on another road, the Cumberland Valley Rail Road. A little more than a year ago I passed along this same route on my way to Dickinson College.[22] Little did I think then that I would ever pass over the same road on my way to war! It was the least of my thoughts that I would ever be a soldier. "Thus the fates roll." We are short sighted ignorant creatures. We know not one day what will befall us the next. Whilst traveling from Harrisburg to Carlisle I was sorely troubled in mind. The reflexion, that I was about one year ago passing over the same road through the same beautiful valley, to the fame of knowledge, was sad to the extreme. Then I was full of hopes for the future. Honor, fame and pleasure seemed to be almost within my grasp. Then I thought soon to reach forth my hands and pluck bright honor from the hill of science. All that heart could desire was mine. But now alas! how changed! I am now a hungry, weary soldier. No ray of hope lights my gloomy mind. All bright anticipations of honor, fame, pleasure and usefulness are cut off. The short time that I will be able to stand the hardships and exposure of a soldier's life shall be dragged out in gloom and sorrow. Farewell bright hopes of my earlier days; I shall never realize you. I gladly forego all the pleasures and honors that the world can bestow that millions yet unborn may enjoy the blessings of Constitutional liberty. At Mechanicsburg the young ladies turned out enmass to cheer us as we passed. This town is the seat of Irvine Female College.[23] The ladies of the College waved their handkerchiefs to us and encouraged us by telling us to fight for our country. Such fair ladies I never before saw. "The boys" were charmed by their beauty. They declared that they would go back there when the war was over. The greatest demonstration along our route was made at Carlisle. Here the cars stopped for about fifteen minutes. I shall attempt no description of the enthusiasm which was here manifested. Many of the soldiers fell in love with the town. It was a little after dark when we got to Carlisle. We passed in sight of Dickinson College. My feeling may be imagined not described. "Farewell Old Dickinson," I ejaculated. The night was dark and rainy. We arrived at Hagerstown, Maryland about 1 o'clock in the night. We remained all night on the cars. I suppose that some of "the boys" slept; there was but little sleep alloted to me. Guards were placed at the doors of the cars. I was detailed for this duty.

Nov. 2—This morning about daylight we put on our knapsacks, got off the cars and were formed in marching order. We were then marched up into the town, (the cars stopped in the outskirts of the town) and commanded to halt. After going through the regular formula of "dressing up," etceteras were commanded to rest at ease. I did rest and at ease too. I struck a beeline for Williamsport. When I got half way from Hagerstown to *Gulielmi portus* [Williams port] I stopped at a farm house and got an excellent breakfast. I then set down by a comfortable fire to wait till the regiment came along. Dinner was prepared before the regiment came. I therefore had an opportunity to satiate my craving appetite. Late in the afternoon passed the regiment. I waited till they got some distance ahead, not wishing to be in the rain any longer than I could help. I intended to overtake them but in this I failed. I fell in with two boys of Company K. We reached Williamsport a short time before sundown. Part of the regiment was quartered in some old warehouses on the banks of the Potomac. The rest of the regiment pitched their tents on a hill near and over-looking the river. It rained hard all day. The wind blew hard while we were pitching our tents and the rain was falling in torrents. We laid floors in our tents with boards. Our blankets were wet.

It continued to rain till late in the night. The atmosphere was very chilly. The water ran through our tents. On the whole this was the hardest night that I ever experienced. This evening the Potomac was fordable.

Recapitulation—The boys enjoyed, I believe, the trip hither very well. There was considerable grumbling for the want of something to eat. I am sorry to have to record that there was much disgraceful pilfering. In Ohio one of Company K fell off the cars through a bridge. He got badly hurt. He was taken to Pittsburg where he has since died. This should be a warning against standing on the platform of the cars. On Saturday night I was so wet and cold that I could not sleep, yet I was consoled by the thought that I was laying on the banks of the Potomac.

Nov. 3, Sunday—This morning the river was pretty swollen too much so to be fordable. Drift wood was floating down the stream. I took a walk into the cemetery which is nearby where we encamped. Otto Holland Williams, a Brigadier General in the Revolutionary War and founder of Williamsport, is buried here. Williamsport was founded in 1787. The General died in 1794.[24] In the forenoon I went to an old mill and spent several hours writing. We could see men on the Virginia side of the river today, supposed to be the rebel pickets. In the afternoon we moved our camp about one mile northeast of Williamsport. We are now encamped in a clover field. The name of our camp is "Camp Lamon." I have heard the expression, "He lives in clover," meaning he lives well. We literally "live in clover" but it is quite certain that we do not live very well. Tonight we had to go almost supperless. It's painful and yet laughable to see the boys eating pieces of raw fat bacon. One man actually picked up meat skin and ate it. It was clear today.

Nov. 4—We were not required to drill today. It was clear today so that we could dry our blankets and clothes. We have excellent water here. The country seems quite hilly to suckers but the natives call it level. The soil is of a yellowish color. It does not resemble the rich black loam of Illinois. From the looks Illinoisians would say that it is no account. Such is not the case for it produces well. The soil in this part of the state is what the people here call lime stone soil. Our camp is in Washington county. Hagerstown is the county seat. Williamsport, on the north bank of the Potomac and six miles southwest of Hagerstown, is a poor dilapidated village. It is also on the Potomac and Chesapeake Canal. This canal extends from Alexandria in Virginia to Cumberland in Maryland. The Potomac River is not navigable to this point. The village contains about 2000 inhabitants. It also has one bank, a Presbyterian, a Methodist, a Lutheran and a Catholic Church and several large stores. This village seems to be far behind the times; old style postage stamps are in use here yet.

Nov. 5—This was a beautiful day. There was no drill today till in the afternoon when we were taken out on battalion drill. There were some good resolutions passed in our tent last Sunday evening viz: that no swearing nor card playing be allowed in the tents and that a portion of each evening be spent in singing and that we have prayer before retiring of a night. So far these rules have worked excellently. A soldier of the 1st Virginia regiment was buried today. He died with the consumption. This warns us to be ready for the coming of the Son of Man. It rained tonight. The band endeavored to give a false alarm but failed. One man of our company is sick with the measles. William Gesford is his name.[25]

Nov. 6—This was a gloomy morning. I was detailed for guard. The election for state and county officers in this state came off today. There were 2 tickets, a Union ticket and a Peace ticket. The Peace ticket is considered secession in disguise. This was a hard night on guards, being dark and cold.

Nov. 7—I have nothing to record today. The election returns show this state to be loyal to the Union.

Nov. 8—This morning Hank Gott and I took a ramble.[26] We went up the river about three miles from Williamsport. Got plenty of persimmons. I stopped at a house on the banks of the Potomac River to get something to eat. There were two large girls in the house. They told me that they had nothing cooked. I was hungry and weary and they administered not unto my wants. On our way back to camp I asked an old woman for some bread and butter. She excused herself by telling me that she was poor and had a large family to provide for. She said that her husband was a weaver and that he could not get any work to do. I told her that I did not wish anything without paying for it. We got back into camp tired and hungry at three o'clock P.M. This afternoon thirty-one rebel cavalry appeared in Virginia, in pursuit of two women, who were fleeing from Martinsburg, Virginia. The women hid themselves in a house. When the rebels approached near the river our troops planted a cannon in the road between Williamsport and the river. They then fired three times at the rebels. The first shot fell short; the other two scattered the "secesh." They soon disappeared. It is not known whether any body was killed or wounded or not. The women then came out from their hiding place and came to the river. The provost marshall sent a boat over after them. What news they brought from Martinsburg I have not been able to learn.

Nov. 9—This is a rainy dreary morning. It continued rainy all day. I amused myself by writing letters and reading the Greek Testament. I wrote four letters. We did not drill today.

Nov. 10, Sunday—This is a beautiful, clear morning. We cannot get to go to Williamsport to church. There is but little Sunday for soldiers. At 1 o'clock P.M. we were inspected. When the inspection was over the Colonel formed us in close column. The band then played a tune. The Chaplain prayed, made some announcements and preached a short discourse from the text, "The fool hath said in his heart, there is no God." I once heard President Sturtevant preach from the same text, in the chapel of Illinois College.[27] At the close of the sermon the regiment sung, "When I can read my titles clear." To see the soldiers, with their knapsacks on their backs, standing in ranks, was a very interesting sight. Several men of our company are sick with the measles. The rebels were reported to be throwing up entrenchments across the river near here. At about 8 o'clock tonight the long roll was beat. The Colonel galloped around through the camp commanding, "Fall into ranks, boys, quickly." The boys rolled up their blankets and put on their knapsacks. In less than five minutes the regiment was in ranks ready to march. Some, in the midst of the haste and excitement, left their blankets, knapsacks, canteens and haversacks. The Captains, Lieutenants and high privates supposed that the enemy were in close pursuit. The Colonel marched us around over the parade grounds for a short time, then, drawing us up in line of battle, he said, "Drill is dismissed." The boys were considerably excited but not scared. They acted cooly, more so than could have been expected. I expected soon to see Richmond, as a prisoner of war, not being very fleet of foot, I knew that my chances to escape were not as good as that of most others. I was never more merry. I noticed one woman of the regiment greatly terrified; she stood shedding tears profusely. The alarm was gotten up by the Colonel to try our pluck. It was satisfactorally tested. I am not aware that any one shrunk from his post of duty.

Nov. 11—There were several cases of the measles today. Some were taken to the hospital in ambulances. We were drilled by Lieutenant Colonel Osborne. Osborne knows but little about military tactics. We spend most of the day in our tents doing nothing. We have yet had to drill only about two hours in the day.

Nov. 12—We had company drill this morning for the first time since we have been on the Potomac. The day was beautiful. At battalion drill today Colonel Light made a few remarks, showing the reason why a column was ever drawn up in close order. "The reason," he said, "was for strength. A thousand men are stronger in a compact body than they would be scattered over a ten acre field. Each man supports his neighbor." He illustrated this fact by the fable of the bundle of switches. Bind them in a bundle and they cannot be broken, but take them singley they can be broken with ease. This reminded me of my Classical days in Illinois and Dickinson Colleges.

Nov. 13—I was detailed for guard. Several of our men being sick, our time to stand comes oftener than it otherwise would. One man of Company I was accused of stealing a pistol from a man of Company G. He was tried by a "Courtmartial" and found guilty. He was condemned to be confined in the guard house five days, on bread and water, and half a month's wages to be retained from his monthly pay. This was published as a special order today at dress parade. The night was warm and clear, excellent for guards.

Nov. 14—"Watchman tell us of the night." Before one o'clock, my sleep was disturbed by the Corporal of the "third relief." At one the third relief was put on guard. For two long hours we stood guarding our beats. The moon had almost disappeared behind the mountains before we were relieved. Whilst at my post, early in the morning, a fellow comrade handed me a letter from a "good" friend. The following extracts will show that its contents were such as are calculated to cheer up the desponding spirits of one, who in the midst of company, yet liveth alone. "Not receiving an answer to my letter for so long, I thought perhaps you had not gotten it. You cannot imagine how sorry I was that I did not see you, the night you passed through. (Carlisle, Pa) I was down town, by Mr. Mille's Shoe Store looking for you, in every direction, but all in vain. Hopes once cherished are now blighted. One year, many, many are the changes that have taken place in that short space of time. Could the language of many hearts be read, on them would be written, we met, we loved, we parted, six small words, yet how much of happiness or misery is concealed within them." Many other soul-cheering things were written in the letter. It rained tonight.

Nov. 15—Today we received full particulars of the naval expedition.[28] The news is encouraging in the extreme. The news from Kentucky and Eastern Tennessee, received today, is scarcely less encouraging. The loyal people of East Tenn have arisen in their might and destroyed the bridges of the East Tenn & Va Rail Road. Our Chaplain, who went to Washington a few days ago, returned today. After dress parade he made a report of his mission to the Capital, in a short off-hand speech. He mounted a barrel, the soldiers gathered around him eager to catch every word that fell from his lips. This was a cold rainy day. It was distressing tonight after we retired to hear the soldiers in different tents coughing. Many, O how many are contracting colds that will terminate their lives. Many will be the victims that will be sacrificed on the altar of Southern ambition. The blood of the innocent already cries to heaven for vengeance. There is a just God who will not turn a listless ear to their cries. Let traitors beware. The day of retribution is not far distant.

Nov. 16—This was a cold and windy day. We were not drilled today. Colonel Light, at dress parade, read some of the articles of war to the regiment. The few comments, which the Colonel made showed clearly that he is no orator; this does not prevent him from being a good Military officer. There was not bread enough for dinner, some of us, myself among them, did not get even a crumb. I had nothing for dinner but some rice. At supper time no bread was yet provided. There was fair prospect of many of us going to bed hungry. Late in the night bread was brought into camp. A piece about the size of a lady's hand was given to each one of us. A poor apology for a supper to a hungry soldier was this. There is no necessity for thus starving the soldiers of the United States. The fault belongs to villainous officers. No body is to blame of course! You must expect to suffer privations many for your country.

Nov. 17, Sunday—"Set thyne house in order; for thou shalt die and not live." Isaiah 38,1. First Lieutenant Richardson of Company A died last night. His disease was the Typhoid Fever. His remains were sent home this evening. He lived in Wilmington, Illinois. How true is the Latin proverb, *In media vita sumus in morte* [In the midst of life, we are in death]. Surely "All flesh is grass." I know not what had been the character of the deceased. This should warn us all to be ready. Life at longest is short. We must all soon yield to death. Death knocks equally at the doors of the rich and the poor. In the afternoon we went out on inspection, at the close of which, Chaplain Macreading preached a short sermon. There was a prayer meeting tonight in the Chaplain's tent. I did not attend owing to the pressure of the multitude.[29]

Nov. 18—A company from New York came into camp today. I do not know whether they intend to go into our regiment or not. We did not do much today. To do nothing is the hardest work a man ever did.

Nov. 19—I was detailed again for guard today. This morning we received the news of the Archtraitors, Mason and Sidell, being captured on board an English steamer.[30] The wicked should not go unpunished. Let their heads pay the debt for playing the traitor. Lieutenant Richardson's remains, which were started home last Sunday, were intered this afternoon in the cemetery at Williamsport. He was sent as far as Harrisburg, Pennsylvania. Transportation could not be obtained further, not being money enough in his company to pay the expenses, his remains were sent back to Williamsport. The 39th Ill and 12th Mass attended the funeral. I being on guard could not go. Two soldiers of Company I were arrested tonight and put into the guard house. They, by some means, got the countersign and went down into town. A Sargeant and two privates were detailed to go to arrest them and bring them back. The sentinel, whom they passed, was also put into the guard house.

Nov. 20—This was a cloudy morning. Nothing but the regular routine of camp occured today. The health of the regiment is improving; all of Company I, who had the measles, are convalescent.

Nov. 21—Colonel Light, who went to Harrisburg, Pennsylvania a few days ago, returned today. He brings the welcome intelligence that the regiment will be paid off tomorrow; he also says that our arms are on their way hither. I was detailed for fatigue duty. The duty to perform was to carry water. Myself and some of my comrades went out after persimons. I got lost from them. A chance to enjoy the pleasure of solitude was offered to me. I had a very interesting ramble over the hills not regretting in the least that I wondered off from my comrades.

Nov. 22—This morning we received good news from the Eastern Shore of Virginia. The report is that 3000 rebel troops in Accomac County have disbanded and returned to allegiance. This news, if true, is much better than to have heard of the same number of rebels being killed in battle. Among the criminals sentenced today was one charged of using abusive language to one of his comrades. The specification was that he called his comrade "a son of a bitch." He was condemned to work one day on the regimental parade ground and to ask forgiveness of his comrade in the presence of his commanding officer. The parties both belong to the 1st Virginia Regiment Volunteers. The paymaster has been paying the troops here today. It rained tonight.

Nov. 23—Between three and four o'clock this morning our tent blew over. At the time rain was falling in great torrents. Most of the mess were "held in the embraces of sweet sleep." "What is the matter boys; what is the matter?" ejaculated some of the mess in astonishment. "O what will I do! What will I do? I am so sick," exclaimed a convalescent comrade. "Get up boys, get up and help hoist the tent, or I'll kick you out," in anger vociferated the head of the mess to four brave soldiers, who were buried in the ruins and had not yet extricated themselves from the destruction in which they were involved. "Get off me, till I put on my pants," said one, who was endeavoring to array himself in his apparel to an other, who was trying to crowd under the fallen tent out of the drenching rain. Four men deserted us in our trouble; two of them were convalescent. Soon all the rest were at work driving stakes and stretching the tent. In less time than it takes me to record it the tent was hoisted and staked down. The cause of the catastrophe was this; the tent when dry was stretched tightly. When the cold rain wet it, according to a well known principle of Philosophy, the tent contracted thus pulling up the stakes; a very light gust of wind blew it over. I have heard of dry jokes. This was certainly not a dry one, there was too much water mixed with it. The long-wished for day has come at last. The paymaster, a welcome guest, visited our camp today or rather our regiment. We were paid off. From some mistake in the pay rolls, we were paid only for one month and seven days, amounting to sixteen dollars and three cents. Part of the regiment was paid in United States treasury notes and gold, the rest in gold and copper. The money was needed. The boys are in good spirits.

Nov. 24, Sunday—Whilst lying in our tents, this morning, we heard the church bells in Williamsport, summoning worshipers to the house of God. We are compelled to be here, in the midst of profanity and vulgarity, during the Sabbath. At night, in company with a sergeant, I attended church in Williamsport. Captain Slaughter, of Company G, preached a war sermon. The text was Romans 13th chapter 1, 2, 3 & 4 verses. He showed that all governments are ordained of God. He proceeded to show the benignity of this government by the good which it has confered on us. Next he showed the wickedness of the present rebellion. Its wickedness was magnified by the benignity of the government; it was also gotten up by broken vows. Fraud and deceit characterized it. Floyd was the meanest traitor from Caeser to the present time.[31] At the close of the discourse the congregation united in singing the last stanza of the "Star Spangled Banner." The discourse was a very able one. After all was quiet in camp tonight a villain, of Company E, endeavored to break into Captain Phillips' tent. Men had been detailed to guard the head quarters of Company I. The sentinel commanded him to halt three times; the villain paid no attention. The sentinel fired at him with a pistol and hit him in the thigh. The rascal fell down exclaiming, "I am killed, I am killed, go away and let me die here." The sentinel discharged his duty in shooting the thief.

Nov. 25—I got a pass for the day for a friend and myself. We went to Hagerstown. We started across the fields and traveled over meadows, wheat fields and through forests. After traveling thus for three or four miles, we, at length, reached what, to our surprise afterwards, we learned to be the Baltimore and Ohio turnpike. We traveled, as we supposed, towards Hagerstown about two miles, when we met a negro and a white man. I asked them how far it was to Hagerstown. They told us that we were going in the opposite direction from the town. On further inquiry we learned that we were traveling towards Ohio and that to go to Hagerstown we must go back the same way that we had come. A boy gave us incorrect directions, thus causing us to walk near four miles for nothing. Hagerstown, the county seat of Washington County, is quite a handsome town. It contains, I should judge, about 6000 inhabitants. We took dinner at the United States Hotel. I felt very awkward eating at a table. We returned to camp near night fall. Thus ended a very pleasant day. I increased my library some. *"Tempus fugit"* [time flies].

Nov. 26—I was detailed for guard. There was a rumor of a skirmish at Hancock today. I do not know how much of truth there is in this report, whether there is any at all or not, I am unable to say. The day and night were fine for guards being clear and dry.

Nov. 27—This was a cold, cloudy and rainy day. There was nothing to relieve the dullness of camp. Don't know how long we will have to lie here doing nothing, hope not long. I should like to be in "Dixie."

Nov. 28—This morning I received two letters, one from Pennsylvania the other from Maryland. There is just now great excitement in camp, what is in the breeze I know not. Perhaps, before the record of the day is closed, the cause will be revealed. It is known, Colonel Light has been deprived of his command. The news, which has just been received, caused intense excitement and indignation. It was about half past twelve o'clock when the intelligence was made known in camp. The companies fell into ranks and were formed in line of battle. The Colonel mounted, on his charger, addressed the regiment as follows, "Fellow officers and soldiers. I have to take my leave of you. By some political intrigue, I know not why, I am deprived of my command. Farewell officers and soldiers." The Colonel reined his horse around to start. Some of the officers prevailed in him to tarry for a short time. Several of them made short speeches. I could not hear what they said, excepting their regrets at having to part with our Colonel and their determination to use their utmost endeavors to have him restored to his command. The rear rank in the meantime marched backwards about four paces and the front rank faced about. The Colonel rode between the two ranks, which were standing face to face, with his hat in hand, Lieutenant Colonel Osborne and Adjutant Marshall leading his horse. Officers and soldiers took their hats off. "Good bye boys," said the Colonel as he rode through the ranks. Many tears were shed both by officers and Privates. It was truly an affecting scene to see the

Regiment standing bathed in tears. Many a war worn veteran wept like an infant. *"Stabat miles dolorosus. Juxta miles lacrymosus"* [a sad soldier stands beside a weeping soldier].[32] The high heads and proud looks of many were brought down. Many, in whom one would have supposed the fountain of tears was long since dried up, gave expression to their grief by profuse weeping. As for myself I partook largely of the common sorrow. Tears were not wanting to my eyes, but before they were dry, I was laughing at the many ludicrous remarks, which I heard, uttered it is true in sadness. Money was soon made up to defray the expenses of an investigation of the cause of the Colonel being discharged. A donation, for his own benefit, was also made by the noncommissioned officers of the regiment. Captain Munn, of Company A, was dispatched to Washington to investigate the matter and, if possible, to have the Colonel restored to high command. Colonel Light had a firm hold on the affections of all his command, officers as well as privates. He is a plain unpretentious man. In stature he is tall and rather sparely built. He has an excellent military bearing. His voice and demeanor are commanding, but not harsh. He never manifested that contempt of those under his authority, so common to officers of his rank. As to the Colonel's qualifications for the position he held there can be no doubt of his competency; having served several years in the regular army. Report says that he also served in the Florida and Mexican wars. By his men, he was regarded as a good commander, a brave soldier, an excellent man, a loyal citizen and, what is more than all and embraces all other virtues, a true Christian. If my information be correct he is a member of the Clark Street Methodist Church. He is a poor man so far as riches are concerned; "Let none admire that riches grew in Hell." This evening gloom prevails throughout the camp. We were not prepared for such an action by the war department. When it was known in camp that the Colonel was discharged it would be difficult to say which was the most manifest indignation, surprise or sorrow. I fear that this was a fatal stroke to the regiment. Some declare that they will serve under no other Colonel. There is a mutinous spirit, to some extent, manifest in camp. I think that it will be pacified without anything serious resulting. For the present Lieutenant Colonel Osborne takes command.

Nov. 29—All that I have to write is that I have nothing to write today. It has been too rainy and muddy to drill today. Since writing the above I have learned of the death of a private in Company G. He was interred today in the cemetery at Williamsport. Let his remains rest in peace on the banks of the Potomac.

Nov. 30—This afternoon we were inspected. There was no other duty to perform today. It has been raining for several days. This is the beginning of sorrow to soldiers.

December 1, Sunday—Welcome, Old Hiems. For the "Poor soldier's" sake be sparing of your storms. Lay not thy frigid hand too heavily upon us.

Often permit the genial rays of the sun to penetrate thy dismal domain. Relent of thy wonted rigor. Be not apathetic in thy sway. Hasten to give place to thy successor, Blooming Spring. As thou hast found us jovial, rejoicing and in good health, so transmit us to the season that is fragrant with flowers, melodious with the notes of the wild warblers, enlivened with the hum of industry and vested in natures most beautiful garb. Today I finished reading the first Epistle of John, in Greek. John seems well worthy of the title, "The disciple whom Jesus loved." He seems to breathe forth love in almost every sentence he utters. This Epistle has been called, "God's love letter to the Church." I have heard learned men say that the article is always used with Christos in Greek. This is not true. In the following passages it is not used 1st John 2nd 1–4.2 It is questioned, among the doctors, whether the Iota subscript should be written under the alpha in the inflection *av* of the present infinitive mood. The regular ending of the infinitive is *eiv.* In contracts of the first form it would be, if written in full, *qeiv;* it is, perhaps, never so written. Alpha and epsilon contracts into long alpha. If the Iota subscript is omitted, how will you account for it. It has disappeared by no regular principle of language. It is then lost sight of entirely; this is not characteristic of Greek language. One of the many beauties of this language is that it does not lose one jot or tittle. If a single letter disappears in a word it can be accounted for on the principles of contraction, syncopation or euphony. Hence we conclude that the correct inflection of the present infinitives is *av.* Both forms are used by Classical Authors. In the Epistle under consideration we find both terminations. This afternoon we attended Divine services on the regimental parade ground. The regiment was formed in a hollow square and faced inwards. Chaplain MacReading then mounted a box, in the center of the square, prayed, sung and made a few remarks. Hampton's Battery and a cavalry company were also in attendance.[33]

Dec. 2—Detailed for guard. We moved our camp about half a mile from our camp ground in the clover field. We are now encamped in the timber. This was a clear day. The night was cold.

Dec. 3—Captain Munn returned from Washington today, having performed his mission. The reason why Colonel Light was discharged is satisfactory. The investigation shows that he deserted the regular army in 1857. He was a Corporal in the 1st Cavalry, he went on furlough and did not return. In 1860 he enlisted again in Chicago and was apprehended in St. Louis. He was tried by the courtmartial for deserting. The court found him guilty and sentenced him to receive 50 lashes on the naked back well laid on, to be drummed out of the service and to be branded on the left thigh with the letter D. The sentence was approved and was executed, excepting the last which was revoked by the commander in Jefferson Barracks, A.M. 1860. The unbounded confidence which both officers and privates had in the Colonel was simply misplaced.

Dec. 4—Nothing of interest marked the day. Companies I and B went to Williamsport to attend the funeral of a private of Company B, who died in the hospital. All things not being ready the funeral obsequies were not performed.

Dec. 5—There was inspection of the companies this morning by the company officers. I have made a mistake. On the 4th nothing of interest occurred. The recorded for the 4th took place on the 5th. The company inspection recorded on the fifth was on the 6th. This is to rectify the above mistake.

Dec. 6—The record of this day has already been made. The prospect of going to Romney, Va cheers up our discontented spirits. I never enjoyed better health than at present.

Dec. 7—We heard cannonading this evening up the river. The firing commenced about 4:00 p.m. and continued till dark when it ceased.

Dec. 8, Sunday—The firing was kept up at intervals during the night. Heavy cannonading was heard this morning till about noon when it ceased excepting an occasional shot. At 9:00 a.m. there was company inspection; in the afternoon preaching by the chaplain. One sentiment uttered by the chaplain I cannot subscribe to. He prayed for the refugees among us who could see their homes from which they had been driven by "Barbarians." The Southerners, though rebels (and that too against a benevolent government), are not Barbarians. The firing heard yesterday and today was in the vicinity of Clear Spring, seven or eight miles above here. The rebels endeavored to destroy a dam by firing canon balls at it. The federal forces returned the fire. The skirmishing was kept up for about 20 hours. The rebels burned a barn on this side of the river by throwing a shell into it. The firing was all done across the river that is the rebels were on one side and the Federalists on the other. A detachment from each company of this regiment went up tonight to reinforce the federal troops.

Dec. 9—Detailed for guard this morning, all is well. The detachments sent up the river returned today.

Dec. 10—We received additional intelligence from the skirmish up the river. The rebels consisting of a force of about 400 infantry and 200 cavalry were driven back with a loss of 13 killed and several wounded. This was on Sunday. The rebels left their guns but returned after night fall and took them off. The dam which they endeavored to destroy was not damaged excepting the wood works. The only casualty on the side of the Unionists was one man seriously wounded.

Dec. 11—I am on fatigue duty today; have to carry water. The weather for several days has been very beautiful more like spring than winter.

Dec. 12—Got a pass this morning and went to Williamsport. Took dinner at the hospital. Captain Munn, who was sent to procure arms for this regiment returned today. He told us that the arms were in Hagerstown and instead of 2000 there were 3000. When the captain made this announcement Major Mann proposed "three times three cheers for Captain Munn."[34]

Dec. 13—The weather is cool but very pleasant being dry and clear. Last night we slept with our clothes on and knapsacks packed ready to march at minutes warning. There was a slight apprehension of an attack by the rebels. Our slumbers were not disturbed. Our arms have been received at last; late in the afternoon they were distributed. The boys were glad to get them. Tonight many of the boys amused themselves by scouring their bayonets, cleaning their guns and making many ludicrous remarks about their skill and shooting. Whilst most of my fellow soldiers were thus interesting themselves, I was reading Paradise Lost, completely absorbed in the beauties, which abound therein.[35]

Dec. 14—Today [we] were drilled by squads in the manual of arms. In the afternoon we went out and made trial of our arms. They gave entire satisfaction, shooting accurately 900 yards. We fired three rounds apiece. This was more shooting than all the rest I ever did in my life. When having hold of a gun I'm extremely awkward. Our arms are rifled muskets, made in Springfield, Massachusetts, patented in 1858. The ball, which is used with them, is conical shaped hollow at the base.

Dec. 15, Sunday—The wind rustling in the pine trees awoke me early this morning. This is a doleful sound, fit Herald indeed of the approach of the day, pleasant if rightly spent, but if perverted, as it is by the United States Government, extremely melancholy. To my dislike I was detailed for guard. I verily believe there is no excuse for violating the Sabbath so much as is done in the Army. The reviews, inspections and parades so common on Sabbath are unnecessary. This is the day appointed for Sabbath but to me it is no Sabbath at all.

Dec. 16—The cooks have been busy today preparing rations for three days. We are to take up the line of March in the morning. Where our destination is we know not, the prevailing opinion is that we are going to Romney, Virginia to join General Kelly.[36] The prospect of soon seeing active service cheers up the boys. Inaction among soldiers breeds discontent. Soon we will be in "Dixie," if the conjectures are correct, shall we all ever return to our homes! Reason says no; experience echoes no; conscience reverberates the reply and warns us all, all to be ready. Some of us will certainly fall, whether you or I is not known. Mortal man cannot penetrate the future. As for me, being confident that I am in the line of duty, I am resigned to the will of him that rules over all and doeth all things well. Tonight some of the boys of Company I had a dance. How lightly they rush into danger! Gen Lamon came to Williamsport today. The report came into camp tonight that he had countermanded the order to march; this cast a gloom over the camp so far as known.

Dec. 17—After making the necessary preparations we took up the line of march about noon today. When the regiment was drawn up in line of battle preparatory to starting Gen Lamon rode in front of the line, took off his hat and made a short speech. I should judge that he is a better orator than general. "Attention, battalion shoulder arms, right face, column, forward march" was commanded by Colonel Osborne. With alacrity we stepped off, glad that we were going to escape inactivity. The regiment presented a fine appearance with bayonets glistening in the sun. The day was clear and warm, the roads dusty. We started northward on the Greencastle turnpike, traveled on this road about two miles then turned to the left, on the Baltimore and Ohio pike, our route was now due west. The country, over which we passed, is well improved. The soil is very fertile, not however so rich as that of Illinois. The surface of the country is moderately hilly. The Regiment halted several times to rest. There was no demonstration of patriotic feeling, no such a display of flags as the times demand. The sick were sent up on a canal boat. Our destination is Hancock, Washington County Maryland. When we arrive there Col. Osborne is to report to General Kelly at Romney, Virginia and await further orders. We reached Clear Spring about sun down, where we are quartered for tonight. The regiment is quartered in churches and school houses. Company I is comfortably quartered in a school house. Most of the boys are now either asleep or out in town. I am seated in a chair and writing on a desk for the first time since I have been in the services. I was greatly surprised, when we got into this town, to find a very handsome and smart little village. Clear Spring two miles from the Potomac River is romantically situated near the foot of North Mountain. The scenery is quite picturesque. There are four churches, several school houses, an academy, two hotels and a goodly number of stores; there are also some very fine private residences. The inhabitants are the most hospitable of any that we have found since being on the Potomac. The town is very neat and clean. The location is healthful. The town takes its name from a large spring in its midst. The spring has no medical virtues. Population about 700. Saw many beautiful ladies, who reminded me of my own "Dear Sadie." As long as life lasts I will remember Mr. and Mrs. Boyd of Clear Spring.[37] I was far away from home, a stranger, a weary, hungry soldier; they invited me into their house and gave me an excellent supper. Many other hungry soldiers enjoy their hospitality. If we are permitted to return home with pleasure will we relate this kindness toward us to our mothers and sisters. Soon we expect to meet the enemy. We will not disgrace ourselves. Be of good cheer. The distance traveled today is about 13 miles. From Williamsport to Clear Spring is seven miles. We did not come to direct route. I had finished writing my diary for the day and commenced reading "Paradise lost" at the ninth book, when the "long roll" was beaten. We fell into ranks quickly and were marched down to Four Locks, distant 2 1/2 miles, on double quick much of the way. It was about 10:00. Most of the boys were sleeping when the command fall into ranks was given. The night was clear. In the light of the full moon our bayonets glistened. When we got almost [to] the "Locks," the command, "halt, load at will" was given. Out I took a cartridge and bit off the end, by mine awkwardness I dropped and wasted the powder. This was my failure. The next trial I succeeded in getting my piece loaded. When near the river we were halted in a muddy lane.[38] After standing for about half an hour the voice of the Col. was heard, "column about face, forward march." Back to Clear Spring we marched, without seeing the enemy. At about 2:00 we were again resting our weary limbs on the floor of the school house. An attack was apprehended at the "Locks." When the command, "about face," was given, a volley, not of musketry, but, of oaths, was discharged by the boys. They were very mad.

Dec. 18—A report came into town this morning that the enemy were endeavoring to cross the river at Dam No. 5. The Dam is four miles from Clear Spring. We were marched to the dam; the result was the same as last night, we did not see the enemy. We "about faced" and marched back to Clear Spring, where we rested till 2:00 p.m., when we again took up the line of march to Hancock. Our knapsacks were hauled in a wagon thereby relieving us of a great burden. In the middle of the afternoon we crossed North Mountain. The ascent is graded. When on the top we halted. Here a grand scene is presented. That part of Virginia known as a valley district was visible. The country appeared to be a vast forest interspersed with occasional clearings, oases in the desert. A large plantation seemed not larger than the playgrounds of a child. The valley below was dotted with houses, once the seat of comfort, peace and pleasure but now suffering the penalty of rebellion. At the foot of the mountain could be seen the Potomac winding its serpentine course around the hills. Far away in the distance could be discerned a dim outline of the Blue Ridge, appearing like a cloud in the horizen. To the Southeast was Williamsport plainly to be seen. By the aid of a spy glass the officers saw a rebel camp. This place is called "Fair View" and it well deserves the name. There is a house of entertainment called "Fair View Inn." The descent was more difficult to most of us than the ascent. After crossing the mountain the country is more hilly than that of our previous journey. For several miles our route lay along the river. Virginia was in sight. We reached Hancock at about 9:00 in the night. We were quartered in school houses, churches and warehouses. The distance from Clear Spring to Hancock is 15 miles.

Dec. 19—I took a walk this morning before breakfast. I walked across the entire state of Maryland and one mile into Pennsylvania! In Fulton County, Pennsylvania at Gobin's, two miles north of Hancock, I got my breakfast. Mrs. Gobin not only gave me a good breakfast but also one day's ration. She invited to call again if ever I passed that way. Such acts of kindness as the above shall long be remembered. Hancock, on the Potomac River, contains about 1500 inhabitants. It is a place of considerable business. In neatness of appearance, beauty of location and hospitality of its inhabitants it is not equal to Clear Spring. In the afternoon we crossed over into Virginia. Our feet have touched the "Sacred soil." We are now in Dixie's land. We crossed the river in a ferry boat. One company crossed at a time. When across each company aligned itself and gave three cheers for "Dixie." Opposite to Hancock is the Baltimore and Ohio Railroad. For the night we were quartered here, Companies I & G. in a barn.

Dec. 20—An artillery Co. of the regular army came here from Romney, last night, en-route, as they supposed, for Washington. I witnessed them ford the river this morning. The water run over the cannons. They had six brass smooth-bore pieces. Our regiment was today divided; it was stationed on the Baltimore and Ohio Railroad from Hancock Station to Great Cacapon. At the former place, in a brick house, the property of a rebel, the headquarters of the Regiment are kept. About noon today four companies went up the road on a freight train. Two companies stopped at Sir John's Run. At this place the rebels had burned the depot. Companies I & G. went on and are now stationed at Great Cacapon. A very costly bridge across Great Cacapon Creek had been burned by the rebels, a new one has just been completed. The companies stationed here are to guard this bridge. Picket guards are sent out one mile in different directions to guard roads by which an enemy might approach. The railroad from Hancock to this place, distant 10 miles, runs within a few rods of the Potomac River. The scenery is very romantic. The road now winds around a mountain then runs straight across a narrow valley. Here over head hangs an immense cliff of rocks. The bottoms of the river are very rich but narrow. Great Cacapon is a mere railroad station, no town. We are quartered in two houses deserted by their former, rebel, occupants. The one in which Company I is quartered was used for a store and residence. This is quite the desolate looking place. The blight of rebellion is plainly visible here. The ruins of bridges, deserted houses and fields with fences destroyed all combine to attest the evils of Civil War. There are but few able bodied men in this country; they are either in the rebel or union army or have been driven from their homes. This county, Morgan, gave a majority for the Union last spring, when the ordinance of secession was submitted to the people.

Dec. 21—Today was spent in fixing up our quarters. The day was very blustery and cold. The boys think that we have got almost to the end of the world.

Dec. 22, Sunday—This is Sabbath only in name. I was detailed for picket guard. The pickets are placed on duty at 1:00 p.m.. All the afternoon and night sleet and rain was falling. Three of us were placed to guard a road on the side of Cacapon Mountain. We built us a shelter of straw, like a hogbed. One stood Sentinel, two were under the shelter covered up with their blankets trying to sleep. One man would stand two hours and then wake up another to relieve him. Whilst lying down the sleet poured down into my face. Then thought I of home, of a warm house and comfortable bed. These are luxuries that I, perhaps, will never again enjoy. Till peace is restored I desire not to enjoy them.

Dec. 23—More gladly never did man hail the dawn of day than did the pickets this morning. Long and weary were the hours till 1:00 p.m. when we were relieved. We were wet, cold, hungry and sleepy when the morning dawned. At last the wished for hour came. The relief "hove" in sight. This was my first experience on picket. A scouting party went out late this evening and was gone all night.

Dec. 24—The scouting party, which went out last evening, returned this morning. They brought in some horses, chickens, turkeys and honey. Lieutenant Savage of Company G commanded the party. The Lieutenant administered the oath of allegiance to a man who was suspected of entertaining secession proclivities. What law there is for taking property in this manner I know not. I consider it nothing but stealing. A citizen comes to our headquarters and informs Capt. Slaughter, the commander of this post, that in such a place lives a secessionist. He also volunteers his service to pilot a squad of the men to his house. On the following night, night fit time for such diabolical deeds, the captain sends out a band of thieves, more respectfully called a "scouting party" to steal, or, as Cap would say, capture the property of the man accused of being a secessionist. Of such operations I do not approve. It is violating the laws of which we are fighting to enforce. The man is not given a chance to prove his loyalty. That honest men go out on these scouts no one can deny. This evening I visited a secessionist lady. She has a son in the rebel army in General Jackson's brigade.[39] She talked very intelligently. A very beautiful daughter sat by her side. The damsel said but little. Modesty blushed on her ruddy cheeks. Five other soldiers besides myself were present. And the fair damsel said words so lovely as her looks she could have disarmed, like the Philistine woman did Sampson, and presented me harmless at the feet of the enemy.

Dec. 25—It has been just 1861 years since "peace on earth and goodwill to men" was sung by the heavenly choir. To shepards, keeping watch by night, by an angel was announced the "Glad tidings of great joy, which shall be unto all people." In our country peace is dethroned and Civil War reigns, strife and commotions distract our land. A deadly warfare is now being waged between the two sections of our beloved country, on the one side for the destruction of the best government ever established on Earth, on the other to demonstrate to the world that man is capable of governing himself. By right not by might we shall conquer. *In Deo mea spes est* [In God my hope is]. Can it be that today is Christmas, the birthday of the "Prince of Peace"? Man has forgotten his Savior. Ministers of the gospel have left off teaching men to live peaceably with one another, have girded on the sword and are eager for the fray. Oh! How fallen, how changed are they from him, who said, "Go ye into all the World and preach the Gospel to every creature." How many men are now in the field thirsting for the blood of their fellow man! O humanity, well mayest thou hide thy face in shame! Man alone of all the works of God is transformed into a Demon. May a kind Providence, in mercy hide from my eyes the horrors which seem to threaten this country. To rest my weary limbs in the bosom of my mother earth would be preferable to witnessing the scenes of butchery and misery which are soon to ensue. We arose early this morning to prepare for a journey which we had to take. My ears were not greeted with the wanted, "I wish you a Merry Christmas," but instead oaths! All things being ready we turned our backs to Great Cacapon. Our journey was performed on foot. The walking was rather bad, on the account of a light snow, which had fallen on the night previous. The most difficult part of the route was crossing Cacapon Mountain. We were ordered to march to Bath. Co. I only received marching orders. The distance from Great Cacapon to Bath is four miles, over a bad road even for a mountainous country. We reached our destination at about 11:00 a.m. Bath, the county seat of Morgan County, often called Berkeley Springs, is about three miles from the Potomac River and the same distance from the Baltimore and Ohio Railroad. The town is very romantically situated in a small valley surrounded by high hills. In the midst of the town burst up through the earth the well-known Berkeley Springs, one of the oldest watering places in the United States. The water is about the temperature of blood. The accommodations are excellent for 800 invalids. The scenery is grand. This is a great summer resort. Bath contains 400 inhabitants. The beauty of the scenery, the advantages of bathing and the healthfulness of the location combine to render it a very attractive place. We are quartered in a fine stone house one mile from town. It pains me to see rough soldiers march into the fine well furnished rooms and take possession of the costly furniture. Great taste is displayed in the garden, yard and out houses. All things about the Plantation show that its owner was a man of taste and means. The possessor is in New Jersey. The house was occupied by a tenant, to whom notice was given to vacate it to make room for Company I. The tenant and landlord are both Union men. Three companies of the 39th regiment Illinois, a company of the fourth artillery of regular army are now in or near Bath. I visited the artillery company in their quarters. The cook gave me a cup of coffee, a piece of meat and some crackers. I took a bath in the Berkeley Springs. This closes the record of a very gloomy Christmas. It is now late in the night; my fellow comrades are lying around me asleep. There is no hope for the morrow.

Dec. 26—Nothing to do was characteristic of the day. The company had nothing to eat, excepting what it got of its own accord, from before daylight on the 25th till late in the evening on the 26th. Thus the fates roll. Nobody is to blame. The government furnishes plenty for its soldiers but they cannot get it.

Dec. 27—Hunger is gnawing at my bones. It is now about 12:00; we have had nothing to eat today. In the afternoon we get our breakfast! It consisted of "slapjacks," sour pork and coffee. The slapjacks tasted sweetly.

They are made as follows: mix flour and water, add a little salt, stir this composition until it has attained the consistency of dough; then frying in dirty grease: if the grease is not to be had fry it dry pan, frequently turning the cake to prevent it from burning. This makes a very delicious dish for hungry soldiers. I would not recommend it to anyone unless he is very hungry. "Appetite is the best sauce."

Dec. 28—For all that was done today, it might as well appear as a blank in my diary. The name of the Plantation in which we are quartered is "Fruit Hill." There are a great many fruit trees on the place. The cherry trees are some of them one foot and a half thick through the trunk and proportionately high. The apple trees are almost as large. At the foot of the hill, on which the house stands, are some large weeping Willows, the diameter of whose trunks is two feet or more. The soil of this county, Morgan, is poor; it is mostly slate stone soil. The county was formed from Berkeley and Hampshire counties. Berkeley Springs was in Berkeley County; hence the name. This part of the state was included in the grant to Lord Fairfax. He is said to have had a summer residence at Bath. There is a small house in town which tradition says belonged to General Washington. Lord Fairfax donated 50 acres, around the Springs, to the state of Virginia, *"pro bono publico"* [for the good of the public].

Dec. 29, Sunday—I was again on picket guard. No person was allowed to pass without a written pass. The day was beautiful. There was nothing to remind one that it was Sabbath. The day passed off quietly. There was nothing to do but to keep watch and examine passes; if they were correct the bearer was permitted to go on his way, if not we were instructed to arrest the bearer and bring him or her to headquarters. We arrested nobody. There were three of us at the same place to guard a road. The Chaplain returned from Illinois a few days since. He preached in Bath today; picket duty prevented me from attending. Tonight a man was making around the pieces of the artillery company. The Sentinel challenged him three times to halt. Each time he retreated. The Sentinel then fired at him five times. We were not well instructed in the duties of picket guards. Something was evidently wrong. To give an alarm we discharged our pieces. Other pickets did likewise. When we had fired our guns my two comrades retreated to the quarters of the company. I ran a few steps into a field and loaded. I then took position behind a large tree near the road. Not seeing an enemy I went back to my post in a few minutes. I was anxious to discover what was the matter, whether we were attacked and if so where the attack was made. For this purpose I was swift to run around over the hills. This about 9:00. The companies fell into ranks ready to repel the enemy. When the cause of the firing was known the excitement subsided and we were left to our reflections. Our post was on the top of Warm Spring Ridge. On this Ridge are many pine trees. The night was very dark. The wind was high. In the distance, on the mountain top, it could be heard blowing among the trees, making a noise like the rushing of many waters, or the tread of cavalry. Now the purchase nearer and gradually dies away till it sounds like the sigh of a person lamenting the loss of a priceless treasure, a friend, true and dear. Again many men seem groaning in the agonies of death. All sorts of sounds it assumes, excepting of merryment. The wind rustling among the leaves of the pine trees is an awfully solemn sound.

Dec. 30—Day dawned and our hearts were filled with joy. During the night we extinguished our fire, we were therefore, quite chilly. At 9:00 a.m. we were relieved. This day's record would be the same as other days of inaction. Nothing remarkable.

Dec. 31—We were drilled in the manual of arms this morning. At 2:00 p.m. we went to town to be "mustered in for pay." We have to be mustered in once in a month. This is the way in which a company "is mustered in." The company comes to a "support arms." Then in the presence of a "mustered in" officer the roll is called. Each man answers "present" and immediately without the command being given, comes to an "order arms." When we came back to our quarters, before breaking ranks, Lt. Waller said that secessionists were about 15 miles below filling up the ditch on the Baltimore and Ohio Railroad. He said that we want to go down and take them. All that thought themselves able to stand the trip and to take some of "the pills," if necessary, he wanted to step two paces to the front. About 60 of the company volunteered to go. We expected to start about 9:00 p.m. with today's rations in our haversacks. I, among the rest, volunteered. Forty rounds of cartridges were given to us. Some of the boys wrote to their friends that they expected to meet the enemy tonight. After roll call we went to bed expecting to be called up soon. We were not called up but slept and slept on till day dawned and we awoke and found ourselves all safely launched into a new year. Thus ended the year 1861, which year shall ever be memorable for the present wicked rebellion.

The end of volume one.

Volume 2

HANCOCK, MARYLAND, JANUARY–MARCH 1862

The men of the Thirty-ninth Illinois spent a comfortable Christmas and New Year's Day in their "well provided for" outposts around the numerous hot springs resorts in north central Virginia.[1] In early January 1862, they received a warning that an enemy force under General Thomas J. "Stonewall" Jackson was approaching Bath, Virginia. Colonel Osborn immediately readied his command, and on January 3 elements of the Thirty-ninth began skirmishing with Jackson's lead units. The next day, the duel with the Confederates continued as the Illinois soldiers withdrew from positions at Bath, Great Cacapon, and Alpine, to cross the Potomac and join forces concentrated at Hancock, Maryland, under Brigadier General Frederick West Lander. The Confederates approached Hancock but did not cross the river. Instead, Jackson opened an artillery bombardment against the town. On January 5, Jackson sent his cavalry commander, Colonel Thomas Ashby, to demand the Federals' surrender. Lander refused, and the next day the Confederates withdrew.

A week later, when word came that Jackson was advancing on the Union base at Romney, Virginia, the Thirty-ninth Illinois was shifted west to Cumberland, Maryland. Though Romney was abandoned, Jackson surprisingly did not move on Cumberland, and five days later the Thirty-ninth boarded railroad cars and moved farther west to New Creek, Virginia, where they briefly became part of General William S. Rosecrans's command. In early February 1862, the regiment moved again, this time to Patterson Creek, Virginia, to rejoin General Lander's division. The soldiers lived in railroad cars while they set to work protecting and repairing the Baltimore and Ohio Railroad. Some of the men crossed the Potomac and visited Bath where they were shocked to see the destruction that had been wreaked by the Confederates upon the property of Unionists in the town. During the celebration of George Washington's birthday, officers read the soldiers a series of resolutions that congratulated their Illinois brethren serving in the West for recent victories, particularly the capture of Fort Donelson, Tennessee. Calling for all loyal citizens to continue the fight, the resolutions concluded:

> That the inauguration of that traitor Jefferson Davis as president of the so-called Southern Confederacy upon this, the birthday of the immortal Washington, is an insult of the deepest dye to the memory of the Father of Our Country and to every lover of free institutions, and that we pledge ourselves to avenge the insult whenever and wherever we meet him or his emissaries.[2]

On March 9, 1862, the regiment left their now-familiar railroad cars and marched to Martinsburg, Virginia. Camped near the town, men from the Thirty-ninth Illinois, defying threats from the local townspeople, raised the U.S. flag over the Martinsburg courthouse. The Thirty-ninth was assigned to the Second Brigade (under Colonel Jeremiah C. Sullivan), Second Division (under Brigadier General James Shields), Fifth Army Corps (under Major General Nathaniel P. Banks), and Army of the Potomac (under Major General George B. McClellan). According to General McClellan's plans, Banks's Fifth Corps would secure the Shenandoah Valley and then shift the rest of Banks's command east to protect Washington, while McClellan coordinated a convergence on Richmond from the east and north. By early March, Banks had his corps ready to move, and on March 12, his command marched south and occupied Winchester, Virginia. *—S.R.W.*

★ ★ ★ ★ ★

—"Tis distance lends enchantment to the view."

January 1, 1862—"If thou beist he—But O how fallen, how changed!" So unlike last New Year's Day was this that I could not realize the fact that this was the day celebrated as the beginning of the year. I have not written any for several days. This is the seventh day of the month. The exciting scenes through which we have passed since writing has erased from my mind the things which occurred during the days of inactivity from the 1st to the 4th.

Jan. 2—Twenty of Company I, myself among the rest, went out to forage. We were commanded by Lieutenant Waller. We brought some corn and hay, taken from Buck's farm. Buck is an Adjutant in the rebel army. His farm is six miles from Bath, on the road to Winchester. The boys went into the house and some of them rendered themselves very obnoxious to a lover of politeness and a respector of virtue. Ungentlemanly and unsoldierlike language was used to two ladies. A woman, who respects herself, should always be respected by man and by soldiers too. The country passed over today is rough and the soil is poor.[3]

Jan. 3—I was on picket guard today. A report came to headquarters this morning the rebels 15,000 strong were advancing from Winchester towards Bath; they were, according to the report 15 miles distant. This report caused but little excitement in camp so accustomed had we become to such reports. Early in the morning Sargents W. C. McMurry and O. P. Nelson, Corporal T. Johnson, privates B. Johnson and Geo Riddle were sent out to reconnoiter.[4] As to their adventures I am not informed. They were surrounded by scouting parties of the enemy, fought their way through, evaded their pickets, escaped to sleep in the mountains. They, on the following day, made their way to Great Cacapon. In the afternoon they returned to the joy of all the Company. Co. D this evening had a sharp skirmish with the enemy. One man was slightly wounded. What damage the enemy sustained is unknown. Major Mann came very near being surrounded and taken prisoner.[5] About dark a messenger came in haste to our post and told us to come to our quarters immediately. Before we got to quarters the company had fallen into and taken position. Quickly we were with our company. We took position on Warm Spring Ridge, between Fruit Hill and Bath, behind the trees, near the road by which we expected the enemy to advance. Bath is just at the foot of the ridge. The snow fell thick and fast. Expecting an attack every minute we stood with our arms in hand. The hearts of many were earnestly desiring that the "Secesh" might attack us. The rebels were encamped about two miles from Bath. Their fires could be seen. It appeared as if they were burning houses. There were three companies of the 39th Illinois Volunteers, part of a cavalry company and one section of the 4th Artillery in Bath. The artillery consisted of two pieces brass smooth bore, one 6-pounder and one 12-pounder.[6] Our whole force did not exceed 315 men. The rebels were variously estimated at from 15,000 to 600. Our determination was to maintain our position or to die. The night was cold, dark and the snow continued to fall. Till midnight we stood in readiness to fire at a minutes warning; there being then no appearance of an attack a heavy guard was stationed along the road and the rest were permitted to go to quarters. I volunteered to guard the road. In the morning we expected to be attacked.

Jan. 4—This morning at 2 o'clock, the 84th Pennsylvania Regiment, part of it, 700 in number, commanded by Colonel McMurry, arrived.[7] The Regiment had just been armed, at Hancock, a few hours before it started to our assistance. At 4:00 this morning we called up, took breakfast and were again in position to receive the rebels with cordiality. We were expecting to be further reinforcements. Colonel McMurry is to command the forces. Major Mann of the 39th Regiment Illinois volunteers, had command previous to the arrival of the 84th Pennsylvania. At about 10:00 a.m. firing commenced. The ball was now opened. The good time had at last come. We were now about to sip the honey of the soldiers life, so thought we, but our experience a few hours after proved that we were sadly mistaken. Skirmishing was kept up for some time. We shelled the Rebels where they were in the woods. Company I was placed to guard the cannons. The rebels appeared to be surrounding us. Firing was kept up to 2:00 p.m. The cannons were occasionally fired at the rebels. None of our men were wounded. How many of the rebels were killed is not known. About 2:00 p.m. we were drawn up in line of battle, now we thought that we were going to strike for our country. Great sorrow caused these words when they fell from the lips of Major Mann, "The Colonel has ordered a retreat." To Sir John's Run we retreated, distant three miles. We had no teams, we were therefore unable to take off our baggage. The retreat was made in so great haste that we left even our knapsacks and blankets, these were at our quarters some distance from where we were posted. The officers lost their trunks. Some of the boys had to leave behind many valuable articles, such as letters from their sweethearts, their pictures and various other things. Our regiment did not want to retreat, they would have preferred to die. Colonel McMurry was cursed when he ordered a retreat. When about one mile from Bath we met 500 men, of the 13th Regiment Indiana, coming to our assistance. The commander of this regiment and Major Mann were anxious to go back to Bath. Colonel McMurry was unwilling to return, "I think that we had better fall back to Hancock, if we can," said he. To have gone back we would've been glad, but Colonel McMurry said, no, and we must obey. We marched on to Sir John's Run, here the 39th Illinois and the 13th Indiana determined to return to Bath and if possible to hold it. We started back and marched short distance when this determination was abandoned and we again retreated. A few men were deployed as skirmishers; they were some distance ahead when a retreat was the second time ordered. They were called back and retreated in great haste stating that the enemy in large force was just in the rear. In the rear was the force far out numbering ours, in front was the Potomac River. There was no bridge, we had no boats. What shall we do? was the question. Our force was 750 strong. The 84th Pennsylvania had gone on to Hancock. The 500 Indianians had only 15 rounds of cartridges apiece. To hazard a battle under such disadvantages would have been madness. It was now about sun down. The day was very cold. The river was deep and swift—"Into it boys, wade it," said Maj. Mann. "Into it" we plunged, for life we waded through the cold stream. If Jordan is a colder stream than the Potomac, a man is excusable for turning back with horror from its brink. The water was waist deep. The Indiana Regiment did not cross the river but went up to Great Cacapon distant five miles. Across the river our clothes were soon frozen on us. We had now to march to Hancock, six miles distant. Thus we made our exit from "Dixie." We went forth with joy but returned with sorrow disgraced and "most mightily" wet too. I was insisted on to take a drink of whiskey. I yielded. My testimony concerning this is that the dram did me no good at all. Two of my comrades and myself stopped at a farmhouse one mile from Hancock, here we fared well. Tonight the rebels threw a few shells into Hancock. The companies of our regiment at the station opposite to Hancock were driven across the river this evening, not however till they had caused several rebels to fall down biting the ground. Co. G. at Great Cacapon was attacked and put to flight. Had we have remained in Bath much longer doubtless we would have been surrounded and cut off.

Jan. 5, Sunday—Considerable snow fell during the night. The rebels made their appearance on a hill across the river early this morning. As we came into Hancock this morning, we met a beautiful young mother, hasting out of town, bearing in her arms an infant; "You are leaving are you?" Said my comrade. "Indeed I am," responded she. General Jackson, the commander of the rebel forces across the river, sent a flag of truce across, demanding a surrender of the town, or he would burn it. He gave an hour and a half for the women and children to leave. General Lander, the commander of our forces, gave him a fitting answer. Colonel Ashby was the bearer of the flag of truce.[8] Our troops were stationed behind the hills, out of reach of the fire of the enemy. Colonel Ashby swore that he intended to cross the river today. A few men were detailed to go to the river to watch the movement of the enemy and to be ready for immediate action, should he attempt to cross. I was one of the detail. Five pieces of cannon could be seen across the river. At 1:00 p.m. the ball was opened. The rebels threw a shell, it fell short. Promptly our artillery responded. Now began the most heavenly music that ever mortal ear was charmed with. For about two hours a brisk fire was kept up. The shots of the rebels nearly all fell short. Certain, if they succeed in destroying a government, they will have to do better shooting than they did today. The heavens seemed rent asunder as the shells and balls whistled through the air. At first our shots seem not to take the desired affect, but afterwards the "Secesh" were scattered to the four winds of Heaven. They could not stand the belchings of our well aimed cannons. As I stood and beheld the firing and heard the missiles whistle through the air, Heaven seemed to be on earth. I was not aware that man was capable of so much enjoyment as the witnessing of the bombardment gave me. What the rebels suffered by our fire is not known. No damage was done to our troops and but little or none to the town. Firing was kept up on both sides till dark. The smoke of the cannon could be seen several seconds before the report could be heard. Hancock was entirely deserted by its inhabitants. Some villainous soldiers entered houses by force and stole things to eat. Such conduct is not right. It is like a certain ancient hunter, whose name I forget, being devoured by his own dogs. I stayed all night at the same place where I stayed last night.

Jan. 6—The "Secesh" gathered in squads on the hill this morning. A few shots dispersed them. They were seen to bring a piece of artillery on the hill when they were fired into by a Parrot gun. This caused them to retreat on double quick without even unhitching from the piece. Several shots were fired at the enemy today but he did not respond. They continued to move their effects from town.

Jan. 7—But little was done today. A few rebels could be seen. Reinforcements began to come into town. Some of the citizens returned today. The weather for several days past has been very cold. The river is nearly frozen over. Tonight the "Secesh" burned a house across the river.

Jan. 8—This morning all was quiet. The rebels are known to have sustained the loss of a few men; various are the conjectures as to the number. Some of "the boys" think that they must have had 100 men killed! My opinion is that the number of their killed does not exceed 10 men!

Almost, if not every, house in town is filled with soldiers. The rebels seem to have retreated last night. This afternoon some of the 39th Illinois Regiment crossed the river, brought over their baggage, such as the rebels had not taken or destroyed. The citizens all returned to their homes today. The third brigade of General Banks divisions arrived today. General Williams is the Commander of this brigade. He is to assume command at Hancock. General Lander is to take General Kelly's command.[9]

Jan. 9—Today we attended the funeral of one of our comrades who died yesterday. He was in the hospital. The hospital is a brick church, in Pennsylvania, one mile and a half north of Hancock. Near this church we buried our comrade, by name M. V. Lyan. Co. I all attended. Death "Cuts down all, Both great and small." It has been good sleighing since Sunday. Today the snow began to disappear.[10]

Jan. 10—This has been a foggy, sloppy day. We received orders to march today. Our destination is not known to us. Wherever we go it will be all right, we will make it so. At dark we started on a forced march to Cumberland, Maryland. The road was muddy, the night dark. At two o'-clock in the night we halted till morning. Many of the soldiers walked on ahead to procure quarters; I was among this number. At three o'clock I stopped till daylight. The country over which we passed tonight is mountainous and thinly settled. It was so warm through tonight the road was very muddy. We had no rations in our haversacks.

Jan. 11—Arose this morning at day light and started on my journey. Traveled in advance of the regiments the rest of the route. We stopped at Gillman, a small village, for breakfast, at 9 o'clock a.m. The lady at whose house we stopped was very hospitable. At this town there is an extensive tan yard. Distance traveled before breakfast was 7 miles. After partaking of a bountyful breakfast we went on our way rejoicing. The next village is Flint Stone. This is small and insignificant. The road was muddy again today. The squad with which I traveled reached Cumberland at 3 o'clock PM. The country traversed today is mountainous and poor. I saw the Allegheny Mountains for the first time in day-light. I have passed through this range three times, but in the night. The beauty of the scenery did much to alleviate the hardships of this day's march. The main body of the regiment arrived about dark. The distance from Hancock to Cumberland is 40 miles.

Jan. 12, Sunday—I attended Sabbath school at the Methodist Protestant church, in the afternoon, and taught a class. In the evening I attended church. Stayed all night at Joseph Young's. Setting down to a table and sleeping on a good bed reminded me of better days than I expect to again enjoy. "Man wants but little here below, Nor wants that little long."[11]

Jan. 13—I saw Mr. Weber, this morning, a college friend—Alas! Alas![12]

Jan. 14—Cumberland, the capital of Allegheny County, Maryland, is the second city in the State, excepting perhaps, Frederick. It is disputed as to which of these is the larger. Cumberland is the western terminus of the

Chesapeake and Ohio Canal. Coal of a superior quality is abundant in the immediate vicinity; iron ore is also found. The country around is poor for agricultural purposes. There are many fine buildings. The churches, school houses and other public buildings speak well for the enterprise of the inhabitants. The streets, though narrow, are well paved with stone. The city is lighted with gas. This also is a place of considerable historic interest. Fort Cumberland and Will's Creek are noted in the early exploits of General Washington.[13] Excepting a well, which the general had done in the Fort, the last vestige of it has disappeared. The ground only, where the fort was, is pointed out to the inquirer. The courthouse, a private residence and an Episcopal Church now stand on the ground where once stood Fort Cumberland. Washington was a mere youth when he built this fort. The site selected is a hill on the banks of the Potomac River, overlooking Virginia. The city is at the mouth and built on both sides of Wills Creek; this Creek is crossed by a fine iron bridge. Population about 8000. There was nothing done in the military today worthy of note. I was impressed with a sight which I beheld on the street tonight. A soldier of the 110th Pennsylvania Regiment had become so intoxicated that he was unable to take care of himself. The night was cold. He was lying in the street suffering. A little boy came along and saw his condition. He took him by the hand and was trying to get [him] to some comfortable place for the night. The boy was fearful that the soldier would freeze.

Jan. 15—We are quartered in the basement of the Lutheran Church, on the corner of Baltimore and Centre streets. There was preaching this evening at the Methodist church. The house was crowded, mostly with soldiers. It was difficult to hear what the preacher said for the coughing.

Jan. 16—We have received a new uniform. The pants are pale blue, the coats deep blue or black. There has nothing of interest transpired since our arrival at this place. Two funeral processions passed our quarters today. The death of two soldiers will sadden the hearts of friends at home.

Jan. 17—I took a walk to the mountains this afternoon. With great labor I ascended to the top of Wills Mountain. For all my toil and labor I was amply paid when on the summit. Beautiful far beyond the powers of description was the scenery presented to my view. Just at the foot of the mountain, in a valley surrounded by hills and mountains lay Cumberland. To the East and West mountain seemed piled on mountain. I descended on the opposite side from which I made the ascent. So steep was it, in places, that I was compelled to lie down the ground, take hold of huckleberry bushes, that grew among the rocks, and swing myself over a precipace down for several feet. I returned to camp via the "Narrows." This is a deep gap in Wills Mountain through which a creek of the same name flows on its way to join the Potomac. On both sides of the creek the mountains rise almost perpendicularly several hundred feet above the bed of the creek. On one side is a railroad on the other is the

Baltimore and Ohio Turnpike. This gap is called "The Narrows." Perhaps the greatest work in Cumberland is the viaduct across Wills Creek. It is made of brick; built at an immense labor and cost to the railroad company.

Jan. 18—I was detailed for guard today. My post was in the St. Nicholas hotel to guard General Kelly's room. I was reading a newspaper when the general stepped out of his room. I did not see him till he was near where I stood, "Salute an officer," said he. We received orders to march New Creek, 21 miles above Cumberland. We got on the cars at about 2 o'clock p.m., switched, backed, run forward and acted the fool generally till 5 o'-clock p.m. Then run to the viaduct and stopped two hours and then started off. Thus our journey was after night. We were loaded on a freight train like so many hogs. We slept on the cars tonight.

Jan. 19, Sunday—It has been raining all day. We are living in box cars. Companies A & F. are in Cumberland. New Creek is a station on the Baltimore and Ohio Railroad, in Hampshire County Virginia. This is a small town containing only a few houses. In a beautiful Valley among the Allegheny Mountains, on the north branch of the Potomac River, lies the little town of New Creek, which takes its name from a creek that "Flows fast by." On every side are high mountains. Across the river, in Maryland, is Queens Point, a high mountain. Near the summit are three large rocks, resembling somewhat, huge pillars.

Jan. 20—This was a rainy day. We endure living in the cars well, but do not enjoy it at all. West of and on a hill overlooking the town is a cannon 12 pounder. On this hill also are entrenchments, breast works and a ditch. The cannon is nine feet and 4 inches long; it is a siege piece. Read the ninth book of "Paradise Lost." Last night the 5th Ohio Regiment came.

Jan. 21—Still raining. The 66th Regiment Ohio volunteers came on the cars last night. They are direct from camp. When we came the 1st Virginia cavalry and the 5th Virginia infantry were here. What such concentration of forces at this point means we know not. This afternoon late we were moved across the river to the Maryland side. We are now at Black Oak Bottom Allegheny County, Maryland.[14]

Jan. 22—At last the rain has ceased and the sun again shines. Black Oak Bottom is a mere stopping place for the cars, distant from New Creek 6 1/2 miles. There is a switch but nothing else to indicate that is a station. The situation is in a valley, on the river, with mountains on the east and west. The trees on the mountain tops are covered with ice, which in the light of the sun presents a beautiful appearance.

Jan. 23—At night we place straw on the floors of the cars and then spread our blankets down on it. A man lies down across the car next to the one end, on his side. In the rear of him, in the same manner, both fronting to the end of the car, another man lies; a third man takes a like position. Then a man, skilled in works of art, places his foot on the posterior parts of the individual, who has just lain down, and crowds them up close together. In like manner three more men are disposed of and so on till the car is filled to its utmost capacity. Then we spread blankets over us. Thus crowded in edge ways and "keyed up," like a floor, we lie and, if we can, sleep. When a man turns over he knocks fire out of his bones against those of his nearest neighbor.

Jan. 24—The regiment was "paid off" today. "The boys" now have plenty of money. This evening and tonight it snowed. We are momentarily expecting orders to make some move. We are, perhaps, one fold of the "Boa Constrictor," which is to crush out this "wicked rebellion." Doubtless the day of "masterly inactivity" is near at a close. If so the iniquity of the so-called Southern Confederacy is filled up. Its days are numbered, "few and evil have they been." On the day that General McClellan moves with the "grand army" Jeff Davis and Co. had better take passage to the Fejee Islands.[15]

Jan. 25—This morning we were taken back to New Creek, where we are now lying, expecting soon to have something to do.

Jan. 26, Sunday—This was a cold day. The ground froze up solid last night. We have to consult the almanac to tell when Sunday comes.

Jan. 27—"And o, it fills my soul with joy, to meet my friends at home; Home, home, home again." So heard I officers sing tonight as I passed by the car, in which they were. To hear such songs melts the hearts of men who can stare death in the face without fear or trembling. There was nothing done today worthy of note.

Jan. 28—This was a rainy morning. A few days ago I finished reading "Paradise Lost." With delight have I perused its pages till Adam and Eve were expelled from the garden till "They, hand in hand, with wandering steps and slow, through Eden took their solitary way."

Jan. 29—It rained again today. If rain be the tears of heaven we should be consoled with the thought that it sympathized with us. There are some egregious lies in circulation with regard to the skirmish at Bath.

Jan. 30—There is more sickness at the present time in the regiment than ever before. Our quarters, in the cars, are very uncomfortable. Whilst we were at Camp Mather, we received the Chicago morning papers, sometimes the evening papers also; at Benton Barracks the St. Louis morning and evening papers were regularly received; at Williamsport the Baltimore and New York papers were received one-day behind the Times, at Hancock the same as in Williamsport, at Cumberland, Black Oak Bottom and New Creek the Wheeling papers were received regularly.

Jan. 31—I was on picket guard today. The post, on which I was stationed, was one mile from camp among the Allegheny Mountains. The day was cloudy; the night very dark. In the latter part of the night it snowed. Nothing extraordinary occurred during the day or night.

February 1—"Let there be light," was uttered by Divine command. There is now a charm in the sound of the word light to me such as never before.

The word is in Latin, Lux, in Greek, Phos. By picket guards the dawn of day is watched with intense interest and hailed with great joy. This morning, when the light of day appeared over the mountain tops, I felt greatly cheered up. My weary limbs seemed refreshed. I was no longer tormented by the loss of sleep. This was a wet disagreeable day.

Feb. 2, Sunday—This was a clear day; the sun shone all day for the first time since we have been quartered on the cars. The cars are poor quarters for soldiers. Hope that our stay here will be short.

Feb. 3—It snowed today. Masterly inactivity rules the day. Something great is to be done, in a few days, we are continually told. "The few days" have not yet come. From early dawn till after dark the snow continued to fall. Report says that we have marching orders; we are to go down the road to guard it as it is rebuilt. I do not know that there is any truth in this report. "There shall be wars and rumors of wars."

Feb. 4—This was a cloudy and cold day. As usual nothing was done more than common. The boys amuse themselves by making finger rings and pipes out of Laurel root. One battery came here today. This looks like making the "Secesh" get from the happy land of Canaan. There is now a heavy snow on the ground.

Feb. 5—This was a very cold morning; it was also clear. We are now momentarily expecting to leave this place. Hope that our sojourn on the cars is nearly terminated. At 11 o'clock a.m. the steam was let on and we were moving down the road. Near Patterson's Creek we stopped and are yet quartered on the cars. Patterson's Creek is eight miles below Cumberland. It is a beautiful stream. At the mouth of this Creek is a station, on the Baltimore and Ohio railroad, of the same name. Country around mountainous, with beautiful valleys between. This is in Hampshire County, VA. From Patterson's Creek, this evening, six flat boats were taken down the Potomac River. Between Cumberland and this place are many troops also several pieces of artillery, perhaps 75 pieces. General Lander has command of these forces.

Feb. 6—We lay on the switch and did nothing today, excepting stand guard. There has been all day a movement of troops down the river, on the railroad, the road follows a course of the river. I was this evening detailed for guard. We had to guard some cars loaded with hay. Wherever there is a half bushel of potatoes or a peck of beans or hay enough to bed a mule there a guard must be placed to keep his lonely watch. There are a great many things done in war, which it would be difficult to find any reason for. But why should not this be the case? War is unreasonable. When there is no reason in a thing itself, how can we expect to find any reason in anything connected with it? The weather continues unsettled. Time drags heavily on our hands. The hope of a "forward movement" soon being made only keeps up our spirits.

Feb. 7—There was nothing done today worthy of note.

Feb. 8—Ditto

Feb. 9, Sunday—Nothing to remind one of the Sabbath. There has been no meetings in the regiments, to my knowledge, since we left Williamsport. The Chaplain has gone home on furlough.

Feb. 10—We are lying in the cars on a side track doing guard duty. We daily mount between 75 & 50 guards. The weather is yet very unpleasant.

Feb. 11—This evening General Lander went down the road. The general is five feet and eleven inches tall, hair dark and turning gray, eyes blue, complexion light. His eye is very piercing; his nose is sharp and rather long. He wears long hair, his face is unshaven, he has not a heavy beard. Age about 45 years. There is, if I mistake not, fight in the general. Time will soon show.

Feb. 12—I was on guard today. There were three of us on the post. We had to guard a "Secesh" family. Whenever any of the family wanted to go any distance from the house to attend to business, a guard would accompany them. The man of the house is quite old. Whilst guarding him to the sutlers I had an opportunity to converse with him. He complained bitterly of his rails having been burned by the soldiers. I told him that the greatest destruction of property that I had ever seen was along the Baltimore and Ohio Railroad, where the rebels had destroyed costly bridges. "Virginia built and paid for these bridges," said he, "and she had a right to destroy them." He said that they were destroyed by the order of the governor of the state. "Which is governor of the state Pierpont or Getcher?" Asked I. "Getcher," he said. He thought that there would be four years of feeling of enmity between the North and the South. His secession proclivities were very patent to anyone.[16]

Feb. 13—This was a clear warm day. The blue birds merrily sung their spring songs. Had it not been for the snow on the ground the day would have seemed like a day in April. The troops have mostly left here, the Yates Phalanx, (39th Illinois) only remains.

Feb. 14, Saint Valentine's Day—The Saints day was gloomy.

Feb. 15—I got a pass and went to Cumberland today. Some prisoners, who were taken by General Lander at Bloomery Gap, arrived at Cumberland on the afternoon train. There was a large throng of people to see them. The privates were poorly clad. They belong to the Virginia State Militia. Quarters will be furnished them free of expenses.

Feb. 16, Sunday—This day I spent in Cumberland. In the morning I attended church at the M. E. Church, in the afternoon Sabbath school, and in evening church again. This has been Sabbath not only in name but reality.

Feb. 17—I endeavored to procure a pass from the Provost Marshall, this morning, but did not get in time to take the morning train, so I did not return to Patterson's Creek till in the afternoon.

Feb. 18—I was on picket guard today. My post was on a mountain. The day was warm and clear. We kept a sharp lookout for "Bushwhackers." The night was pleasant. No trouble occurred. The countersign was Fort Donelson.

Feb. 19—Today we received the glorious news from Tennessee. Fort Donelson is ours. 15,000 prisoners were taken. This news is good enough without any comment. The day was rainy.[17]

Feb. 20—This afternoon there was a dress parade for the first time since we left New Creek. T. O. Osborne has been commissioned Colonel of the Regiment, Major O. L. Mann Lieutenant Colonel and Captain Munn Major. Osborne and Munn are very unpopular with the Regiment. The boys have nicknamed Col. Osborne, "The Bull of the Woods," "The Buffalo Bull," "The Bull Pup" and "The Regimental Bull." O. L. Mann is the most popular of any of the Regimental officers. Against him there is no complaint. At dress parade, this evening, Lieutenant Colonel Mann spoke of our victory at Fort Donelson. "The news," said he, "comes leaping over the telegraph wires by lightning that General Siegel, that great German military man, who can gain a victory and retreat as well as advance, has taken General Price and all his command 'prisoners.' In view of this fact and the recent victory at Fort Donelson," said he, "I propose that we give three times three cheers and a tiger. Hip, hip, hip," "hurah, hurah, hurah, hurah, hurah, hurah, hurah, hurah, hurah." Then the royal Bengal Tiger then made the mountains of Virginia reverberate with his roar.

Feb. 21—There was nothing done today at Camp Kelly. The number of prisoners taken at Ford Donelson is 14,000. Generals Buckner, Bushrod, Johnson and West are among the officers taken. The Illinois soldiers have nobly shown to the country and to the world that they fear not to die for their country.[18]

Feb. 22—This is Washington's birthday. At 11 o'clock a.m. The regiment was drawn up in a hollow square, on a hill opposite to Kelly's Island. The band played a soul rousing tune. Colonel Osborne said, "prayer will be offered to the God of our country, by the Chaplain." I should have said that in the center of the hollow square was a stack of straw. On this stood the Colonel, Lieutenant Colonel, Major and others who addressed the regiment. The Chaplain offered up prayer. The Colonel then made a short and eloquent speech. Washington's farewell address was next read by the Chaplain. Capt. Slaughter then made a short and pointed address. The set of resolutions was read by Lieutenant Rudd and was unanimously adopted.[19] The resolutions complimented our fellow soldiers of the West for their bravery at Fort Donelson. It was also declared, in the resolutions, an insult to the people of the United that Jeff Davis should be inaugerated president of the so-called Southern Confederacy on Washington's birthday and that this insult should be avenged. Major Munn then made a few remarks. He said that Jeff Davis' term of administration would be short. He said that we had the Rebels surrounded and if Jeff Davis wished to leave he could not get out of the limits of the so-called Southern Confederacy. "We have possession of every route leading into Richmond," said he. This last assertion is simply untrue. The band played Yankee Doodle and the regiment was drawn up in line of battle and fired three volleys. Thus was Washington's birthday celebrated by the Yates Phalanx, 39th Regiment Illinois volunteers.

Feb. 23, Sunday—This evening I was detailed to act as Sergeant of the guard. This was a very fine day. The Blue Birds could be heard singing.

Feb. 24—This was a stormy day. We are now, 8 o'clock PM, ordered to march immediately. Momentarily we expect to start. We are to go on the cars at first. Where our destination we know not. What we have to do we are also ignorant. Perhaps we're going to meet the enemy. We will not disgrace our state. Honor awaits the brave.

Feb. 25—We went to bed last night as usual. At midnight the cars started. They run very slowly. When we awoke this morning we were at Sir John's Run, where we were to be stationed, quartered in the cars. Three companies, D, I & K went to Bath today on a reconnoitering expedition; the party was commanded by Lieutenant Colonel Mann. We made no discovery of any consequence. The citizens told us that Jackson's force consisted of 17,000 men and 30 pieces of cannon. After Jackson's brigade left the town General Carson's Militia came in and remained there until two weeks ago.[20] The fine stone house, on Fruit Hill, in which company I was quartered, with all the furniture was burned. The barn was also destroyed with fire. The fences around the plantation; a great deal of it had been used by the vandal hordes of Jackson for fuel. Not content with using and destroying what they needed they even leveled to the ground a stone fence. The trees on Warm Spring Ridge were all cut down for several acres. Two men were arrested by order of Lieutenant Waller. In the arrest of one I assisted. Lieutenant Colonel Mann released them. One of them invited me to his house to get dinner. I accepted the invitation. His wife was glad when she saw him come back released. An interesting little boy of his had been crying ever since he had been taken into custody, for about an hour. My heart was touched when I saw how his family were grieved. Many a loyal citizen is accused of being "a secessionist" by their domestic foes, who would seize on any opportunity to do them harm. We should be very cautious whom we arrest for treason. Better let the guilty go unpunished than to punish the innocent.

Feb. 26—A reconnoitering party was sent out towards Winchester this evening. The party consisted of 90 men besides officers. Capt. Woodruff took command of the party.[21] We had started but a short time before it commenced snowing. On Warm Spring Ridge we turned to the right, leaving Bath on the left a short distance. We again soon came into the Winchester Road. The road was uncomfortably muddy and the branches and creeks were swollen. About sun down we halted for supper. We took in our haversacks one day's rations; we also took with us our blankets. This is the road on which Jackson's Army came to Bath, Hancock, Great

Cacapon and Romney. The fences on both sides of the road are all burned up. There seems to have been an indiscriminate destruction of rails for several miles. The people complained of having been robbed of household articles such as provisions. The fence of Buck, Rebel Adjutant, was burned. Friend and foe seem to have suffered equally. Buck's house had also just been burned down when we passed, the fire had not yet gone out; some stacks of grain were burned. The torch of the incendiary has been kindled, in this part of the country. By Jackson the county was laid waste. We could see houses or rather shelters made of pine limbs, which the rebels had constructed to protect them from the storms. Poor deluded fellows! Had it not been for their designing, unprincipled and villainous demagogues they and we might now be at home enjoying the blessings of peace. Night came on and with it almost Egyptian darkness. In the early part of the night there was a light shower of rain. Not a star was to be seen. On we marched through mud and water. The night was so dark the men could scarcely see ten feet. "Halt," commanded Captain Woodruff. On learning the cause we saw in front of us a deep creek, called Sleepy Creek, to us at the time a significant name. The next thing was to get across Sleepy Creek. We sent back to the nearest house and got four horses. Thus six men crossed at a trip. In this manner we crossed Sleepy Creek. Through fields and brush, over rocks and ditches we pushed on our way, frequently turning out of the road. Dry feet was a rare thing among us. To me, some of the branches, which we had to wade, were knee deep. In a dark hollow we came to a halt. The officers charged us to be as noiseless as possible "or our cake is dough." We knew not yet what was to be done. Onward, onward with difficulty we made our way. Now we came to a log house, such as are common in this country. Here we took a prisoner, leaving a guard over him we continued on our way for one mile, then arrested another rebel. At one o'clock in the night, we reached the house of the guide. Here we laid down on the floor as many as could find room. The rest, I among them, went to the barn. We enjoyed the luxury of a short nap, with our wet clothes on.

Feb. 27—At four o'clock we were aroused from our slumber and after partaking of a breakfast, prepared by the girls, sent a detachment of ten men one mile to take some prisoners. They had better success than we anticipated, they took five prisoners. In one thing we were disappointed. A company of cavalry had been camped three miles from the "Ultima Thule" of our reconnaissance.[22] We intended to surprise them, but when within three miles of the camp we learned that "the bird," as usual, "had flown." Before daylight we left the house of our guide that the neighbors might not see us there. This we requested to do to save the property of our host from being destroyed by his rebel neighbors. The distance we went was 15 miles from Sir John's Run. After getting our prisoners together we started back to camp. The number taken was seven, some of them militia. When the darkness of night had cleared away we found ourselves in a beautiful valley. On the right was Sleepy Creek Mountain, on the left Cacapon. Nothing extraordinary occurred on our return to camp. The prisoners were treated with respect. Our boys gave them blankets, lugged their napsacks for them and other acts of kindness.

Feb. 28—We were mustered in for pay this morning. Seven companies, Co. I included, went to Alpine, on the cars, and stopped there all night. Alpine is opposite to Hancock, Md. I have before called it Hancock Station.

March 1—This is the month dedicated to Mars, the God of war. From the present indications many will bend a suppliant knee to his throne. Many will fall victims to the *misanthropos theos* [the man-hating gods]. We have wintered on the banks of the Potomac River, at no time more than three miles from it. The past winter has been an unusually warm one, the River has not been frozen over at any time during the winter. I now behold what I never expected again to see. I felt certain that the exposures of a winter campaign would be more than I could endure. The exposures truly have been great but I now, in good health, behold the ushering in the Spring. Not once since being in the services have I been unable for duty. This morning we moved down to Sleepy Creek, distant 7 miles from Hancock. A bridge is being built across this Creek. This was a beautiful day. On the opposite side of the Potomac River from us, in Maryland, is a little village, Mill Stone Point. "Our flag is there." Capt. Phillips returned today.

Mar. 2, Sunday—The work on Sleepy Creek bridge went on today, the same as if it had never been said, "Thou shalt remember the Sabbath day, to keep it holy." General Lander died with the "Diphtheria" at Paw Paw. He was a brave soldier but I doubt it whether he was a good general. He was very wicked, not regarding the command, "Thou shall not take the name of the Lord thy God in vain." Swearing is not only a violation of the law of God but also of the Articles of war for the government of the army of the United States. Why should officers, who are fighting for the enforcement of the laws, violate them daily, even hourly? Swearing is also an ungentlemanly practice. That individual, who is sunk so low in degradation as to swear in the presence of a lady, has forfeited his title to the honorable appellation, Man. General Lander exposed his men too much, the consequence is that out of an army of 10,000 men 1600 have been in the hospital sick at the same time.[23]

Mar. 3—It rained nearly all day. The day, which was gloomy, gloomy in the extreme, was a fair index to my mind at the time. Darkness prevails. The war is not yet over. Blind fanaticism yet sways the minds of the Southern people.

Mar. 4—A soldier's life is hard. There is but little pleasure in wandering about from place to place without any place that one can call "Home." Home what a world of meaning in the word. To the ear of the weary wanderer it is music. How many a soldier, when heroically enduring the privations incident to his situation, thinks, "It will not be so when I return home!" Erase from his mind the hope of ever returning home and you plunge him into depths of unfathomable despair.

Mar. 5—I was on picket guard today. In the afternoon I went to Dr. Johnson's Mill, on Sleepy Creek, four miles from camp. The country is poorly cultivated. The bridge across Sleepy Creek was, today, completed. All the Regiment, except Company I, went down to Back Creek. Report says that General Shields takes General Lander's command. May it be true.[24]

Mar. 6—To my joy the gray streaks of light appeared in the Eastern horizon. The night was too cold to be pleasant. Nothing of a war-like character occurred. This evening, at roll call, there was an election to fill the vacancies occasioned by the physical inability of the first and second Corporals. G. Riddle and J. W. Weedman were elected.[25]

Mar. 7—What was the origin of the name Sleepy Creek I have not been able to learn. The creek is a very sluggish stream; it lazily courses its way to the river. From its resemblance to a sleepy person, moping about without any vitality, may have suggested the name. What ever gave the name to the creek it has been very appropriate since we have been here. We sleep from dark till sun up. Tonight we were moved down to Cherry Run, distant about four miles. This station is near the line between Morgan and Berkeley counties, it is in the former County. We expect soon to be ordered to Martinsburg.

Mar. 8—The report was circulated this evening that General Shields had come and was at a certain house nearby. The band of the 39th Regiment Illinois volunteers serenaded the supposed General. After playing several tunes the Mann (man) made his appearance on the portico and responded in a few words, thanking the band for the compliment. He closed by requesting the band to play "Anna Laura." Several soldiers assembled to hear the Gen. speak. But "the ass was let loose among the arms." We learned that General Shields was not here and that we had been addressed by Lieutenant Colonel Mann.[26]

Mar. 9, Sunday—A comrade and myself crossed the river in a skiff. The object of crossing was to visit an old Fort which stands near the river bank, on the Maryland side.

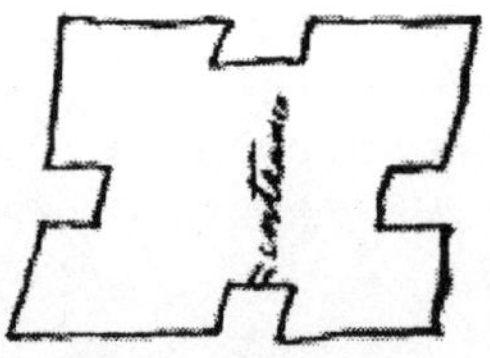

The above is a rough sketch of the fort. The walls are built of rough limestone laid in mortar. They are about twelve feet high and three feet thick. The area occupied by the works is one acre and a half. The walls, which are now beginning to fall in, are overgrown with poison vine. Within the walls grow some large trees, one apple tree in particular attracted my attention; judging from its size it must have been planted by a generation long since passed away. The country around is quite level. By whom this fort was built is a matter of conjecture. It is said that there is no account given of it in history. The general opinion with regard to it is that it was built as a defense against the Indians, when this part of the country was "The far West," a frontier settlement. The name by which it is known is Fort Frederick. It is in Washington County, Maryland about ten miles below Hancock. It is evidently a very old work. Time has left marks on it that cannot be mistaken.[27]

Mar. 10—This morning, at two o'clock, we received orders to prepare three day's rations and be ready to march, with knapsacks and blankets, at 8 o'clock this morning. The cooks got up and went to cooking but before they had the rations cooked the order was countermanded and they went to bed again. General Shields actually has arrived! We're glad to be commanded by a man, once a citizen of Illinois. The General says that our regiment looks like it was badly neglected. He expressed a determination to find out the cause and to remove it. Said he, "I will give you plenty of fighting to do and if you disgrace Illinois you had a damn sight better never return home." We are now encouraged with the hope of soon having pleasant weather. Today we heard the frogs croaking.

Mar. 11—We bid farewell to the cars this morning. Whilst lying in them during the bad weather the Regiment became somewhat demoralized. After loading our baggage into the wagons we took up the line of march for Martinsburg distant 14 miles. We traveled along the railroad. For several miles the track has been torn up by the Secessionists. The ties in places are burned. A great many cars and engines have been destroyed in and near Martinsburg. The day was beautiful and the road was good for foot men. The country, Berkley County, is well improved. We saw but little demonstrations of patriotism. The people, what few we saw, looked decidedly sour. At North Mountain Station two flags were floating in the breeze of heaven. One of them had been in the possession of the rebels and re-captured by Company D.; we gave three cheers for it. We reached Martinsburg at sun down. Our flag was there. On the courthouse our flag was hoisted and General Shields made a short speech. The federal troops are in possession of Manassas! Martinsburg, situated on Tuscarora Creek is a handsome town of 3000 inhabitants. It is the county seat of Berkeley County. The streets cross each other at right angles. Saw several fair ladies but they could not bestow on us a single smile. We marched out one mile, towards Winchester and bivouaced. We got some straw and spread our blankets on it with the moon and stars smiling lovely on our faces. We had a comfortable night's sleep.

Mar. 12*—Winchester delinda est* [Winchester must be destroyed]. I hope that we may be spared the painful necessity of destroying it. A beautiful Spring day was this. The forenoon we took up the line of march to the devoted city. Our teams had not yet overtaken us. We halted, after traveling three miles, and when the teams over took us cooked dinner. The road traveled today is good, being the Valley Turnpike. The country is good by nature and art. It is in a high state of cultivation. The improvements are good. There is a great deal of stone fencing and many fine houses. The country is level and the land productive, being of the quality known as limestone land. The scenery is grand, on the right is North Mountain on the left and far away in the distance is the Blue Ridge. The farms looked as if the folks had gone from home. There were but few men to be seen. The women looked sad. Perhaps they have husbands, sons, brother or lovers in the rebel army. We passed through two small villages. The first, Buckle's Town, consists of only a few inferior houses on each side of the road and a brick Church. This village is 2 miles from Martinsburg. The second is Bunker Hill. This is a small village in Berkeley County. Here there are two churches and a large stone mill. This is the farthest point reached by General Patterson last summer. It is now dark; we are halted to cook supper. We expect to march on tonight. We are 11 miles from Winchester. What there awaits we know not. We did not march.

Mar. 13—At the sound of the drum, at 3 o'clock a.m., we arose from our beds of leaves and cooked breakfast. At half past four we started on our way. Light had not yet appeared. This part of the state is called "the Valley District"; it is probably the best part of the state. At 9 o'clock a.m., we reached our camping grounds. It is two miles from Winchester, on the road leading to Martinsburg. We now have our tents pitched for the first time since we left Williamsport. We have the Sibley tents. Jackson left Winchester day before yesterday. He took off all his guns and stores, excepting forage; a great quantity of which he burned. "The devoted city" was not destroyed. The rebels call General Jackson "Stone Wall Jackson." I was not aware that a stone wall could be moved so quickly as he moves. Swift footed Jackson, I think, would be a better name. He is too fleet of foot for us to catch him. For him to run is better than to fight.

Mar. 14—Winchester, the county seat of Frederick County, is the largest town in Virginia west of the Blue Ridge, excepting Wheeling. The town is well built, the streets crossing each other at right angles. It is supplied with pure water, which is conveyed into the town through pipes from a spring one mile distant. The houses are built chiefly of brick and stone. There are many fine residences here. A number of churches, a female academy, "The Valley Female Institute," the Eastern State lunatic asylum are among the benevolent institutions.[28] There are or rather have been two weekly papers published at this place. A market house, the courthouse, stores, two of which are bookstores, hotels to make up the business part of the town. The scenery around is enchanting. Twenty miles distant is the Blue Ridge. The population of [the] town is 6500. I could discover no union feeling what ever among the citizens. The ladies in particular "looked daggers at us." "You can't subdue us" is on the lips of everyone. Sen. Mason's residence is in the north part of town. It is on a hill in the midst of a beautiful grove. The house is built of rough limestone plastered on the outside; it is two stories high. The plastering on the outside is beginning to fall off. The house has a dingy appearance. It is the headquarters of the 5th Connecticut Regiment. Over the residence of traitor Mason float the Stars & Stripes. This with my own eyes I have seen. Today at a few miles from here there was a skirmish. A few prisoners were taken by our forces. We could hear the firing.[29]

Mar. 15—It rained all day. This sort of weather gives soldiers "the blues." Inside of our tents is wet and muddy. In this mixture of mud and water we make our beds and, if we can, sleep. The rebellion is not yet crushed. The war still rages with unabated fury. Since hope has taken its flight from my mind I now dismiss fear. "Suffer death rather than disgrace."

The End of Volume 2nd

Volume 3

MARCH–JULY 1862

On March 11, President Lincoln removed General McClellan from overall command of the Federal armies so the general could concentrate his full attention on the campaign against Richmond. Even so, the armies continued to pursue McClellan's strategy. While McClellan shifted the majority of his army from Washington to Fort Monroe and marched west up the peninsula between the York and James rivers, against Richmond, Banks was to use his army to clear enemy troops from the upper regions of the Shenandoah Valley. Once done, Banks would then leave a holding force in the valley and dispatch units east to cover Washington and cooperate with General Irving McDowell's army as it marched south from Fredericksburg to join McClellan outside Richmond.

On March 19, the Thirty-ninth Illinois, still assigned to Jeremiah C. Sullivan's brigade in Shields's division, left camp near Winchester and proceeded south toward Strasbourg, Virginia. The Confederates, under Stonewall Jackson, withdrew behind a shield of cavalry beyond Strasbourg. Banks, acting upon an erroneous report that the Confederates had left the valley, returned his command to Winchester and began shifting the majority of his men eastward, leaving only Shields's division at Winchester. Jackson, under orders to keep Banks's army from leaving the valley and joining the attack on Richmond, quickly moved his small command toward Winchester, with the intention of defeating Shields and drawing Banks back to the valley.

Late on the afternoon of March 22, the Thirty-ninth Illinois with the rest of Shields's division was turned out and moved south to meet the approaching Confederate forces. Shields initially arranged his forces to cover the various roads leading into Winchester; the Thirty-ninth was positioned along the Romney Pike west of Winchester. An engagement flared south of Winchester, and Shields, riding toward the sound of the guns, was badly wounded by artillery fire. Command passed to Colonel Nathan Kimble. Shields, who believed they were facing only cavalry, directed Kimble to drive the Confederates from the fields the following morning. Kimble, however, realized he was facing Jackson's entire army and placed his men in a defensive position south of Winchester.

On the left of the Union forces, Sullivan's brigade, with the Thirty-ninth on its extreme left, was positioned on a ridge overlooking the village of Kernstown directly facing the Confederate army. To Sullivan's right and out of sight of the Confederates stood Kimball's brigade, with Tyler's brigade in reserve behind them. The Confederates demonstrated in front of Sullivan's brigade at Kernstown while Jackson sent the majority of his army against the Federal right. Kimble countered by sending forward Tyler's brigade. The two sides met west of Kernstown, and although the Confederates gained an initial advantage and held off the Union attacks, Kimble brought his brigade into action. Soon the weight of numbers and a shortage of ammunition forced the Southerners to withdraw. Throughout the battle, the Thirty-ninth Illinois remained on the Federals' extreme left, supporting an artillery battery.

Defeated and forced from the field, Jackson had nonetheless accomplished his mission. Banks called back the divisions he had dispatched eastward and consolidated his army at Winchester. For a second time, Banks started his forces down the valley, this time determined to defeat the Confederates. Jackson again withdrew in the face of superior numbers. With Shields's division in the lead, the Thirty-ninth Illinois spearheaded the advance, skirmishing with Jackson's rearguard. By April 4, 1862, the Federals occupied Strasbourg and went into camp. Over the next few weeks, the Thirty-ninth Illinois guarded bridges against Confederate raids.

On May 10, 1862, the Thirty-ninth Illinois and the rest of Shields's division was ordered to march to Fredericksburg to join General McDowell's command, preparing to march south to join McClellan's army north of Richmond. At Fredericksburg the western troops found themselves under tighter discipline "so they might harmonize more fully with the popinjay soldiers from Massachusetts and the Eastern states." The harmonizing did not go too smoothly and altercations broke out, as the men from Illinois felt obliged to teach the easterners better manners.[1]

At Fredericksburg, the Thirty-ninth took part in a grand review where President Lincoln, Secretary of War Stanton, and the British ambassador Lord Lyon joined McDowell for an inspection of his army. Lincoln, while riding past the troops, spied the Thirty-ninth regimental colors and acknowledged the soldiers from his home state. That night he made a brief tour of the regiment's headquarters.

Before McDowell could make his march toward Richmond, Jackson regrouped his command and struck at threatening elements of General John C. Fremont's army moving from the Allegheny Mountains toward Jackson's base at Staunton, Virginia. Jackson defeated the Federals at McDowell and drove them from the Shenandoah Valley. Then, after receiving reinforcements, he turned on Banks's weakened army. Banks attempted to make a stand at Strasbourg, but Jackson shifted his army east at New Market. Using Massanutten Mountain to screen his advance, Jackson continued north and captured Front Royal. From there he moved west, threatening to trap Banks at Strasbourg. Banks immediately withdrew up the valley. The Federals attempted to make a stand at Winchester but, quickly overwhelmed, fled to Harper's Ferry.

Jackson's tactics so disrupted the Union plans that McDowell, instead of joining McClellan, was sent to the valley with three divisions, including Shields's. At the same time, General Fremont again moved his forces eastward in hopes of pinning the Confederates between his men and those from McDowell's command. Jackson managed to avoid the trap and defeat both Fremont at the Battle of Cross Keys and the lead elements of Shields's division at Port Republic. Shields's second brigade—containing the Thirty-ninth Illinois as well as the Thirteenth Indiana, the Sixty-second Ohio, and the Sixty-seventh Ohio, and now commanded by Brigadier General Orris S. Ferry—did not arrive in time to take part in the battle of Port Republic but did assist in caring for the wounded.

Once united, Fremont and Shields contemplated following Jackson, but Shields's division was again sent eastward, this time to Alexandria, Virginia. Jackson, with no interference, moved his army to the outskirts of Richmond to join Robert E. Lee's army. There, he took part in the Seven Days' Battle that drove McClellan from Richmond and back to Harrison's Landing on the James River. As a result of the Confederate attack, the Federals dispatched additional reinforcements, including the Thirty-ninth Illinois, which along with two brigades from Shields's division was sent by boat from Alexandria, Virginia, to Harrison's Landing where they were assigned to General Erasmus D. Keyes's Fourth Corps. The regiment arrived in time to witness—but not engage in—the battle of Malvern Hill on July 1, 1862. Though the Federals won a great victory at Malvern Hill, the next day the army retreated to Harrison's Landing. There McClellan attempted to restore morale and demanded an additional hundred thousand men before launching another advance on Richmond. —*S.R.W.*

★ ★ ★ ★ ★

March 16, Sunday—The poor soldier, the poor soldier! The Sabbath smiles not for him. The usual bustle and excitement characterized the day, which differed, only by the ordinary drills being omitted, from the other days of the week.

Mar. 17—I was on chain guard today. The 39th Illinois regiment is in the second brigade. The 13th Indiana, 5th Ohio and 62nd Ohio are in the same brigade. Colonel Sullivan of the 13th Indiana is acting Brigadier General of the brigade. Brigadier General Shields is commander of the division in which we are. This and General William's divisions constitute the Fifth Corps, commanded by Maj. Gen. N. P. Banks.[2]

Mar. 18—Early this morning some of the regiments of infantry and artillery began to move south ward. Four Batteries, consisting of six pieces each, commanded by Lieutenant Colonel Daum, the first, second and third brigades of infantry, General Shield's Division and two or three companies of the 1st Michigan Cavalry constituted the entire force.[3] General Shields to command in person. To the music of the bands, with regimental and state colors unfurled to the breeze of heaven, we took up the line of march "Dixieward." Truly we looked as terrible as "an army with banners." The following was our outfit, three day's rations in our haversacks, which consisted of crackers, raw bacon, ground coffee and sugar, each man took a tin cup, canteen and blankets we tied up into a round roll and tied the ends together and swung them over our shoulders. We exercised our own judgment about taking our overcoats, some took theirs others did not. I took mine and was well paid for carrying it. Sixty rounds of cartridges were dealt out to each one of us. Our cartridge boxes hold only forty rounds, the remaining 20 rounds we carried in our pockets. All day the sun shown brightly. The slow and steady tread of infantry could now be heard. A grand sight was it to see this array of men, with highly polished guns, marching at right shoulder shift arms. The universal opinion with us was that we were marching to the battlefield. All hearts were joyful. Do or die, was written on every countenance. Two men from each company were detailed to act as pioneers. They each one took an ax. Into Winchester we marched, the band playing "The Red, White and Blue." Out of windows and doors gazed old women, fair young ladies, little girls and boys. There were comparatively few men. Sad were the looks of the women. We marched out on the road to Staunton which is 92 miles from Winchester. Slowly we marched frequently halting to rest. Two miles from Winchester is Mill Town. This village consists of a few residences and two stone mills, one called Union Mills was built in 1800. The other, Mill Town Mills, built in 1834 is the finest mill I ever saw any place. There we saw, what I believed to be true demonstration of patriotism. A man and two women cheered the Union. It was not what they said but what they looked makes me call this "a true demonstration." The next village we passed through was Kern's Town. This is a small place, with a hotel, a church, stores and residences. Bartonsville is next, aside from one princely residence it is a village un-noteworthy. Next on the list is New Town. This consists of rows of houses on each side of the Turnpike, extending along it for about half a mile. Here there are some fine residences, there are also churches, stores and hotels. As thou goest southward towards Staunton, Middle Town is next to be passed through by thee. Like most of the towns in Virginia it is small. The country passed through today is good. There are many fine residences. They generally stand off some distance from the road. The grounds around are ornamented with shade trees. The farms are large and well improved. Along the road there is much stone fence. The wheat, which is now beginning to grow, looks well. In justice to the Rebels I must say that they had not devastated the country. The fences remained intact. I wish that I could say the same of ourselves, but truth forbids. Before us rails vanished. When we halted to rest many of the boys would tear down stone fencing merely to make a comfortable seat. The stern looks of the inhabitants plainly told us that we were in the midst of a hostile people. When the sun was about one hour high we heard firing ahead. This enlivened us all, made us to forget our weariness. "Halt, order arms, load at will," was heard along the lines. This looks like fighting, thought we. "Bang, bang, bang," we heard ahead. On quick time we marched off. Soon we halted and opened ranks for the artillery to pass. In a gallop four batteries rushed the drivers putting whip at every jump. The earth trembled beneath the tread of the horses. The scene was a very excitable one. The artillery having passed, we marched on towards the scene of action. At this time an officer rode along and said, "Hurry up, boys, we will soon have some fun." The sun was setting behind the mountain when the firing ceased and we met cavalry men, who told us that there had been a skirmish with rebel cavalry, infantry and artillery and that rebels retreated burning the bridge across Cedar Creek. One of our men was wounded. Half a mile from the battlefield we bivouaced, in an open field. The cannons were placed in position, on a hill, defiantly looking southward. In the rear of them we bivouaced, ready for action at a minute's warning. Back from where we slept on our arms, fires were built of the rails, extending half a mile along the road. This was done, perhaps, to deceive the enemy as to our position. I saw General Shields sitting on his horse, looking on with complacency. I do not know how we can avoid burning rails when on the march. I hate to see such devastation. I reckon that we will have to consider it one of the evils of war and not be troubled about it. It was late in the night before we came to a halt. We slept comfortably beneath the canopy of heaven. On the following morning our blankets were white with frost. The distance marched today was 17 miles.

Mar. 19—On the end of a little stick I stuck a piece of bacon and held over the fire to roast; this and a cup of hot coffee and crackers made as good breakfast as ever I ate. My appetite made up for what it lacked in quality. Early we were again on the march. A temporary bridge across Cedar Creek was constructed. The bridge had burned and fallen into the water. Across these fallen timbers boards were laid, on which we crossed in two files. Thus we crossed Cedar Creek, on the ruins of the bridge, destroyed by the rebels, while it was yet burning. The bridge was a noble structure, about 100 feet long. The stone abutments yet stand as a monument of rebel vandalism. There was no reason for burning this bridge, as it did not retard our progress in the least. The creeks were shallow so that we could have easily forded it. About one mile from the creek was an encampment. The fires had not yet gone out. The enemy had left but a few hours before. When near Strausburg firing was heard a short distance beyond the town. We halted and the artillery went on. General Shields and staff went ahead to choose a position for the cannon. After the position was taken and the cannons planted we were marched up and formed in divisions, ready for battle. The cannons were on the crest of a ridge. The infantry was drawn up in the rear. Boom went a volley of six guns, the earth quaked and the heavens seemed rent asunder. We were now commanded to fix bayonets. "What, are you going to give us a charge the first thing?" was the thought of many. Being behind the hill we could not see what was ahead. Several rounds were fired by our cannoneers but the enemy did not respond. The enemy retreated and we had no fight after all. This was one mile from Strausburg. The rebels burned a bridge on the Manassas Gap railroad. This road runs from Manassas Junction on the east to Mount Jackson on the west. The bridge burned is a mile or so from Strausburg towards Edinburg. This was another piece of wanton vandalism. From Strausburg to Edinburg is but a few miles. In this direction the road intersects no other; it is therefore of no importance whatever to us. Neither did it aid the rebels in their retreat. Strausburg is 18 miles south of Winchester, in Shenandoah County. It is on the Manassas Gap Railroad. It is a dingy looking village with about 500 inhabitants. On the outskirts of this town, near the banks of the Shenandoah River we bivouaced. The Shenandoah is a beautiful stream. On each side it is lined with willows. It rained through the night. Our blankets were thoroughly soaked in the rain. This is a part of the many hardships which a soldier has to undergo. Our three day's rations run out of the end of this, the second day, at least this was the case with many of us. Our knaps were moistened with rain.

Mar. 20—Our haversacks were emptied after we had eaten our breakfast. At 10 1/2 o'clock a.m. we started back to camp, which was 20 miles distant. The day was cloudy and occasionally light mist was falling. The road was a perfect mortar bed about two inches deep. We penetrated 55 miles into this, for a few months past, *Terra incognita* [unknown territory]. This is the same route I traveled a little more than a year ago. A short time after dark we reached camp tired and hungry. Thus terminated our three day's march, which I do not know whether to term a pursuit of the enemy or a reconnaissance in force. We had wet blankets to sleep under tonight.

Mar. 21—This was a wet disagreeable day. We could not dry our blankets and clothes. Nothing extraordinary occurred today. Lying in the mud is very unpleasant. In camp we are confined to narrow limits. "Thus far thou shalt go and no further." Does not suit a freeman.

Mar. 22—The day passed quietly till late in the afternoon, when Ashby's Cavalry made an attack on our outposts near Winchester.

"The long roll" was beat and we fell into ranks and went on double quick to Winchester. When we got through the town, on the outskirts, we halted and loaded our pieces. We learned that Colonel Ashby's Cavalry had engaged ours and that there had been a little skirmish. General Shields' arm was broken in the engagement. We were commanded to "about face" and were marched out on the road to Romney five miles from Winchester. The regiment was placed on picket. At about midnight we were relieved and were marched back to camp where we slept till morning.

Mar. 23, Sunday—Today will hereafter be memorable in the history of our country. We met the enemy and after a hard battle victory is ours. All glory be to Him who ever defends the right. *Quem Deus vult perdere prins dementat* [Whom God wishes to destroy, he first makes mad] is the only reason why I can imagine that Jackson attacked us. We were called out at 1 o'clock p.m.. Three miles south of Winchester the rebel forces of Jackson met true Union steel to their total defeat. It is thought that Jackson was led to believe that most of the Union troops had left Winchester and that his possession of the town would be unobstructed. In this he was deceived. General Shield's division was two or three [miles] east of Winchester. All the morning skirmishing had been going on. At 2 o'clock p.m. the ball was opened on a grand scale. The line of operations extended for about two miles, that is from the extreme right to the left was two miles. Kernstown lay between contending forces.[4] Cannonading along the line of action commenced the exercises. The scene was terribly grand. For several hours all Satan's powers seemed combined to spend their fury on Earth. The missiles of death began to fall everywhere. Now a shell from the enemy falls in the midst of a squad of our cavalry, good heavens! How the dirt flies! They put spurs and away they galloped. We were drawn up in line of battle in a wood on the right of the enemy, the 39th Illinois and 62nd Ohio occupied this position. We were commanded to lie down. The shells in quick succession passed over us. Their whistling through the air no longer seemed like music to charm the ear but like a fiendish hissing. All the Furies of Hell seemed to be let loose. The powers of darkness were contending with the powers of light. The Rebels opened on us from two batteries, thus compelling us to go through the fierce ordeal of a cross fire. The shells fell a few feet in front of us and passed over our heads too close to be comfortable. We lay on our faces close to the ground. One man lying by my side was wounded in the hand by a canister. Two pieces of Captain Clark's battery came to our relief at this juncture.[5] We were ordered to change our position further towards the left. Whilst we were executing this movement the rebel batteries paid special attention to us. Capt. Clark now began to respond to the cannons of the enemy. The 39th Illinois Regiment was stationed in the rear of these two pieces to protect them. A brisk fire was kept up on both sides for some time. A shell struck a stump a few feet in front of us. The fragments of the stump flew in every direction. The battle continued to rage with unabated fury, chiefly between the artillery. Clark's two pieces finally succeeded in silencing the rebel guns which had been playing on us with such furious intent but without any success. Col Sullivan had command on our left wing. A messenger came to him and told him that Colonel Kimble wished to see him.[6] "Colonel Osborne," said Sullivan, "if the enemy makes an advance before I return, don't retreat. I will be back soon." "Of course not," cooley replied Col. Osborne. Co. D of the 39th Regiment Illinois was deployed as skirmishers. They made three or four of the rebel cavalry bite the ground. Late in the afternoon hostilities ceased excepting on the left flank of the enemy where the hardest fighting was done. Volleys of musketry could be heard. Soon the firing became incessant. There was one continual sound not unlike a very heavy hail storm. With intense anxiety we watched the probable result of the battle. For some time it was doubtful which would gain the day. It was a hard contested field. At last our anxious suspense was somewhat relieved; we saw that the rebels were losing ground. Finally they began to retreat. The firing was now all done by our men. With terrible fury this part of the battle raged for two hours when dark put an end to hostilities. This for the time it lasted was one of the hardest battles that has been fought during the present war. During the day, signals were displayed from all parts of the field to Winchester. The signals made use of large white flags with a square red spot in the center; at night lights were used. They could be seen waving over all parts of the field, a victorious field! Colonel Murray of the 84th Pennsylvania Regiment was killed whilst bravely leading his men.[7] Colonel Osborne and Lieutenant Colonel Mann acted as cooly as if they had been on battalion drill. What I saw and know to be true I have written. Further, lest I should err from the truth, I forbear to write. When they shall have become a part of the history of our country then and not till then will the truth be known. We bivouaced for the night on the field. The groans of the wounded loaded the air. The cattle bellowed, said to be occasioned by the smell of blood. The horrors are indescribable. I could have enjoyed myself better at church than on the battlefield. The whistling of shells, cannon balls and bullets have no charm, at least they had not on this memorable day. The smell of gun powder is too Satanic to be agreeable. There are men who vainly boast that they like the battlefield and are eager for the fray. Such men either deceive themselves or they are transformed into beasts. No man of sense will say that I am a coward when I frankly confess that I have no love for the battlefield. Our regiment sustained no loss, one man only was slightly wounded.

Mar. 24—We were out before daylight this morning and started in pursuit of the flying enemy towards Strasburg. There was skirmishing all day with the rear guard of the enemy. We would place our cannons in position on a hill and fire a few rounds and then move forward to another position. We marched by divisions through fields tearing down fences whenever they were in the way. We halted for the night near Cedar Creek.

Mar. 25—The pursuit was continued five miles beyond Strasburg. The dead and wounded of the enemy were left along the road. Today there has been skirmishing. We bivouaced five miles from Strasburg by the Manassas Gap Railroad.

Mar. 26—Nothing of importance occurred today. Skirmishing was kept up. We received our tents and have gone into camp five miles from Strasburg. All quiet on the Upper Potomac.

Mar. 27—Skirmishing was still kept up. Wearied out we are now encamped.

Mar. 28—Firing is still heard. The weather is fine. General Shields issued an order, complimenting the officers and soldiers of his command for the bravery in the recent battle near Winchester. He congratulates them on having opened the campaign on the Potomac. "Let them inscribe 'Winchester' on their banners and prepare for other victories."

Mar. 29—This was the first quiet day for one week, there has been no firing heard today. What is going on in the world we are unable to tell; we receive no newspapers. Our camp is in a hollow between the Valley Pike and Manassas Gap Railroad.

Mar. 30, Sunday—This was a wet dismal day a fair index to my feelings. Instead of the church bell we hear the unmusical sound of the drum, telling us that the hour for roll call has arrived or that we must fall into ranks without delay for dress parade. If witnessing card playing all day and hearing profanity be the proper way to keep the Sabbath holy then today was well spent.

Mar. 31—I was on guard today. The operations of the month, which today ends, have not been unworthy of its name. Many have been the victims that have been sacrificed on the altar of the bloody and ever to be tested God, Mars. Whilst writing an involuntary sigh escaped my breast, a sigh for other scenes than the scenes of conflict and blood. The regiment went out on picket this afternoon. All the camp guards were relieved excepting three, who guarded the commissary. I was one of the three. The weather fine.

April 1—This morning I joined the regiment, which was two miles from camp. We received marching orders and did not return to camp. Onward towards Staunton we marched. The scenery was beautiful. In the valley of the Shenandoah are some good farms. The Shenandoah River is a most lovely little stream. On our march today we witnessed some of the devastations of the Rebels. The bridges on the Manassas Gap railroad were all destroyed as also those on the Pike. Fences had been burned. We passed through Woodstock, 26 miles from Winchester. Woodstock, the county seat of Shenandoah County, contains about 2000 inhabitants. It is an ancient looking town. We did not possess it without opposition entirely. Ashby fired a few rounds at us with his cannon; our artillery responded. On our side no damage was done. The town is on the Manassas Gap railroad. The same paucity of men and patriotism characterized this town as the others through which we have passed. We marched four miles out on the Pike and bivouaced in a wood. I was very unwell today; it was with difficulty that I marched. All our baggage was back at the camp which was 11 miles distant.

Apr. 2—All day I lay prostrate on my back unable to sit up. The roar of the cannon occasionally disturbed the quietude of the day. There was nothing for us to do today.

Apr. 3—My health was too poor for me to take note of what went on today. I was consoled with the thought that I could rest my weak limbs on the banks of so beautiful a stream as the Shenandoah.

Apr. 4—This and the two days previous taught me that to lie sick on the ground without even a tent for a shelter is a thing not at all pleasant to perform.

Apr. 5—Our naps this morning were interrupted by drops of rain falling on us.

Apr. 6, Sunday—My health began to improve. Late in the afternoon our tents were brought to us. This day was very unlike Sabbath.

Apr. 7—We are now encamped in a grove between the pike and the road leading to Luray, near Edinburg. The regiment went out on picket. I, for the first time, fell behind. About noon today it commenced sleating and continued all night.

Apr. 8—Still continued to sleat all day. The Regiment returned from picket at 10 o'clock a.m. All quiet on the Shenandoah.

Apr. 9—Still continues to sleat and is quite cool. The mud is very deep. The trees are laboring under a load of snow. I am again able for duty. Intelligence of the victories at Island No. 10 and Pittsburg Landing was received this afternoon. It caused great rejoicing in camp.[8]

Apr. 10—The storm has finally subsided and the Earth again visited by the genial rays of the Sun. Somehow or other a report got out that our regiment was to be stationed on the Manassas Gap railroad to do guard duty. This caused great indignation among the officers and soldiers.

Apr. 11—Old Sol was still mindful of us today in dispelling the gloom of winter. The trees are disemburdened of their load of snow. Winter seemed disposed to encroach upon the rights of Spring. Sunshine and shade join hands. The news of the sinking of the Merrimac came into camp tonight. This and further particulars of the capture of Island No. 10 and our victory at Pittsburg landing, on the Tennessee River, caused unbounded enthusiasm. The valley resounded with cheer after cheer. The bands of all the regiments played stirring airs. All the Fifth Army Corps seemed to be enjoying a universal jubilee from dark till midnight. Several of the bands serenaded General Williams. The war is progressing in a satisfactory manner. The dark night of rebellion is passing away. All are up, standing on tiptoe, anxiously looking to see if the dawn of day can be discerned. We await with trembling hearts the day when shall be born on the wings the lightning to all parts of the land the joy begetting word, "Peace." Soon may the day be.[9]

Apr. 12—I took a walk to Edinburg this afternoon. This is a small village on the Shenandoah River and the Manassas Gap railroad. The village has no appearance of comfort. It is almost a "deserted village." In it are two churches. There was a review of General Shield's Division in the afternoon. The General was able to ride in a buggy. He looks badly.

Apr. 13, Sunday—There was Divine services in the several regiments by order of the Secretary of War to return thanks to Almighty God for his single blessings on our arms. God rules the Universe and in his hands are the destinies of nations. He is present in the most minute affairs of men. He also exercises his care over all the works of nature, which are the works of his own hands. Not a spear of grass grows but by his command. God cares for even the least particle of powder that a soldier ever put into his gun. On every bullet discharged by a soldier He either smiles or frowns. To such a great and glorious Being be all praise for all the good we enjoy, for all that we hope for now and hereafter. One year ago our flag was disgraced at Fort Sumpter. Dearly have the impious hands, that caused it to trail in the dust, paid. The star spangled banner is destined, ere many months more shall have elapsed, to be unfurled to the breeze of heaven in every part of the South. *Vi et armis* [with force and arms] it shall be restored.[10]

Apr. 14—The announcement that the Merrimac was sunk seems to have been premature. The sinking of her is reserved for another feast. There was an inspection of the troops of General Shield's Division this afternoon. This was thought to be preparatory to some movement, which we are soon to make.

Apr. 15—One year ago today President Lincoln issued his proclamation calling for 75,000 troops to suppress the rebellion. Since then nearly 700,000 troops have volunteered to serve their country and have been armed and equipped and put into the field. We, it is true, have suffered some reverses. Many victories have crowned our efforts to sustain the government among the most important of which is the change of public opinion in the loyal states. In the beginning of our troubles there were not wanting those who empathized with the secessionists. Many good men, who have since proved themselves patriots, to avoid the evils of civil war were willing to let "the South alone." We are now a united people. There is but one sentiment; viz the government must be sustained at all hazards and that civil war though a great evil is not the greatest that can be endured. A dissolution of the union would be a greater evil. Our regiment was paid off today. The weather is changeable.

Apr. 16—Today was beautiful. The early spring flowers are in bloom. The snow today disappeared on the mountain. We took 84 of Ashby's cavalry prisoners today. At dark we fell into ranks, the roll was called and all that were unable to march stepped out. The rest were ordered to hold themselves in readiness to march at a minute's notice, with three day's rations in our haversacks. This we apprehended would be a sleepless night to us. *"Aut vincere, aut mori"* [either victory or death] is the motto inscribed on my gun sling.

Apr. 17—Our apprehensions turned out to be correct. At one o'clock in the night we were aroused from sleep, fell into ranks and marched to the regimental parade ground and were formed in line of battle. All General Shield's Division was on the move. Not a drum was heard, all was done quietly. The moon was shining in all her loveliness. Viewed in the stillness of the night all nature wore a beautiful aspect. Peace and serenity invested all things, save man alone who was plotting the destruction of his fellow men. Along our lines we heard the command "load at will," this executed and after a good deal of right dressing etc. We took up the line of march southward. After passing through Edinburg a short distance we heard a few shots of random firing between our advance guard and the rebel pickets. We continued marching and halting to rest occasionally hearing firing ahead. There was light skirmishing all along our march as far as Mt. Jackson. This village on the Manassas Gap railroad and Mill Creek contains about 100 inhabitants. At this place the secessionists have erected three large buildings used by them for hospitals. Their sick had been moved to Staunton one month ago. Yellow flags were still floating over the hospitals. Nearby were several newly made graves, there rest the remains of poor misguided soldiers. The rebels burned two bridges across Metal Creek at Mt. Jackson, one a railroad bridge the other the Pike bridge. We had to wade Mail Creek while the bridge was in flames and fragments of it floated down in our way. About a quarter of a mile from Mt. Jackson we halted and took dinner. Afterwards a large force "about faced" and marched back across the creek. We turned to the left, up Mill Creek marching in a northwestern direction for about two miles where we crossed the creek and bore southward. Mill Creek well deserves its name from the fact that about every quarter of a mile there is a mill on it. The road we had to march over was miserable. We passed through Forestville, a small village. Here we found some professed union people. The women wore linsey dresses and had a good old-fashioned look. From this village we took the county road leading to New Market, which is 6 miles distant. Near the North Branch of the Shenandoah 2 miles from New Market, in a wood, we bivouaced for the night. Mt. Jackson is not the terminus of the Manassas Gap railroad as represented on most maps. The road has within a year past been completed to Timberville, a small village 15 miles distant from Mt. Jackson.

Apr. 18—The chief event of today was crossing the North Branch of the Shenandoah River. There is no bridge at the place where we crossed. The water was about 3 feet deep and very swift. The manner in which we crossed it made truly a ludicrous spectacle. The boys emerged from their pants and drawers and in a half nude state heroically waded across. The day was warm which added to our comfort. New Market, (Novum Forum) in the southwest part of Shenandoah County, is a town of about 1500 inhabitants. It is a place of considerable business. There is here a female seminary. About one mile east of town we encamped. We made ourselves as comfortable as we could in houses which we constructed of pine boughs. In the afternoon it commenced to rain.

Apr. 19—The valley from Martinsburg to New Market is good but it is better improved between Martinsburg and Strasburg than it is between Strasburg and New Market. The 39th Illinois Regiment, part of the 1st Vermont cavalry and two pieces of cannon were sent across Massanutten Mountain into Page County. Companies B, D and I and part of Co. H of the 1st Vermont cavalry were sent to the Columbian Bridge on the road to Gordonsville. The bridge was guarded by some rebel cavalry, who on our approach set fire to it and fled. Our cavalry made a gallant charge, exchanged a few shots, captured some horses and took some prisoners; they also extinguished the fire before the bridge was damaged. We took up our quarters in a large log barn. It rained all day.

Apr. 20, Sunday—So gloomy was today that I could not realize that it was the Sabbath.

Apr. 21—Still continued to rain. Colombian Bridge is 12 miles from New Market.

Apr. 22—There was nothing but the regular guard duty done today.

Apr. 23—The sun once more, after four day's absence, made his appearance in all his splendor.

Apr. 24—It snowed this morning till the ground was white. Beautiful Sunny South this is.

Apr. 25—The companies of the 39th Illinois Regiment marched to the White House Bridge, where the rest of the regiment was stationed. This bridge is across the Shenandoah River on the pike from New Market to Sperryville and 9 miles from the former place. Our tents were brought up and we went into camp again.

Apr. 26—All quiet on a Shenandoah.

Apr. 27, Sunday—Company I was sent out on picket today. The day was beautiful. Snow on the Blue Ridge and green wheat fields in the valleys below presented a strange contrast.

Apr. 28 —A clear, serene and quiet day is all that I have to record today.

Apr. 29—I received a letter from a rebel cousin, who was taken prisoner at Ft. Donelson and is now in Camp Douglas in Chicago, Illinois. He seems to be treated better by the "Yankees" then he expected.[11]

Apr. 30—This morning we were "mustered in for pay." All through the long and dark night of rebellion many an anxious inquirer has been asking "Watchman what of the night?" The night is rapidly disappearing. With joy the dawn of peace is hailed. Soon we shall lay aside the implements of war and resume our wanted vocations.[12]

May 1—This the first day of the merry month of May was clear and serene, indicative of the political calmness which we expect soon to enjoy. The cloud, which was at first not larger than a man's hand, has been accumulating till now it over hangs us in all its blackness, but the darkest hour is just before day, soon it will have spent its fury and we will again bask in the genial sunshine of peace.

May 2—All continues quiet. The natives say that this has been a very backward Spring. The farmers are behind with their work.

May 3—We are again resuming our accustomed drills which were suspended during the unsettled weather of the winter and spring.

May 4, Sunday—Company I was sent out on picket to guard the bridge. All the rest of the regiment marched up to the Colombian Bridge this morning. The day was delightful.

May 5—There seems to have been a stampede among the colored population, 40 of them came to the bridge early this morning enroute for the North. They were from Rapponnock County and assigned as the reason for escaping from their masters (they were all slaves but one) that they were to be sent South in a few days. They said that hand cuffs were already made for them. There were two women the rest were all men and boys. They had traveled all night. The commander of the post thought it contrary to his instructions to let them across the bridge, they, therefore, had to devise other means to cross the river. Some of them struck for the Colombian Bridge about six miles above. A short distance below the bridge, which we were guarding, and in sight of it, was a skiff, the owner of which had to get out of the river, when the negroes came along to prevent them from crossing in it. Led by one of the 1st VT Cavalry about 20 of the negroes seized the skiff, carried it to the river and crossed in it. One old negro man was riding a horse branded "E. S." Company I is here alone, of course Capt. H. M. Phillips is commander of the post. The name of the post office at the White House Bridge is Massanutten, the orthography is variable. It is sometimes spelt Massanuten but the natives spell it Massanutten.

May 6—I went three miles from camp to guard a man who wanted to go on an errand. The people are disappointed with the "Yankees." They find them much better men than they expected. The "Yankees" were represented as a miserable set of fellows.

May 7—I was on picket today. We were reinforced by two companies of the 2nd Massachusetts Regiment. They are a mean low life set of scoundrels. They committed gross outrages on some of the citizens, even insulting the women in the dark hours of night, a fit time for such diabolical deeds. It would be a pleasure to shoot such demons-in-human-form. A company of the 1st Michigan cavalry relieved the company of "Green Mountain Boys" who were here.

May 8—The news of the evacuation of Yorktown created little or no sensation among the boys of Company I. Some of them were sorry; they wished to hear of the rebels getting a good thrashing.[13]

May 9—From conversing with the citizens I am led to believe that there are but few secessionists at heart in this part of the State, though their sympathies are with the South. What could be more natural, when we consider that their sons, husbands, fathers, brothers, lovers and neighbors are in the Southern Army, that the people should sympathize with the South? Soon perhaps there will be something to record in my diary, we are under marching orders.

May 10—Two deserters came in this morning from General Taylor's Army, of a Louisiana Regiment. They said that they were tired of fighting for nothing, declaring that they had nothing to fight for but the fun of the thing and too much of it is no fun. One of them said that if he had any property in the South he might stop and fight some longer but he said he had nothing—no plantation, no negroes and nothing but what he had in his pocket. They were both very poorly clad. I was on guard today. All quiet.[14]

May 11, Sunday—There is a great fire burning on the Massanutten Mountain and the Blue Ridge, which causes it to be very smoky in the valley below.

May 12—The day was dry and clear. At about 1 o'clock p.m. General Shields Division commenced crossing the river at this place. At sun down the 39th Regiment Illinois Vols came along and we fell into line and took up the line of march. Some days previous we had turned over our tents to the quartermaster, expecting to get gum blankets. Our regimental quartermaster was too negligent to procure the blankets for us. Hamburg is a small village containing a church and a few residences mostly log. Near this village we bivouaced in a stony field, two miles and a half from Luray.

May 13—After the accustomed preliminaries we were again on march. Today the road was very dusty. The day warm. Luray, the county seat of Page County, contains about 600 inhabitants. There is the one street of any importance. In the town are some very respectable looking buildings. Hawks Bill Creek, a beautiful stream, flows through the town. General Shields had guards all through the town, on every quarter to protect private property. No soldier was allowed to enter any house or yard. It would be difficult to laud the Gen. too highly for this. We did not have to lug our knapsack, they were hauled for us. The country passed over today is hilly and the soil poor. Nothing extraordinary occurred. At Luray we took the road to Front Royal. This surprised some of us; we expected to keep the Sperryville Pike. Front Royal is 25 miles, in a northerly direction, from Luray. We bivouaced on a creek six miles from Front Royal. The distance marched today 21 1/2 miles. It rained in the night, thereby rendering us very uncomfortable. We were a tired set of union soldiers when we halted.

May 14—It rained all day. We marched six miles. The road runs through a beautiful pass five miles from Front Royal. The road is built at the foot of a high precipice. Looking to the right is an awful cliff of rocks, in the crevices of which grow cedar trees, apparently taking root in the solid rock, they are very tenacious of their hold. On the left is the Shenandoah River, or as it is when translated into English, "Daughter of the Stars," the name is thought to have originated from the clearness of its water. Front Royal is the county seat of Warren County, it is one mile from the main stem of the Manassas Gap railroad. A road from the main stem has been built to the town. The situation is in a valley surrounded by hills. The scenery around is grand. The town is an insignificant place, of 500 or 600 inhabitants. There is but one fine house in the town. It is a residence in the outskirts on the road to Luray. We were quartered for the night in a hospital.

May 15—There are here two large hospitals built by the rebels. They are models of comfort. Each building is capable of accommodating about 1000 patients. They are two stories high, frame with stone foundations neatly plastered on the inside. Attached are out houses for cooking, ice houses etc. The foundation is laid for another building of the equal magnitude to those completed. Nearby is the graveyard where the soldiers who died in the hospital were buried. I counted 135 graves. Some of the bodies had been exhumed and taken home. At the head and foot of each grave is a pine board, on the one at head is painted in black letters the name of the deceased, the Regiment and company to which he belonged and the date of his death. Most of the poor fellows had come a long way to die in a bad cause. Virginia, Maryland, North Carolina, South Carolina, Alabama, Georgia, Louisiana and Arkansas regiments are represented in the "necropolis." They had all died within a few months. Peace be to their remains. They are no longer the tools of the Southern aristocrats. In the afternoon we left our comfortable quarters and set out on the march in a heavy rain. The road runs in a southeasterly direction. We took the road leading from Front Royal to Gaines' Cross Roads. The march this afternoon was across the Blue Ridge. Along up the side of the Ridge are some splendid farms, with fine residences, better clover fields I never saw any place. The women at one fine house waived their handkerchiefs as we passed, the boys responded with loud cheers. We crossed the Ridge at Chester's Gap, leaving Manassas Gap 5 miles to the left.

Owing to the fog and rain we could not have an extensive view of the country. Dark found us on the top of the Ridge. Late in the night, after marching 8 miles, we halted till morning on the eastern slope of the Blue Ridge, in Rappahannock County. From Front Royal to Gaines' Cross Road is 17 miles. How we were to sleep was the question to be decided. Two comrades and myself bunked together. By a strategical movement we got possession of the end gate of one of our wagon beds, and laid it on the ground it being three feet wide our bodies were thus kept out of the mud. On this we spread our knapsacks, unbuckling them, then our blankets. On this bed we slept very well in the rain.

May 16—Continued stormy. Distance marched today 9 miles. Encamped before night at Gaines' Cross Roads. Had plenty of hay to sleep on. The country passed over poor. Scenery romantic. Towns passed through today one Flint Hill a small village and Rappahannock County. There was skirmishing between our advance brigade and part of Ewell's forces.

May 17—Fair weather again. Country gradually becomes more level as we march eastward. Crossed the Rappahannock River as usual by wading. Much of the land today is poor, the improvements are good. There were but few natives, excepting negroes, visible. Distance from Gaine's Cross Roads to Warrenton 19 miles. Marched till after dark and encamped near Warrenton, in Fauquier County. Nothing extraordinary occurred today. Our teams were far behind so that we did not get supper and ready to go to bed till midnight.

May 18, Sunday—The sun shone out resplendently. When day appeared the light revealed to us a beautiful country moderately undulating, diversified with groves and cleared ground, in the far distance was Blue Ridge. Nearby was the beautiful town of Warrenton. All these varieties made up a grand scene. The illustrious John Marshall late Chief Justice of the United States was born in this county. Warrenton is the county seat of Fauquier County. There is a railroad from this place to the Orange and Alexandria railroad, distant ten miles. This is a very aristocratic looking town. Doubtless some of the F. F. V.'s reside here. Many of the residences are fine structures. The streets are tastefully ornamented with shade trees. A fine courthouse, a jail, four churches, two academies, one for males the other for females, stores, hotels and residences make up the town. Population 2100. On a magistrate's office I saw the following Classical inscription, "Nullius addictus jurare in verba magistra" [Bound to swear allegiance to no master]. Negroes seemed to compose the greater part of the inhabitants. They were well dressed and appeared happy. Heard the church bell the first time for many weeks. Soon after noon we were again on the march. The teams went before consequently we made slow progress. We marched about 8 miles and encamped, it was after dark. Nearby was a force of 5000 or 6000 encamped. General Drury was in command of them. The weather pleasant.[15]

May 19—We marched about one mile this morning and are now encamped in a field near the O & A railroad. The country gives evidence of a poor system of agriculture. Our encampment is near Catletts Station. We received a mail today, the first for about ten days. Did no marching.

May 20—Started on the march early this morning. The teams went ahead. Our pioneers cut out a road for some miles through the timber. The country passed through is very poor; the soil is worthless. The surface of the country is level. The improvements are inferior. We passed but few houses. There is no crop at all being raised. Saw only a few natives. The farms are in a bad state of repair. The old-fashioned Virginia rail fence is the only used in this part of the State. Truly this looks like a land of starvation. Much of the land once cultivated has been thrown out and is now over grown with a thick growth of young pine. We suffered considerable today for the want of good water, it being scarce and the day being warm. We encamped in a field near a small creek, in Stafford County, about 12 miles from Fredericksburg. Distance marched unknown as we traveled through woods and fields without any regard to regular beaten paths. (I have made a slight error. On the 20th we laid in camp and did nothing of importance. The notes under May 20 are correct, after substituting May 21. This correction rectifies the mistake.)

May 22—We started in good season this morning but owing to some unaccountable vexatious delay did not march more than a quarter of a mile before noon. The country presented the same barren appearance as yesterday. Desolation holds supreme sway. Our march was through Stafford County today. One old man said that he was glad to see us this and in Page County, where some ladies displayed a small flag and at a house on the western slope of the Blue Ridge are the only indications of a union feeling that I saw on the way from Massanutten to Fredericksburg. We passed through Falmouth, a small village on the Rappahannock River, in Stafford County about two miles above Fredericksburg, an hour before sun down. Finally we halted late after night in a plowed field two or three miles below the village. On our arrival here we learned that McDowell had a large force in the immediate vicinity. His force is daily augmenting.

May 23—We went into camp about half a mile from where we bivouaced last night. Took a bath in the Rappahannock River; it is a muddy stream. There are three bridges across the river, a railroad bridge, one constructed of canal boats and a pontoon bridge, these have all been built by General McDowell. The rebels burned two bridges. There are several boats which were burned by the rebels at the water's edge when they evacuated the place. I could not get permission to cross the river over to Fredericksburg, but from the view that I could get of the place it is an ancient looking town and one of considerable importance. There was a grand review of the troops at this place today by President Lincoln, Secretary Stanton and General McDowell. Before Shield's Division was reviewed it was dark so that I could not get much of a sight of the Dignitaries. I was anxious to review them. It rained unmercifully tonight thus preventing us from sleeping. There is no pleasure in sleeping out in the cold rain.[16]

May 24—This was a rainy disagreeable day. We drew small tents large enough for three men, they can easily be carried in a knapsack. Late in the evening we received orders to be ready to march in the morning. Agonizing rumors were afloat in camp to the effect that General Banks was surrounded at Strasburg and likely to be taken with all his command.[17]

May 25, Sunday—In compliance to orders General Shield's Division took up the line of march or rather countermarch. We marched on the same road that we came into Falmouth on. We encamped on the Creek where we encamped on our forward march last week.

May 26—No new features in the country, being the same as previously traveled. Various and conflicting rumors continued to circulate at par. We are now halted at Catletts Station to cook supper. Our orders are to procede immediately to Manassas Junction. Something is to be done. Our Country may expect every man of us to do his duty. It's now sun down. After dark we started on the march. The night was cloudy and dark, a light sprinkle of rain falling. The road was rough. At 10 o'clock in the night we halted till morning. This night march was very laborious on the men. Our teams did not arrive till one o'clock, consequently we were without blankets till that time, there was but little sleep allotted to us.

May 27—Early in the morning we were again on the march. The day was warm. The country to the Junction from our encampment, 7 or 8 miles is a level plain, watered by several small runs, the largest of which is Broad Run. The plains of Manassas were covered with a golden yellow flower. The soil is very poor. We marched within a mile and a half of the Junction, here we filed left and took the road to Strasburg. How far is it to water? was the question asked by many thirsty soldiers. Without dinner or any breakfast excepting hard crackers we marched till sundown and then halted for the night. This Division has now been on the march for 15 days on half rations. In the present age this is barbarious. For several miles around Manassas Junction there are dead horses scattered along the road, the stench of which is sickening. The country is completely desolated, the houses around which are huts of the meanest kind, are deserted. The rails have all been burned.

May 28—When I took up my blankets this morning I found that a black snake had shared my bed with me. He was snugly sleeping under my blanket. For its impudence its life atoned. Nothing extraordinary occurred on the march today. The day was cool and fine for traveling. Early in the morning we passed through Haymarket, a small village in Prince William County. This is an old weather beaten village presenting no appearance of comfort or taste. The next town we passed through was Thoroughfare, in Fauquier County. It is at the foot of a ridge, a spur of the Blue Ridge. The town consists of a few houses and a large stone mill. At this place is a deep gap in the Ridge called

Thoroughfare Gap. Through this gap flows Broad Run, the Manassas Gap railroad runs. The country until we crossed this ridge was poor. After crossing the country becomes better. Between this and Blue Ridge is a beautiful Valley, well improved, called "The White Plains." In the afternoon we passed through White Plains, a neat little village on the Manassas Gap railroad in Fauquier County. In it are some handsome residences with nice flowers in the yards. The country around is delightful. Before Virginia disgraced herself it would have been a desirable place to live to one fond of rural scenery. We passed in sight of Salem, leaving it to the left. Rector is an insignificant town. Near it we encamped for the night. Along the road we saw the graves of Southern Soldiers. At Thoroughfare Gap two companies had been placed on picket, they were the 104th NY Regiment. Their Regiment left without relieving them. They burned their tents, clothes, knapsacks etc. and made their way to Manassas Junction. They had too many luxuries with tents on picket!

May 29—We were preparing to move on when the order came that we would not march today. Guards were placed around the camp to keep soldiers from straying off. I was on this detail. The day was warm. The men are very tired, we have been long marching. Orders came for us to march, so against dark we were moving. We left trains behind. The road over which we marched was very rough. The men were greatly fatigued from loss of sleep and long marching. At about two o'clock a.m. we halted till morning.

May 30—As we approach the Blue Ridge the country becomes more hilly. Marksham is the first on the list of towns passed today. It is a small village on the railroad near the foot of the Blue Ridge. We passed through Manassas Gap. This is a pass in the Blue Ridge, through which passes a wagon road and the railroad to which the gap gives a name. The Ridge is about two miles through at this point and the elevation above the surrounding country is so small that one would hardly think that he was crossing a range of mountains. The Gap is a quarter of a mile wide, on either side of which are the lofty heights of the Blue Ridge. Instead of a mere mountain pass the Gap is a narrow valley in a high state of cultivation. Rich clover fields, fragrant flowers, emitting a sweet perfume, springs of pure water, a salubrious atmosphere, to which add the beauty of the scenery all combine to render this little valley a second Paradise. Fruit trees are abundant. The inhabitants have not altogether neglected the improvement of the country. The gap is 8 miles from Front Royal. In the Gap is Piedmont, a village consisting of a few scattered houses. From this place to Front Royal is very hilly. At noon we halted and took dinner. In the afternoon there was heavy shower of rain. Our cavalry made a charge on the enemy at Front Royal and beyond and took between 150 and 200 prisoners. Some 30 of our men, who were taken at Strasburg were re-captured, two of them belong to the 39th regimen Illinois, one to Company I. In the affair 9 of our men were killed including one Captain, and several wounded. What loss the enemy sustained is not known. The enemy burned the rail road depot at Front Royal. I have been informed that our cavalry succeeded in saving the bridge across the Shenandoah River, this one mile from town. We learned that several men of Co. I, 39th Illinois Regiment were taken prisoners at Strasburg. They had been sent to the hospital there.[18] The second brigade General Shield's Division marched through Front Royal out on the road to Luray. Near the town, in a clover field, we halted for the night. There was a thunderstorm and hard rain in the night. Our teams being left behind, many of the boys were without tents or blankets exposed to the merciless rain all night. Some were more provident and carried their small tents and blankets with them. I was not caught, as the saying is, napping. We carried our blankets along. Of our gum blankets we made comfortable tent and making a bed of our woolen blankets we enjoyed a good night's sleep.

May 31—We are lying in the clover field, where we halted last night. It is cloudy with the appearance of more rain. In the afternoon we, the second brigade, were ordered out just as if we were going on a long march. We marched through Front Royal out on the Winchester Pike. After marching a short distance from town we were ordered to halt. Now a tremendous cheer went up from the front of the column. Gen. Ferry, who has command of the second brigade, rode back with his staff. Soon we discovered that the brigade was countermarching. What the object of this movement was we could not learn. I think that it was a mere ruse. All we had to do was to march back to camp, "retake and possess" our former camping position.

June 1, Sunday—The sun shone brightly this morning. Cannonading was heard in the direction of Strasburg at 7 o'clock a.m. At ten o'clock the brigade was marched out on the Strasburg Pike to the river. Here we halted for half an hour. Some cavalry men came riding back, who had been to Strasburg. They said that Banks had attacked the enemy in the morning and had routed; they also told us that Jackson had already retreated above Strasburg. The order was given us to countermarch. So back through Front Royal we marched taking the Pike to Luray. We did not halt till late in the night. Being very cloudy the night was dark. We marched 9 miles from Front Royal. We got our suppers and went to bed. The rain, in the latter part of the night began to pour down into our faces. Until this we rested well.

June 2—Cannonading was again heard in the Shenandoah Valley in the forenoon. The day was extremely warm. Late in the afternoon there was a heavy rain with a terrific thunderstorm. We were at the time halted in a wood near Luray. The main body of our forces halted west of Luray, between it and the White House Bridge for the night. The 39th Illinois Regiment was sent in to within half a mile of the bridge. Company I was detailed to do picket duty at the bridge or rather where it was. A party of the enemy's cavalry had been sent from New Market by Jackson to burn it. They accomplish the order at 4 o'clock this morning. All was quiet during the night. It still continued to rain.

June 3—Things remained in status quo. One of General Shield's aids crossed the river in a skiff, walked up on the hill, and was fired at. Five or six men were sent across to make a reconnaissance. Nothing of importance was discovered by them. It continues to rain. The river is very high and still rising, it is too deep to ford. We are back again to the place where we started on our march to Fredericksburg. It has been just three weeks since we left here. There has been a great change since then to the appearance of this valley. We have marched about 250 miles. The boys learned one bad trick of our fellow soldiers of the East. I refer to counterfeiting the Confederate treasury notes. Our boys bought them of Eastern soldiers for a mere nothing and pass them to the citizens. I disapprove such operations. It is unworthy of a high minded man. What has transpired in the Shenandoah Valley within three days past we have not yet learned.

June 4—It rained hard all last night and today. Nothing of importance occurred in this region. No communication has come, disappointment in our expectations to bag Jackson and bad weather discourages the boys. All hopes of a speedy termination of the war have vanished.

June 5—We received marching orders earlier this morning and were soon in the act of executing the order. It was very tiresome marching, the road being muddy. As good luck would have it we had only to march to the Colombian Bridge, distant 7 or 8 miles. The Rebels burned this bridge also. We went into camp back of the hills near the river. Boats are being built at this place.

June 6—A fine morning once more was this. From present indications we will soon be on the march again. Go where we may it will all be right. The indications were correctly interpreted for soon after writing the above we were marching. Opposite General Shield's headquarters we halted. The General came out and inquired for Colonel Osborn. The Col being pointed out to him he walked up and addressed him as follows. "Good morning Col.," (shaking hands cordially) "did you receive an order from me?" "No sir I did not," replied the Col. "It must have gone astray," said the Gen. "The order is to detail one of your companies to go across the river. Detail Co D. I want them to go across and drive those fellows out of the woods. Report to Colonel Daum at the bridge, he will set the company across." The above order was soon obeyed and [we] were marching on down the river. We did not, however, go far, for we filed left into an open field. Here the Brigade was drawn up in close order, forming three sides of a hollow square. General Ferry then rode up, took off his hat and made an eloquent speech. He complemented his command highly for the alacrity with which the men had performed their recent arduous duties. "You started from Newmarket," said he, "on an eight day's march to join General McDowell's Corps. You had no rations excepting hard bread, coffee, sugar, salt and beef on the hoof. On you marched over mountains and through defiles cheerfully performing the hardships incumbent upon you. You join McDowell and on the very day that you were to have marched to Richmond, there substantially to terminate the war, we received the intelligence that the feeble column of Banks was being driven across the Potomac by the overwhelming numbers of his wiley foe. This Division on the very day it was to have marched on the right of the advance of General McDowells column towards Richmond was ordered back. And rightly so too because it was our old foe whom we thought that we had laid in the dust at Winchester. Without a murmur you endured hardships, the most severe that I have ever seen any command endure since I have been in the federal service. Marching under a burning sun and through pelting rains, by day and by night, you reached Front Royal, in the vicinity of which we expected to meet 'Stonewall' Jackson, there to batter down his wall." The Gen. went on to say that the enemy escaped the mesh which we set for him and retreated up the Valley and how that we marched from Front Royal without rations and benefit of the river etc. He also with regret spoke of another thing, stealing from the citizens. His manner of address was persuasive. "Come cease this marauding. Refrain from anything that will cause an unpleasant recollection in your soldier's life. *Do nothing that will tingle in your consciences when you return to your peaceful homes.*" This last sentence ought to be written among the stars, where every soldier in the Army could read it, while walking his lonely beat as sentinel. Whoever is so vile as not to give heed to this advice is unworthy to be a soldier in the union army. Regardless of all principles of honor it is too true there are many who will still persist in stealing. We rested on the grass about two hours, after the Gen was done speaking and then marched one mile further down the river and encamped.[19]

June 7—This was a beautiful morning, a saying which has become rare of late. All remained quiet in camp during the day.

June 8, Sunday—In the afternoon the 39th regimen Illinois marched to Luray, where after dark it encamped. A report was received of our fourth brigade having a fight with Jackson's forces in which our men were repulsed. The battle was above Colombian Bridge. None of the particulars were learned.

June 9—Still fighting up the river, the camp was alive with various rumors, but from them it's impossible to sift the truth. We remained in camp all day, in a field, on the Sperryville Pike, in the outskirts of Luray.

June 10—It rained all day. There was nothing more than the common camp routine done today. Have not yet learned the facts of the battle up the river. "Old Mother Rumor" with her many tongues represents it as having been a very serious affair to the Unionists. Our wounded have been brought to Luray.

June 11—We get newspapers about once a week. There is certainly an expedition in contemplation for this Division. All the tents, excepting the small ones we got at Fredericksburg, knapsacks and surplus clothing have been turned over to the quartermaster and sent to Front Royal. Previous to starting to Fredericksburg, on the 12th of May, all the tents, excepting one to each company for the officers, were turned over to the quartermaster. They are now no exceptions made in favor of them. The recent battle was at Port Republic in Rockingham County. It seems that Col. Carroll, acting Brig Gen. of the fourth Brigade was sent up to burn a bridge. Instead of burning it he endeavored to hold it.[20]

June 12—At one o'clock this morning the 39th Illinois Regiment and 30 men of the 1st R. I. Cavalry started out of camp as was thought to surprise a band of Guerrillas. When we arose the moon was eclipsed, the size of eclipsed was about ten digits. Nothing of importance occurred from a day's hard tramp through the mountains. We took two prisoners and took, captured or stole some horses. The day's march might be termed a scout, a regimental picnic, or perhaps more properly, a stealing expedition, everlasting infamy is attaching itself to our army.

June 13—We moved half a mile to our Brigade. Our knapsacks were returned and the officers' tents. This seems like a crazy fit of somebody.

June 14—The weather is very warm. The wheat is ripening for the harvest very fast.

June 15, Sunday—The Division began to move towards Front Royal. The second Brigade started at 12 o'clock noon. The day was very warm and the road dusty till the afternoon when there was a shower of rain. We marched 8 miles and encamped on the banks of the Shenandoah River. The night was too cool to be pleasant.

June 16—Started on the march late in the forenoon. Distance marched 10 miles. The day was clear and pleasant. We encamped on a creek within a few rods of where we bivouaced when on our first march to Front Royal. The night was so cold that we could not sleep comfortably under two woolen blankets in a tent.

June 17—Struck tents and took up the line of march early this morning. Went into camp on a hill, one mile from Front Royal, at ten o'clock a.m. We had to lug our knapsacks on this march, on account of not having transportation. There are many dead horses and mules along the road. Since encamping here a soldier of the 62nd Regiment Ohio volunteers whilst bathing in the river got drowned. We received our mail today which to most of the boys was an interesting event.

June 18—The second Brigade was paid off today for two months. The 39th Illinois Regiment voted on the adoption or rejection of the new constitution for the State. It was rejected by a unanimous vote almost, there being but two or three dissenting votes. On guard today. All quiet in the Department of the Shenandoah.

June 19—The weather is fine. We again get the daily papers. "Injustice is everywhere written."

June 20—We held an election today to fill the vacancies in our company which have lately occurred. J. D. Lemon was elected 1st Lieutenant, E. S. Waller having resigned, Samuel Gilmore 1st Sgt. And J. B. Craiger 2d Sgt.[21]

June 21—Early this morning we started to Manassas Junction. Our baggage was transported by railroad. The route was the same as that we marched two weeks ago from the Piedmont district to Front Royal. The day was pleasant. Encamped near Marksham Station, in Fauquier County. This is in the Manassas Gap, by Railroad 14 miles from Front Royal. Distance marched today 14 miles. It is now sun down. I have written my diary for the past two days in our present ephemerial camp, using a stone wall fence for a desk. All quiet in the region of "The Daughter of the Stars."

June 22, Sunday—A bright and beautiful Sabbath was this. Early in the morning we were violating the command, "Thou shalt remember the Sabbath day to keep it holy," by marching. We passed through Salem. This is a small village on the Manassas railroad. Encamped 1 1/2 miles from The Plains, between it and Thoroughfare.

June 23—The morning was warm. All things moved off quietly. There is a great paucity of news. The idea that the war be over against the 4th of July has been abandoned by most. The regular system of evacuation which the enemy seem to follow will certainly prolong the struggle. A Southern Confederacy is certainly not among the most improbable of human events. We started on the march about noon. The march was quite pleasant, excepting the dust, till in the afternoon. Then a small cloud was visible over the mountains. At first it attracted but little attention, but soon it began to increase in size and blackness. The distant thunder now told us that a storm was inevitable. Late in the afternoon we marched through Haymarket and halted in an open field to prepare for the fury of the impending storm. The thunder roared and the lightning flashed. The rain falls in great drops slowly at first but soon we were in the midst of a pelting storm. The rain fell so fast that in a few minutes the face of the earth was flooded with water. Cheer after cheer went up from the boys whilst marching through the drenching rain. The noise made by them was surpassed only by the sharp claps of thunder, which was terrific. Little brooks were swollen into large creeks, having to wade these, the work of completely soaking the clothes was thoroughly done. A halt was ordered in Pine Grove. This afforded but little protection from the unmerciful power of the boisterous Storm King. Such is a soldier's lot. We halted for the night about two miles from Haymarket. At this town we left the road to Manassas Junction and took the road to Bristoe Station. The Boys made comfortable beds of boughs. So they enjoyed themselves as well as they could under the circumstances. "A rainbow at night is a sailor's delight."

June 24—Early we struck our tents and were on the march. We marched two miles to a grove and halted till afternoon, when we were again marching onward. Another storm similar to that of yesterday was allotted to us. We reached camp near Bristoe, on the Orange and Alexandria Railroad, here we pitched our shelter tents with the prospect of lying camp for some time. Our knapsacks were returned to us.

June 25—This was a clear day. We are now encamped near Bristoe, a mere station on the Orange and Alexandria Railroad, in Prince William County 4 miles from Manassas Junction. The encampment is on Broad Run. This stream unites with Bull Run below the junction and the latter thus increased empties into the Potomac River. General Shields went to Washington this morning. It is reported that he intends to resign. He is very indignant on account of the rejection of his nomination by the Senate to be Major General. Col. Osborn has command of the second Brigade, General Ferry of the Division.[22]

June 26—There was a general inspection of the Division today. As usual it was a grand Bore. The weather is fine. The daily papers are regularly received on the day that they are published.

June 27—The nights are not so cold as they are in the Shenandoah Valley. Everything was very quiet in camp today but the good news read on dress parade compensated for this. The first and second Brigades, the third Indiana Cavalry and the reserve artillery are ordered to hold themselves in readiness to be shipped to Alexandria, on the cars, in the morning, as soon as transportation can be furnished, preparatory to joining the Army before Richmond. This is just as I would have it. It has been my desire to be a part of "The on to Richmond army." "Old Stonewall" Jackson came very near cheating us out of this honor by his rapid descent down the valley of Virginia. The boys are generally pleased with the idea of going to Richmond, some of them however would prefer not to go there.

June 28—Early in the morning we took breakfast, struck tents and were ready to move on towards the Rebel Capital. After loading our baggage we fell into line and marched to the railroad, distant about half a mile. Here we halted, front faced, right dressed, ordered arms, fixed bayonets and rested till the cars arrived. We had to lie around in the sun till noon when the train made its appearance. No regard seems to have been in view to our comfort. Two Regiments, the 39th Illinois and 13th Indiana, were crowded on a train of box cars large enough for half the number of men. Inside, on their tops and platforms the cars were crowded to their utmost capacity. At 1 o'clock p.m. the engine was set in motion and the cars began to bear their living freight to Alexandria, distant about 40 miles. At Manassas Junction the car stopped 15 minutes. Manassas will hereafter be one of the Classical spots of our country. The following is as near the origin of the name as I can trace it. In the Gap, through Blue Ridge, which bears the same name lived a hospitable Jew by the name of Manasseth. Here [he] kept a house for the entertainment of the weary traveler. That they might stop with Mannasseth for the night, travelers would put up before night or travel late to reach his house where they were always sure to be welcome. The name of the Hebrew was transferred to the Gap in the Ridge. Hence long ago it was called Manasseth Gap. After the lapse of time the name became corrupted into Manassas. Some of the old men in Page County, Prince William, Fauquier and the City of Alexandria and perhaps in other localities still call it Manasseth. The original name has become so obsolete that there is no hopes of its being called anything else but Manassas. From the Gap the railroad takes its name and where the Manassas Gap railroad forms a junction with the Orange and Alexandria Road is called Manassas Junction. South and west of the junction is, as I have before described, a little plain country. At the Junction have been erected several board houses for temporary use. One is struck with the displays in large letters "New England House," "New York Saloon" etc. Passing on towards Alexandria the country becomes broken and hilly. For several miles on the Northeast side of Bull Run the country is covered with a dense growth of trees and under brush. So thick are the trees and shrubs that it is impenetrable to mortal men. The hills are high and steep cut up by many deep ravines. Bull Run is a sluggish stream about 30 yards wide. The water is muddy and of a yellow color. Manassas certainly was a very strong position in front but approached by the way of Winchester, Strasburg and Front Royal it is entirely defenseless. Passing through on the cars I could get but a glimpse of the fortifications. After crossing Bull Run the country is well watered with limpid streams of pure water. Along the railroad are no towns but several stations. The entire line of the road is guarded, small squads of soldiers being stationed every few miles. Near Alexandria the country is much better than on Bull Run. The train reached Alexandria about 4 o'clock p.m. and after a great deal of vexatious delay run out to the place assigned for our encampment. This is on an open green in upper suburbs of the city, near the river. Alexandria, the county seat of Alexandria County, is on the Potomac River, 7 miles below Washington. The river here is a fine body of water being about 1 mile wide. The city is built with great regularity; the streets cross each other at right angles, they are well paved and Macadamized. There are some fine public buildings and residences. Fairfax Seminary is an ornament to the place. The Marshall Hotel is the house where Col. Ellsworth was slain. It is a brick building three and a half stories high of no uncommon pretensions. The American flag now floats over it. The citizens of this place seemed to take extra pains to make themselves pleasant to the soldiers. Alexandria does not appear like a city in a rebel state, there is too much life in all departments of business. The stores are well filled. Here I was in the best bookstore that I have seen since leaving Chicago. Population of the city 12,000.[23]

June 29, Sunday—Went to the river to wash before breakfast. One Brigade of Shield's Division was on the two boats "North America" and "Georgia" anchored out in the river. The steamer Louisiana went up loaded as I supposed with sick and wounded from the Army before Richmond. She had a hospital flag floating. Steamers and schooners are continually passing up and down the river. Late in the afternoon we packed up, fell into ranks and marched to the river for the purpose of embarking for Fortress Monroe. After lying at the wharf opposite to where we were encamped two hours, we marched down the river to another wharf, stacked arms and lay around until our baggage was loaded. Finally we went aboard, five companies of the 39th Illinois embarking on the steamer Metamora, among these was Company I. Gen. Ferry also went on this boat. It was about 11 o'clock in the night when we embarked. The boat lay at anchor till morning.[24]

June 30—The morning was foggy till the sun rose and cleared it away. Earlier we were steaming down the Potomac. The Metamora, next the John Tucker and then the Young America started at the same time. The Young America was soon left far behind. The first object of interest that we passed was Fort Washington. This is situated on the Maryland side on a point of land, commanding the river from below for some distance. The walls are built of stone. A band came out and played Hail Columbia as we passed. Our eyes had scarcely been taken off the Fort till the opposite side of the river attracted the eyes of, not all, but most of us. Mt. Vernon, a name sacred to every American, was now in sight.[25] There rest the remains of him whose name is a synonym for unselfish patriotism. In reverence to the departed hero the Metamora, as is the custom of boats, tolled her bell whilst passing Mount Vernon. This Classic spot is in Fairfax County, Virginia six miles below Alexandria. The mansion is on a hill by the river. So densely wooded is the hill that the passer by can only see the roof of the house in which George Washington resided. Strange to say some of the boys could sleep while passing Mt. Vernon! Along the river are many fine plantations. There are no towns below Alexandria. At Acquia Creek was a camp of soldiers. From Alexandria to its entrance into the Chesapeake Bay the Potomac is a fine stream. It gradually widens to its mouth where it is between 15 and 20 miles wide. One is at a loss to tell when he enters the bay. The ride on the calm bosom of the Chesapeake was very pleasant, a short rest from the fatiguing marches we had recently had to perform. On the right far away in the distance could be discerned blue "skirts of timber." We for the first time understood that "Tis distance lends enchantment to the view." On the left land could not be seen. At one time we were entirely out of sight of land. At the mouths of the Rappahannock, York and Back rivers we could see light houses. We were too near the land to have a fine view of the sunset. The only monsters of the deep that we saw were porpoises, which stuck up their ugly black heads out of the water. Night spread her sable curtains on the face of the waters and we rode calmly on. In the wake of the boat the water sparkled like fire this presenting a beautiful phenomenon. At about 10 o'clock in the night lights in Hampton Roads hove in sight. The lights on the shipping was a grand sight. We cast out anchor and lay in the Roads till morning.

July 1—The light of the morning revealed to us the fact that we were in the midst of a forest of masts. Shipping of various kinds was anchored in the Roads. River steamers, small schooners, ocean sailing vessels, steam ships, men-of-war, gun boats, propellers and tug boats were all represented numerously. Nearby was Fortress Monroe on Old Point Comfort.[26] The Fort covers 257 acres of ground and mounts 335 guns. On a point of sand between the fort and the water are the two huge guns "Lincoln" and "Union." They look like two large black bears.[27] One mile south of Fortress Monroe, in the Roads, is a fortification in course of construction called the Rip Raps.[28] Among the curiosities of the shipping was an English man-of-war and a Brazilian man-of-war. We lay in Hampton Roads till about noon, when we started for City Point 100 miles up the James River. Soon was the Metamora under full headway steaming up the James River. We passed over the water where the Merrimac made such dreadful havoc with our shipping off Newport News and where she was beaten by the Monitor. Our boat passed within a few rods of the wrecks of the Congress and Cumberland. The Congress had been burned to the water's edge. The Cumberland was sunken. Her wreck speaks eloquently of the devastations of war. Her masts are several feet above the surface of the water. All of her crew and guns, I was told, went down with her. The next object of interest was James Town on the north bank of the river. It is situated on a level peninsula. The site seems to have been well selected. All that remains of this ancient town is the ruins of a building said to have been the first Church ever erected on the Western Continent. The ruin is a brick pile, probably 12 feet high and 5 feet square. Some thought that the ruin was part of the main building and that aperture was a doorway. I am inclined to the belief that it was a chimney and that the opening in the side was a fireplace. The bricks are laid up in good order and are in a good state of preservation. The rebels had heavy batteries at this place; at many other places were deserted batteries. On both sides of the river are some splendid plantations. The greater part of the land near the river is covered with a heavy growth of woods. The surface of the country is level. The river was lined with different sorts of craft. Contrabands could only be numbered by the boat loads. They were on canal boats, men, women and children. Steamers crowded full of soldiers, schooners loaded with forage, Sanitary Commission boats, guns boats and canal boats loaded with niggers were all either anchored or going up the river. Our fleet was conveyed up the river from Berkeley's Landing by a gun boat. There are no towns on the river but mere landings. The wharf at City Point was on fire. Above this place, about six miles, we cast anchor and lay till morning. It was after dark before we cast anchor. We heard of the awful battle which had been raging for several days. We could see the flash of cannons but not hear the report. Twenty-four prisoners were brought aboard the Metamora tonight.[29]

—The American flag waived over the wreck of the Cumberland till the wind blew it into tatters. "It was nailed to the mast." This is similar a tradition of our flag in Martinsburg, Va. When the rebels made such wholesale destruction of the cars and engines belonging to the Baltimore and Ohio Railroad Company. The flight was on the engine, which was doomed to taste the fiery element. Fuel was piled around the engine and set on fire. The flag though wrapped in the burning flame was impervious to its touch. The iron horse was destroyed and yet strange indeed the bunting was unhurt. The Rebels being enraged took it and soaked it in turpentine and cast it into the fire. Still it would not burn. Being defeated the second time in their nefarious design they tore the flag into pieces. How dear tearing subsequent events have shown. Many respectable citizens of Martinsburg pledged their word for the truth of this, having been eyewitnesses of the transaction. The distance from Alexandria to the mouth of the Potomac River is 100 miles; thence to Fortress Monroe 100 miles; thence to City Point 100 miles making the distance from Alexandria to where we lay in the river tonight over 300 miles. The wheat fields along the river were harvested.

July 2—Early this morning we run down the river below City Point to Harrison's Landing. We passed the Monitor. "She looks like a Yankee cheese press on a black raft" is a good description of her. The forenoon was rainy. At noon we went ashore with three day's rations in our haversacks. All our baggage was left on the boat. After lying on the shore till dark when we were marched 3 or 4 miles out into the woods, where we slept in the rain and mud till morning. Such mud as we had to march through it was never a lot of mortal man to leave in it the vestige of his foot. The Regiment became scattered. Some got lost and could not find their comrades. I was among these unfortunate ones.

July 3—The Rebels began to annoy one part of our lines by throwing shells. The 1st & 2nd Brigades Shield's Division was sent to settle up this Secesh Battery. We were not much troubled with it. We were drawn up in line of battle and permitted to rest in place. I lay down the ground and amidst the cannon's roar fell asleep. Whilst dreaming of meeting friends at home in the parlor the "Command attention fall in" broke my nap. Our brigade was placed on picket. All through tonight there was occasional firing.

July 4—Before daylight this morning bang went a volley of musketry; the reserve were up and in line in a minute. A wild Irishman of the 67

Ohio came running back bare headed saying that his regiment was dispersed and that he saw the men falling around him thick. This proved untrue. I was detailed to chop down trees. A great deal of timber is being felled and entrenchments throwed up. There was skirmishing along our lines during the day. This was rather a hard spent Fourth of July. Our Company was placed on an advance picket post this evening. We as much expected to be attacked, following morning as we expected to eat breakfast.

July 5—We were disappointed. The Secesh did not come. We occupied an advance post till evening when we were relieved and sent back to the reserve. Nothing extraordinary transpired today. Cannonading and musketry was heard along our lines but these are of daily occurrence and have become stale.

July 6, Sunday—All concurred in the belief that this would be a hard and the last Sabbath with some of us. We were drawn up in line of battle to receive the enemy. Litters were made to carry off the wounded on and men detailed for this purpose. It is the duty of the musicians of the regiment to carry off the wounded, but our Corps of musicians was not deemed sufficiently strong. The battle did not take place. In the afternoon the second Brigade was relieved from picket duty and went into camp near the river. Some of our regiment have friends in the 8th Illinois cavalry; it is interesting to see them meet. In camp some distance from the front we were permitted to take off our clothes to sleep for the first time during the past week.

July 7—The Army of the Potomac is in Turkey Bend on the James River, above the mouth of Chickahominy, in Charles City County. The position is being strengthened by throwing up entrenchments, digging rifle pits and felling trees. This county is noted as having given birth to two Presidents of the United States; Harrison and Tyler. In the afternoon I was detailed to work on entrenchments; the shovel handle blistered my hands.[30]

July 8—At 2 o'clock a.m. the regiment was called up, formed in line of battle on the parade ground; we were then ordered to stack arms and get breakfast. It was thought that the enemy would make an attack early in the morning. We were called up to be ready for the conflict. All passed off very well until noon when the regiment was detailed to work on the rifle pits.

July 9—The weather is very warm. The landing the army is stationed on is covered with a dense wood consisting chiefly of pine and oak trees. There is also much swampy land; the soil is poor. How the early explorers could give such glowing accounts of the fertility of Virginia I cannot understand. Good water is scarce. This is certainly a sickly climate. Perhaps disease will do with the Army what the enemy have failed to do. All has been quiet along our lines. The Rebels are reported to be falling back to Richmond.

Conclusion

In looking over my diary I find many mistakes in composition. If I should never return home it is my wish that my journal should be burnt. I have written much of the present volume, as it were, with my pen in one hand and gun in the other. This is a simple narration of facts as they have come under my observation.

End of Vol 3rd

Volume 4

HARRISON'S LANDING, VIRGINIA, JULY 1862–MARCH 1863

At Harrison's Landing, the Thirty-ninth Illinois joined the Fourth Corps (under Brigadier General Erasmus Keyes) as part of the Second Division (under Brigadier General John James Peck), Third Brigade (under Brigadier General Oris S. Ferry). Though the regiment had arrived in time for the battle at Malvern Hill, the men did not participate. Instead they went into the large encampment at Harrison's Landing, where they remained while the Union army commander, General George B. McClellan, sparred with Lincoln and the War Department over future campaigns. McClellan demanded additional reinforcements before renewing any advance on Richmond, while Lincoln and his advisors were loath to give any more troops to a general who had already squandered an opportunity to capture the Confederate capital.

While the bickering played out between McClellan and his superiors, the Federal soldiers suffered under the heat of a Virginia tidewater summer. On August 3, 1862, McClellan was directed to leave Harrison's Landing and take his army to Fort Monroe where it would be transferred to northern Virginia. On August 5, before McClellan left, he dispatched forces under General Joseph Hooker to reoccupy Malvern Hill, only to recall them two days later.

On August 14, the Federals began their movement from Harrison's Landing to Fort Monroe, and two days later the landing was completely evacuated. Keyes's Fourth Corps with the Thirty-ninth Illinois were the last to leave. While one division of the Fourth Corps was sent north, Peck's division and the Thirty-ninth Illinois remained on the peninsula until they were assigned to the Department of Virginia. The regiment then moved to Yorktown and, after a brief stop, marched to Fort Monroe, where they boarded a transport with the rest of General Peck's division and proceeded to Suffolk, Virginia.

The Federals had initially occupied Suffolk, situated on the Nansemond River about twenty-four miles east of Norfolk, in the spring of 1862. The town was an important commercial and agricultural center, served by the Norfolk and Petersburg as well as the Seaboard and Roanoke railroads. Arriving at Suffolk on September 3, 1862, the Thirty-ninth Illinois settled down to garrison duty and the construction of a line of fortifications stringing together eight forts and fourteen miles of trenches. The regiment also joined raids and fought a series of skirmishes in October and December 1862 against Confederate forces along the Backwater River.

In early 1863, Peck's division numbered among the reinforcements being assembled for a joint expeditionary force against Charleston, South Carolina. On January 5, the Illinois soldiers marched southwest from Suffolk to the Chowan River. The short march proved pleasant as the men found ample forage to supplement their army rations. The ingenious and resourceful regimental band, at one point, even used the bass drum to hide a piglet that had been appropriated from a local farmer.

Once they reached the Chowan River, the men boarded transports and rode to New Bern, North Carolina, to join the Eighteenth Army Corps.

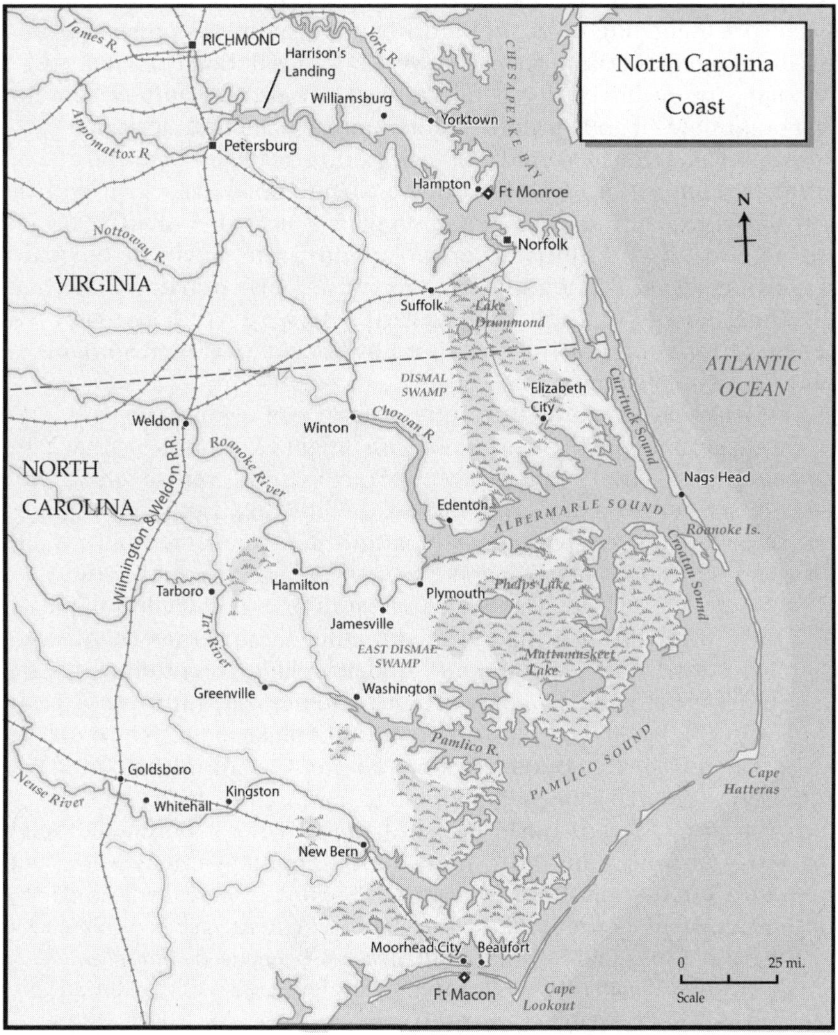

The regiment paused at New Bern, then proceeded by rail to Morehead City, North Carolina, and again by transports to South Carolina. Heavy swells made for rough sailing, but soon the weather cleared. On January 22, 1863, the men arrived in Port Royal Sound off Hilton Head Island, South Carolina, the headquarters of the Department of the South.

The Thirty-ninth Illinois bivouacked on St. Helena Island with the rest of the units from North Carolina, under the command of Major General John G. Foster who had brought elements of the Eighteenth Corps from North Carolina for a joint expedition against Charleston. At Port Royal the navy had been concentrating the majority of its ironclads, including the *Passaic* class monitors, which were improved versions of the original monitor that had fought the *Virginia* at Hampton Roads. According to the initial plan, the army was to seize the outlying Sea Islands at the mouth of the harbor, capture the Confederate works, and establish artillery batteries that would support the ironclad attack against the harbor forts. The overall army commander was Major General David Hunter, a solid administrator but not an aggressive field commander. It was expected that Foster, formerly a member of Fort Sumter's garrison in 1861, would command the field army. Upon his arrival, Foster enthusiastically undertook his duties yet often neglected to keep Hunter informed. Hunter was not pleased. The senior commander resented Foster's activity, considered him insubordinate, and eventually forced him out of the department. By the time the navy was ready, the army command was in such disarray that it was unable to provide any effective service.

While animosity and controversy swirled among the generals, the soldiers on St. Helena Island enjoyed a brief respite from active campaigning. Many took the opportunity to explore the Sea Islands and the town of Beaufort. When a Northern expeditionary force had captured the region in November 1861, not only the Confederate military but also the white property owners had all fled. Nearly eight thousand slaves were left behind. The Federal government eventually stepped in and with the help of Northern missionaries began an assistance program to provide food, clothing, schools, employment, and pay for the slaves. The area was also used as a recruiting ground for African American soldiers. Many saw the efforts at Port Royal as the first step in a comprehensive reconstruction program aimed at uplifting the slaves and granting them citizenship.

By the end of March 1863, the final preparations for the Charleston attack were in place. The Union squadron at Port Royal, under the command of Rear Admiral Samuel Francis Du Pont, was ready to sail. The flotilla consisted of the ironclad frigate *New Ironsides,* the tower ironclad *Keokuk,* and the monitors *Weehawken, Passaic, Patapsco, Nahant, Nantucket, Montauk,* and *Catskill.* At the same time, Hunter readied his forces, and the men on St. Helena Island prepared to embark. Although Hunter had some ten thousand men, he had no firm plans other than to be in a position to occupy Charleston should the ironclads prove successful. Otherwise, the attack would be primarily a naval affair. —*S.R.W.*

★ ★ ★ ★ ★

—What he did, saw and heard.

—*Patria perpetua esto* [the fatherland is forever].

July 10, 1862—This was a very quiet day, not the usual amount of firing being done. "Old Sol's" rays were scorching. The day was extremely warm, almost hot. Prof. Lowe made a balloon reconnaissance this morning.[1]

July 11—The day was rainy and is disagreeable. To lie in our shelter tents all day without room to move unless one gets in the mud or water is by no means pleasant. Nothing exciting transpired today.

July 12—The sun shone out this morning, drying the mud and thus rendering camp life tolerable. It is generally thought that the enemy will not attack us here.

July 13, Sunday—Today was more like Sabbath than any day for some months past, there being services in the adjoining regiments. The Chaplain of the 8th Illinois Cavalry preached to the 39th Illinois Regiment. His discourse was practical.[2]

July 14—The 39th Illinois Regiment is in the Second Corps, commanded by Brigadier General Keyes, Peck's Division and Ferry's Brigade. In strolling around over camp this afternoon we saw a board nailed to a tree on which was an index, pointing to a camp, with this inscription "Headquarters of the Army of the Potomac." Headquarters constitute a considerable camp of itself. Here the American Napoleon with his staff stays. Including staff, bodyguard and servants the General has a long train of Satellites. Among other things is a printing press. We next visited Lowe's balloon. This is kept continually inflated with gas and daily makes reconnaissances. On one side of it is painted in large letters the word "Intrepid," on the other is a spread Eagle holding in its talons the American flag, in its beak is a picture in a splendid frame.[3] The picture is a portrait of McClellan. The house where President Harrison was born is the next object of interest. This is a large brick building, two and a half stories high. In its day it was a fine residence; the style of architecture is antiquated. The situation is beautiful being on an eminence overlooking the James River, which is here about one mile wide.[4] This once fine estate is now sadly laid waste. There is scarcely a rail to be seen on it, having all been burned by the stern necessities of war. The mansion is used for a hospital for sick and wounded Union soldiers. Around the house is what might be called a hospital camp. There are tents, enough to accommodate at least one full regiment, filled with sick and wounded soldiers. The Signal Corps has a station on the top of the house. Such is the place where President Harrison was born. Well was it for him that his eyes closed in the slumber of death before such dreadful calamity befell our country as that in the midst of which we now are. Here and there is a grave where rest the remains of a poor soldier, who died far away from home without a kind friend to speak one gentle word or soothe a single aching pain. Amid the clangor of arms they died and were consigned to the bowels of the Earth. A pine board at the head of each grave with the name of the deceased is all that marks their resting place. Soon will they be forgotten. Such is the reward of unselfish patriotism.

July 15—The camp of Ferry's Brigade was today arranged in regular order; the tents are placed in streets running parallel to each other. The day was extremely warm. The Rebels of Petersburg, Va console themselves with the knowledge that the position occupied by the Army of the Potomac is the hottest place in Virginia. "There is no place," say they, "out of Tophet like it." There was a refreshing shower of rain in the evening.[5]

July 16—Lowe's balloon, "Intrepid," made an ascension, 1000 feet high, the length of the rope by which it is drawn down to the ground, this morning. All was quiet along our lines today. The day was clear and very warm. In the evening, after sun down, there was a cooling shower of rain and thunderstorm.

July 17—A warm day, balloon ascension, dress parade and a shower of rain in the evening, the same as yesterday, make the record of the 17th of July.

July 18—The day was cloudy and cool. Nothing transpired to render the day notable. There is no prospect of any active operations in the Army of the Potomac soon.

July 19—The day was moderately cool. We had been notified for two successive days that General Keyes would inspect this Brigade at ten o'clock a.m. We therefore prepared to receive the Magnus Apollo. Before the appointed time on each day the order was countermanded.[6]

July 20, Sunday—The morning was peaceful and calm. At 10 o'clock a.m. was company inspection. The day was very warm. The rations which are now issued out to us consist chiefly of crackers, a poor quality pork mess, fresh beef, coffee and sugar, rice and beans. With such rations during the warm weather it is not strange that there is much sickness in the army. Crackers, fat meat, sugar and coffee is enough to kill anybody.

July 21—The morning was pleasant till Old Sol's rays began to pierce too keenly the Earth. Ferry's Brigade was inspected this forenoon by General Keyes, being on guard I escaped this red tape torture. In the evening late the 39th Illinois Regiment went out on picket. All was quiet today.

July 22—The day was pleasant, there being a cool breeze in circulation. There has been for several days a great scarcity, in the Army of the Potomac, of any news exciting or interesting. Laziness prevails. In the afternoon the regiment came in from picket.

July 23—At daylight in the morning and at 9 o'clock in the night a cannon is fired from one of the gun boats. These are called the morning and night guns. The former calls forth the soldiers to the active duties of the day, the latter reminds them that the time to retire and extinguish the lights has arrived. We have again resumed the duties of a camp of instruction. From 7 o'clock till 9 o'clock a.m. is company drill, at 10 a.m. Company inspection; 5 till 7 p.m. Battalion drill closing with dressed parade. Company H of the 39th Illinois volunteers arrived this evening; this company has not been with the regiment but has been guarding prisoners at Camp Butler, Ill.[7]

July 24—I was on a detail to chop down brush in a swamp. The water and mud was knee-deep. All the living creatures that I saw inhabiting the swamp were two mice and a stupid lizard.

July 25—*"Aura popularis mutat"* [the pleasure of the people changes]. Colonel Osborn is more popular with his regiment than he was a few months ago. The names by which he was then called have now become obsolete. Lt. Colonel Mann is despised by the regiment. Thus fluctuates public opinion. So changeable is it that it is not a sure criterion to go by. Today the 39th Illinois was paid two months wages by Major Patton.[8] After tattoo this evening the band of the 13th Indiana serenaded the major. The band played a few tunes and sang a song. Major Patton was then called for, he thanked the band for their complement and said that he had some bottles of wine and invited them to step forward and drink. This over the band played a song and speeches were made thus keeping up the Bachanals till some time after the taps were beaten to extinguish the lights. This was at the Headquarters of the 39th Illinois. The shoulder strap gentry can commit offenses with impunity.

July 26—I was tormented this morning with a violent headache. Ferry's Brigade was reviewed in the forenoon by General Peck. There was also Brigade drill by the same general. In the evening there was a shower of rain.

July 27, Sunday—There was company inspection in the morning and dress parade in the evening; this was all that we had to do today.

July 28—Inspection, battalion drill and dress parade make the record of today. The day was very warm.

July 29—There was Brigade drill by General Peck this morning. Rumor says that Ferry's Brigade is under marching orders and that we will soon again resume active operations; that this may be true is my wish.

July 30—There was a grand review of Peck's Division by the Commanding General. Four pieces of cannon were drawn up in line and fired a Brigadier General's Salute. When we returned to camp Gen Ferry said that he wanted this brigade and this regiment to prepare to fight this afternoon. "Begin" said he, "by eating a hearty dinner so that you will be able to endure the fatigue. Have your guns thoroughly in order and then stack them on the parade ground. Let each man have sixty rounds of cartridges, forty in his box and twenty in his pocket. You must not think of anything else but licking them because we can't retreat if we would, and it will be a good while before they can get us out of this camp." A second Merrimac is expected to come down from Richmond to pay our fleet a visit.[9] Had she have attempted it today she would have been warmly received. Ten of our gun boats were drawn up in line of battle to welcome her with shot and shell. The Galena was furthest up the river; she was a short distance above Jordan's Point, the Monitor was next; the names of the others I did not learn.[10] By order of General Peck this Division is to consider itself on duty in the field. The men are not to leave their camps but are to be ready to take their position in the rifle pits. Each man is ordered to have one hundred rounds of cartridges and three days rations at hand. Pickets are admonished to be vigilant and closely to watch the movements of the enemy. From present indications I will soon have something else to record, if spared to tell the tale, besides "All quiet in the Army of the Potomac."

July 31—Up to the present all is quiet. Perhaps with the expiration of the present month many of us will also expire. The long roll would not surprise us at any minute. We don't know what hour that we will have to "face the music." The morning was cloudy with the appearance of rain. The usual calls were given, as if nothing uncommon was expected. At 11 o'clock a.m., the rain began to fall and continued all day. The day passed off quietly; the war-like voice of Mars was not heard.

August 1, 1862—This month began in a great uproar. A little after 12 o'clock in the night heavy cannonading commenced and was kept up for near an hour. The firing seemed to be from our gun boats down the river from where we are encamped; our encampment is nearly opposite Jordan's Point. We were called into ranks and formed in line of battle on the parade ground. We there stacked arms and went to our quarters but were in readiness to "fall in" at a minute's warning. The boys turned out far better than they do for drill or dress parade. The cause of the firing, as near as I have since learned, is this; the Rebels fired from the opposite side of the river on some of our transports. After allowing them thus to amuse themselves for a while the gun boats gave them a few rounds which caused them to skedaddle in haste. Some negroes on our side were killed, no other casualty happened.

Aug. 2—In the forenoon there was division drill conducted by General Peck. To an entire Division of the Army maneuvering in the field is a grand pageant. In the evening the 39th Illinois was sent on picket. Just when we reached the post the signal gun fired so we obeyed its demands and lay down on the ground and were soon "held by sweet sleep." We were not placed out as vedettes but were held as reserves. All was quiet today. If the Rebels attack us in our present position they will not find us unprepared for their reception, nor will they manage to surprise us. Our officers are too vigilant for a repetition of another Shiloh affair. There is now but little talk among the boys about when the war will end. The settled conviction is that it will continue for some time yet.

Aug. 3, Sunday—The 39th Illinois was relieved from picket duty in the afternoon. While out all was quiet. O when shall war cease and our land have rest! May Heaven put an end to this unprovoked rebellion. O God of mercies put a stop to this fratricidal contest. Eradicate from the hearts of the people North and South all malice and hatred towards each other and may unity and love again be restored. Thou art able to speak the word "Peace" and the evil passions of the abbettors of our present troubles shall subside. Cause Discord to take its flight from our land never again to return; then will we sing unto thee, "Mercy and truth are met together; righteousness and peace have kissed each other. Yea, the Lord shall give that which is good; and our land shall yield her increase." Then will we no longer see fair fields laid waste; no longer will families flee from their homes of comfort, houses will no longer be food for the torch of an infuriated soldier.

Aug. 4—All was quiet today. We depend on the New York and Philadelphia papers for the latest and most reliable news from the army of the Potomac. This is a curious fact but nevertheless true and illustrates the difficulty that a soldier has to get the news in his immediate department. An expedition of Cavalry, infantry and artillery was sent out this evening up the river. Their destination is supposed to be Malvern Hill.

Aug. 5—Cannonading was commenced early this morning on the river. Our men who went up last night were thought to be making themselves heard. The Division of General Peck was ordered to hold itself in readiness to march at any minute with two day's rations in haversacks. This began to look like that there would be something else to write besides, "All quiet today." The morning was cloudy. The boys are in good trim to fight. The full particulars of the firing today I could not learn. The enemy had to skedaddle. The 39th Illinois was sent out on picket tonight. After marching about 5 miles we reached our post late in the night. Porter's mortar fleet went up the river last night. Our forces possessed Malvern Hill with but slight loss. Hooker's Division was the one chiefly in this engagement.

Aug. 6—The post which Company I, 39th Illinois Regiment had to occupy was in an open space between two heavy bodies of timber. Three large persimmon trees furnished a shade to protect the boys from the sun's rays. There all day they lay some of them playing cards, others asleep. Some of the more enterprising went into the neighboring woods and picked black berries which here grow in great abundance. Nothing occurred to disturb the Peace of the boys save when some officers came along when they had to put on the accouterments and fall into ranks ready to salute if the officer came near. General Peck visited the lines. In front were cavalry vedettes. The Regiment was relieved from picket late tonight and took a position behind our entrenchments where they slept on arms till morning.

Aug. 7—Our forces evacuated Malvern Hill last night. The rear guard came in this morning. There was a continuous move of artillery all night. The 39th Illinois was relieved early this morning and returned to camp. In the evening Ferry's Brigade was again ordered out with three days rations in haversacks. The brigade marched out in the direction of Malvern Hill about three miles from camp. Pickets were sent out in advance and the men slept on their arms. The night passed off quietly. Something extraordinary is doubtless going on in the Army of the Potomac. I think most likely an evacuation of Peninsula has been in contemplation for some time past.

Aug. 8—Our lines were made very strong to prevent the possibility of anyone passing them. Then the men, both vedettes and reserves, were kept on the "qui vive." Cavalry patrolled the road between the different posts night and day. Our vedettes and those of the enemy were but a short distance apart, almost within "ear shot." All was quiet today. Company I was sent out from the reserve on picket at night.

Aug. 9—There was occasional random firing during the day but nothing of importance transpired. Huckleberries grow plentifully around Company I's post. These were quite a luxury to the boys; they were also a timely auxiliary to their subsistence department as some of their haversacks were by this time well nigh depleted. The company was relieved at dark and back to the reserve which lay in the edge of a pine woods.

Aug. 10, Sunday—The regiment was called up and formed in line of battle before daylight ready to receive an onset from the enemy. This was rather a war-like commencement for the Sabbath but the day passed off quietly. The weather is exceedingly warm.

Aug. 11—Men were detailed from the regiment to go to camp and pack up the baggage and load it on a boat. This leaves no doubt about there being some movement going on. What it is we have no means of knowing but I still cling to the opinion that McClellan is evacuating. Being three miles out from camp in the woods we have no chance to observe the movements. At daylight this morning a Major General's Salute was fired. A gun was fired at intervals of about an hour apart, all day. At sun down a National Salute was fired. All the operations for two weeks past, I think, has been with reference to the move now on foot.

Aug. 12—Early this morning there was firing ahead of us, either by our pickets or scouting parties. I did not learn which. The boys were soon in line of battle ready for action but the enemy has not yet, 9 o'clock a.m., made his appearance. All quiet in front. The morning is very warm. The remainder of the day was quiet. Two days rations were hauled out and issued to the men. Capt. Phillips and his 2nd Sergeant started to Illinois to recruit for the Regiment.

Aug. 13—Ferry's Brigade still on picket. It is not yet known what move is afoot. There are three conjectures with the boys. Some think that we are going to advance direct on Richmond; others believe that we are going to cross the Peninsula to the vicinity of White House, on the Pamunky River. The third opinion is that we are going to evacuate the Peninsula and consolidate the Army of the Potomac with the Army of Virginia and advance on Richmond from the north and at the same time protect Washington. This latter supposition I think most likely the correct one. The Army of the Potomac is not yet ready to move on to Richmond. To prove this needs no argument. Facts, sufficient to verify this, are patent to all. As to the Second conjecture the question may be asked why McClellan should change to his former base of operations on the Pamunky which was untenable when before occupied? The James River is admitted to be a better base of operations than the York and Pamunky. If McClellan were compelled to fall back to the James River under the protection of the gun boats how can he now assume offensive operations against Richmond from his old base? Since his repulse the Army of the Potomac has received few reinforcements, two brigades of Shields Division, I think, are all whilst the ranks have been thinned by sickness. Thousands have been sent to Northern hospitals. Those who hold the second opinion think that Burnside is somewhere in the vicinity of White House.[11] It is true that we are ignorant as to Burnside's whereabouts. For ought that we know he may be on the Pamunky or he may not. But why should not Burnside have come up the James River and McClellan thus reinforced have moved on to Richmond direct from Harrison's Landing? Drewry Bluff and obstructions in the river may be the answer. On account of these he could not have the cooperations of our gun boats. I object to these reasons first because I believe that Fort Drewry could be taken, the obstructions in the river cleared and the Confederate gun boats destroyed.[12] If this cannot be done we certainly could take Richmond as easily without the assistance of our gun boats by moving direct on it from Harrison's Landing as we could by going the way of White House. With regard to the third supposition it may be said that the Peninsula is of no importance to us only as a road to Richmond. If, by trial, it proved to be an impassable road then the quicker we get off of it the better. If reports be true as to the number of troops the Confederates have in and around Richmond they can hold McClellan at bay and at the same time send a force in the direction of Gordonsville large enough to defeat General Pope and, if not to take Washington, at least to cause the loyal people from Maine to Maryland to fear and tremble. It is also certain that in our present position we are surrounded by the enemy. Both banks of the river are in their possession thus our transports have to run a gauntlet of about one hundred miles. Not a single steamboat can pass up or down the river without a convoy of gunboats. Could the enemy blockade the James River then they could capture the entire Army of the Potomac unless reinforcements were sent to it within three weeks. Our own safety, the protection of Washington and a consolidation of forces may necessitate an evacuation of the Peninsula. To evacuate doubtless would be a very perilous undertaking. Such a thing might be that we are going to cross the river and cut off communication between the Confederate Capital and its Southern dependencies. The above are mere speculations. Time alone will prove all things. I confess that I feel great anxiety as to the movement now going on. I hope that it will work together for the good of the Union. Perhaps a chance to observe the movements in camp would have modified the foregoing speculations but of this I have been deprived being on picket three miles from camp. Today we received the news of the battle near Culpepper Courthouse between Banks and Jackson. It was not very decisive either way according to all accounts yet received. Bank's men fought heroically against great odds. The battle was one of the hardest that has yet been fought during the war. This will render the ninth day of August notable in our Country's History.[13]

Aug. 14—Everything seemed to be on a dead standstill. The sick of this army have, during the past week, been sent off to General hospitals. The weather has become less warm so that it is now quite pleasant. Company I was sent out from the reserve on picket this afternoon. At night we could plainly hear the tattoo of the rebels and at the same time that of our own camp. There was some firing during the night by the pickets but nothing serious occurred.

Aug. 15—We could hear the drums beating in our camp at two o'clock this morning; the drumming was kept up till daylight, what it meant we could not tell. Today drafting is to begin in the loyal states. All the forenoon we could hear the drums of the Rebels. It was evident that the camp of the enemy was nearer to us than our own. In the afternoon we were ordered in; all the pickets were drawn in. A few cavalry were thrown out in the rear. When the pickets arrived at the rendezvous of the reserve they found that the Brigade had all gone. They were in the rear of what they were certain was an evacuating force. There were eight companies of them. After marching into camp the several companies joined their regiments. The Brigade was relieved of two weeks in succession picket duty. During that time their men slept on the ground and were not permitted to take off their clothes. When returning to camp we found that the main body of the army had left. The tents were mostly struck and the men were all ready to move. Ferry's Brigade started once but was ordered back so we slept in camp till near daylight.

Aug. 16—We were called into [formation] before daylight this morning, not even taking time to get breakfast, and took up the "line of march." It was yet a mystery where we were going. Some thought that we were going to march on to Richmond but this notion was abandoned when they saw the column moving down the river. The next question was were we to march or go aboard transports. All hopes of the latter had not vanished till we were outside of the entrenchments and we heard the command "load at will" along the lines of the different Brigades. This assured us that we were elected for a march. There was but little valuable property belonging to the government was left or destroyed. A considerable sprinkling of tents were left standing, this no doubt being done for a purpose. The troops were withdrawn in splendid order, Keyes Corps left in one body. Whether this was the last to withdraw from the camp I could not learn. After leaving the entrenchments we marched in a southeasternly direction till we passed Charles City Courthouse, then direction was North the rest of the day. The surface of the county is [?]. The soil is of a grayish color and quite sandy. Corn, wheat, oats, potatoes, beans and peas are the chief products. The country is well improved; there are some fine plantations with fine residences and beautiful shade trees. Charles City Courthouse is the county seat of this county. It has a courthouse, a jail, a county clerk's office, a hotel and an Episcopal Church. The courthouse is a small one story brick building. It looks like an Illinois Country school house. When we consider the fact that this is one of the oldest Counties in the State and that in it were born two Presidents of the United States, one is surprised to see such poor public buildings. It certainly shows a small public feeling. Near this hamlet is a little creek of clear water. This with two or three other small runs was all the water courses we crossed today. The timber consists chiefly of large pine trees. The growing corn is poor. I noticed on a sandy hill cactus or prickly pear growing wild. A short time before sun down [we] halted in a corn field to bivouac for the night, about 5 miles from Charles City Courthouse. The men then addressed themselves to preparing supper. Many of them had done some little unlawful foraging so to add to their regular rations. They had such luxuries as green apples, peaches, tomatoes, roasting ears and potatoes. These cooked in soldier's style were quite a treat. The day was cool in the morning but warm in the middle of the day. The road was very dusty.

Aug. 17, Sunday—We were called up before daylight this morning to get breakfast and at sunrise were on the march. The direction marched today was Southeast. The country presents the same features as that passed through yesterday excepting that there are not so many fine plantations and it is more densely wooded. Pine trees of immense size and height constitute the forest mostly; there is some Oak about 7 miles from the Chickahominy and hemlock in the swamps. At about 12 o'clock noon we came in sight of the James River and soon after we beheld the Chickahominy. This latter river we crossed about half a mile above its mouth on a pontoon bridge 2000 feet long. The bridge was supported by 96 boats. Beams were laid across the boats and on the beams planks were fastened and then covered with straw. The boats were held fast by anchors. This made a very secure bridge though it was rather tottering. We were here told that the Army had been crossing ever since Thursday, the 14th. The Chickahominy River is the boundary line between Charles City County and James City County. Considerable historical interest is attached to this stream. We bivouaced for the night in James City County seven miles west of Williamsburg. The marching today was very fatiguing. We were marched rapidly not even halting to cook dinner. The dust was almost suffocating. The men suffered greatly for water. The day was very warm.

Aug. 18—We took up the line of march at daylight. The artillery and baggage trains crowded the road so that in marching today we had to undergo a great deal of extra labor. Early in the morning we passed through Williamsburg, the county seat of James City County. The situation of the town is on a level plain surrounded by dense forests of pine and oak, near the York River. This is a very antiquated town. There are some fine residences. The town is regularly laid out, the streets are ornamental with shade trees. William and Mary College is located here. This is the oldest institution of the kind in the United States excepting Harvard University. The College is in the western part of the town; it is a handsome brick edifice two stories high. A lunatic assylum, three churches and the county buildings are here located. Williamsburg was the capital of the state of Virginia till 1779.[14] The main street is about one mile long. Population near 2000. The town is rendered notable by the battle recently fought here between the Federal army and the Confederates. The battle was east of town in an open field. The Confederates were here strongly entrenched. The federals had to approach through a dense woods to almost within rifle shot of the first earthen works. The trees were scratched and scored by the bullets and cannon balls. The Confederates shot too high. For several rods in the woods the trees bore the marks of the missiles of the cannon. The houses of the town were nearly all closed when we passed through. I did not see more than a dozen grown white persons. There were a good many negroes and some white children. Dreary indeed was the appearance of Williamsburg. At noon we halted 6 miles east of the town. Here we bivouaced for tonight. Wagons and soldiers were passing all night. Apples, pears, peaches, Irish potatoes, sweet potatoes and roasting ears were "seized by the boys." This is contrary to the articles of war and General McClellan's orders. But in spite of these the boys will "forage." The surface of the James City County mostly level. There are some hills of considerable height. Heavy pine forests cover the greater part of the county. Some of the land swampy; in these grow tall hemlock trees. The soil is poor being very sandy. The country looks like a howling wilderness, a fit habitation for frogs, skanks and vultures only. The improvements are poor.

Aug. 19—Ferry's Brigade was mustered this morning in accordance with an order issued by the President. At about 8 o'clock a.m., marching orders came; we fell into ranks, took arms and were ready to start. The command rest was then given. This command we continued to execute till the next morning. The road was all this time crowded with soldiers and wagons.

Aug. 20—"I see the man," said Cyrus, and rushing forward to avenge himself of his supposed injuries, fell in the beginning of the engagement. Cyrus had conducted his army up into the interior of Asia with great skill and ability. Amid the many difficulties with which he had to contend he was remarkably cool and self possessed but, when his forces were drawn up in battle array against those of "The Great King," he saw Artalereus, then he lost all control of himself. He became reckless of his life, rushing forward regardless of all danger, he fell a victim to foolhardiness.[15] This morning when orders came to be ready to march at 6 o'clock I determined at all hazards to go on in advance of the Brigade that I might have time to visit Yorktown and the surrounding objects of interest.[16] Accordingly a comrade and myself were at sun up winding our way over the hills and through the woods of York County every inch of which is classic soil. We traveled through the woods and fields to avoid the dust of the roads. The thought of Washington, Cornwallis and more recently of McClellan and Magruder urged us on; and we were actually to see the place where the Revolutionary war was substantially terminated and the heavy works which the rebels had thrown up for the defense of Richmond; these thoughts stimulated us to quicken our steps anxious to lose no time. It would be impossible to describe the fortifications unless we had have had more time to examine them. The first work that we came to is on the road leading from Williamsburg to Old Point Comfort. This is a strong work; the earth is thrown up about 5 or 6 feet high and near 15 feet thick. In front of this is a ditch about 6 feet deep and 10 feet wide at the top. There are platforms for large siege guns & magazines for storing away ammunition. Near each piece is a barrel sunk to hold water in. The number of angles and curves are so unintelligible to those who are ignorant of the art of war, they are so numerous that the uninitiated is almost bewildered upon beholding them. This is a part of the main line of defense extending from the York to the James Rivers. In front of these are other works of less importance. From the Old Point Comfort road to York River the works are on a ridge, in front is a deep ravine and the trees were felled. A few rods in the rear is a hollow through which flows a clear stream of water. At the foot of the hill are several good springs. In this hollow is an excellent road so that the rebels could move troops around through the entrenchments without observation. There are heavy water batteries on the river opposite to Gloucester Point. The river at this place is not more than one mile wide while just below the Point it is about two miles wide. At Gloucester Point the Rebels had heavy batteries. The position to defend the river is certainly a very strong one. The batteries on the two sides of the river ought to have blown any common boat out of the river. The works so far as we examined are very strong and display good engineering skill. The position is excellent. The enemy were unable to take off all their large guns. Some of them were blown up, some spiked, some were dismounted by burning the carriages, others were left uninjured. We noticed several 8 in. siege howitzers burst into fragments. Shell, shot, grape and canister were scattered around promiscuously. On most of the guns was painted the following "Gen. Cap J. B. Magruder Yorktown"; on one was "Gen. Hill."[17] We next passed on to visit relics of the Revolutionary war regretting only that we had not more time. But before prosecuting our researches further we went to the river to enjoy the luxury of a bath in saltwater. Saltwater extends above Yorktown. Whilst sitting on the bank to cool off we saw two porpoises. There are two wharfs at the landing. There were three or four steamers and several schooners anchored in the river. Troops were going aboard of the transport Merrimac.[18] The next thing to be procured was dinner; this was no small object to accomplish. After looking around for some time we found a negro baking corn cakes to sell to the soldiers; of him we bought sufficient hoecake to supply our wants. He also made coffee for us. The chief cook of the establishment where the contrabands are fed prepared some beef steak for us. Our appetites being satisfied we continued our researches. Two hundred negroes are employed by the government at Yorktown. The cooking for them is all done at one kitchen. It was quite interesting to see the cooks boiling rice and beef in large iron ovens for 200 men, women and children. The cooking is done by colored men; the Chief or "boss" of the establishment is a sailor and has been engaged in the West Indies and Coast trade nearly all his life. He is an intelligent free man. Magruder built several comfortable board houses for hospitals. These are now used for negro quarters and as hospitals for our sick soldiers. Yorktown, the county seat of York County is situated on the north bank of a river of the same name 11 miles above its mouth. The situation is beautiful being on high ground commanding a fine view of the river. The town consists of about 60 old weather beaten houses; we were told that they were all built before the Revolutionary war. On the bank of the river is a small Presbyterian Church; nearby it is a cemetery in which are some old graves. The following is an inscription copied from one of the tomb stones: "Here lyes the body of Suzanna Reynolds daughter of William Rogers. Who departed this life March 29th 1768. Aged 60 years." The church which once stood here was a fine building, it was destroyed by the British. The river bank about 58 feet high. On it are yet to be seen the water batteries built by the British during the Revolutionary War. They were excellently constructed and are in a good state of preservation. There are two tiers of them, the lower batteries are near the waters edge, the upper batteries are on the top of the bank. Some of these batteries are repaired and used by the Rebels. The Federals seem determined to perpetuate their name in Yorktown. As we entered the town we saw posted in large letters Burnside Street. The main street running parallel with the river is called McClellan Avenue; the other streets crossing this at right angles are called Halleck Street, Van Allen and Ellsworth. These names will no doubt be very obnoxious to the Sensitive Southrons. At the foot of the river bank is shown the place where the cave was in which Lord Cornwallis is said to have hid after he was whipped. East of town in an open elevated plain is a small cedar railing fence. This encloses the spot of ground where Lord Cornwallis delivered up his sword to General Washington. A stone till recently marked the place, but this has all been carried away in small pieces by the soldiers as relics of the Revolutionary War. At the time of our visit there was no trace of the monument left. The railing fence, which encloses the Classic Spot, is beginning to go in the same way that the monument was destroyed. Against this species of vandalism we protest. These monuments of our country's past history belong to the people of the United States in general and persons have no right to despoil them to gratifying their own individual curiosity. Around this renowned spot are buried 300 union soldiers. The place is enclosed by a new rail fence. On the head board of each grave is marked the name of the deceased with his regiment company and date of his death. On two of the head boards we noticed the following inscription; "Stranger, Army of the Potomac"! In town we saw a man "who has come down to us from a former generation" Sam Page by name. He is a negro 103 years old! And has been a slave all his life. He lived in James City County during the Revolutionary war. When the battle at Yorktown was fought he heard the cannonading 25 miles distant. Lord Cornwallis stayed in his master's house. He said that he wanted to be free when he was young but now he did not care anything about it; he was so old that it would do him no good. Having visited a few of the objects of interest we hastened on to join our regiment. We found the Division bivouaced about two miles east of Yorktown.

Aug. 21—The boys were engaged today in catching crabs and oysters. These are abundant in a creek near which we are encamped. They catch crabs by letting down a line with a piece of meat fastened to the end; this the crab seizes hold upon and it is then gently pulled to the top of the water. A dip net is then slipped under it and the deluded victim is lifted from the water. The manner by which the crab moves is curious. It does not go straight forward but makes a flank movement; it walks sideways. This reminds me of the fable of the crab in Andrew's Latin Reader.[19] I took a short scout through the country. York County contains 70 square miles of territory. The surface is hilly and broken. There are good springs along the ravine. The soil is sandy and poor. This country has been severely blighted by the effects of the present Civil War. Considerable of the surface has been dug up by two contending armies. Acres of the timber have been felled and then set fire to. The fences in places have all been destroyed. The face of the country presents blackened and wasted appearance. Desolation holds undisputed sway. Egypt after the ten plagues could scarcely have presented a more desolate appearance.

Aug. 22—The Division begins to assume something of the appearance of a regular camp. Whilst I was bathing in the York River this afternoon the regiment was sent out on picket. The York River is a beautiful stream, the channel is deep and straight. Down the river the view extends far out on the Chesapeake Bay. Vessels can be seen up the stream so far off that they appear like a black speck in the sky. At West Point the river divides into two streams and forms the Pamunkey and the Mattapony rivers.

Aug. 23—The regiment returned from picket at 12 o'clock m. We have orders to march in the morning to Fortress Monroe. The greater part of the Army of the Potomac has left the Peninsula. It remains to be seen whether or not the Peninsula is entirely evacuated. The evacuation of Harrison's Landing was a complete success and reflects great honor in the Commanding General. At night the camp presented a lively scene, the men were cooking their rations for the march. Later in the night it commenced raining most of the boys were poorly prepared for this sort of weather. My bunk fellow and myself were completely drowned out. We took refuge in an empty ambulance till about midnight when the driver came along and "ousted" us out. So but little sleep was allotted to us tonight.

Aug. 24, Sunday—Early this morning we were executing our marching orders. The road not being blockade by wagons, as usual, we had a chance to "go in on our nerves," or rather on our legs; and in we did go as the distance marched today over muddy roads fully testifies. Our limbs were stretched over about 24 miles of Virginia's Sacred Soil. At noon we halted near Big Bethel for dinner. This is 13 miles northeast of Fortress Monroe, in Elizabeth City County. Big Bethel is an old frame church on the road from Yorktown to Hampton. The house is white washed on the outside and plastered on the inside. On three are galleries, perhaps for the accommodation of the colored part of the congregation. The building is nearly destroyed, the weather boarding is torn off and the seats entirely demolished. Around this house in which was wont to be preached, "Peace on Earth and goodwill towards men," are some breast works bearing evidence of having been hastily thrown up behind which the Confederates were posted in the late battle. The road leading to Hampton runs nearly south for several miles. In front of this road near the church is a ravine which is nearly always dry, in this also the Confederates were posted. Big Bethel has been described as being "Nothing more than a large brick church," this is incorrect, it is a frame building. The country through which we marched today is poor and partakes of the same desolation already described. Near Hampton are some fine residences and the plantations are in a moderate state of repair, the desolating influences of war not having been so severely felt here as elsewhere. There were but few native white persons to be seen today. We passed through Hampton in the evening and encamped about half mile east of it. The day was cool and very pleasant for marching, when we halted for the night the breeze from the Bay was too cool to be comfortable.

Aug. 25—We have seen much of the desolations of war. Houses have been destroyed, fences burned, stone walls torn down, fruit trees spoiled, railroads torn up, bridges burned, cars and locomotives destroyed and in fact the whole face of the country blighted; as bad as all these are, worse still was the burning of Hampton.[20] Here a sad spectacle is presented to the eye. One may well pause and consider the evils of war of which this town is a monument. Hampton is the county seat of Elizabeth City County, situated on the north side of Hampton Roads, four miles northwest of Fortress Monroe. This was a beautiful town before the present civil war broke out. The streets cross each other at right angles. The houses were nearly all brick buildings. Through the town passes Hampton Creek; this is deep and is a harbor for vessels. The Creek is now crossed by three bridges, one of which is a pontoon. This being only three or four miles from Old Point Comfort, the noted summer resort and watering place, was the abode of some of "The first families of Virginia." The streets which were a few months ago promenaded by the elite of the South are now so many thorough fares for Army wagons, soldiers and negroes. The walls, within which once echoed the voices of Virginia's fair daughters, are now blackened ruins. Fine brick houses are now large piles of broken bricks. Scarcely a house was spared from the devouring flame. What is the cause of this fashionable town being now mouldering in the dust? is the inquiry. The answer is short and sad, the answer that a negro gave me to this question is that "Mr. Magruder came down and burnt it." Early in the war the Confederates burned the town to keep it from falling into the hands of the Federals. The houses on the east side of the Creek were not destroyed, but this was only a small part of the town. A large Academy for ladies is among the buildings which escaped. Among the ruins I noticed an Episcopal Church built in the shape of a cross. This was a fine edifice, the bricks are said to have been imported from England. Hampton in its day was a lively place having a population of 1600 inhabitants, stores, churches, hotels etc. made up the town. The burning of Hampton may be by some termed "a piece of wanton vandalism." This phrase is not half severe enough for some Demons, in the disguise of human form, attached to the union army. Acts which they have committed in the cemeteries of Hampton would disgrace a Hottentot. Tomb stones are broken into pieces. The graves are defiled. The tombs of Foreigners, who died far away from their native land, are dishonored. The last tribute of respect of the friends of the departed are spoiled. These things I have seen with my own eyes. I like to give the union army a good name so far as it can be done consistent with truth and no further. I am glad however to know that there are but very few in the army who would commit any such depredations.

Aug. 26—Fortress Monroe is situated on Old Point Comfort in Elizabeth City County, Virginia, at the entrance of Hampton Roads into the Chesapeake Bay. The Point forms a semicircle. The extremity of the point, on which the fort is built, is only a few rods from the mainland and connected with it by a bridge; following the curve of the point around it is about 6 miles. The body of water between the Point and the mainland is called Mill Creek. Around the Fort is a town of considerable business. Besides the government workshops and bakeries there are several stores, a hotel, a post office and a handsome Catholic Church. Large guns, shot and shell might be estimated by the number of acres of ground they cover. There are some residences with nicely shaded yards; the fig tree is here to be seen. Exhibiting our pass to the Sentinel we were permitted to pass within the Fort. Our examinations of the Fort was very imperfect as we were not allowed to leave the gravel paths. A railroad runs through the fort then extends to Hampton. The grounds within the walls are laid off into walks and are ornamented with beautiful shade trees. Workshops, barracks, officers' quarters and other necessary concomitants are here for the comfort of the garrison. There is also a Catholic Church in the fort. The General Headquarters are in a fine two-story brick house; the yard is ornamented with shrubery and ornamental trees. In front is a row of cannon balls piled up in the shape of small pyramids. The Fort is surrounded by a deep ditch, which is walled up with stone and filled with water. The garrison look like holiday soldiers. They have not seen such hard times as the "veterans" of the field. Old Point Comfort is a noted summer resort and watering place. It has been visited during the summer season by every President of the United States. The shape of the Point is beautiful to behold. Starting out from the mainland it gradually curves forming a rainbow. The furthest point that it reaches from the mainland is about two miles; it then gradually approaches within a few rods of the mainland. The body of water in the concavity thus formed is what is known as Mill Creek. The Point forms a cone the base of which is about two miles in length. The Point is covered with timber for about half its length, the rest is a sand bank. The sand is drifted up into hillocks several feet high.

Aug. 27—There is a large camp west of Mill Creek, between it and Hampton, the name of which is Camp Hamilton. The soldiers here constructed barracks of boards for temporary use. Here also is a hospital called Mill Creek Hospital. There are here stables for jaded horses. On the whole Camp Hamilton is "quite an institution." A philanthropic gentleman from the North has fitted up a house in Hampton and teaches a school for the Africans. The house is two stories high, the lower story is used for a school room, the upper for a Chapel. The school room is furnished with alphabetical charts and cards with quotations from the Bible. This is certainly an inviting field of labor and if well cultivated will yield an abundant harvest. Near Hampton are hospital buildings enough when completed to accommodate several thousand patients.[21]

Aug. 28—Ferry's Brigade was ordered to be ready to embark this morning. The supposition was that we were going to Suffolk. During our sojourn at this place the weather has been very pleasant. The chief inquiry now is "What is the news from Pope?" This we hear on every hand and at all hours of the day. We held ourselves in readiness all day to move at minutes notice, but the "notice" was not given. All quiet.

Aug. 29—The sun rose brightly, dispelling the gloom of night and shedding its genial influences on the face of the Earth. We had the same orders as yesterday but did not "move." Nothing of interest in this vicinity today. All quiet on the Lower Peninsula.

Aug. 30—In the afternoon Carolus Clara Aqua and myself hired a negro to take us across Mill Creek to Old Point Comfort.[22] We embarked on a sailboat and went darting through the water like an arrow through the air. The distance was about two miles to where we landed. The point of disembarkation was where the timber ceases and the sand sets in. In front was spread out the Chesapeake Bay. Here and there were to be seen the white sails of vessels either arriving or departing. The water lashed furiously against the beach and then it would recoil till meeting a gust of wind, it was heaped up into a wave and driven on it appeared as if it would submerge the land for some distance but on its first collision with the land it was burst to pieces and retreated to its own domain. The waves keep continually lashing the beach making a great noise but they advance "Thus far and no farther." To the right following the Point and on the extremity of it was Fortress Monroe. The sand is drifted up into hills 30 or 40 feet high. To the left the Point is covered with a shruby growth of timber, consisting of live oak, pine, persimmons and grape vines. Where we disembarked is a cemetery in a shady and secluded place. Union Soldiers have within the past year been interred here. Perhaps 1000 soldiers are here buried in the sand. We saw a coffin which our negro told us had been washed up by the waves. In it were some locks of human hair. We were told that the soldier who had been buried in the coffin was interred in another grave in less proximity to the water. Our rambles complete we got into the boat and sailed back to the mainland. When near the shore the negro stopped the boat and carried us out on his back to the shore. We returned to camp and found that the right wing of the 39th Illinois Regiment had gone! They embarked at Fortress Monroe. So we were left with a few other stragglers to fall in with the left wing, which was ordered to start in the morning at 5 o'clock.

Aug. 31, Sunday—Vale, Peninsula! The left wing struck tents this morning and marched down to the Roads to embark. The boat which was to take the right wing up yesterday evening got aground in the mouth of the Nansemond River and lay till this morning, having to wait for the same boat to go up and return we were delayed till noon. After being thus vexatiously delayed half a day we went aboard the steam ferry boat Stepping Stone and started on our way to, we were not quite certain where.[23] The boat headed towards the James River, leaving Sewell's Point about a mile and a half to the left. When the boat passed the mouth of Elizabeth

River we were sure that our destination was Suffolk. Nearly opposite to Newport News the Nansemond River empties into the James; up the former river our boat headed. Off Newport's News was considerable shipping. Near the mouth of the Nansemond River spoils had been driven across and on the banks batteries were erected. There is only a narrow passage for boats. The river is difficult to navigate being crooked and shallow in places. Up the river for several miles the banks are high and the country tolerably well improved. Arriving within 10 or 15 miles of Suffolk the country on both sides of the river is low and swampy. The river is very narrow, being only 200 or 300 feet wide. At dark we reached Suffolk and quickly disembarked. We marched through town out to camp. Tents were pitched ready for us, these the 13th NY Reg't three months men had occupied. They are wedge tents with plank floors. To us these were a great luxury.

September 1—(Exit Summer, enter Autumn) We are again in a comfortable camp with a prospect of remaining here for several months. The camp is regularly laid out; wells are dug for each company. There is a good parade ground and all other necessary appurtenances.

Sept. 2—Guard mounting and dress parade make up the record of the day.

Sept. 3—*Non habro scribire nova* [I'll have nothing new to write].

Sept. 4—One hundred and eleven prisoners were brought into town today. They were new recruits, unarmed, on their way to Richmond to join the Rebel Army.

Sept. 5—The days are warm and the nights are cold. The water, which we have to use, is very poor, the wells being shallow. From all appearances this is a sickly place.

Sept. 6—The news from Washington is very exciting and discouraging. The Union army has been defeated and the national Capital is the second time besieged. This is a disgrace to the nation. The enemy now threatens to invade the loyal states. About two months ago Richmond was a beleaguered city; but the Rebels by defeating McClellan raised the siege of Richmond and were then enabled to hurl their forces against Pope and drive the combined armies of Virginia, the Potomac and Burnside's Army into the forts around Washington.

Sept. 7, Sunday—Company I went out on picket this morning. The day was quiet. The forces at this place consist of Ferry's Brigade, the first Delaware, third & fourth New York, third Delaware, the 11th Pennsylvania cavalry and one battery of artillery. Gen. Mansfield is commander of the post.[24]

Sept. 8—Our company was relieved from picket this morning. The two Delaware Regiments left here this evening on the cars. The railroad is in running order from here to Norfolk, there is also a railroad to Portsmouth. Our supplies and mail are sent up the Elizabeth River to Norfolk or Portsmouth thence by rail to Suffolk. The distance is 28 miles.

Sept. 9—A scouting party was sent out on an eight days expedition. The party was composed of infantry, cavalry and artillery. Three companies of our Regiment, A., C. & D., were sent out.

Sept. 10—Maryland is invaded! Hill, Jackson and Longstreet have crossed the Potomac. Frederick, Md has been occupied by the Rebels. The people of the North are just beginning to realize the fact that the war has actually begun. Pennsylvania is thoroughly aroused; the people are rising up as one man and preparing to defend their state. The loyal people of the country will have to taste of the bitterness of war, perhaps their homes may be desecrated by the ruthless invader but this will have a salutary effect. The lesson will be dearly learned. The sojourn of the Rebels north of the Potomac will doubtless be short and full trouble.[25]

Sept. 11—There is too much guard duty to do for the number of men able for duty. The men have to go on guard every other day. This morning was rainy. No news yet from our scouts sent out on the ninth instant. The day was rainy. In the afternoon our scouts returned. No enemy was seen by them.

Sept. 12—Nothing of interest occurred today. In the evening Company I was sent out on picket. All was quiet during tonight. The weather is very warm. The record of today is very meager.

Sept. 13—Company I was relieved from picket this morning and returned to camp. All was quiet today.

Sept. 14, Sunday—I spent the day in Suffolk. In the morning was Sabbath school and church. The attendance at Sabbath school was small. The number of scholars belonging to the school is 75 or 100; they were not all present. The attendance at church was about one-half soldiers the rest citizens. The preacher was a son of Dixie. He preached a sermon from a text alluding to the Isthmean games; the subject was very well handled.[26] This was the M E. Church South. The building is a fine two-story edifice. The inside was very clean and neat. In the afternoon was services at the African Churches for "the colored population." Suffolk is a dull place on Sunday. We could not get our dinners in the town but by diligent inquiry we found some pies to sell which was a substitute for dinner.

Sept. 15—Suffolk, the county seat of Nansemond County, is situated at the head of navigation on the Nansemond River. It is 85 miles southeast of Richmond. It is quite a handsome town of about 1500 inhabitants. There are several fine churches and residences. The principal street is well shaded; trees are planted on each side and also in the center of the street. For railroad connections see Lloyd's map. Small boats run up here.

Sept. 16—All quiet today. I was on guard. Company I was sent out to tear up the railroad track tonight.

Sept. 17—Company I was sent out again this morning to tear up the railroad. We went out about 9 miles. The country is level and sandy. Pine forests cover the greater part of the surface. The improvements are poor. Corn and beans seem to be the chief products raised. The corn is very poor, beans are planted with it. The blades of the corn are all stripped off and tied up in small bundles. This when well cured is excellent provender. The day was very warm. After destroying the railroad, for about two rods, we returned to camp in the evening, confident of having done nothing to amount to anything.

Sept. 18—We were called up at 4 o'clock this morning and formed in line of battle. We then stacked arms and went to our quarters. The morning passed off quietly. An attack is expected here. Gen. Dix is at this place to take command in person during the engagement. New troops have been arriving for several days past. The Rebels will have a hot time if they attempt to take Suffolk.[27]

Sept. 19—Two wheeled carts are the vehicles used in this [area]. The people hitch a horse or mule or an ox to one of these carts and drive into town with their marketing. It is no uncommon sight to see a woman driving an ox harnessed to a small cart. The carts look something like the picture of an ancient chariot. Two horse wagons are hardly ever seen. The inhabitants appear as if they belonged to another century and "have come down to us from a former generation."

Sept. 20—Company I was sent out this morning on the Edinton road to support a battery. There was a thunderstorm in the night and heavy rain; the boys were thoroughly drenched.

Sept. 21, Sunday—There was preaching in the regiment this afternoon from the text "He was speechless."

Sept. 22—Company I went out on the Sea Board & Roanoke railroad and tore up the track and hauled the rails into Suffolk. We run a train of cars out. We had orders to tear up one mile of track.[28]

Sept. 23—Our company went out on the cars 15 miles on the Norfolk and Petersburg Railroad, in the direction of the latter named place, to guard hands at work on the road. The hands were mostly negroes; they worked well. The gauge of the road is being changed; it is too wide for our engines & cars. The surface of the country along the road is level and covered with heavy pine forests. We did not see a single good plantation; they are small and poorly improved. The houses are for the most part log huts. The soil is poor as the stunted corn attests. It seems to be well adapted to the culture of sweet potatoes alone, which grow to a great size. We passed through Windsor, a station on the road containing a store, hotel and a few residences.

Sept. 24—One hundred men were detailed from each regiment in our brigade to fell timber and work on entrenchments; a corresponding number of men were detailed from the regiments. General Peck is in command at this post; he arrived yesterday. The report now is that General Wise is to retake Suffolk & Norfolk. Let him try it.[29]

Sept. 25—Our regiment changed its camp today to the east of town. Heavy details were made for fatigue and picket guard. The men are on duty everyday.

Sept. 26—The work of felling timber and fortifying is still going on with promptness. The day was clear and pleasant.

Sept. 27—Nothing extraordinary marked the events of the day.

Sept. 28, Sunday—"Prepare war," Joel 3:9. The regiment was detailed this morning to fell trees and dig rifle pits. At 4 o'clock a.m., the troops here were under arms. A man in Co. G was killed while chopping by a tree falling on him; he survived but a few hours. When we go out to slash timber or to work on entrenchments we take our arms. What day we will awake to a scene of conflict and carnage is uncertain but that an attack will be made here ere long is the opinion of all.

Sept. 29—We finished the rifle pits. The Rebels will be warmly received if they visit us. A man of our company met an accident by which he lost an eye. He was in the timber slashing and a limb struck him in the eye.

Sept. 30—The days are very warm from 11 o'clock a.m. till 4 p.m. The nights and mornings are cool and refreshing. The forces here have to be under arms half an hour each morning, from reveille till half an hour afterwards. There are here at the present time near 10,000 infantry, one regiment of cavalry and two batteries of artillery.

October 1—The morning was serene and clear; quiet prevailed all along our lines. Soon, perhaps, this quietude will be exchanged for the clash of resounding arms.

Oct. 2—We today enjoyed "inglorious ease," *"transtulit gloria mundi"* [passes the glory of the world].

Oct. 3—In company with a friend I examined our defenses today. They are yet incomplete. Beginning at the Petersburg and Norfolk railroad, as the left, is a redoubt two miles east of Suffolk near where the railroad crosses a canal. Towards the right our rifle pits, in a corn field. About 1 1/2 miles from this redoubt is Fort Dix commanding the Edinton road and mounting ten guns. It is a square work enclosing an area of about 100 yards square. Within is a magazine for ammunition. The fort is surrounded by a ditch about 10 feet deep and 12 wide. The work is in the edge of a corn field commanding the country in front and to the right and left for some distance, the timber being felled. Lieutenant James is the engineer under whose direction the fort was built.[30] From the fort to a belt of woods on the left are rifle pits for one regiment. To the right are the rifle pits of the 39th Illinois, in an open field; to the right of these are the rifle pits of the 67 Ohio. These are in front of a dense woods; in front of the pits the trees have been cut down. These are the strongest works of the time that we saw anywhere along our line of defense. The next is the position of the 101st Pennsylvania. Their rifle pits are in a heavy woods that in front of them being cut down. The next work is Fort McClellan commanding the road to Somerton. This is similar to Fort Dix but not quite so large; it mounts the same number of guns. About 1 1/2 miles to the right of this another fort was being thrown up; between these two forts are rifle pits. To the right of this on the bank of a creek is a fort mounting 4 guns commanding the road to Blackwater. This is the best position of any that we examined. To the right of this extending to the Roanoke and Seaboard railroad are rifle pits. This is the extreme right of our defenses as we understood the position. There is a vast amount of slashing done in front of our defenses. Before the Rebels expell the "Yankees" from Suffolk they will have plenty of work to do. Some of the regiments were ordered to take their position in the rifle pits tonight. Here we slept till morning, nothing occurring to interrupt the quietude of the night. There was a skirmish on Blackwater. One man killed.

Oct. 4—The drummer of Co. B died and was buried according to military honors today. Colonel Osborn returned from Illinois where he had been recruiting for the regiment. He had poor success.

Oct. 5, Sunday—No familiar hymn reminded us that today was the Sabbath. Instead of dressing to go to church we had to scour guns and clean our uniforms preparatory to inspection. We could hear the Church bells in Suffolk but could not go without a pass signed by the commander of the company and countersigned by that Colonel of the Regiment. Slavery and polygamy have readily been termed twin relics of barbarity. War is not a relic of barbarity but is barbarity itself. Are not all who are engaged in it Barbarians?

Oct. 6—Slashing timber and digging in the trenches was the business of the day. This evening a new regiment, the 132 New York, came on the train from Norfolk. It belongs to the Empire Brigade, Gen. Spinola is the commander of the brigade; he is also here. Several nationalities are represented in this regiment, English, German, French, Irish, American, Spanish and Italian are in it. The cars were running during the night bringing in other troops. Some of our released prisoners returned to the regiment tonight also some of our men who have been in hospitals.[31]

Oct. 7—Heavy details were made to work on the fortifications and build bridges.

Oct. 8—Virginia has many natural curiosities. Her medical springs, caves, mountains and, greatest of all, Natural Bridge are well known to the tourist. Scarcely less notable than these, but far less known, is Lake Drummond, in the midst of the Dismal Swamp. For three hours had we been slowly riding down the Canal, through the swamp, the sides of which are lined with a dense growth of cane, when all at once was spread out before us a beautiful lake. Surrounded by the swamp, which is rightly named Dismal, it appeared like "a jewel in a swine's snout." The lake is about 6 miles long & 5 miles [wide]; its greatest length is SouthWest and Northeast. Several years ago, our informant could not tell when, a stock raiser was hunting his cattle when he got lost in the swamp. After wandering around for several days he came to the sheet of water which is now called from the name of the discoverer, Lake Drummond. He made a raft and crossed the lake on it. Ten days was Mr. Drummond in the Swamp subsisting on berries, roots and whatever else "the country afforded." The Lake looks like a black cloud; the water is black, when it is dipped up into a vessel it has the color of weak lye; the color of the water in the swamp ditches is the same yet it is pleasant to the taste and wholesome. The lake abounds in fish of a superior kind; they sell for more in the market than fish caught elsewhere. Six of us procured passes early in the morning and set out for the lake.[32] We hired two negroes, Sam and Tom, to take us down. The boat which we chartered for the trip was what the natives call a skiff, it is used for carrying lumber out of the swamp on; it was 60 feet long and about 5 feet wide. The negroes propelled it with two poles one at the bow of the boat fastened like a lever for prying, the other at the stern. The negroes placed their shoulders to these poles or levers and pushed the boat along they walking on the tow path. This is the way that lumber is gotten out of the swamp; thus negroes are used for beasts of burden; nay even worse mules are often towed into the swamp by negroes! Two mules are put into one of the boats like that we chartered and are towed down the canal in the manner described. We embarked at the water tank on the Norfolk and Petersburg Railroad, 10 miles from Lake Drummond our destination. By laboring hard Sam and Tom made the lake in about three hours. The canal is four feet deep and 9 feet wide at the top. The tow path is much of the way nothing more than a small log on which a white man could not walk. Sam and Tom could get over them with as much agility as a goat. The name of this canal is Jericho Canal. The Dismal Swamp is too well-known to need a minute description by me. The land is soft and spongy and in places miry. One has to ponder well his footsteps or else he will sink deep into the mire and clay. There is but little solid ground. Cane 15 feet high grows so thick that a person cannot see into it ten feet. The swamp has long been noted for the vast quantities of lumber taken out of it. Gen. Washington was engaged in this business, he had a canal cut which to this day is called Washington's Ditch. The most valuable timber is Cypress and Juniper. From these vast quantities of shingles, Cooper's stuff, rails and other kinds of lumber are made. The swamp is owned by a company which pays a certain price for the lumber manufactured. The work is mostly done by negroes. To facilitate the getting of the lumber out of the swamp several ditches are cut from the dry land similar to the one already described, the names of these are Jericho Canal above mentioned, Southwest ditch, Washington's ditch, Dismal ditch, a ditch leading to Hamburg in North Carolina and a feeder of the Dismal Swamp Canal. These all empty into Lake Drummond. Running out from these canals are corduroy roads. On them lumber is hauled in carts with mules to the canals. The mules are taken in, as I have already said, by negroes in boats. The men who work at this business go into the swamp and camp. They are very healthy. The water is said to be extremely wholesome. Sam told me that he had worked in the swamp for 25 years and had never been sick in all that time! The other kinds of wood besides that above mentioned, which we saw, are black gum, soft maple, beech, white bay, green bay, paw paw and some others. There are plenty of fox grapes. Black bear are numerous, there are also deer, raccoons and foxes. At the mouth of Washington's ditch lives a man by the name of Prentice Duke. He has been living here for 4 years, fishing, hunting and making shingles. He took us into his cabin and entertained us hospitably at a reasonable price.[33] Fishing was rather dull, we however caught enough for a mess. The "Coup de grace" of the excursion was a ride on the lake by moonlight. Myself and a comrade chartered one of Mr. Duke's small boats and, whilst our fellow excursionists were fishing, took our boatman Sam and went out on the lake to enjoy the beauty of the scene. The full moon had risen above the tops of the tall trees which surround the lake. Not a speck of cloud obscured the brilliancy of the stars or marred the beauty of the "Fair Empress of night." A gentle breeze fanned the bosom of the lake, just enough to make it a little rough. Over the waves like an arrow shot our boat. Now she raises with the wave now she descends into the abyss between the swells. On we dart and with greater force Sam plyes the oar till we almost fly. Now a wave strikes the bow of our boat and bursting we are sprinkled with the water; but we heed not this, the night is warm. The woods in our rear gradually grow dimmer and dimmer till they look like a black streak in the horizon. On we dash when ahead we discern a black belt in the horizon which proves to be the timber on the other side of the lake. The gale now begins to subside till there is "a great calm." Sam steered for the Hamburg Canal which he missed only a few rods. Near the timber on the opposite side from which we started the lake is as smooth as a pane of glass. We run up into the mouth of the canal and halted for a few minutes to reconnoiter and then run back on the lake a quarter of a mile where we stopped to behold the beautiful scenery spread out before us. This can be imagined not described. The reflection of the moon and stars in the water, the placid bosom of the lake with its irregular shores skirted with woods add to these the stillness of the night made up a scene which had so many charms that we were completely carried away into the ideal world. Not a sound could be heard, not even a rustling among the leaves. A supreme stillness over spread all. We broke the silence by discharging a pistol. The report was a sharp quick sound. In a few seconds we could hear the echo along the woods in the distance, which sounded like volleys of musketry. The echo was at first loud than it grew fainter and less distinct till it gradually died away in the distance. We now had to recross the lake to the place whence we started. Leisurely we rode along over the smooth surface amid the sublime stillness of the night. There was no noise to be heard save the splashing of the oars in the water. We reached Mr. Duke's at about midnight. A good mattress was furnished us which we made good use of the remainder of the night. Thus we had a moonlight ride of 12 miles. Our comrades, who were fishing did not return from the lake till a later hour. Thus we spent the eighth of October one of the pleasant days that we have enjoyed since being in the United States Army. Lake Drummond has no natural outlet. The lake is as high as the tops of the chimneys in Norfolk.

Oct. 9—We arose at daylight and after fishing and getting breakfast we started back to camp at 9 o'clock a.m. There was a light fog on the lake this morning. The ride up the canal was rather tedious but we had excellent opportunity to see the far famed Dismal Swamp which compensated for the tedium of the upward journey. A fire broke out 8 years ago in the swamp and burned over a large portion of it, consuming lumber and killing trees. The course of the fire can plainly be seen; the swamp in those places is bare of trees, excepting the dead trees which were killed by the fire and yet stand. Three men were burned to death in the conflagration. When we got within two miles of the water tank some New York soldiers were coming down the tow path; when they espied us they took the back track on the double quick supposing that we were Rebels. The day was very warm. Our passes run out yesterday. We reached camp at about 3 o'clock p.m.

Oct. 10—I was on camp guard today. Nothing extraordinary marked the day. "Old Mother Rumor" with her thousand tongues is busy in camp circulating the report that Ferry's Brigade is to be sent home to recruit etc. Etc.

Oct. 11—The afternoon was rainy. We received the news of a hard battle at Perryville, Kentucky. The account of it is very meager. There is now but little talk of an attack at Suffolk.[34]

Oct. 12, Sunday—The day was rainy and gloomy. I was detailed for picket in the afternoon. All night we had to stand out without a shelter and all night it rained.

Oct. 13—The day was damp and rainy. "The Relief" came around at 4 o'clock p.m. and we were permitted to return to camp. After returning from picket we esteem our tents a great luxury. A night's sleep, on our wooden bunks, is sweet.

Oct. 14—The weather continued rainy during the day. All has been quiet in this vicinity for several days. Fortifying is about done.

Oct. 15—The sun shone out again; his appearance was welcomed by the soldiers. The accustomed drills were resumed today; they had been suspended while so much chopping and digging was to be done.

Oct. 16—The regular routine of camp duty, and nothing else, constitute the record of today.

Oct. 17—The old stereotyped phrase "All quiet on the Potomac," has again come into vogue.

Oct. 18—Since the recent rain the nights have been quite cool and the middle of the day is quite warm. Several cases of ague have made their appearance in the Regiment within a few weeks past.

Oct. 19, Sunday—Upwards of 100 negroes came into Suffolk from North Carolina this morning. They consisted of men, women and children. The greater part of them was afoot and carried a heavy load of stuff but some were in carts and one wench was riding a mule. This is, perhaps, the first fruits of Lincoln's Emancipation Proclamation; if so it has ripened prematurely.

Oct. 20—The day was warm and the night cool. "Old Jack Frost" made his appearance tonight for the first time this fall. The frost was light.

Oct. 21—This afternoon two Brigades were reviewed by General Ferry. The roads were very dusty.

Oct. 22—All the troops at this place, excepting the cavalry, were reviewed by General Peck this morning. Ferry's Brigade constituted the first line, Wesels's [Wessells's] the second, Spinola's the third and Foster's the fourth. The artillery, three batteries, was formed on the right. General Ferry commanded. Col. Osborn commanded Ferry's Brigade. The men made a splendid appearance.[35]

Oct. 23—In the afternoon there was brigade drill by Gen. Ferry. An idea that we are going to winter here seems to prevail. The boys have began to build log huts.

Oct. 24—The pickets of this brigade were relieved this morning and we were ordered to be ready to march at 5 o'clock p.m. with three day's rations and blanket. At the appointed hour we fell into ranks and marched out on the road to Blackwater River. The force consisted of Ferry's and Foster's brigades, two regiments of cavalry with two small howitzers and one battery of artillery. Gen. Ferry commanded the expedition. The cavalry went in advance, next was Ferry's Brigade, the 39th Illinois first, and the artillery in the rear. We marched till about midnight when it was discovered that we had taken the wrong road, the cavalry had gone on another road, the one which we should have taken. We came to a halt and were ordered to lie down and sleep two or three hours. We spread our blankets and were about to drop off into the sweet embrace of Morpheus when the report of a cannon was heard in the distance; it was one of the howitzers which the 1st NY Mounted Rifles had with them.[36] Gen. Ferry ordered the Colonel to wake the men up and get them under arms. So [we] were disappointed of a nap in the sand. After counter marching two or three miles we took the right road. With weary limbs and heavy eye lids we marched on to Windsor, in the Isle of Wight County, which we reached between two and three o'clock, where we halted till daylight, enjoying a refreshing sleep.

Oct. 25—Before we had time to get breakfast the order to "fall in" was given. This order we obeyed with as good grace as we could with an empty stomach. Without anything extraordinary occurring we marched, in a zig zag course to Blackwater River. The artillery was placed in position on the banks of the River and shelled the woods on the opposite side. Skirmishers were also sent out who fired across the river at the

Secesh. The 39th Illinois was drawn up, (or rather down!) in position to support a battery. We stretched our weary limbs out on the ground and soon fell asleep. The cannonading and musketry was good music to sleep to. It was about 2 o'clock p.m. when the firing was commenced and it was kept up quite brisk a few rods in front of us. While the affair was going on we were engaged in a very comfortable nap. Two or three hours afterwards when we awoke all was quiet and our cavalry were crossing the river. We next addressed ourselves to preparing something to eat. Soon coffee was boiling over blazing fires and salt pork was being boiled. These with our "hard tacks" made as good a supper as we needed. Arrangements were made for the night, pickets were thrown out and every other precaution against a surprise taken. At 8 o'clock in the night the pickets were called in and we started back to camp. At 12 o'clock we arrived at Windsor where we bivouacked for the night.

Oct. 26, Sunday—It commenced raining before daylight this morning. After breakfast we resumed our campward march. We came in on the Petersburg Road and cross the Nansemond River on the draw bridge. At 2 o'clock p.m. we got into camp. The distance marched was at least 50 miles. What was accomplished it would be difficult to tell. The men were very much fatigued. The sand was two or three inches in the road over which we had to travel. The expedition I suppose might be termed a reconnaissance in force. A short time before we reached camp it began to rain furiously. The rest of the day and the night were stormy.

Oct. 27—The day was dismal and dull nothing exciting going on. Towards night the storm began to clear away and the sky was bedecked with many a star. Owing to the storm the mail boat did not arrive at Norfolk today. Consequently we were deprived of the pleasure of hearing from the "dear ones at home."

Oct. 28—We have premonitions of the approach of Winter. There was, this morning, a tolerable heavy frost. The sound of the hammer and ax can be heard building winter quarters; this the soldiers do at their own risk, they have no assurance that they will stay here one week. Heavy details for guard and fatigue were made this morning.

Oct. 29—Nothing of interest occurred today. The work on the fortifications here is not quite done!

Oct. 30—Log huts are beginning to take the place of our wedge tents. The boys have, for several days, been busily engaged in building. Cannonading was heard at Fortress Monroe today. This we learned to be occasioned by the trial of some new guns.

Oct. 31—It was my luck to be detailed to work on Fort Halleck today. This fort is near where the Petersburg and Norfolk railroad crosses the Jericho ditch. It will mount six guns.

November 1, 1862—So heavy have been the details for a few days past that I had to shovel dirt again today. The weather has for some days past been fine. The health of the troops good.

Nov. 2, Sunday—I attended church this morning at the Episcopal Church. The Minister preached a sermon from Hebrews 1:14. General Peck was present and participated in the services.

Nov. 3—There was regimental inspection this morning. The Colonel said a few unpleasant words to _____ about a rusty gun.

Nov. 4—On picket today; posted on a dim path in a dense wood. The night was clear, cool and very still. Not even a leaf on the trees appeared to move.

Nov. 5—Warm and clear day. Fort building and quiet reigned today.

Nov. 6—Fort Halleck had to have some more sand shoveled on it today. Guess it'll take to Christmas to finish it.

Nov. 7—When we awoke this morning we found the ground white with snow and it was still snowing. All the day was stormy alternating with snow and rain. The snow was about an inch and a half deep. This is "the Sunny South."

Nov. 8—Cloudy day but no rain or snow. Fort Halleck was again my sorrow.

Nov. 9, Sunday—The storm has subsided but by looking out of the tent evidence of it is yet to be seen. The trees are not yet disemburdened of their load of snow. At 1 o'clock p.m. the English men-of-war Cadmus and Petsel, lying at anchor in Hampton Roads, fired a salute in honor of the birthday of the Prince of Wales. We could plainly hear the firing. The day was unseasonally cool.[37]

Nov. 10—There was a heavy frost and slight freeze this morning. My vocation today was fort building. I am not aware that knowing how to conjugate the "mi verb" is any advantage to one shoveling sand.

Nov. 11—Duty same as yesterday. The weather is quite pleasant again.

Nov. 12—This forenoon there was a grand review of the troops at this place by Maj. Gen. Dix. There were four lines of infantry, Ferry's Brigade being the first. The cavalry was on the right and the artillery on the left. When the train on which the Gen. came arrived, a salute of 13 guns was fired; the same number of guns was also fired when he came out on the field. Gen. Ferry gave the commands. Dix was accompanied by Gen. Peck. Colonel Osborn commanded Ferry's Brigade. The troops made a good appearance. The day was very pleasant neither too warm nor too cold, neither was the ground muddy nor dusty. The review was in a field in front of Fort Dix.

Nov. 13—The pickets on the Petersburg Pike were fired on at about midnight. One of our men was killed and one wounded. The forces were called out on arms at 4 o'clock this morning, ready to receive the enemy should he advance in force. An affair occurred between one of the 62nd Ohio volunteers and the 132nd New York which came near causing a riot. This is an illustration of the ill feeling between the Eastern and Western troops. The new regiments from New York in particular are hated bitterly by the men of Ferry's Brigade. The Western men think that they are far superior to their Eastern comrades as soldiers. The bounty paid to the new regiments irritates ill feeling which the soldiers of the

West have for those of the East.[38] What is the real cause of the grudge between the soldiers of the two sections of the country would be difficult to tell. It is probably owing to a local pride, which to say the least is a selfish patriotism. I am proud that I am an American, but I feel no pride that I am a native of Illinois. What is any particular State, only as a member of the glorious Union? Dismember the country and who will then boast that he is a resident of Massachusetts, a New Yorker, a Virginian, or an Illinoisan, a native of the New England States, the South or the West? What respect that the name Pennsylvanian, South Carolinian, Ohioan or that of any State command abroad? American is the name which serves an aegis of protection around a man in any part of the world. A sectional feeling between the soldiers is wrong. It was this which entered largely into the origin of our present national troubles. I am for my country, my whole country and whoever is engaged in the effort to put down the present unprovoked rebellion and to restore the Union to its pristine glory, whatever else may be his faults, or in what part of the world he may have been born or what his color is, while he is so engaged, my friend, a friend whom I can take by the hand and sincerely say to him "God be with you." Even more I would, if necessary, share with him my rations or blanket. This may be called abolitionism or any other sort of ism which demogogues may see fit to call it, but the true name is Unionism.

Nov. 14—I was on picket today. General Peck came galloping along the lines. The sergeant called out the guard to present arms. But before the guard could turn out the general rode past. "You are too late, too late," said he. A greatly to be deplored occurrence took place tonight. I refer to the stoning of Gen. Spinola's Headquarters; it was doubtless done by a few malcontents of Ferry's Brigade. The house occupied by the Gen. belongs to a wealthy "Secesh," who left with his family a few days ago, for "parts beyond" the Blackwater river. The house is just without the lines of the camp of the 39th Illinois. Before the family left Colonel Osborn and Major Mann boarded with them; since they have left, the Gen took the house for his Headquarters.

Nov. 15—After dress parade Colonel Osborn formed the regiment in a hollow square and cautioned the boys against further riotous demonstrations. It is to be hoped that there will be no further trouble. The Colonel's popularity with the men of his command will have a beneficial effect in allaying the agitated prejudice of the boys.

Nov. 16, Sunday—This was a cold boisterous day. A mind conscious of rectitude causes a genial sun ever to shine within one's breast, the light of which dispels black cares. A sense of being in the discharge of duty to God, Country and man creates an inward pleasure which nothing can mar. It is a priceless treasure of which thieves cannot deprive one.

Nov. 17—I was detailed today to work on Fort Halleck. The day was warm and clear. A Scout went out to Blackwater this afternoon. Cannonading was heard late in the evening. Marching orders may be received at any minute by the 39th Regiment Illinois Volunteers.

Nov. 18—Cannonading was heard all day at intervals on Blackwater.

Nov. 19—This afternoon our reconnoitering party returned. There was some artillery skirmishing with the enemy, no musketry fighting; no damage was done on our side.

Nov. 20—The date passed off without anything of interest occurring. In the night there was a heavy rain.

Nov. 21—On camp guard. The day was cloudy and rainy. Another fort is being built to the right of the rifle pits of the 67 Ohio Volunteers. This makes six forts defending the approaches to Suffolk.

Nov. 22—Quiet prevailed today.

Nov. 23, Sunday—The day was clear and pleasant. No passes were given this morning to go to church, excepting to squads under the command of a non-commissioned officer.

Nov. 24—On picket. The night was clear, cold and frosty. There was no disturbance along the lines.

Nov. 25—This morning there was some target practice with the guns on Fort Dix. The target was a small cedar tree about half a mile from the fort. One shot cut the tree down. The day was very pleasant.

Nov. 26—We awoke this morning to find a rain storm in progress. Sunshine and dust, rain and mud, cold nights and frosty mornings constitute the chief variety of Camp Suffolk. Digging, drills and grand reviews have become too stale to be of any interest, unless perchance the women who attend the reviews are interested. An order came to be ready to march, at 11 o'clock a.m., with forty rounds of cartridges and three day's rations in haversacks. We were prepared to march when, a short time before the appointed hour, the order was countermanded. This was received with joy by the boys as they were not particularly [eager] to exchange their comfortable huts for a march in the rain and mud.

Nov. 27—The clouds cleared away during the night and there was a heavy frost and a considerable freeze. Detailed to work on Fort Dix. Our pickets were relieved by soldiers who are unable to march and the details for fatigue were discharged at noon. This is considered as ominous of a expedition, on which we are soon to start. In fact we are momentarily expecting orders to get ready to "fall into ranks." Whether we are going merely on a reconnaissance or not is to us unknown.

Nov. 28—Nothing of special interest transpired.

Nov. 29—Detailed to fell timber in the swamp, where the water was half a foot deep.

Nov. 30, Sunday—Regimental inspection and muster this morning. The weather very pleasant. Sad thought is it that we should be under the necessity of waging war against our fellow citizens. But whether they will never again be our fellow citizens or not is extremely doubtful. If "to doubt is disloyalty," I for one, am disloyal. Exit Autumn. Enter Winter.

December 1—At 2 o'clock p.m., on expedition, composed of the 39th Regiment Illinois, 62nd Ohio, 130 NY, 103 Pennsylvania and 6 Mass infantry, and the 11 Pennsylvania cavalry with two howitzers, and one section of battery Z, 4th U.S. and two sections of battery G., 7 Mass, started out in the direction of Franklin. Colonel Spear of the 11th Pennsylvania cavalry had command of the expedition.[39] We marched out about 8 miles from Suffolk and bivouaced for the night. Rails were burnt after the old campaign style. The night was cloudy and threatened rain but fortunately for us the threat was not carried into execution. While we were halted to rest this afternoon three interesting looking young ladies drove along in a two wheeled cart drawn by a small ox. This was such a ludicrous sight the boys could not help laughing.

Dec. 2—At 3 o'clock a.m., we were again on the march. It was yet very dark which made the marching laborous. Soon after sun up we reached Carsville, where we halted only a few minutes. This is a small village on the Seaboard & Roanoke railroad in the Isle of Wight County 14 miles from Suffolk. Two miles from Carsville we encountered a body of rebels variously estimated at from 300 to 800 men. The 11th Pennsylvania cavalry made a gallant charge and took 25 prisoners, besides wounding several, and some small arms and a rocket battery. Our loss was none. The engagement was a hand to hand one between our cavalry and that of the enemy. The infantry had halted at a church before the enemy was discovered and were not brought out into action. The prisoners were Georgia Conscripts. Their uniforms were multiforms! Having gone as far as orders permitted we started back to camp in the afternoon. About 10 miles from Suffolk we bivouaced for the night. The night was too cold to sleep much. We built large fires of rails and would lie down around them. Occasionally a short nap would come to our relief. With joy we hailed the grey streaks of light after a long and dark night. Cheer up.

Dec. 3—At the dawn of day it commenced raining, which continued all day. Of this expedition there is but little more to write. By the dint of hard marching through rain and mud we reached camp at 1 o'clock p.m. This was in many respects the best conducted expedition that has been sent out from Suffolk since we have been here.

Dec. 4—Nothing of special interest to record; the day was clear.

Dec. 5—Two Pennsylvania regiments, the 175 & 185 Conscript, have been sent here within the present week. The day was rainy. This evening the 158th NY Regiment came to Suffolk.

Dec. 6—This morning at 4 o'clock, when I went on guard, the moon was partially eclipsed. The size was about four digits. The day was very cold.

Dec. 7, Sunday—It was my luck to be on picket today. Our post was at edge of the Dismal Swamp, in a dense woods. The night was very cold. Being on the reserve, we were not altogether deprived of sleep. Three of us made our bed together. We spread our gum blankets on a pile of cane; on this we lay down and covered with three woolen blankets. We slept very comfortably. In the morning the gum blankets, on which we lay, were covered with frost as was also the top blanket, with which we were covered.

Dec. 8—Brigade drill in the afternoon. Clear cold day. Winter claims his own. Shelter tents were issued out to the soldiers today.

Dec. 9—The weather clear and cool. Considerable freezes of nights. Ice thick enough to bear up a man.

Dec. 10—Three drills and dress parade today. Company and battalion drill in the forenoon and brigade drill afternoon.

Dec. 11—Fine morning; all calm and peaceful, nothing to disturb the quietude of the camp. The quiet beginning of the morning did not endure long. At 11 o'clock a.m., with 60 rounds of cartridges and three day's rations in haversacks, an expedition commanded by Gen. Ferry started to "Blackwater." At about sun down we halted to get supper and a short time after dark resumed the march again. There were many bad mud holes in the road so that the artillery & wagons could scarcely get through. We would march a few rods and then halt a half an hour or an hour. At 11 o'clock we had marched only about two miles from where we halted for supper. Passed through Windsor about midnight. The night was cold and frosty. To march a short distance till one's blood is heated up, and then halt for an hour, and lie down on the frozen ground is far from pleasant. I should have mentioned as a part of the expedition a pontoon train. From this we thought that we were to cross our Rubicon, the Blackwater. All night we were on the march. The suffering from fatigue, the want of sleep and the cold, when halted, was great. Some of the boys, many of them, heap execrations upon the heads of President Lincoln, Gen. Peck, Gen. Ferry and "the damned Abolishionists." It is a disgrace that they should be so far overcome with evil as to act such an un-soldierlike manner.[40]

Dec. 12—At sun up we reached the end of our destination. There was an unimportant skirmish with infantry and artillery. Our loss was two men killed and between 15 & 20 wounded. A part of the 10th Indiana Regiment crossed the river in small boats and took 15 prisoners, one of whom was a Captain. The Rebs were in rifle pits so that our men had an unequal chance with them. Well we did not cross the river but Gen. Ferry ordered the pontoon to be burnt. We also lost one wagon which broke down and was burnt. It looks very much like the expedition was a failure. We certainly lost more than we got, saying nothing about the fatigue of the men. At 12 o'clock m., we started back to camp. Bivouaced for the night near Windsor.

Dec. 13—Took up the line of march at 5 o'clock this morning and reached camp before noon. The weather was clear all the time that we were out this time.

Dec. 14, Sunday—Nothing noteworthy transpired today. General Peck left this morning to be gone 20 days to New York. General Ferry is command at Suffolk.

Dec. 15—The weather is like Indian Summer.

Dec. 16—We have not received the daily regularly for one week. There is great anxiety with regard to the Army of the Potomac. Burnside is fighting is all that we know.[41]

Dec. 17—Cold weather. On picket today. Being on the reserve we could sleep a little at night. We had a house made of pine boughs; in the center a fire was kept burning. We were thus enabled to keep tolerable comfortable. Bad was the news received this evening. Burnside by a tremendous effort and a great loss of life was unable to dislodge the enemy from his strong position on the South side of the Rappahannock River. He recrossed the river under the cover of night.

Dec. 18—The cars have been running from Suffolk for three days & nights, bringing in reinforcements.

Dec. 19—Detailed to work on Fort Union; this, situated at the right of the rifle pits of the 67 Ohio Volunteers, is diamond shaped and the largest of the forts around Suffolk. The slashing was set on fire today. At night the scene was something similar to a prairie on fire in Illinois but far less grand. Robert Halloway has been promoted to drum major.

Dec. 20—The morning was very cold. A Pennsylvania drafted Regiment has been here three days without tents.

Dec. 21, Sunday—All quiet today.

Dec. 22—On camp guard.

Dec. 23—A nice warm day, like one of the smoky days of October. There was this evening what is called "a stag dance." The Colonel & Adjutant participated.

Dec. 24—Orders this evening to be ready to march with three day's rations in haversacks; to be a permanent move. Prospect of rather an exciting Christmas.

Dec. 25—Dull Christmas. Lieutenants treated Company to apples. Contrary to orders guns were fired all through the last night & today. The weather seemed more like a mid September day than Christmas. On guard at Brigade Headquarters. Night so warm that I could sleep out comfortably.

Dec. 26—Heard the blue birds sing like a spring morning. Still have marching orders.

Dec. 27—The day was rainy. No movements of troops today. Rain poured down all night.

Dec. 28, Sunday—The 132nd Regiment NY volunteers & the 171st Pennsylvania drafted militia left this morning; their baggage was loaded on the cars. The 132nd New York set fire to their quarters. Men from the 39th Illinois were detailed to strike the tents of the 171st PA after they had left; it was my ill luck to be on this detail. They have had a few cases of the small pox in this regiment. Some of us perhaps will have this loathesome disease as we had to strike this hospital tent. The sun shone all day. We kept our ears pricked up momentarily expecting to hear the order "fall in." As to our destination we are in the dark.

Dec. 29—Two regiments of Corcoran's Irish Legion came this evening from Newport News; the rest of the Legion is coming. The weather is fine.[42]

Dec. 30—The 67 Ohio Regiment left on the cars this morning, going towards Norfolk, VA. The day was slightly rainy. All goes well; Soldiers were arriving and departing during the day.

Dec. 31—Mustered for pay this morning; six months pay is now due us. Company I was detailed to go on picket but it was relieved soon after it went out. We had orders to strike tents and be ready to march at 8 o'clock a.m. tomorrow morning. The 62nd Ohio Regiment left this evening on the cars. This completes the record of the year of our Lord one thousand eight hundred sixty-two, an eventful year in our Country's History.

January 1, 1863—If the year 1863 have as good a termination as it has beginning all will be well. The day was clear with a chilly wind blowing. We have not yet struck tents but such an order is momentarily expected.

Jan. 2—All quiet today and nothing to chronicle.

Jan. 3—The weather fine. Today everything in status quo.

Jan. 4, Sunday—Attended church in the forenoon and afternoon at Suffolk, the 13th Indiana Regiment was put into Foster's Brigade. Deep regret at having to part, they came to our Regiment tonight and bade us farewell. The 39th Illinois went over to their quarters to bid them adieu. Speeches were made. Orders to march in the morning at 7 o'clock.

Jan. 5—Early in the morning the drums and fifes of our martial band were calling us forth to prepare to march. In obedience to the call the soldiers, some of them grumbling & cursing, got out of their bunks and invested themselves with a United States uniform. It was almost 10 o'clock a.m. before all the preliminaries were completed and the order forward march was given by the "Magnus Apollo" of the column. The 39th Illinois volunteers and the 176 Pennsylvania militia, escorted by a part of the 11th Pennsylvania cavalry with two mountain howitzers constituted the column. General Ferry commanded in person. The baggage was mostly sent via Norfolk. The boys had to lug their knapsacks and shelter tents. We marched out on the Edenton Road. The day was very warm; some of the boys took off their shoes and marched barefooted. The road runs across portions of the Dismal Swamp. These places had to be crossed on planks about two feet wide supported by piles three or four feet high. The infantry had to go across by single file. We halted half an hour at noon for dinner, after which the march was resumed. The country is very level and the soil sandy. By far the greater part of the surface is covered with primeval pine forests. The improvements are good; most of the houses are built of wood and are handsome edifices. They are shaded by trees that look like they might have been planted by the first English settlers. Among the products of the soil are corn, cotton, sweet potatoes and orchard fruits. Cattle, horses, hogs and negroes are raised to a considerable extent, the latter are, or rather were, very numerous. All the cattle which we saw were very inferior. We marched in Nansemond County, VA till in the afternoon but when we crossed the line into North Carolina we did not know. Passed through Holly Grove after dark. This is a small village of Gates County, N. C. About one mile from this village we bivouaced for the night. The boys were very tired. Many curses were heaped on Gen. Ferry's head for marching so late. Distance marched 20 miles.

Jan. 6—At 5 o'clock a.m. we arose; prepared breakfast and at 6 o'clock took up the line of march. Today we were in Gates County, North Carolina. The topography and products of the Country are the same as that through which we passed yesterday. In the afternoon we passed through Sunbury; this is a small village consisting of a few residences, stores et cetera. The boy's feet were very sore from the previous day's march. Dr. Woodward, of the 39th Illinois volunteers, pressed all the carts along the road to haul the knapsacks for the boys.[43] With blistered feet and wearied on we toiled through the sand. To add to the hardship of marching it began to rain at 4 o'clock p.m. Some of the boys are strongly opposed to Lincolns proclamation of freedom.[44] They curse abolitionists and negroes and wish them all in Tophet together. They would rather see the Union dismembered than to see the slaves of the South emancipated. But they are by no means martyrs to their doctrine. Many of them were today glad to get negroes to carry their knapsacks. When one of these loud pro-slavery men would get a little tired he would compel a negro to come along and carry his knapsack and gun. After marching about 18 miles we halted, at 4 o'clock p.m. and bivouaced for the night. This was about three miles from the Chowan River. Two prisoners were taken today but General Ferry released them. "Ego" went to a farmhouse and got supper. The farmer, or more aristocratically, the planter was very hospitable and entertained us with the best he had. He had no coffee nor sugar, wheat is used here as a substitute for coffee. But his daughter, about 14 years old, was the chief attraction to "Ego." She was quite communicative and expressed her sentiments freely. She was attending school in Hertford when the war broke out but had been at home ever since. She expressed a contempt for free schools and said that she would never go to one again; she had attended a free school one week! She did not like to associate with the "Piney Woods folks." This is what the poor are called in North Carolina. She said that she had some near relations among them but she did not care anything about them. To the inquiry whether she was for the Union or the South she said that she was neither one. She sang both Union and Secesh songs, she said. According to her report most of the men in that part of the country were for the Union and the women were secessionists. This county Gates gave a majority of votes in favor of the State remaining loyal to the Union. A Union Co. of cavalry was raised here and is now stationed on the Chowan River above Holly's Landing.[45] There are many churches along the road from Suffolk, VA to Edenton, NC but no school houses. The night was dark and cold.

Jan. 7—Started on the way at 8 o'clock a.m. The boys were some of them short of rations. "How far is it to the river?" was asked by many. The answers were as various as the inquiries were numerous. No two persons would give the same answer. But what was more aggravating still we got no nearer to the river till we were almost there. There are mile posts on the Edenton Road with notches in them instead of figures to mark the distance. One notch for each mile from a certain place, which the inhabitants understand. Finally at about noon the cry went up "I see the river, I see the river" and such cheering as Ferry's Brigade only can do. *"Visto el rio"* [I see the river], said I, thus improving my scant stock of Spanish. Before us was the broad Chowan. This was at Holly's Landing about ten miles above Edenton. Here we embarked for parts further South. We pitched our tents, got dinner and strolled around till 4 o'clock p.m., when we had dress parade. An order, issued by General Ferry, was announcing the time that several calls would be sounded, among the rest was inspection at 10 a.m. Regimental, these calls were to be observed while we remained here. We were waiting for boats to come "to take us away" and the boats came soon after dark. We went to bed and had a splendid foundation laid for a good night's sleep. At 12:00 midnight we were aroused and struck tents and embarked. The 39th Illinois and two Companies of the 176 PA went aboard of the steamship Eastern City. The rest of the 176 PA went on a boat very similar to the Eastern City but I did not learn the name of her. The wagons and some of the horses were put on a steam ferry boat. Our fleet consisted of these three vessels. After embarking the boys lay down and slept till daylight.[46]

Jan. 8—At 4:00 a.m., we weighed anchor and started down the Chowan. The river is near two miles wide where we embarked and it gradually grows wider as it nears the Albemarle Sound, into which it empties. It is a noble stream. Each bank is covered with dense pine forests. There are no cities nor towns of importance along the river. The day was cold and cloudy. Soon after daylight we entered Albemarle Sound. This is a fine body of fresh water. It extends 60 miles inland & is from 2 to 15 miles wide. From Albemarle we passed into Croatan Sound. Croatan Sound is a narrow pass separating Roanoke Island from the mainland and connects Albemarle and Palmico Sounds. To the East of the Island is Roanoke Sound. We left Roanoke Island to the left. We did not pass near enough to have any thing more than a distant view. All that we could see of it is that it is a long narrow island covered with timber. Opposite the northern end of Roanoke Island and between Albemarle Sound and the Atlantic Ocean are the Kill Devil Hills. These are high sandy hills, presenting, when viewed from a distance, something of the appearance of huge snow drifts. Nearly opposite to the southern end of Roanoke Island, where Croatan Sound unites with Palmico Sound, is Stumpy Point. This is low and marshy. The extremity of the Point is composed of several islets. These are covered with tall grass. One of my fellow soldiers, but who was, for the time being, transformed into a fellow tourist, could see some resemblance between these islets and stumps; hence we inferred that the name "Stumpy" was given to the point. There are some huts on the point, which we supposed to be the abodes of fishermen. A few rods out in the water is a light house. Passing through Croatan Sound we came into Palmico Sound. This is a body of saltwater 80 miles long and from 9 to 25 miles wide. Loggerhead Inlet connects the sound with the Atlantic Ocean. Hatteras Island was far to our left; we could only see it far away to the East, appearing very much like a blue cloud in the horizon. During the day we passed three or four light houses. Soon after dark we entered the Neuse River. At midnight we cast anchor and lay till morning. It is reported on good authority that two negroes were thrown overboard. All the circumstances seem to confirm the report. The brutal affair occurred after dark tonight while we were running up the Neuse River. According to the report it was done by soldiers of the 39th Regiment Illinois volunteers. The negroes gave no cause whatever of offense.

Jan. 9—When the light cleared away the black darkness of night we saw that we were anchored in the Neuse River about one mile below Newbern. The morning was cold and rainy but the clouds soon cleared away and the day was tolerably pleasant. There was a considerable amount of shipping lying at anchor off Newbern. By far the greater part was two mast schooners, there were seven or eight gun boats and a few steam boats and tugs. The Eastern City arrived off Newbern several hours ahead of the other two boats of our expedition. During the passage down coffee was made on the boat for the boys. The kitchen was on the starboard side of the vessel. When the coffee was ready the boys would rush to the starboard thus causing the boat to careen so that she could scarcely run. The boat was very much crowded, the bunks were full and the floor of the gang way was covered with union soldiers; so many of the boys had to make their [bed] wherever they could find room for their carcasses and run the risk of being tramped on, spit on etc. To guard against such a calamity I made my bed out on the deck and in daytime was up on the hurricane deck in order that I might see what was to be seen. We lay at anchor till noon when we disembarked at Foster's wharf Newbern, NC. We were on the boat about 36 hours all of which time the weather was very calm. We marched out about three miles from town and pitched our shelter tents in an open field. Here we found the 62nd and 67th Ohio Regiments. The boys were very hungry. The 67 Ohio made coffee for us. Our baggage has not yet come.

Jan. 10—The day was rainy. Hallowell, the base drummer, and myself went out into the woods, built a fire, wrote our diaries, from the time we left Suffolk, VA.[47] We built our fire between two pine logs, which, if a line were drawn from the butt of one to butt end of the other, would form an isosceles triangle. We would change our seat from one of the legs of the triangle to the other according to the way the smoke would blow. We had a gum blanket stretched on four stakes for a shelter from the frequent showers of the day. Our fire was in a dismal looking place, an edge of a swamp. Around us were large pine trees, hacked for turpentine. This is what I believe the natives call "a pine orchard."

Jan. 11, Sunday—The day was clear and warm, flies and bugs were sailing around through the air; this seems quite strange for the middle of winter. There was company inspection at 10 o'clock a.m. We are encamped in a dreary looking place. It is in a small sandy field surrounded by dense pine forests and swamps. The trees in the swamps are covered with long hoary moss, which resembles, somewhat, coarse hair. From the limbs of the trees long bunches of the moss are suspended.

Jan. 12—On guard. Our Regiment moved into the woods and pitched our tents. Our baggage and convalescents came up today. We laid aside, for the present, shelter tents and re-occupied the wedge tents.

Jan. 13—Newbern, NC, the county seat of Craven County, is situated on a triangular shaped piece of ground just above the junction of the Trent with the Neuse River. The town is on the right bank of the Neuse River and on the left of the Trent; it is about 40 miles from the mouth of the former river. The town has an old dilapidated appearance; the houses are mostly built of wood and are very much weather beaten. The streets are not paved nor graded. There are a few tolerable good business houses and some of the residences have some appearance of comfort and neatness. But as a general thing the town wears a sad gloomy aspect. There are comparatively few citizens living in the town at present. Scarcely any other human forms meet the eye but soldiers and negroes. Hotels, churches, stores and a courthouse are among the public buildings. Newbern, previous to the rebellion enjoyed considerable trade inland by means of a railroad running from Beaufort to Raleigh, the capital of the State, coastwise by the Neuse River, which is here about two miles wide and empties into Palmico Sound. The Trent River is not navigable. There was an extensive business done in turpentine, tar pitch and rosin, large quantities of which was annually exported. In the vicinity cotton is raised to a considerable extent; excellent sweet potatoes are produced in great abundance. The business now is mostly done by the "Yankees" but few of the citizens being engaged in mercantile affairs. There are plenty of stores, sutters, oyster saloons, grocery stores, eating houses etc. All, with but exceptions, kept by Northerners. One firm, Dibble, has issued checks, redeemable in trade, which [are] current in town and surrounding country. There is a daily paper published, "The Newbern Progress."[48] This was the title of a paper published before the town was taken by General Burnside, on March 14th 1862, and the "Yankees" kept the institution going. The place is lighted with gas. The population I should suppose, before the war was about 6000. A negro told me that "a cession of folks lived here before the war." I was just as ignorant as I was before the

Sable gentleman gave me this information. The market is regulated by the Provost Marshal. Farmers bring sweet potatoes, corn meal, poultry, pork, etc to market for several miles around. We saw sweet potatoes, corn meal and chickens which had been brought 75 miles in small boats. Cedar Grove Cemetery is in town! It was opened A.D. 1800. It is enclosed by a stone wall and is shaded by large Cedar trees. The stone of which the wall is built is of a very peculiar formation. The stones are composed of numerous shells and pebbles firmly cemented together; this is said to have been done by the action of the sea. The enclosures are in a bad state of affair. I noticed tomb stones manufactured at the following places viz: Wilmington, NC, Baltimore, MD and Taunton, MA. Newbern, Newberne, New Bern the name of this town is spelt the three above ways; the first is most common.[49]

Jan. 14—We are in the second brigade, third division, eighteenth army corps and the Department of North Carolina. Colonel Osborn commands the Brigade, Brigadier General Ferry commands the Division and Maj. Gen. Foster is commander of the Department. There is here a large force, perhaps 40,000. Ferry's Division is composed of two brigades, Osborn's and Col. Howell's. Osborn's or the second brigade made up of the following regiments viz: 39 Illinois, 62 & 67 Ohio volunteers and the 176 Pennsylvania militia.[50]

Jan. 15—The turpentine season is from the first of March till Christmas. A small box is cut in the tree near the ground and the trees are hacked about an inch deep beginning just above the box and extending up the trunk of the tree. The turpentine runs down the tree from the incisions made in its trunk, with a tool made for the purpose, and is caught in the box. It is dipped out of the boxes once a week. As many boxes as one hand can dip in a week is called "a crop of boxes." The turpentine after being collected from the trees is taken to the distillery and distilled; it is then ready for market. Our recruiting officers returned to the Regiment today with a few recruits.

Jan. 16—The day was damp and chilly. We have not got much news since we have been here, consequently we do not know what is going on in the outer world.

Jan. 17—The day was cold; a frost fell during the night. We are not now, as we were a few days ago, serenaded by the frogs and crickets.

Jan. 18, Sunday—Attended church, in the afternoon, at the Episcopal Church in Newbern. After dress parade a state banner was presented to the regiment by Col. Osborn on behalf of Gov. Yates. Col. Osborn made a few appropriate remarks to which Lt. Col. Mann responded. When the banner was handed to the Color Sergeant three cheers were given for Governor Yates. The banner is made of blue silk, with yellow fringe and golden tassels. On one side is a large portrait of the governor, above the portrait is a semicircle of stars and under it on a scroll, in large letters, is "Yates Phalanx 39th Regiment Illinois Infantry." On the other side of the banner is the coat of arms and motto of the State of Illinois and the motto of the United States. Above the Eagle is a semicircle of stars; under is the name and number of the Regiment. On the top of the staff is perched an eagle. Cost of the banner $400.[51]

Jan. 19—By order of the Colonel the boys began to build log huts today. The weather continues cold and chilly. No news yet from the "outer world."

Jan. 20—The regiments of Ferry's Division marched to an open field, on Trent River, one mile above the camp, for a review. A rain set in before they got to the field and prevented the review from being had; the regiment were ordered back to their quarters. There was a hard rain in the night. Our tent was by no means impervious to the pelting shower.

Jan. 21—The morning was damp and cold. There was to have been a grand review of all the troops around Newbern, on the south side of Trent River but on account of the stormy weather the review was not had; thus the weather did for us what General Foster was unwilling to do, viz; gave us rest.

Jan. 22—The day was damp, dreary, dismal, dark, desolate, disconsolate, discouraging, disheartening, dismaying, dispiriting, displeasing and distressing.

Jan. 23—The 62nd and 67 Ohio Regiments struck tents this morning and left on the cars, probably for Morehead City. The other regiments of the second Brigade are under marching orders. Went to town in the afternoon and visited Fort Totten. This is an earth work for the defense of New Bern.

Jan. 24—It seems that the sun has deserted the Earth; it has not shown its face for nearly one week. The weather continues damp and drizzly. Tonight, after all honest men ought to have been in bed, a row was raised by some drunken officers. More oaths than blows were used.

Jan. 25, Sunday—No familiar hymn reminded us of the return of this day of rest. The reveille was sounded at 4 o'clock a.m. & at six we struck tents and were off on the expedition the destination of which was mystery to the "uncircumcised gentiles." At Newbern we get aboard the cars and went to Morehead City, distant 34 miles. This place, and not Beaufort as laid down on some maps, is the terminus of the Atlantic & North Carolina Railroad. The 176 Pennsylvania militia came down on the same train with us. The train was made up of platform cars. The battlefield of Newbern is three miles southeast of town on the railroad. There are some light earth works thrown up by the Rebels and in front of these the timber is slashed. The country here for a short distance is quite broken; there are steep hills and deep ravines. The enemy certainly had a good position, but they did not make a good use of it.[52] At two other places along the road are breast works. The country between Newbern and Morehead City, with the exception of the narrow strip just described, is low and flat. The greater part of the surface is covered with pine trees; there is also much boggy land. The soil is sandy and almost worthless. There are no more improvements of any consequence. The only business to be done is making turpentine, tar etc. There is but one town along the road and it consists of a few miserable looking houses. Morehead City, situated on a point of land between Bogue Sound & Newport River, opposite to Beaufort, is a small town of about 200 inhabitants. There is here a wharf with a railroad track so the cars run out to unload their freight near the boat on which it is to be loaded. Here we embarked at 1 o'clock p.m.; the right wing on the Sentinel. We run out into the sound a few rods and cast anchor: so here we lie off Beaufort with the prospect of not starting out for several days. Fort Macon, Beaufort, Morehead City, Bogue Sound, Newport River, Old Topsail Inlet and the Atlantic Ocean are all in sight. Transports, schooners and small steamboats are lying at anchor in the harbor. Some of the transports are loaded with troops; others are being loaded as fast as they can embark.[53]

Jan. 26—Troops are embarking all day. Lighters were busily engaged carrying baggage & soldiers from the wharf to schooners & transports. The day was clear and warm. We began to feel the monotony of lying at anchor in harbor. Charleston is on the tongue of all on board; the Officers of the boat are positive that the expedition is to take this City, they also say that Bull's Bay is the place of rendezvous. It is rumored that General Butler is to have command of the expedition.[54]

Jan. 27—Last night was cloudy and windy. At daylight there was a shower of rain. Wind continued to blow through the day. General Foster passed around through the harbor, this morning, in a steam boat, and inspected the fleet.

Jan. 28—The wind increased to a furious gale. The harbor is a very safe one; it is almost surrounded by land. The shipping here lay safely at anchor in a smooth harbor while the Atlantic was violently agitated. We could see its white capped waves dashing over Bogue Point, two miles distant. The steamer Mary Sanford arrived this morning from the North with mail for the army at this place.[55]

Jan. 29—The gale subsided so that by noon a small boat was sent ashore for the mail; this being the first we had received for more than ten days, great anxiety was felt in its distribution. No papers were brought aboard. In the middle of the afternoon the sailing craft of the expedition began to start out to sea, soon after General Foster passed through the harbor in his boat and gave orders to the Captain of each transport to get his vessel underway and go to sea. An hour before sun down we were passing out through Old Topsail Inlet into the Ocean. We passed under Fort Macon. This is built on Bogue Point; it is said to be one of the strongest forts built by the United States. There are two tiers of guns mounted on the parapets; the inner tier is higher than the outer one. The sea was very rough, although the gale was light, and the boat heaved. Soon the wind blew harder and the boat heaved more. At dark the wind had increased to a furious gale and the boys were giving the contents of their stomachs, gratuitously, to the Atlantic Ocean. Many heads were stretched over the bulwarks and stuck out of the portholes bowed in reverential adoration to Old Neptune.[56] This night will be remembered by many a union soldier as a night of misery. Some of the boys stayed on deck; these were not so sick as those who were below. The wind whistling through rigging of the vessel made a doleful noise. The gale increased and increased till it arose to the dignity of the storm. The ship tottered like a drunken man. Soon my curiosity to witness a storm at sea was satisfied. Late in the night one of the sail yards broke and the vessel labored hard to ride the waves. The boys were crowded together, like hogs, so thick that it was impossible to walk over the floor without stepping on them. The creaking of the ship, the groans of sea sick soldiers, the crashing of boxes, barrels and other plunder and the roaring of the sea all combined to make a horrible noise. The vessel made but little way during the night. The wind was what the sailors call "a southwester."

Jan. 30—The storm raged furiously all day and all day were the boys lying prostrate with sea sickness. There they lay, three hundred men crowded together on the lower deck; vomiting on blankets! A big sea would occasionally dash through the portholes and completely drench the involuntary worshipers of Neptune. There was an awful stench, which was very sickening, perhaps not quite equal the Black hole of Calcutta. One soldier, who was lying at my side, wished for a corner in his mother's hog pen; it would have been a palace. No one was able to help another; all were in a helpless condition. "O stand the storm, it won't be long. We'll anchor by and by," had to us a literal meaning. The ship made no headway today; she just about held her own.[57]

Jan. 31—During the night the storm subsided and this morning the weather was calm and the sea smooth. Most of the boys were well and ready for their rations of "hard tacks & salt horse." The day was very pleasant and towards evening the sea was as smooth as glass. The color of the water is sky blue. When off Charleston we heard artillery firing. All day and all night the ship run smoothly and the boys had rest from vomiting.

February 1, Sunday—At 5 o'clock this morning we arrived off Port Royal and lay till after daylight, when the boat run in. A number of the vessels of the fleet had arrived but none of the sailing craft. The vessels anchored in two lines extending up and down the harbor. Various reports were circulated this morning with regard to a rebel ram running out from Charleston and attacking our blockading squadron. The right wing of the 39th Illinois volunteers embarked on the transport Sentinel, three companies on the Gen. Meigs and two companies on the schooner Skirmisher. Colonel Osborn and staff were on the Miegs, so was Col. Mann also. Capt. Linton, Acting Maj., had command on the Sentinel.[58]

Feb. 2—The schooners began to come in this morning. We lay still at anchor in Broad Bay off Hilton Head SC. This harbor, I should think was too open to be safe from storms. The body of water, in which we are now

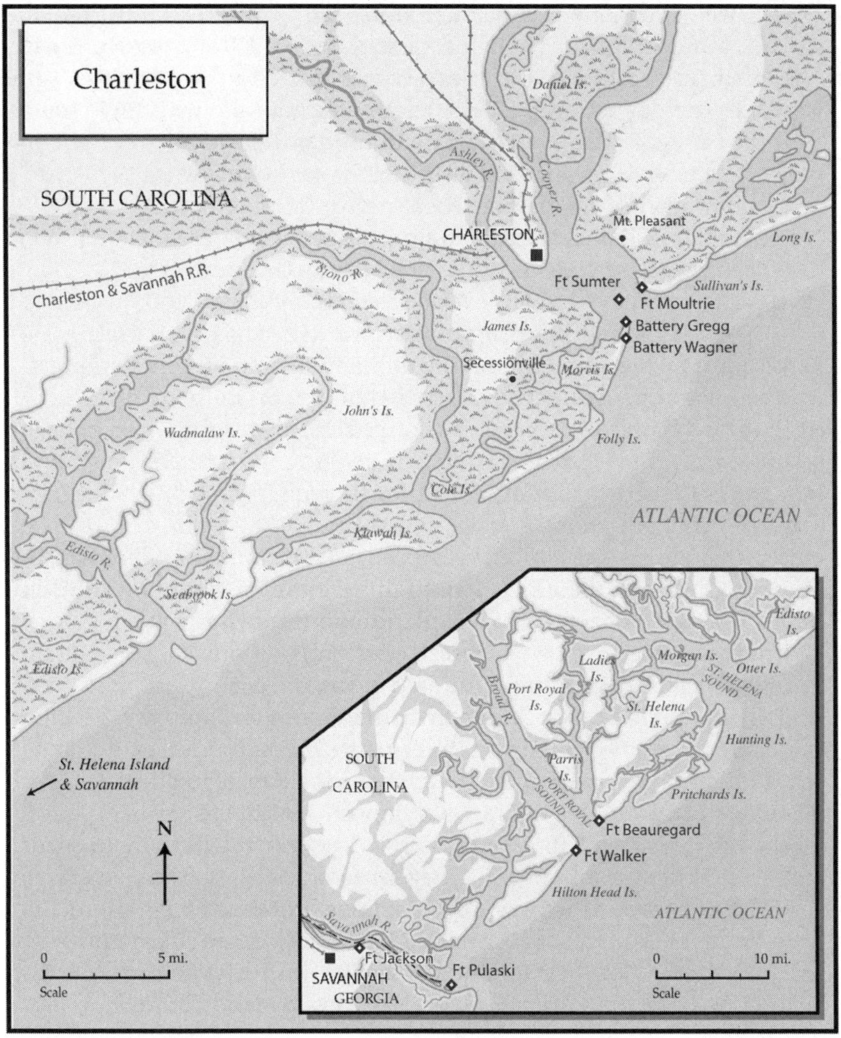

anchored, at the entrance to the Ocean is marked on maps Port Royal Entrance and a little further up it is called Broad Bay. Coosawatchie River puts into the bay further up. Hilton Head is to the left as we pass in.[59]

Feb. 3—The day was warm and calm. The fleet presents a grand sight after night, with the lights hung up in the rigging of the vessels, add to this the soft rays of a half-full moon and the reflection of the stars in the water and the scene is most enchanting. But the soldier walks the deck and looks melancholily at these gentle beauties; there rankles something within his breast which beats not in unison to the lovely scene, which is spread out all around him.

Feb. 4—Twelve schooners, which left Morehead City at the same time that we did, came in today. The wind blew quite hard from the Northwest. The harbor is so open that the vessels were tossed to and fro with great violence. The day was very cold and the soldiers were shivering around, with the capes of their overcoat turned up over their heads; yet there was no ice to be seen! In the evening the boat was run further up the bay to a more secure part of the harbor. There is now here a considerable fleet lying at anchor off Hilton Head. No troops have as yet disembarked. What the expedition is to do is a mystery to the uncircumcised Gentile.

Feb. 5—The gale of yesterday was succeeded by a rain today. One day passes away and another comes. "Hard tacks," coffee and "salt horse" make our daily rations. We have no variety in anything, excepting the weather. The boys are justly getting tired of the sort of living.[60]

Feb. 6—The day was cloudy, rainy and cold. Nothing of interest to record today. No news yet! Demoralization is beginning to appear not only in our own regiment but in all the others heard from. Sad, sad indeed is this to reflect upon, but it is nevertheless true.

Feb. 7—There was a light frost this morning. The day was clear, warm and pleasant; the boys could take a much needed airing on the hurricane deck.

Feb. 8, Sunday—General Ferry's Division disembarked at noon today; the 39th Illinois volunteers were aboard transports just two weeks, some of the other regiments longer. We had no sooner come ashore, on St. Helena Island, and stacked arms than the scattering in every direction, exploring the Island. Following the example of many comrades, I started out on a ramble of observation. Walking, in an Eastern direction, three miles, we came to Dr. Jenkin's plantation. The doctor left when Port Royal was taken, and the plantation is now inhabited by negroes. Mr. Bryant, and family, a government agent to superintend the negroes, occupy the mansion. This was a fine plantation. The mansion is a fine, large frame building; it is two stories high and a veranda extends along the entire front both above and below. The yard is tastefully arranged, laid off into flower beds and walks. The house stands on a slight eminence. A few rods from the front door runs a creek, to which a wharf is built, for embarking on pleasure excursions. There is a small village of negro quarters. Everything that a southron could desire Dr. Jenkins seems to have had. But now how different! He is a fugitive and a stranger has his plantation! Here is material for reflection. This is a sad spectacle. Negroes cultivate the plantation, under the superintendance of Mr. Bryant, for the government. A school is taught for the colored children by a white lady that they call "Miss Lucy." Asking two boys who made them, one very promptly answered, "Mr. Jenkins, sir." This was my first adventure in South Carolina.[61]

Feb. 9—The day was so warm that it was more pleasant in the shade than in the sun! The nights are damp and cool. Troops were disembarking all day. In the afternoon I was on fatigue. We had to unload commissary stores from a boat. The wharf being incomplete we had to unload with a lighter. The men were compelled to wade knee-deep into the water and haul out cracker boxes, barrels of pork, beef, beans, rice and salt. A pretty rough introduction to soldiering in this Department.

Feb. 10—Some Pennsylvania and New Jersey soldiers got into a row with a lot of negroes, who lived near the encampment of the soldiers. Ten or twelve negro houses were burnt, their corn was destroyed and their hogs killed. The soldiers, generally have a bitter enmity towards the negroes. Any, that plead for even the most common rights of the negro, do so at the risk of their popularity with their comrades. "Damned nigger" is a very common epithet and coupled with it is "Damned Abolishionist." This is true, not of any particular regiments only, but generally so far as my observation extends, which has by no means been limited. The white and the black races cannot live together without serious detriment to both. Wherever they come into contact, the white will be the domineering race.

Feb. 11—The weather seems like summer. I saw negroes making garden today. Young chickens are plenty, the trees are green, the frogs can be heard croaking, snakes are to be found, an alligator was shot today by a soldier and in fact everything has the appearance rather of summer, or at any rate spring, than winter.

Feb. 12—The 39th Regiment Illinois volunteers was paid 4 months' pay today, almost 8 were due to. Each soldier is allowed $42 per year for clothing; the clothes that he draws are charged to him at a fixed price and if he does not get $42 worth he is paid the balance in money at the end of the year: all over $42 per year is retained from his wages. The boys nearly all overrun the $42. Some of the boys got only three or four dollars after settling up their clothing account and paying the sutter, both of which were retained by the pay master.[62]

Feb. 13—"Guards will pass M Sovereign & Randolph to Beaufort and returned this day. Signed: R. C. H. D. M., O.L. Mann, Lieutenant Col. Comd Reg." Furnished with the above pass we set out early in the morning to explore St. Helena Island and to relieve our pockets of some of our "green back" in Beaufort.[63] We took the main road leading from Land's End to Beaufort. The road runs in a northernly direction and is a good sand road. We found it very fatiguing for pedestrians to travel over; nevertheless we, the heroes of a hundred forced marches and fifteen scouts to Blackwater, were able to stretch our bones over three miles per hour. St. Helena Island, in Beaufort District SC, is situated at the mouth of Broad Bay, or as it is put down on some maps Broad River, and is a large island. The Island is elevated 7 or 8 feet above the level of the sea. The surface is level and more than half of it is covered with trees. It is cut up by numerous creeks, which are affected by the tides. At flood tide they are deep and are no insignificant bodies of water but at low tide they are mere sloughs. Much of the surface is taken up by swamps, which are the abode of alligators, frogs and water snakes. The swamps are grown up thickly with tall bull rushes. The soil is very sandy and, to a sucker, looks to be very poor. The most important product of this and the adjacent Islands is sea island cotton; among the other productions are sweet potatoes, corn and oranges. Pigs and chickens are raised in great abundance. The chickens are hatched year round; so that at any time of the year the inhabitants can have young chickens fried! The woods resound with the notes of birds of different plumes. Rabbits, crows and quails afford amusement for the sportsman. Of the trees the famous Palmetto, live oak—valuable for shipbuilding, the green bay spoken of in the Bible and a very pretty evergreen and pine are the most common. The trees are mostly of a scrubby growth. There were many fine plantations on the island. The fine mansions of the planters are occupied by those, who were, a few months ago, their chattels, in many cases. The Government has agents over the island to superintend the negroes. And there are not wanting good ladies, who esteem it a privilege to forge the comforts of home and refined society to teach the children of this long oppressed race of the human family. These teachers are generally highly accomplished young ladies, who might, if they saw fit to remain at home, move in the highest circles of society. To them the path of duty is not only the path of safety but the path of pleasantness also.[64] Ignoring self and turning a deaf ear to the sweet words of society they have nobly come hither to these sandy islands and to this pestiferous climate not to see their own but the good of others. Here is true philanthropy, the practical results of Christianity. Only He that is "Love," the "Great I Am," can reward them. The negroes were preparing the land to plant cotton on; men, women, boys and girls were busily engaged. The land was left from last year's crop thrown up in ridges three and a half feet apart. The only implement used by the hands was a huge hoe. With them negroes were "turning over the ground." They dig down the ridges into the furrows between. This process is neither so good nor expeditious as plowing. The language spoken by these people is a Mongrel English strongly impregnated with negroism, which makes it very difficult to understand.[65] They have scarcely no idea at all about distances. Our colored cook told us that it was nine [miles] from camp to Beaufort. After traveling five or six miles, it was still nine miles to Beaufort. The answers they gave us to inquiries about the road were real amusing. "Hold the main road," said one, "and when you come to the first Church there are two roads; one goes so and one so; don't take the one that goes so but take the one that goes so." "How far is it to Beaufort?" asked we of a stout lad. "Three miles, after you get off dis one mile, sir," answered he. To the same inquiry another answered, "Furder sir." "Well how far?" we asked pressing the question. "I've walked about three miles, sir." "Where did you come from?" "Beaufort, sir." An old man answered the same question thus; "you are purty near to de water, jist go right down dar, sir." These are a few of the ridiculous answers we received, but it is impossible for me to translate them and do justice to "Sambo." One more dialogue I must not omit to give. "How far is it to Beaufort?" "A ways, sir." "About how far?" "Not bery fur, sir, jist right down dar." We passed two churches, at each is a cemetery. The first is in a dense forest. The trees are loaded with long grey moss, the same kind that abounds in North Carolina, which gives to them a mournful appearance.[66] The looks of the place is very appropriate for a burying ground. Even the trees seem to be in sympathy with the bereaved friends of the departed. The church is a neat little building, painted white. The next church is a large brick building; it is now used for a school house. Through the windows we could see alphabetical charts, cards with passages of scripture on them and wreaths of cedar hanging up. On the wall, made in large capitals of cedar boughs, is this inscription, "His people are free."[67] A short distance beyond this church, two white ladies riding in a buggy, with an Ethiopian driver were met by us. We raised our caps and they acknowledged the salute by bowing to us. A little further on we met a fair young lady. She was in a buggy and a young African was sitting at her feet. After her ran two or three dozen black urchins, girls and boys from 7 to 14 years old. She appeared like some fair Diana with her long train of attendants. Rapidly she speeds by, recognizing our salutation by a polite bow. In a moment she is out of sight and we are left in doubt whether or not our eyes have been deceived. But our doubts were dissipated when a negro, who was at work hard by, told us that they were "school misses" to teach the black children to read and write. At 1 o'clock p.m., two hours later than we had counted on, we arrived at Beaufort River opposite to the town of the same name. Owing to some cause the ferry boat was not running today; so we paid a negro 50 cents to take us across the river, which is here about quarter of a mile wide, in a skiff. We went to a dining saloon and ordered some ham and fried eggs, next some baked beans. Apple pies was the next course ordered and lastly plum pudding. We had hot coffee, bread, butter and molasses. After eating till we were full to the tongue we asked for our bill. The proprietor informed us that it was the moderate sum of $1 a piece. We were now ready to attend to other matters. Beaufort, the seat of justice of Beaufort District, South Carolina, is a handsome village and contains a population of about 1500 inhabitants. The streets are regularly laid out and are nicely shaded with China trees, live oak and other kinds. Some of the residences are handsome buildings; they have verandas reaching from the top to the ground. The situation is high. The town is on Port Royal Island. On the approach of the Union troops the inhabitants all, excepting one man, fled. The place is now occupied by Northerners and negroes. Considerable business is done. A weekly paper, "The Free South," is published. After completing all our business we went down to the wharf to see if we could get passage to Hilton Head; in this we were unsuccessful.

The boat was not to go down till morrow morning. We next set ourselves about procuring lodgings for the night. After hunting the town over for a vacant house and finding none, we stopped at the Stevens Hotel, where we had good bed and, therefore, a comfortable night's rest.[68]

Feb. 14—The sergeant of the guard objected to us going on board of the boat because our pass was not signed by the Commanding General of St. Helena Island but he told us that if we would get transportation from the post quartermaster we could go. To get this we had no difficulty whatever. So we went aboard the steamer Wyoming and started for Hilton Head at 8 1/2 o'clock a.m.[69] We had a pleasant ride down to Hilton Head, distant about 15 miles. The shores on either side of the river and bay are low. Several creeks put in, some of which are deep enough for vessels to run up. We saw two schooners apparently standing on the land among the bull rushes, but when nearing them we saw that they were lying in a small creek, which was so narrow that the vessels seemed to reach nearly across it. After a ride of near an hour we arrived at the wharf at Hilton Head, the Wyoming had a flat boat in tow and made slow time. Hilton Head is a point of land, at the junction of Broad Bay with the Ocean, extending out into the water; this is also the name of the Island. The Headquarters of the Department of South Carolina are on Hilton Head Island. There are here Government buildings, sutter's stores, saloons & etc. making quite a business place. There are here large quantities of ordinance and commissary stores. Hilton Head Island is in Beaufort District, South Carolina. It is a low sandy island. The place has been well fortified since its occupation by the Union forces. The wind was blowing hard and the sand was flying, at the time of our visit. To keep men on this island is certainly a punishment which none but scape gallows are worthy of. At 2 o'clock p.m., we took a boat, which runs between this place and Land's End every two hours, to return to camp. The distance across the bay is about six miles. Nothing further of note occurred in this adventure. We arrived safely at camp, 24 hours nearly behind time.

Feb. 15, Sunday—The forces of Foster's Expedition are turned over to Gen. Hunter, Commander of this department. This is the 10th Army Corps. Two Divisions are encamped on St. Helena's island, Naglee's & Ferry's; the former by seniority of rank has command of the forces on the Island. Order was issued on dress parade this evening forbidding officers or privates from leaving the Brigade camp without a pass signed by the commander of the Regiment or Brigade. The innocent have to suffer with the guilty.[70]

Feb. 16—The day was cold and cloudy. Nothing of special interest occurred today. Money seems to be to the boys "The balm of Gilead"; we hear now no grumbling. Since pay day there has been some gambling and drunkeness in camp.

Feb. 17—We were ordered, today, to hold ourselves in readiness to embark at two hours notice.

Feb. 18—The order for us to hold ourselves in readiness to embark at two hour's notice was today suspended and a grand review was ordered tomorrow. Grand reviews are unpopular with the boys and they elicit many curses from them. Some of the regiments embarked but they debarked again and repossessed their former camping grounds. This put them to considerable inconvenience more than merely striking and pitching tents, for a regiment hardly ever breaks up camp but what the boys burn a great amount of stuff useful to a soldier in camp, such as boxes, barrels, wash tubs, boards and bunks. These articles are generally piled promiscuously together and the torch is applied. There was a shower of rain in the forenoon and in the afternoon the sun shone out.

Feb. 19—Heavy canonnading was heard, during the day, in the direction of Savannah; the cause of which was unknown to us. Some conjectured that it was the bombardment of Fort Jackson. Didn't have the "grand review."[71]

Feb. 20—Pleasant weather. Quiet day. Rumor says that Gen. Burnside is to be here in a few days, with his old 9th Army corps, to take command in this Department. This would suit the men of the Department of South Carolina. Hunter may be a good General, for ought I know to the contrary, but he is decidedly unpopular and has not the confidence of the men of his command. That a General may be successful is indispensable that he should have the confidence of his men.

Feb. 21—All quiet today and nothing of special interest to record. New York papers of the 17th instant were received today. Not much news in them. The people of the North are not so united as they ought to be.

Feb. 22, Sunday—Washington's Birthday. The vessels in harbor were decorated with many flags. They presented a gay appearance with the national colors, streamers and signal flags of brilliant hues flying. In the afternoon there was brigade inspection of the second Brigade, preparatory to a "Grand Review."

Feb. 23—The men were ordered to build bunks, at least 8 inches high from the ground. In the afternoon battalion drill and dress parade; thus the record of today.

Feb. 24—There was a grand review today of all the troops on St. Helena Island. At half past ten in the morning the regiments were formed and marched to the ground selected for the review, this was in an old cotton field about two miles from camp. There were present 19 regiments of infantry, no cavalry nor artillery. Gen. Hunter was the reviewing Officer and Gen. Naglee the Commanding. The Brigades were drawn up in columns, the first regiment of a brigade was in front, the second to the rear of this and so on. The next brigade was formed in the same manner, on a line with the first and a few paces to the left. The same arrangement held all through. When the several brigades were thus formed the men were ordered to rest at will. Near 15 minutes elapsed before Gen. Hunter came on the field. But when he "hove in sight," the command "attention battalion" was passed along the lines. First the command was given by the General commanding in the field, then by the Generals of divisions, next by brigade commanders, then by Colonels of the regiments and lastly by the Captains. The ranks of the regiments were opened and when General Hunter arrived within a few paces of the center of the first regiment of the brigade the command present arms was given when each rank of all the regiments presented arms, the colors dropped, the officers saluted and the drums beat. General Hunter acknowledged the Salute by taking off his hat. He then wheeled his horse around and passed back to the right of regiment and down in front of it between the line Officers and the front rank; he rode in a slow walk and seemed to look at each soldier individually. After riding in front he passed along in the rear and thus he reviewed each regiment and each individual Soldier. This part done, the Gen. took his position and the following commands were given and executed; "Battalion, Close order, march, By companies right wheel, march, right dress, march in review, forward, guide right, march." Thus we marched, describing a parallelogram. At the center of the second side described was the position of General Hunter. There he sat on his horse, just outside of the geometrical figure above referred to. A few paces in the rear was his staff. While the regiments were passing he uncovered his head and sat with hat in hand. Passing in review was the closing scene of the exercise. This was not so grand and pompous as some other reviews I have taken part in, but there was certainly more common sense by far in it than I have ever witnessed. There were present quite a number of Officers of the Navy. Of Hunter's personal appearance, I would simply say that he exactly comes up to the idea I had formed of a General, when a child, from pictures in Geographics and school Histories.

Feb. 25—All quiet during the day, on St. Helena Island. Distant firing heard in a Southwesternly direction. At night we were lulled to sleep by the roaring of the Atlantic Ocean.

Feb. 26—The birds were singing gaily, early this morning, and everything wore the appearance of Spring. The grass growing, the trees budding and a soft breeze blowing, oh how delightful! The 176 Regiment Pennsylvania left for Beaufort, SC, and the 39th Regiment Illinois Volunteers was ordered to plant shade trees in front of their tents.

Feb. 27—On guard. Three Corporals elected in Company I. Not present and did not know anything about it till election was over.

Feb. 28—Mustered for pay this morning. Drum Major Hallowell was shot in the leg. The ball passed through the fleshy part of the leg above the knee. A soldier of the 62nd Ohio had a pistol apart showing it and the Drum Major was sitting nearby when the pistol accidentally went off and inflicted a flesh wound.

March 1, Sunday—We received the mail this afternoon. The North is divided! Traitors are tolerated in Illinois! There are unmistakable evidences of an attempt being plotted to unite the Northwest with the South. Vile miscreants are openly advocating this measure. The prospect of restoring the Union to its pristine glory is good in the field, but at home the prospect is gloomy. May the country be saved from ruin.[72]

Mar. 2—On fatigue today. Had to load commissaries stores from the bark Milton on the transport Collins and the steamer Convoy. Put ten day's rations for 350 men on the Collins. On the Collins was a striped pig. The stripes were parallel to the spinal column. The pig was of a bluish color and the stripes grayish. "The striped pig" was the butt end of a considerable merriment when I told my mess mates of it after returning to camp. "Are you sure it was a pig?" "And it was a striped pig?" "Was it an orphan pig?" The above is specimen of questions asked about the pig.[73]

Mar. 3—Col. Osborn made a patriotic speech to the 39th Regiment Illinois Volunteers. No sacrifice, he thought, was too great to make for the preservation of the Union. He was willing to fight Northern traitors as well as Southern rebels. A series of resolutions, to the same purport, were read and adopted unanimously by a *viva voce* of the regiment. No disloyal sentiment can find lodgement in the 39th Illinois, unless perchance it be in the dark corner of some coward's heart. Heavy cannonading was heard all through the night, in a southwest direction.

Mar. 4—Regular routine of camp duty. Day and night cool.

Mar. 5—Had to guard beef cattle tonight. Moon full and calm weather. Harbor by moonlight beautiful. Pleasant reflections and good resolves. *Crux Christi est sola mea spes. Deo et Filis* [the Cross of Christ is my only hope, God and Son].

Mar. 6—Beautiful morning. Within all is peace and calmness. By faith in the Redeemer we will one day be able to exclaim "Thanks be to God who giveth us the victory." O blessed thought worth more than all the World can give. Finished reading the memoirs of Captain Hedley Vicars of the English army. He warred not only against the enemies of his country but also against the common enemy of mankind, even Satan. The victory was his through the blood of Christ. O that there were more such soldiers, in the Union army, as he was! Then could we go forth in the name of the God of hosts to battle for our country.[74]

Mar. 7—Took a walk out to a plantation this afternoon, and saw a negro grinding corn. The mill, I suppose, was the same kind as those used in the days of Abraham. A round stone, about 3 feet in diameter, is fastened in a box and on this another stone, of the same size, is placed. In the center of the upper stone is a hole way into which the corn is poured, there is also another hole cut half through the stone, in which a stake is placed upright for a handle. About one pint of corn is poured in at a time and a man takes hold of the handle and turns the upper stone upon the nether. The meal works out into the box and, when it is full, the meal is taken out and put into a sack. Such is the manner of grinding corn in aristocratic South Carolina, in the year of our Lord, one thousand eight hundred and sixty-three! One hand can grind three bushels per day.

Mar. 8, Sunday—There was a prayer meeting this evening of a few boys of the 39th Illinois. Mr. Brown, who is in the services of the Christian Commission, was present and opened the meeting by reading the 7th of Matthew. There are but few in this regiment who have been kept steadfast to the Cross of Christ. Alas how few! Yet there are some who have not polluted their garments.[75]

Mar. 9—Nothing more than the regular routine of camp duty.

Mar. 10—On brigade guard. A bird serenaded me while on duty as a sentinel tonight. Received mail today.

Mar. 11—Brigade drill this afternoon by Colonel Osborn.

Mar. 12—Warm days and cool damp nights. Some of the regiments on the island have been practicing embarking and loading in small boats. We expect to have to land under the fire of the enemy.

Mar. 13—The widow of the late General Lander was presented to the 39th Illinois and 62nd Ohio regiments this afternoon. The boys gave three cheers for the lady.[76]

Mar. 14—On brigade guard today. Rather often on duty. "It is an evil wind that blows no body any good." By being on guard today I missed a hard job. The 39th Illinois practiced disembarking in small boats; the boys to jump out of the boats, when they got near the shore, and wade to land & form in line of battle.

Mar. 15, Sunday—In the afternoon Dr. Croshers taught a Bible class and in the evening there was a prayer meeting. Lieutenant Col. Mann was present at the meeting and led in prayer and spoke. Dr. Croshers is the second assistant surgeon of the Regiment; he was sent to us while we were encamped at Suffolk and a short time before we left there. He seems to be an active Christian. The prayer meetings and Sunday school were held under two live oak trees. These trees have wide spreading tops and the branches are very thick. They resemble, in shape, large apple trees. Two of them, growing near each other and overlapping their tops, form the shelter beneath which a few, who amidst the sins and vices of camp have remained steadfast in the faith, meet to worship God. There seems to be a feeling in the regiment of the need of something more than mere human supports in these times that try men's souls. Lord, help us to be watchful.[77]

Mar. 16—Nothing more than common today. Warm & sand blowing.

Mar. 17—Nothing worthy of note.

Mar. 18—On regimental guard.

Mar. 19—All quiet. No visible prospect of the expedition leaving here soon. There seems to be but one opinion here as to the future movements of the expedition that has been here for some weeks past; the prevalent opinion is that Charleston is to be attacked. Seven or eight of the new iron clad boats, "Monitors," have been lying in the harbor for some time.

Mar. 20—Took a walk this afternoon to the Navy yard, which is on a creek emptying into the harbor above Bay Point. The Montauk & two of her sisters were lying up the creek. Could see the dents in the turret of the Montauk at Fort McAllister; her smoke stack was riddled. Day cloudy. Camp life is again becoming monotonous.[78]

Mar. 21—The day was cool & rainy. It was very disagreeable to be penned up in our tents without the means of keeping comfortably warm unless we went to bed. To relieve the despondency of the day a mail was received.

Mar. 22, Sunday—On brigade guard. The weather cleared off and in the afternoon the day was pleasant.

Mar. 23—Today was remarkable as being one year from the battle of Winchester, VA. Pleasant weather again. The 100th NY Regiment left today on transports; destination said to be Coal Island, above Charleston.[79]

Mar. 24—A party of us started on an excursion to Shell Island, this morning, but we did not get a boat and we had to return to camp. This was to be regretted on account of the difficulty of getting a pass signed by the Colonel and approved by the Brigadier General. The day was very rainy.

Mar. 25—The regiment was inspected, this morning, by Colonel Osborn. The Colonel was more critical than common about the arms, clothes and equipments. The weather was fine again. There is not so much despondency among the soldiers as there was one month ago.

Mar. 26—General Hunter reviewed the troops on St. Helena Island today. There were present at the review 12 regiments, all infantry. There was an order issued today, by General Hunter, attaching the 85th Regiment Pennsylvania Volunteers to the brigade, at present commanded by Colonel Osborn, and giving Colonel Howell, of the 85th PA, command of the brigade which is thus composed of the 39th Illinois, 62nd & 67 Ohio and the 85th PA Regiments. Colonel Osborn, I suppose, will take command of the 39th Illinois again. The above is the military record of the day. There was a prayer meeting this evening under the live oak trees.

Mar. 27—On guard today. Saw the iron-clad Keokuk lying in the harbor; she has two turrets. General Steven's brigade embarked last night & this morning. Stood on my beat at night and talked Spanish to the man in the moon.[80]

Mar. 28—Nothing to chronicle of importance. Day warm & clear.

Mar. 29, Sunday—Rained all day without cessation. Thunder & lightning in the morning. Heavy gales of wind through the night. Tent leaked so that it made a very good shower bath.

Mar. 30—Cold & windy. More like a day in February than March.

Mar. 31—The day was disagreeably cold, though not freezing. There is prospect of soon moving from here. We are ordered to embark instanter. "Charleston" is in the mouth of every body. May it soon fall is the wish of all loyal persons. From all appearances April will not pass off so peaceably as March. We are now doubtless on the eve of important events. Our success will be as God wills, and we are encouraged by the thought that He is interested in the affairs of men and is ever on the side of right.

End of Volume 4

Volume 5

FOLLY ISLAND, SOUTH CAROLINA, APRIL–AUGUST 1863

On April 3, 1863, after nearly a year of preparation, Rear Admiral Samuel Francis Du Pont took his ironclad squadron out of Port Royal Sound to attack Charleston Harbor. That night, the vessels anchored in North Edisto Inlet where Du Pont and his captains made their final plans. General David Hunter joined the navy at North Edisto Inlet with army transports carrying nearly ten thousand soldiers. His bickering with General Foster had sabotaged any active role for the army, but Hunter did plan to land troops on some of the outlying islands south of Charleston Harbor in order to be in a position to occupy Charleston once the ironclads captured the city.

On April 4, the Thirty-ninth Illinois, along with elements of General Ferry's division, landed on Cole's Island where the men threw up new entrenchments. The following evening, as the ironclads prepared to cross the bar and enter Charleston Harbor, the Federal soldiers were shipped from Cole's Island to neighboring Folly Island, a seven-mile-long barrier island covered by sand dunes and dense pine and palmetto growths. Over the next two days, the soldiers moved to the island's northern end and looked across Lighthouse Inlet to the Confederate positions on Morris Island, a fortified island that made up the outer, southern lip of Charleston Harbor. From their vantage point on Folly, on April 7, the Federals were also able to watch the naval attack against the harbor's fortifications. Du Pont and his commanders, unwilling to take their vessels through the Confederate obstructions running from Fort Sumter across the ship channel to Sullivan's Island, turned back and, after a fruitless bombardment of Fort Sumter, withdrew.

With the ironclads retreating, the Union soldiers pulled back three miles and constructed a line of entrenchments across the island. The failure of Du Pont's attack and Hunter's obvious inability to initiate any land assault prompted officials in Washington to revamp their plans. While the Army and Navy departments searched for new commanders, Hunter was ordered to maintain his positions off Charleston and Du Pont was instructed to keep his ironclads ready for future operations.

By May of 1863, new commanders had been selected and a campaign planned. Brigadier General Quincy A. Gillmore led the army, and Rear Admiral John Dahlgren took command of the navy. The operation called for the use of Folly Island as a jumping-off point to capture Morris Island.

Once the island was secured, breaching batteries would be built at its tip, Cumming's Point, which was a mere one-half mile from Fort Sumter. After Fort Sumter was bombarded and captured and the harbor obstructions removed, according to plan, the ironclads would enter the harbor and capture Charleston.

On July 10, 1863, after building masked batteries on the northern end of Folly Island, the Federals launched an amphibious assault against Morris Island. Under cover of fire from the Union ironclads, the landing force overran the Confederate batteries at Lighthouse Inlet, but they could not capture the whole island because of Battery Wagner, a strong earthwork stretching across it. On July 11, an assault on the barrier failed. A second and larger attack launched on July 18 and spearheaded by the Fifty-fourth Massachusetts, a regiment of white officers and African American soldiers, was also defeated. The attacking force suffered severe casualties; and the Thirty-ninth Illinois, which had been held in reserve during the campaign, was shifted from Folly Island to Morris Island in case the Confederates launched a counterattack.

No such attack occurred, but Gillmore, denied access to Cumming's Point, opened siege against Wagner and began the construction of breaching batteries in the center of Morris Island, two miles from Fort Sumter. The work was hard and hot. The soldiers soon came to refer to their shovels and spades as Gillmore rifles. Most of the time the Illinois men served in fatigue parties digging zigzag trenches toward Battery Wagner. The Thirty-ninth also provided guards to watch for Confederate sorties. The sick roles increased, but the men kept on working. At last, on August 17, 1863, the Federals opened their bombardment of Fort Sumter. Seven days later, although it was destroyed as an artillery position, the Confederates still refused to surrender the fort.

Facing Fort Sumter's defiance, Gillmore pushed siege lines toward Battery Wagner, hoping to capture the battery and the rest of Morris Island so that he could launch an amphibious assault on Sumter, capture the fort, and remove the obstructions for the naval attack. The soldiers returned to their digging in the island's hot sands. In late August, the Federals reached and overran Confederate rifle pits a mere two hundred yards from Battery Wagner. The rifle pits were quickly converted into a siege parallel as the soldiers continued their trenching toward Wagner. —*S.R.W.*

★ ★ ★ ★ ★

> —What things, a soldier of Co. I, 39th Regiment Illinois Volunteers, did, saw and heard are herein briefly set forth. It was his constant endeavor that nothing but truth should escape his pen.

April 1st—All quiet in the forenoon; in the afternoon orders to hold ourselves in readiness to embark at any minute. Some of the regiments in

Howell's brigade embarked in the evening.[1] At dark we received orders to "strike tents." Then followed a scene of busy excitement such as is to be witnessed on no other occasion than that of breaking up camp. There was a grand display of pyrotechnics; the burning of boxes, barrels, boards and other things, which soldiers soon accumulate after being in camp and which they have to leave when a movement is ordered, made a beautiful illumination. But the uncertainty of the immediate future robs the soldier of the greater part of the enjoyment of the beautiful & the grand. After tents were struck "the order was countermanded" & we bivouacked for the night.

Apr. 2—Reveille at 4 1/2 o'clock a.m. Went aboard the New England soon after sun up. She was the flagship of the Division. We went out opposite to Bay Point and then turned the boat around & went back almost to the wharf where embarked; here we lay till in the afternoon and then run out and anchored off Hilton Head. Soon after dark we weighed anchor and went to sea. Rough sea & some of us sick. We had in tow a flat boat & 8 surf boats on it.[2]

Apr. 3—At daylight we lay off the mouth of Stono River. We run back to Edisto River and up it a mile or two and at 8 o'clock we cast anchor here and lay till the following morning. Here we discharged part of our baggage on the T. F. Secor & Harriet A. Weed. There were lying in the river 7 monitors, two wooden gun boats and some other vessels. There was a camp of soldiers on Edisto Island.[3]

Apr. 4—About 8 o'clock a.m., we started out and up to Stono inlet. At 11 o'clock a.m., we disembarked in surf boats on Cole's Island. The 100th NY Regiment was encamped here having preceeded us a few days. After Howell's brigade had disembarked there were 5 regiments on the island. Pitched our tents on a rebel camping ground. The enemy half a mile from us.

Apr. 5, Sunday—"The sunny South" has a very treacherous climate. We may go to bed and be very comfortable without any covering but before morning two woolen blankets will not keep us warm. Last night was warm when we went to bed but before morning we were shivering under two blankets and the ground was white with frost. Cole's Island is low and sandy. A few rods back from the Inlet the land is marshy. The shores are lined with batteries, some of which appear to be of quite an ancient date. Fragments of shells are lying around within and back of the batteries. The works are completely dismantled. On the opposite side of Stono Inlet from here is Kiawah Island and on the same side of the inlet as Cole's Island, next to the ocean, is Folly Island. Back about two miles from where we landed is a small village, the name of which I could not learn.[4] Soon after dark tonight we moved our camp down near the shore. A few hours later we were ordered to prepare to march with a day & half rations in our haversacks. At midnight we marched to where we disembarked and went aboard the small steamer Harriet A. Weed and a flat boat towed by her. We were landed on Folly Island about one mile from our camp. The steamer run so near the shore that gang planks were shoved out from the flat boat to the land; so we disembarked dry shod. The rest of the night was spent in marching along the beach, a distance of half a mile and there about face & march back & so on.

Apr. 6—At daylight we started on the march following the beach, in a northeastern direction. There were four regiments, the 85th PA, 100th NY, 62nd Ohio, 39th Illinois, one company of NY engineers & three pieces of marine artillery commanded by a master of the Navy.[5] The whole force was under the command of Colonel Howell. There were no horses along, the officers all walked and the artillery was drawn by men. The sand on the beach was solid and smooth, being over flowed by the tide. We marched to the music of the Atlantic Ocean. At noon we halted to get dinner and to rest, having to lug our knapsacks we were prepared to appreciate an hour or two of rest and more so from the fact that we had but little sleep last night. In the middle of the afternoon we halted till in the night, preferring to making night attack should we find the enemy. We stacked our arms about 100 yards from the Ocean as it then was and some of us betook ourselves to sleep and some to eating, some to reading and some to writing. By night fall we all had advanced far into the interior of the "Land of Nod." At nine o'clock the Atlantic began, as we thought, to infringe upon our rights. Our guns were over-flowed by the tide as were also the beds of some of the boys. Up we had to jump and take the guns out of the water. Then followed considerable confusion but things were soon put to rights and quiet again reigned. We were not disturbed again till midnight, when the tide had subsided and the moon was up, then we were called up to go forth to meet the enemies of our country but the sequel of this shall be recorded tomorrow, if spared to tell the tale. Folly Island, in Charleston District SC, is about 7 miles long & one mile wide. It lies in a northeast & southwest direction and has the Atlantic Ocean on the east. The greater part of the island is covered with trees, consisting mostly of tall pitch pine and Palmetto, live oak, green Bay and occasionally a cedar. There is a dense undergrowth of brush, thorn bushes and briars. The surface is uneven there being high ridges and deep ravines, with here and there a small marshy tract. Each end of the island is barren of any vegetation save a few stunted bushes. The sand is drifted into hills and, being white, after night resembles huge snow banks. There is but one plantation on it, the rest is in a virgin state. There are no roads and on the beach is the only passable way of going up or down the island; this way can only be traveled at low tide. Along the seashore the sand is drifted up into a ridge from 20 to 50 feet high & about 20 feet wide; this looks very much like a breastwork thrown up by man. Back of this ridge is a ravine. Water is very scarce, in fact good water is not to be obtained on the island. The weary soldier is doomed to march along the Atlantic Ocean, suffering & panting for water. Tantalus like he thirsts beside much water. The only way to procure fresh water is to carry spades and dig wells, which can be done in a few minutes. The water is near the top of the ground. We saw no animals and but few birds on the island. Albatrosses fly along the coast, or at least a bird said to be the Albatross.[6]

Apr. 7—We proceeded cautiously along the wet beach at trail arms. This being the second night without much sleep, the boys were very much fatigued. We frequently halted and, notwithstanding the night was chilly, the boys threw themselves down on the wet sand and in a few minutes would drop off to sleep. When the order forward was given the boys would wake up cold and chilly. A short time before daylight we halted and many of us soon fell asleep but we were suddenly aroused, changed front to the rear and deployed a company as skirmishers also one company was deployed and sent forward. Things looked rather squally to one just awoke from a poor nap, enemy both in front and rear! We began to see visions of blood, which fortunately were not realized. Our skirmishers found no enemy neither in the front nor rear. And now having scoured the island from one end to the other, and having found no enemy, the object of the expedition was accomplished and we returned one & a half up and bivouaced. The rest of the day was spent in seeing rather than doing. Fort Sumpter plainly to be seen and the flag on it. Outside the harbor, a few miles, was lying the blockading squadron. Between this and the entrance to the harbor were lying 8 monitors and the New Ironsides.[7] In the forenoon there were a few shots fired by the rebels from shore batteries. The distance from where we were to Fort Sumpter was about 6 miles. After 2 o'clock p.m., the Monitors & Ironsides headed in towards the harbor and, at 3 o'clock p.m., they passed in and the ball was opened. The rebels fired from batteries along from the entrance to the harbor above Fort Sumpter. It did not seem to be the object of our iron-clads to silence the guns of the enemy; they did but a small part of the firing. Yet occasionally we could see a column of smoke rise from the water and in a few instances shells burst over Fort Sumpter. More firing than from any other one quarter was done from Fort Sumpter and that from the *in barbette* guns.[8] We could see the water fly where the cannon balls struck it. Fort Sumpter was enveloped in a cloud of smoke. We could at one time see a vessel under the walls of the fort but we could not make out whether she was a rebel ram or one of the Monitors. A heavy cannonade was kept up for two hours, when the firing almost ceased. We could feel the air vibrate when some of the heaviest guns were discharged. Four of our ironsides were seen to run out of the harbor. There was some random firing in the night. Such were the things seen by us today. We had an excellent night's sleep.

Apr. 8—Not much firing from the rebel forts. The Keokuk is believed to have sunk outside the harbor, not certain. Received mail. In afternoon went down beach to haul up a battery of artillery. Drawed up battery F

3rd NY, 12 pounder Wiard guns. Drew them up behind the timber to conceal them from enemy. Intended to plant them in the night. Kept 39th Illinois up all night to do it. Tide so high had to wait for it to subside; this about 2 o'clock a.m. Men went down to the end of island, next to Morrisons island, to throw up earth works. Did not place the battery in position after keeping us all night shivering around without blankets. Heard some firing in Charleston Harbor late in the night.[9]

Apr. 9—Before daylight moved three miles up the island & half mile back from ocean and paused for a while. Fine day. Nights cool & chilly. Good rest today. Animated with the hope that Charleston, the Great Babylon of the South, will soon fall.

Apr. 10—Still remained in bivouac today. The place is on a ridge covered with a dense growth of small live oak bushes and other tangled brush. The boys trim out the bushes and briars and level down the ground to make their beds. They mat the tops of the bushes together, which shelters them from the heavy dews. There are no tents not even for the officers, they (tents) were left on Cole's Island. The beds of the boys look very much like the beds which rabbits make under a bunch of grass or in a brush heap. Some firing, but not much.

Apr. 11—Received heavy mail this morning. Strange how our letters and papers ever find the way to us in this wilderness place; the good mail-ships bring them safely through. Last night a body of rebels crossed over from Morrison's Island and fired on our pickets, wounded one man and took two prisoners.[10] Our men, according to orders, did not return the fire. The 39th Illinois Regiment thoroughly scoured Folly Island this afternoon. The Regiment was deployed entirely across it and skirmished through the woods. No one can form an idea of the density of the undergrowth. The vines and brush on the island are so thick and tangled that it is impossible for a man to crawl through. Our clothes and hides were torn and scratched terribly.

Apr. 12, Sunday—39th Regiment went to the upper end of the island and relieved the 100th NY on duty as the vanguard there. I was sent out on picket. All quiet through the day. Saw fires on the upper end of Morrison's Island, like burning the stuff of a camp when it is left. Heard rebel drums at sundown. Our post was in a grove of timber on the edge of a marsh & creek between Folly & Morrison's Islands. At ten in the night heard the splashing of the oars of a boat. We took position along the edge of the woods and waited the arrival of the rebels; they did not come. Saw signal lights in the City and vicinity of Charleston. Fleet off Charleston left tonight.

Apr. 13—Heard drums beating in camp of enemy from daylight till sundown, without any cessation. Relieved late in the evening and sent out with the company for reserve picket. Capt. Co. I, 62nd Ohio was shot tonight. He was going to another officers post and got lost. Coming near a vedette the sentinel challenged him; he turned and started back the way that he came from instead of halting as he should. The sentinel discharged his piece at him which inflicted a mortal wound. The Captain soon after died.[11] A few days ago the same regiment was drawing some artillery; the boys started off on the double quick when one fell down and the cannon was drawn over him crushing him to death instantly. Two men of the 62nd were severely wounded by the explosion of a shell which they supposed to be empty. Thus has the regiment suffered in accidents which ought to have been avoided, all since we have been on Folly Island.

Apr. 14—Rainy gloomy day. News from the North is received very irregularly. Company sent out on this evening to be gone for several days. Night dark and rainy. Saw rockets thrown up from Fort Sumpter & Charleston. Posted on the extreme northeastern end of the island. All quiet through tonight.

Apr. 15—Rebels came down on the opposite bank of the river. Some of the boys talked to them. All right today.

Apr. 16—Warm weather and plenty of gnats. These gnats are very annoying, they have sharp bills. On picket tonight; saw rockets & signal lights and heard the tattoo of the rebels. All quiet.

Apr. 17—Cole's Island is evacuated by our forces. Our brigade, on Folly island, is all of Union force in front of Charleston at present. The attack has, for the present at least, been abandoned. One of our gun boats threw a few shells on James Island this afternoon.

Apr. 18—The gnats swarm around so thick at times, that we can scarcely breathe without brushing them away. These insects are about the size of a small pin head. Noiselessly they light on the skin of the victim and the first warning that he has of their proximity is a keen sensation like a cambric needle pricking him. Compared with these gnats, mosquitoes are a luxury to be enjoyed rather than dreaded.[12] The latter give due notice before they make an attack and one is thus prepared for the onset; the former do not make the least noise and therefore take one by surprise. The wood ticks are also very numerous and troublesome; they stick so close to the skin that they can hardly be pulled off. Although we are in sight of the rebels they give us far less trouble than the gnats, mosquitoes and wood ticks. One of our boys exchanged papers with the rebels today; they came across in a boat. On picket today; stood on post till midnight. Saw rockets, other lights and heard the tattoo of the rebels. Three volleys of musketry were fired tonight below one mile and one cannon shot off Charleston; suppose a vessel was trying to run the blockade.

Apr. 19, Sunday—Read 21 chapters in the Bible, learned the three conjugations of the Spanish verb and read a lesson in the Spanish reader. Day as well spent as could be expected, in the woods among the gnats, mosquitoes & woodticks. We were relieved from picket this evening, by Co. D. 39th Illinois, and went back to where the Regiment is bivouacing.

Apr. 20—Our regiment was paid four months wages today by Major Mason. There are, at this time, 5 regiments on this island; they are here in sight of Fort Sumpter, in the presence of an overwhelming force of the enemy. All quiet today.[13]

Apr. 21—We daily hear two guns fired from Fort Sumpter, one at sun up and the other at sun down. The flag which floats over this fortress is plainly visible; O how long shall we be taunted by seeing this emblem of treason displayed there! To die in honorable conflict would be sweeter than to be kept here inactive on the brink of this Gehenna Puros [pure hell, a state of pure misery].

Apr. 22—Folly Island is being fortified. A line of rifle pits extend across the island and there are a few pieces of artillery planted behind sand banks. Roads are being constructed and there is a lookout, in the top of a pine tree, 80 feet high. The engineer corps have made four pieces of cannon of Palmetto logs and painted them black; they are not yet mounted!

Apr. 23—On duty every day, either picket, camp guard or fatigue.

Apr. 24—Nothing noteworthy.

Apr. 25—Fine weather and pleasant night. Fatigue, picket, and camp guard duty in abundance to do.

Apr. 26, Sunday—Got a heavy mail and New York papers of the 14th instant; these contained the first account of the bombardment of Fort Sumpter on the 7th, which we had seen. Although we were eye witnesses of the action, we did not learn the result till we saw New York papers of the above date. It had for some time previous been an undisputed fact that the Keokuk was sunk.

Apr. 27—Beautiful calm morning. All is yet quiet but an attack at any time would not surprise us.

Apr. 28—Stormy day, rain and wind. Nothing new on the Tapis. For two or three weeks Brigadier General Vodges has had command of this brigade; he is in command on Folly Island.[14]

Apr. 29—Pleasant weather. Great dearth of anything exciting or interesting. Rained at night.

Apr. 30—Mustered in for pay. Two regiments, the 4th NH & 6th Conn, landed on the island.

May 1—Walked down to Stono inlet, "Point of the Island." J. E. Hallowell, of the 39th Drum Corps prepared dinner for us; he had biscuits warm, butter, molasses, meat, tea, coffee & sugar. A good dinner to us was this.[15]

May 2—On picket today. Gnats very bad at night.

May 3, Sunday—Relieved from picket in the forenoon and returned to camp. Attended a prayer meeting in the woods at night.

May 4—Rainy in the forenoon but cleared off in the afternoon. Day passed off quietly. There has been a great deal of gambling since last pay day, far more than ever before. Boys that a few months ago would have scorned the thought of being called gamblers, now without shame engage in this business. "O how are the mighty fallen!"

May 5—Clear in the forenoon and rainy in the afternoon. Dress parade at 10 o'clock a.m. Company I on patrol at night.

May 6—The trees have put on a new coat of leaves since we came on this island. The live oak has shed off its last year's leaves and is now decorated with a new dress. The pines look brighter and are far more beautiful than they were; they have a fresh green look. There is scarcely the image of a flower to be found on the island. Berries and wild fruits of any kind are very scarce. There is but little to adorn or render the island interesting aside from the curious specimens of the vegetable kingdom.

May 7—The ocean is yearly encroaching upon Folly Island and gradually washing it away. There are trees lying along the beach which have been washed up. Others are yet standing on the brink of the ocean almost, as it were, vedettes of the forest. The sand is washed away from them; they have ceased to put forth their leaves and they soon will have to bow to the Atlantic.

May 8—I was on fatigue today and was engaged in throwing up a battery on a little mound. Three inches from the top of the ground the mound is a bed of shells, mostly oyster; there were a few conch shells found. We also found small pieces of earthen vessels. This doubtless has been a camping ground for the Indians. It is evident that these shells have been here a long time from the fact that the mound is covered with trees; some of which are quite large. The few inches of soil on top is composed mostly of vegetable matter.

May 9—Went to the Point of the island. Saw some ripe black berries. The Point is being fortified.[16]

May 10, Sunday—Received a heavy mail, New York papers of the 7th instant. Hard fighting at Fredericksburg, VA. Prospect of a great victory. Preaching in afternoon by Chaplain of 62nd Ohio volunteers. Text, "Wisdom is better than weapons of war."[17]

May 11—On fatigue again. Fortifying, boating lookout & clearing off island. On last Friday night power blockading squadron, off Charleston, captured two vessels laden with cotton, trying to run out.

May 12—A vessel run the blockade tonight. Several shots were fired at her but she succeeded in getting into the harbor.[18]

May 13—At the lower end of the island today, a shark was caught. It got into shoal water by venturing up too far at high tide and at ebb tide it got stranded. The boys waded in and killed it with an ax. One man of the 62nd Ohio Regiment was severely wounded in the affair by the shark. The weight of it was upwards 300 pounds and the bones carried away as trophies.

May 14—The flag on Fort Sumpter was at half mast today. A rebel deserter reports that Stonewall Jackson was killed on the Rappahannock.[19]

May 15—On picket. At 10 o'clock in the night there was heavy firing from the blockading squadron. The cause and result, we since learned, was a fleet of vessels came out from Charleston to run the blockade and three large steamers were successful. The night was dark and rainy.

May 16—Rainy day. In the afternoon 4 Rebel vessels came up a creek, which empties into Charleston Harbor, in sight. Could not tell whether they were rams or transports. Firing at night by blockading squadron.

May 17, Sunday—Fine day. Rebels at work on Coles Island were effectively shelled late this afternoon. They skedaddled.

May 18—Dress parade at 8 o'clock a.m., as usual. Regimental inspection at 10 a.m. Clear day. Anxious to get the news. Have not heard anything reliable from the Army of the Potomac for two weeks.

May 19—Regiment on fatigue. Got a mail. News indefinite. Ten men started home on 30 days furlough.

May 20—Blockade running, or rather attempts to run it, are of almost nightly occurrence. The Rebel pickets on Morris Island tell us that they have a new General over there, General Starvation.

May 21—We can hear firing every night, at the blockading fleet off Charleston, but cannot hear anything reliable as to the cause. Five companies, 39th Illinois Regiment went out on picket this evening to be gone five days. Post in woods opposite to lower end of Morris Island. First night all quiet.

May 22—Rebel camps in sight. On duty almost under the mouths of the enemy's cannon. Second night all quiet.

May 23, Sunday—Saw steamer running from Fort Sumpter to Charleston, perhaps carrying some of our rebel brethren to church. Third night quiet, excepting some blockade running.

May 24—Heavy gale blew away the gnats and mosquitoes and thus relieved us of a great annoyance. Fourth night quiet.

May 25—Nothing remarkable. Heavy gale still blowing. Fifth night quiet.

May 26—Cloudy and high wind today. Relieved this evening by 67 Ohio Volunteers. Just across the river from us we saw about 50 men of the enemy at work throwing up earth works. Our five days picket are ended & glad are we.

May 27—Heavy gale and rain. It is far more pleasant to stand on the beach and witness the fury of the Ocean than it would be at sea tossed by the waves and made the sport of the Storm King. In the former case there are no such peculiar sensations in the stomach as there are in the latter.

May 28—Storm still rages. Nothing remarkable, as usual all quiet.

May 29—Storm subsided enough for the mail boat to come from Hilton Head. So we received our mail which was due one week ago.

May 30—The sea was rough this morning. The record of the day is sad. One of our best soldiers was drowned, this morning, whilst bathing in the ocean. The tide was going out at the time and he, venturing too far from land, was unable to get back. In spite of all his efforts the tide carried him further and further out to sea. Two of the boys swam out to him but to save themselves had to leave him in a drowning condition. An effort was then made for some men to go out to him holding to a long rope, but they were too late. I was in my tent when I heard a frightful screaming, as one in intense agony, and soon word flew along that a man was drowning. When I reached the beach he had ceased screaming and in less than a minute after sunk to rise no more. Thus passed away I. S. Baker of Co. I, 39th Regiment Illinois Volunteers. He was highly respected and dearly beloved by all of his comrades. In an hour and a half after he sunk, his body drifted ashore and was procured.[20]

May 31, Sunday—Attended the funeral of our comrade this morning. A little more than twenty-four hours ago he was with us lively and full of hope. Little did he think that his place in the ranks would soon be vacant. But alas how vain are all human calculations! Surely "All flesh is grass." How important then to be ready for that great and awful change. "My Soul be on thy guard." The day was beautiful and the sea was beginning to grow calm.

June 1—On picket. All quiet. Saw rockets thrown up by rebels.

June 2—Relieved at 10:00 a.m., and came to camp.

June 3—Calm day.

June 4—Regiment on fatigue.

June 5—*No tengo que escriber hoy nada* [I have nothing to write about today].

June 6—On camp guard. Mail received.

June 7, Sunday—Hot.

June 8—Nothing of special interest today.

June 9—*Nada hoy que quiero escriber hoy. Todo quieto* [nothing today to write about today. All is quiet].

June 10—100 men of 39th Illinois on sick list this morning.

June 11—Last night a vessel, trying to run the blockade into Charleston, was run aground off the upper end of Folly Island and being set on fire was deserted by her crew, who escaped to Morris Island. She was a two mast steamer with two engines. She was from the West Indies and loaded with tropical fruits and liquors. The fire did not make much headway; it went out or was put out before it got forward the smokestacks.[21] In the evening our men fired a few shots at the ship from the battery in front of our camp. The rebels retaliated by shelling the woods where our pickets were. One negro was killed by a shell; this was all the damage they did us. Five companies of 39th Illinois volunteers went on picket this evening to be gone five days. A party from the 39th Illinois Regiment boarded the grounded blockade runner tonight; they returned safely. A second party went on her, a short time before day, who were less successful. Their surf boat got loose and left them on the wreck.

June 12—Some of the men, left on the wreck last night, swam ashore this morning but four men and sergeant, all of Co. F. 39th Illinois, remained on board all day. It was impossible to send a boat to their relief on account of the rebel batteries on Morris Island. At night they made a raft of plank and succeeded in getting ashore at midnight. A boat was being sent to them when they landed. A little before 5:00 this evening an artillery fight was commenced between the boys of Folly & Morris Islands. The Morris boys paid their respects chiefly to our pickets on the end of Folly Island. But few of their shells struck in our camp although several fell just a few rods in front of our breast works. One shell went schrieking through the air over our heads and lit near the 67 Ohio, cutting away a limb from the top of a pine tree. The last shot the enemy fired was the only one that did us any harm; it struck the trunk of the pine tree about one foot in diameter and cut it down. This tree was standing in Co. K.'s 39th quarters; it fell and smashed up five of their tents. One man who was in one of these tents was badly hurt by the tree falling on him. The Folly boys too replied to their rebel brothers with five or six pieces of cannon on land, and, as the tide was up, a small gun boat came up Little Folly River and opened on the enemy with one gun. Two rebel boats were in sight during the affair and occasionally we could see the water splash over them where our shots struck in the water near them. The affair continued for two hours for which time there was a brisk cannonade kept up on both sides. A large fire was seen tonight in the direction of Charleston.

June 13—Early this morning there were several shots exchanged between our people and rebels; no damage was done on our side. The rest of the day passed off quietly. In the night there was a sharp cannonade, which lasted for about half an hour. None of our men were wounded nor killed.

June 14, Sunday—The day was quiet and pleasant. Gen. Gillmore arrived on the island today.[22] The amicable relations between our pickets and those of the enemy have ceased. They now fire at one another whenever a chance offers itself. Our pickets on the upper end of the island have dug pits to protect themselves from the shot, shell, grape and canister of the enemy. Their positions are so masked that our artillery can play on Morris Island without endangering our own men. At sundown that quietus of the day was broken. The rebels opened on us with considerable fury; this they kept up for half an hour. Our men did not reply. The companies of our Regiment, which were not already on duty, (three C, E & I) were sent out tonight and stationed along the beach from our right battery to the woods where our pickets are. It was my lot to be thrown out as a vedette, in front of the sand hills, along the beach and in the edge of a swamp. We were almost exactly in the range of the guns of the enemy and without any protection whatever. The rebels kept up a regular fire all night at the rate of one gun every twenty minutes. They threw solid shot, shell and grape but mostly shell. The greatest part of the firing was done from a mortar, which threw the shells so high that they would almost go out of sight. The course of the missile through the air was marked by a light similar to a rocket. When it had reached its highest altitude it would start down and at the same time strike up a different tune from that to which it had ascended to its august elevation. Down it would come and, exploding near the earth, with a tremendous crash, scatter its fragments far and near. Now we might have been seen hugging the ground while pieces of a shell were whistling past us in an uncomfortable proximity. In a few seconds after, when the danger was past, we would enjoy a hearty laugh at the ludicrous position one another would occupy. We all got through the night safe although pieces of shells struck all around us. On the whole there is no fun in being shelled at night, for two or three hours is not objectionable if one does not get hurt. Those who have not had any experience in the shelling process better take a soldier's word and not expose themselves to the fiery ordeal.

June 15—Came into camp at daylight well prepared for a day's rest; we did not fail to improve the time. The five companies of our regiment were relieved from picket this evening by the 67th Ohio. The rebels still shell our pickets.

June 16—This evening, half past 5 o'clock, the rebels began to shell the pickets and also our camp. They threw several shells into the camp of the 39th Illinois, but fortunately no one was hurt. The rebs had it all their own way as our men did not respond. Of the pickets one man of the 67th Ohio was killed and one man wounded; also one negro was killed.

June 17—Companies C & I were at work on the entrenchments this forenoon. Across the woods opposite to us, the rebels fired for 15 minutes very heavy guns from two batteries. For a time cannonading was very heavy. We could see the smoke but could not tell what they were firing at. Companies C & I were sent across to Coles Island this afternoon. We marched down to the point of Folly Island and were sent across in a surf boat. We scoured the island but saw no rebels. Placed out pickets and bivouacked. It fell to me to be on picket. The enemy shelled Folly Island through the night.

June 18—Our baggage was sent over to us and we pitched our tents. Tonight there was an alarm in camp; whether false or not is uncertain. Our pickets reported some cavalry prowling around. One thing certain, we had a sweet nap spoiled.

June 19—Four more companies of our regiment came over today, making in all on Cole's Island six companies viz: A, B, C, E, I & K. The rest of the Regiment is on Folly Island. Heavy shower of rain.

June 20—Colonel Howell has command of the brigade; Osborn is in command of the 39th Illinois Regiment. The latter gentleman's aspirations to have his shoulders illuminated with Brigadier's stars is again foiled. Companies C & I scoured the island this afternoon again; no enemy discovered. Very warm day & rain. Sea breeze alone renders the climate tolerable. Better camp than we had on Folly Island.

June 21, Sunday—We had scarcely got our morning toilet arranged and our minds quieted till our orderly passed along the company parade ground. Crying, "Get ready to fall in, boys, immediately with a day's rations." C & I had to go on a scout. There was no necessity whatever of going on this scout on Sunday. It was an open violation of President Lincoln's order with regard to keeping the Sabbath. But, I suppose, some of our newly pledged, dunghill cocks of the military profession would disregard the law of high Heaven and, were it possible, countermand the orders of the Great Jehovah. We scouted around all day. Found the enemy on James Island. They fired across a creek at our men; no one was hurt. Did not return the fire. Left a picket along a creek 1 1/2 miles from camp and returned some time after dark. We had just got to bed when the horrid words of the orderly greeted our ears, "Roll up your blankets, boys, we have to go back on picket." We went back for a reserve of the picket we left when we came in. It would not have been good for the eagles to have fluttered around us then. The boys were justly indignant.

June 22—We were relieved and got into camp at noon. Signed the payrolls. Warm day. Showers of rain.

June 23—On fatigue today. Had to unload lumber, forage and commisary stores from boats and schooners. Warm weather and a superfluity of mosquitoes and gnats at night.

June 24—Paid two months wages today. Rebels shelled Folly Island this evening. Received heavy mail.

June 25—Heat oppressive. Dead calm, not a breeze stirring. Last night a man of the 62nd Ohio was killed while the enemy were shelling Folly Island. Two men were standing talking when a shell struck between them and exploded a few feet from the ground. One was killed, as already stated, and the other was mortally wounded. On camp guard today. Drew new hats & mosquito bars.

June 26—Cloudy day. Mail again. Heavy duty.

June 27—Nothing worthy of note.

June 28, Sunday—Company I on guard on Folly Island. Heavy rain in the afternoon.

June 29—Relieved by Co. B. Heavy shower of rain. Companies E & I are yet on Coles Island; the other companies moved over to Folly today. Heat oppressive. Thunder in the distance.

June 30—On fatigue, carrying baggage. The soldiers are worn out moving camp so often. This would be unnecessary if a man of common good sense had command.

July 1—The boys, who went home on furlough about one month ago, returned today. Mail from New York received. This evening at high tide a Monitor came into the harbor. The knowing ones think that there will be an attack made on Charleston soon. The boys are spoiling for fight. *Guerra al cuchillo* [war to the knife].

July 2—Heavy rain today, the effects of which soon disappeared. It may rain a hard shower early in the morning but before noon the ground will be so dry that one would think that there had been no rain for a month.

July 3—On picket today. Five men of our company received their discharges, dated July 4. They were a jolly set of boys, or least they ought to have been in as much as this was the accomplishment of their long desire. Nothing occurred in the front more than usual.

July 4—The shipping in the harbor was covered with flags. The gun boats Pawnee and Commodore McDonald together fired a national salute at noon. The blockading squadron off Charleston fired the first salute; this was followed by the gun boats above mentioned and lastly by a battery on Folly Island. Otherwise the day was not different from any other day.[23]

July 5, Sunday—There is nothing here on the Sabbath to turn our thoughts from the vanity and frivolity which we are everyday compelled to witness. There is a longing and craving in the soul for something pure and holy, for better associations than the profanity of camp. O how hungreth and thirsteth the soul for the bread of life and living waters! How we wander not knowing whither we tend, like a ship without chart or compass on the trackless deep!

July 6—On picket. Saw rockets of the enemy at night. Mosquitoes very bad.

July 7—All quiet. Three day's rations ordered to be cooked this evening.

July 8—Early in the morning the groves are melodious with the songs of birds of different notes and varied plumages. But as the day advances and becomes warmer this wild and free music gradually diminishes till by noon scarcely a note is to be heard. At times during the heat of the day all animate nature seems hushed in silence, excepting a single Locust once and a while starts up a noise by no means pleasing to the ear, this it continues for a few minutes without at a time. Often when no breeze is stirring and not a leaf or blade of grass can be seen moving, an awful silence prevails as if all nature were listening with intense interest and anxious suspense to hear pronounced the sentence of its doom.

July 9—On picket again: we are on one day and off two; this is too often to be on duty of a night in the swamps of South Carolina. All things are now about ready to make an attack on Morris Island and we are daily expecting to hear the booming of the cannon announcing that the ball is opened. Men have been at work, by night, on the upper end of Folly Island, for some weeks past, fortifying. There are now mounted, as the result of their labor, 42 pieces of heavy cannon and mortars. The forces on the island have, within a few days past, been increased by several Regiments. All day there was great activity in the harbor; steamboats were constantly running up Folly River, to General Headquarters, and down again. Several large transports loaded with troops arrived. A strange looking craft, for removing obstructions, with huge chains and hooks at her bow came in. Thus things stood till about one hour before sundown. Then the Pawnee started up Stono River, the short distance astern followed a Monitor and next was the Commodore McDonald towing a mortar schooner, which has been lying up at Headquarters. Close after these war vessels followed nine transports loaded with troops.[24] This fleet proceeded slowly up the river. When the Pawnee got half a mile above the Village, she threw a few shells into the woods. The rest of the vessels stopped, some above and some below the village. They seemed to have no care about being still; the soldiers were noisy, the watches rang the bells as usual and at night lights were displayed. Two regiments of colored soldiers, commanded by Colonel Montgomery, were aboard some of these transports. The soldiers all wore badges. Some firing along the lines tonight. Thus I saw & heard things today.[25]

July 10—At sunup this morning the attack was made. The batteries on Folly Island opened, in good earnest, the engagement, and for about one hour there was no light work. There was an incessant fire kept up, for that time, with heavy ordinance. We could see clouds of smoke ascending to the sky. The sight very much resembled what we have imagined Gehinna, or the valley of Hinnon, to be.[26] After cannonading near two hours, during which time, we had one man killed, infantry crossed over in surf boats and, making a charge, completely routed the enemy. They fled leaving in our hands all their artillery; the guns were loaded. Quite a squad of prisoners fell into the hands of our men. The rebels did not return the fire till 15 minutes after our men had opened on them. They beat the long roll and finally returned a feeble fire. Evidently they were surprised; it seems that they were unaware that we had been planting batteries on the end of Folly Island. Prisoners say that they were going to attack us this morning; they were anticipated. The 39th Illinois Regiment was ordered up to the head of Folly Island, in the afternoon. The two companies on Coles Island, E & I, packed knapsacks and crossed over to Folly Island. The Regiment, then, excepting three companies A, F & H, which were on duty, marched to the upper end of the island and bivouacked. The men carried with them, besides their equipments offensive, their haversacks canteens and India Rubber blankets. All the rest of our baggage we left in camp. This I mention because we will probably have to bivouac thus for several days. All night artillery and other war material was being taken across the river to Morris island. Everything was pushed forward with the utmost speed.

July 11—This morning, our men made desperate charge on Fort Wagoner but were repulsed. The 76 PA volunteers was badly cut up; the loss in this regiment was very heavy. This showed us that the fort could not be taken by a charge without too great a loss of life; so it must be taken by approaches. They that fight well can dig well. Our boys therefore stacked arms and went to work with spades. Our first line was commenced in the range of the guns of Forts Sumpter, Wagoner and Battery Bee. The enemy, today occasionally threw a shell among our men while they were at work, but they did no damage. Two of our Monitors went in and returned the complement. We could see the shells burst over the rebel works. About three hundred men were engaged day and night loading artillery, ammunition & etc, on boats and ferrying it across the river to Morris Island. All went well today and confidence in our ability to take Charleston inspired all hands to work cheerfully and with alacrity. There is an intense anxiety to see this cradle of rebellion subjected to law and order.[27]

July 12, Sunday—This morning early the enemy made a sortie but they were driven back. Firing from the rebel works commenced early this morning and was kept up all day at intervals. On fatigue today; worked till late in the night. Heavy rain tonight. The river sparkled like fire when the drops of rain fell into it. All goes finely. Cannons, mortars, shot, shell, powder etc., are being hurried across to Morris Island. Everything has to be taken across in flat and surf boats. We hear nothing reliable from James Island although rumors of various kind are rife.

July 13—We were awoke this morning before daylight by a pelting rain which fell in torrents. This was trying to sleep under disadvantages. Three or four of men were killed today and several wounded by shells from Fort Sumpter. Some of our wooden gun boats, off Morris Island, threw shell into Fort Wagoner. A steamer in Charleston Harbor was sunk by our artillery on Morris Island. At night we could see a large fire in the same direction, supposed to be the boat burning. All right yet. Prospects good.[28]

July 14—Record about the same as yesterday. Firing from rebel fortifications and our gun boats responding, fatigue parties working in trenches and hurry in forward ordinance make the record of the day.

July 15—This was the most quiet day we have had since the siege began. The day was very warm, and such is every day. The sand at noon is almost hot enough to roast an egg in. Yet the men work cheerfully under the broiling sun and on the hot sand. The water we have to drink is very poor. At night we sleep on the ground, which is dampened by a heavy dew. This evening the rebels shelled our pickets on the left, on Morris Island; the Commodore McDonald run up Little Folly River and by a few well aimed shots silenced the impudent rebels. A telegraph is erected from Stono Inlet to Morris Island. Today we laid the cable across the river. The New Ironsides crossed the bay.

July 16—Before sunup a heavy cannonade was commenced a short distance west of Seceshville.[29] The firing was very heavy. Gradually the fire receded towards the west, and after an hour's duration it entirely ceased. The Commodore McDonald run up the river and through some shells into Seceshville and the woods to the right of the village. The enemy did not respond. This was after the firing first mentioned had been discontinued. All remained comparatively quiet till about noon when our gun boats began to shell the rebel fortifications. The enemy made a feeble reply from Fort Sumpter and their land batteries. Thus passed the rest of the day; in the meantime our men were busily engaged hurrying up preparations for the great bombardment which is soon to take place. General Gillmore issued an order congratulating the men of his command for the victory on the 10th instant. He especially thanked Brigadier General Vodges and his command for the patience and endurance exhibited by them in the erection of batteries on Folly Island, under almost every conceivable difficulty, and to the brigade of Gen. Strong for their galantry in, for the first time during the war, landing under a heavy fire and successfully carrying heavy batteries of the enemy. This, he said, places us three miles nearer the rebel stronghold, Fort Sumpter; the spires of the rebel city are beginning to loom up in the distance. He exorted the men to emulate their brethren at Emmitsburg and Vicksburg.[30] I have failed before to remark that Gen. Gillmore has his headquarters on Morris Island, near the scene of action and not three or four miles in the rear as is common with some generals of questionable ability as well as bravery. Tonight was severe on our fatigue parties, being one of that number myself, I experienced some of the hardships of war. We worked all night without any supper, loading and rowing boats. Tonight was of an inky blackness, so dark that we could almost feel the darkness. Some said that the rain poured down in torrents but to me it seemed as if there was a body of water from the earth to the sky. Such a hard rain I never saw in any other part of the country but South Carolina. This is the case generally when it rains here. It comes not in the gentle shower but with fury drenching the face of the Earth. The lightning flashed, which for a minute would entirely blind us, and the thunders roared. Hunger, fatigue, darkness and a chilling rain were not enough to dishearten us, but the Captain, under whose orders we were working, was utterly unfit for duty. His management disgusted us. His insolence vexed us. His haughtiness enraged us. He was intoxicated. This discouraged us. But this hard night had its end as all things else have. So we will still be of good cheer. These vexations, privations, deviations, aggravations, defalcations, irritations, exaggerations, misuses, abuses, excuses and this puffing and shuffling and ripping and tearing and cursing and swearing will soon come to an end. We will be citizens again and then ____ and then ____

July 17—Today we had things pretty much our own way. Our fleet kept up a brisk cannonade all the forenoon, in the afternoon the firing was not so brisk. The rebels fired a gun occasionally in response to our ships.

July 18—About noon our land batteries opened on Fort Wagoner; our ironclads and some of our wooden vessels of war took part in the engagement. Fort Wagoner was the object on which the fire of all our guns was concentrated. The rebels responded from Forts Sumpter and Wagoner and Battery Bee, but they did not return shot for shot. The firing was kept up on both sides briskly all the afternoon. About sundown the heaviest cannonading by far was done. Such bombardment seemed more like the fabulous fighting of the Titans than anything human. Perhaps more guns have been at work at the same time during the war but not of such heavy caliber. We were some three or four miles from the scene of action and could hear the shells whistling through the air as if they were but a few rods from us. From this may be inferred the awful noise they made. The hardest of the day's work commenced just after dusk. In two hours a bloody record was made. Mourning was sent to many families on this sad night. Many a brave man of Maine, New

Hampshire, Massachusetts, New York and Ohio fell before the murderous fire of the enemy. Eight regiments made a desperate charge on Fort Wagoner and after gaining possession of part of the works were driven back. From Folly Island we could hear the rattle of musketry and see the flash of their guns. We could distinguish our lines by a sheet of fire. Fort Sumpter was belching forth grape and canister into the ranks of our men, Battery Bee was not idle and Fort Wagoner made dreadful havoc among our men. Under this fire our men fell like grass before the scythe. It is said that 50 percent of the men engaged were placed *hors de combat* [out of action]. This is, perhaps, somewhat an exaggeration. Among the regiments that suffered most were the 62nd & 67th Ohio and the 54th Massachusetts colored regiment. The latter fought like tigers. Their officers suffered severely. Of the 62nd Ohio but three came out unhurt; Lieutenant Colonel Steel was wounded on the parapets of the fort. There has not, perhaps, been more desperate fighting done during the war than our men did on this horrible night. Our loss was great and no advantage was gained. At midnight the 39th Illinois and 85th Pennsylvania Regiments crossed over to Morris Island. We expected nothing else but to go right into battle. Providence managed different. When we crossed, we saw a long train of ambulances and wagons filled with wounded; they were placed on boats and sent off as fast as possible. When passing the hospital the night air was pierced with the cries of the wounded who were having their wounds dressed. The remaining few hours of the night we lay on the beach.[31]

July 19, Sunday—Our wounded were still being brought in this morning. There was a truce this morning during which our men were engaged in burying the dead. I saw graves along the beach where they will be overflowed at flood tide. During the truce I went to the front and from the top of a house had a fine view of Charleston Harbor and its defenses; the suburbs of the City were plainly to be seen. Fort Wagoner is on the northern end of Morris Island, on a point of land between the ocean and the entrance of the harbor. It looks like nothing more than a sand bank, but on testing it proved to be a work of immense strength. Morris Island is a narrow tract of sandy land; it drifted into high hills and appears to be a bulwark between the ocean and the land back of it. There was no firing on either side today. The 39th Illinois was sent out on picket tonight. Companies C, D, G & I were deployed and sent forward. C & D marched up to the ditch of the fort before they were aware that they were so near it. G & I were on the left and did not advance quite so far yet they went within a few rods of the fort. The rebels fired into us from the parapets. The bullets whistled thick and close around us. We lay close to the ground and the balls either passed over our heads or fell short. We lay in this position for a few minutes and then got up and gave the enemy a few shots; this quieted them and the rest of the night passed off without any further demonstration, excepting an occasional stray shot. The tide came up and we had to fall back a few rods. Before daylight we fell to the rifle pits; still we were in rifle shot of the fort. None of our men were killed during the night.

July 20—Under a tropical sun we lay in the ditch, the sand was scorching hot. If a man stood up straight he was liable to get a rebel bullet in his head. A little after noon the regiment fell back, excepting 100 men who were left in the pits to act as sharp shooters. The batteries then opened on Fort Wagoner. Soon after the New Ironsides and two Monitors run up and opened with their guns. The Paul Jones and two other wooden gun boats participated in the bombardment. The practice of the Monitors was very poor, the Ironsides did much better but the wooden vessels did the best. Almost every shot of the latter vessels struck the fort. They would run up, fire and then drop back. The Monitors and Ironsides lay still while they were engaged. The enemy made a feeble response from about three guns, one from Wagoner, one from Battery Bee and one from Sumpter. None of the vessels were struck but the Ironsides, she was not damaged. Occasionally a shot was fired from the direction of Fort Johnson but they fell short, otherwise it would have been a serious thing with our men, for it enfiladed our batteries. All the loss we sustained during the afternoon was one man wounded. Before daylight this morning a ship trying to run the blockade was burned. She made brilliant light.[32]

July 21—Some firing. Paymaster and mail in camp. Got our baggage and established a camp. This is a great luxury to us after lying in the sand and ditches.

July 22—The cannonading today was light. Our folks are still erecting batteries. The rebels shelled our fatigue parties but no damage was done. Howell's brigade, which is now composed of the following regiments, 39th Illinois, 62nd Ohio, 85th Pennsylvania, 67 Ohio and 2 SC, went out on picket after dark this evening. There was a drenching rain. All quiet through the night. Men were at work on the batteries and magazines all night.

July 23—Our sharp shooters fired at the men on Fort Wagoner whenever they attempted to load their pieces; there was no other firing done by either side but that of sharp shooters. Our men were engaged today in erecting a battery of 200 lb. Parrotts. Our brigade was relieved after dark and returned to camp. We had the benefit of another drenching rain.[33]

July 24—Before daylight we were called up and formed in line of battle on the beach. Soon after sunup our ironclads and four other vessels opened on Fort Wagoner. There was a brisk fire for about two hours, when there was a truce for the exchange of wounded prisoners. Our men were still digging nearer to the enemy's works. Duty called me to the front tonight to work in the trenches. The rebels kept up a regular fire on us all night. We marched up in short range of the guns of Forts Sumpter, Wagoner and Battery Bee under a heavy fire. We then took shovels and dug for our lives. When we saw the flash of cannon we would lay down in the ditch and let the shot and shell pass over our heads. The screeching of these missiles over our heads and in such close proximity was far from being pleasant. We had only one man wounded.

July 25—Firing as usual. Our brigade in the front tonight. Constant and at times quite heavy firing mostly from Fort Johnson.

July 26, Sunday—We lay behind a sand bank and the shots passed harmlessly over us. We could see the missiles strike the ground a few feet from us. The day was very warm and the sand drifted like snow on the prairies. Thus we passed the day wallowing in the sand dodging the contents of the guns of the enemy. The whole made a programme far from agreeable. The Sabbath may have been profitably spent but it was not pleasantly. We were relieved at night and returned to our camp where awaited us the few hours rest allotted to us poor creatures.

July 27—Fatigues and exposures too great have been imposed on us. My strength which has been failing for some time was hardly sufficient to keep me going today.

July 28—Sick. Sick and reported to the surgeon for the second time since being in the Army.

July 29—Still on sick list.

July 30—On duty today resolved to fill my place in the ranks or die.

July 31—Heat oppressive. One brigade is kept in the trenches day and night. There have been three brigades on the island, each one has to lie one-third of the time in the trenches. Howell's brigade was sent out tonight. The rebels were quite moderate in the use of their powder; they fired but little and that little did us no harm.

August 1st—Before daylight our men opened fire on the enemy from a mortar battery. The firing was quite active till daylight. We could see the shells of our mortars passing over but in our anxiety to sleep we did not get up to see what work our men were firing at. The day passed off without anything of special interest, shelling have become stale with [us]. We were relieved at night. None of our men were killed.

Aug. 2, Sunday—There is nothing in camp to satisfy the longings of the soul on Sabbath, no services. One turns within to enjoy, aside from the frivolities of comrades, the inner life which the world can neither give nor take away. One may be surrounded by wicked and boisterous companions, placed in the midst of profanity and gambling and yet in his own breast possess peace, tranquility and happiness. Blessed is the man who is thus enlightened from on High. Those who daily strive to do their duty are not left to grovel their way through a dark and sinful world. They not only have an unerring chart, the Bible, but there is a sure monitor within each one's breast which either approves or reproves accordingly as we do right or wrong.

Aug. 3—Foster's Brigade arrived, and landed today, from Virginia. Reinforcements were badly needed, for the men are almost worn out from the arduous duty since the siege commenced. On fatigue tonight; had to fill sand bags. Worked till midnight.[34]

Aug. 4—Time passes rather monotonously, there is so much the sameness everyday. Fatigue, guard, shelling by the rebels and our men returning to complement with interest form the daily curriculum.

Aug. 5—Everything goes after the old sort. Regimental inspection this morning. Hot day and rebels shelled, without doing any harm, the front.

Aug. 6—On fatigue, handling heavy projectiles. Received mail from the North.

Aug. 7—The rebels do not fire so much as they did in the beginning of the siege. The most of the firing they now do is from Forts Johnson and Sumpter; there is but little of Fort Wagoner and Cumming's Point. The 76 Pennsylvania Regiment embarked for Hilton Head this morning. Gen. Gillmore reviewed Howell's Brigade this evening. On post guard late in the evening. On this duty 24 hours. Suffering from the effects of a bad cold.

Aug. 8—Nothing of special interest today. Our regiment was sent to the front on picket this evening; not yet having been relieved from post guard we did not have to go.

Aug. 9, Sunday—On camp guard today; this is too heavy duty for this latitude. The day was hot and unpleasant.

Aug. 10—Awoke this morning very sick, and, at intervals, all through the day was vomiting. The heat was never so oppressive; it appeared as if the hair on my head was burning to a crisp. Thirst unquenchable. This was truly a day of suffering; may we be spared from such.

Aug. 11—At about 2 o'clock this morning the rebels opened on our works from their fortifications. A furious cannonade was kept up by both sides till daylight when things assumed the usual quiet. I did not learn of any casualties on our side. Our regiment was ordered out. Strange how much artillery fighting can be done with so little loss of life. On the sick list. The regiment went to our first line of batteries to fill sand bags tonight.

Aug. 12—Hot, Hotentot, Hotentoter, Hotentotissimus. The usual amount of firing was done today.

Aug. 13—There was considerable firing in the early part of the night. The fragments of one shell, which burst high in the air, passed over our camp.

Aug. 14—It was rumored that our batteries would open on the fortifications of the enemy this morning but it was mere rumor. There was some firing it is true but not more than common. Our brigade was on picket. The rebels did a good deal of firing tonight and at times, for a few minutes, it was furious. The shell, shrapnel, grape and canister fell thick around us. One of our men lying near by me was missed but three or four inches by a large piece of shell; it tore a hole in his blanket. The course of the mortar shells could be plainly seen. They are shot at an angle of 45 degrees, and describe a curve till they reach their highest altitude. In descending they gradually lose the curvature and, if they do not explode in the air, strike the ground at right angles. We could see these shells go so high that they would entirely disappear, for a few seconds, in the cloud; they would appear again coming down out of the clouds. Our batteries responded to those of the enemy.

Aug. 15—Before daylight this morning one man of company H., 39th Illinois was badly wounded in the foot, later in the day a man of Company E same regiment was wounded; there was another man wounded, of what Regiment I did not learn, making three in all during our 24 hours picket. After daylight there was but little firing done but we had to hug our breast works closely through the day, for whenever the rebels saw a man's head above the works their sharp shooters would send several whistling at the "audacious Yankee." The day was cloudy and pleasant. At 8 o'clock p.m., we were relieved and came to camp.

Aug. 16, Sunday—At night the regiment was mostly all on picket and fatigue. On picket to the left of our batteries, fatigue men opened the embrasures of the heavy batteries. Both picket and fatigue parties returned to camp early in the morning. No casualties on our side.

Aug. 17—The much wished for day has arrived at last. Soon after daylight this morning our batteries opened on Fort Sumpter, Cummings Point Battery and Fort Wagoner received the complements of some of our guns; the latter was the object of the concentrated fire of the Monitors, six in number, the Ironsides and some of the wooden gun boats.[35] The fire of our 100 & 200 pounder Parrot guns was directed to Fort Sumpter exclusively. The roar of artillery was awful. The enemy made rather a feeble response; they fired from Fort Johnson and batteries on James Island. Fort Sumpter was inclined to be silent most of the day yet occasionally some of its heavy in barbette guns were fired at the gun boats. The flag on the fort was three times lowered. Towards night the southwest face of Sumpter presented a ragged appearance. The heaviest was done in the forenoon yet a desultorily fire was kept up till dark. Capt. Rogers of the Weehawken was killed; this is to have been done by accident.[36] There was no damage done to our land batteries, as I have learned, no lives lost and but few wounded.

Aug. 18—The early dawn was greeted by the roar of heavy cannon. The firing was not rapid but what it lacked in quantity it made up in quality. The 100 & 200 pounder rifles must have a telling effect on the brick walls of Sumpter. The language of our heart to every shot is "Amen." Two Monitors were engaged for awhile this morning and some of the wooden gun boats fired at long range but, there being a stiff breeze, they hauled off before noon. There was kept up all day a slow but steady fire from the 100 & 200 pounders of our land batteries. The rebels replied mostly from Fort Johnson and two batteries on James Island further to the left these two batteries enfilade our works but they have as yet done us little damage, nor do they seem likely to do much. Far out in a marsh, entirely isolated, to the left of our works, our men have erected a battery of sand bags. This seemed to grow in a night like Jonah's goard, but it was not the work of one night.[37] It stands almost under the muzzles of the guns of a rebel battery on James Island. Nothing seems to be too hazardous for our men to undertake and nothing too difficult for them to accomplish. In the afternoon and at night there was a heavy gale blowing.

Aug. 19—The bombardment was renewed early in the morning. The firing was continued all day but it was not very vigorous on either side. The rebels made a feeble response from Fort Johnson and James Island batteries. They used not more than three or four guns. Forts Sumpter, Wagoner and Cummings Point battery were silent.[38] Two deserters came over from the enemy today. They report that citizens of Charleston have no confidence in their ability to hold the City. The south wall of Sumpter is badly battered. The good work goes on steady and sure. At the close of the day operations cease and quiet reigns through the night broken occasionally by the roar of a cannon. Tonight after we had gone to bed our company was detailed for provost guards. We got up and went to the provosts marshal's office and reported; we then came to our quarters, went to bed and remained quiet the rest of the night; this eleven o'clock. Such are the irregularities of a soldier's life.

Aug. 20—The bombardment was opened in about the same style as yesterday morning. The enemy responded from the same batteries and with no more spirit than yesterday.

Aug. 21—Our company moved camp and went on duty as provost-guards today. The 300 pounder of our battery was bursted this morning. The damage is not irreparable; the gun being only cracked near the muzzle, it can be cut off; men went to work at this immediately.

Aug. 22—Being somewhat more remote from the scene of hostilities our observations were necessarily limited. There were several rumors afloat today, the truth of which is too dubious for me to record here: it was certain that there was some flag of truce business done.

Aug. 23, Sunday—Early this morning there was a brisk engagement between our ironclads and the rebel works on Morris & Sullivan Islands; the vessels dropped back out of range in the course of an hour or so. Fort Sumpter was silent. Her flag staff was shot away and there was a flag on the southwest corner of the fort, a few feet above the parapet. The walls are badly battered.

Aug. 24—We go on guard one day and night and are then relieved for two days. This was our day to go on. The night was stormy; it rained very hard. We had to stay out and take the storm without any shelter whatever, yet we were not more than fifty steps from our quarters. The sea roared furiously and the breakers looked like vast heaps of living fire. This scene in a great degree compensated us for the inclemency of the weather. Considerable firing in the front tonight.

Aug. 25—Rainy day; heavy gale. Sea rough. Ironclads quiet. Our camp is on the beach so near the Ocean that the tide comes up into some of the tents. Cannonading has become, to us, commonplace, too much so to excite any great interest.

Aug. 26—One man of Co. K., 39th Illinois was killed today while on picket and three or four of the same regiment were wounded. At dark this evening the 24th Massachusetts volunteers charged the rebel rifle pits and took them, capturing 68 prisoners. The loss on our side was light, 4 or 5 killed and about ten wounded. The prisoners taken all belong to the 61st North Carolina; they are tired of the service of Jeff Davis. Two lieutenants were taken. The rifle pits charged are about 100 yards from Fort Wagner.[39] The assault was so well planned and so promptly executed that the enemy was completely surprised and many of them surrendered without firing a shot. The prisoners were sent to the Provost Marshall and we, Co. I, had to guard them. They were herded together on the beach and a line of sentinels placed around them. The night was stormy and the rain poured down in torrents.

Aug. 27—The day was cloudy and cool. Still guarding prisoners. But a feeble fire kept up today. Erecting batteries at night. Everything goes well but the time for the consummation of our wishes has not yet come.

Aug. 28—Fair weather again. Very quiet morning. The morning was not a fair index to the entire day, for in the evening and at night the weather was stormy; the rain in the night was very hard. The North Carolina prisoners had to take it.

Aug. 29—Nothing remarkable transpired today.

Aug. 30, Sunday—The record of the day includes the death of the Lieutenant Colonel of the 85th Pennsylvania. He was killed while on duty in the front.[40] There was heavy firing kept up all day and night. The wind blew hard, the sea roars and its waves run high. Ditches, cannon, ocean and ships, these constitute the variety of our daily observation.

Aug. 31—The prisoners, which we have been guarding, were started to Hilton Head this morning but they arrived at the wharf too late for the boat; so they were brought back for us to herd on the beach a while longer. This morning two of the monitors engaged the rebel batteries on Sullivans Island; there was cannonade for about two hours when the monitors drew off. At 2 o'clock p.m., four monitors returned to the attack. The firing on both sides was furious. The engagement lasted just two hours. In obedience to a signal from the New Ironsides the monitors dropped back out of range. At times there was a continuous roar of cannon and the monitors were hid from view by a cloud of smoke. The Ironsides fired only one shot. The rebel prisoners were sent to Hilton Head late this evening thus relieving our company of a heavy charge.

Conclusion

The body of water between Folly & Morris Islands is known by the name of Lighthouse Inlet; it probably takes the name from a lighthouse on the south end of Morris Island built by the U.S. Government but destroyed by the rebels. I have previously called this inlet Little Folly River. Small boats can run into this and soon after the taking of Morris Island, Lighthouse Inlet was made the base of supplies. The inlet is now crowded with light draught boats and schooners. A wharf has been built on both this and the Folly Island side. The amount of business now done here gives the place quite a bustling air. The unloading of commissary, quartermaster and ordinance stores, the busy hum of the machine shops making gabions, sap rolls, platforms, etc., make the place seem more like a town than a mere military camp. Wherever Yankees are, there enterprise is. The rebels have recently been at work with torpedoes but they have as yet done no harm. They sent these infernal machines "flooding down" Lighthouse Inlet at high tide with the intention of destroying some of the boats in the harbor. They have also placed torpedoes between Fort Wagner and our advance works.[41] Siege operations are going on well; much has already been done but more is yet to do before Charleston will fall. Our men have the sixth parallel established. This is, perhaps, 200 yards from Fort Wagner. Fort Sumpter's walls no longer present the smooth and even surface they did before the recent bombardment. It now looks like a vast heap of rubbish and it is almost entirely silent. The number of men killed on our side is rather greater than it was two weeks ago; the daily average is about four men. The health on the island is good. There have recently heavy reinforcements reached this Department. The weather is comfortably cool; a woolen blanket is needed to sleep under of the nights. The weather for several days past has been stormy.

Such is the condition of things in the Department of the South at the end of August 1863. With the close of the Summer closes the 5th Volume of a "Soldier's Diary." It is his wish that the journal should be laid aside and not subject to inspection. If the author should never return home, it is his earnest wish that this and all previous and subsequent volumes should be burned. As a last request he entreats that this be done.

End of Volume 5

Volume 6

MORRIS ISLAND, SOUTH CAROLINA, SEPTEMBER 1863–MAY 1864

As the Federal lines neared Battery Wagner, Gillmore prepared his attack. Remembering the assaults on July 11 and 18, Gillmore and his staff made careful arrangements that left little to chance. On September 5, 1863, the land batteries and warships opened on Wagner. A day later, under cover of the bombardment, Federal sappers reached Wagner's moat. Throughout the evening of September 6, Union regiments occupied the forward trenches. Though not part of the assault force, the Thirty-ninth Illinois served in the grand guard, protecting the fatigue parties as they continued to improve the siege lines. Before the attack got under way, however, Confederate deserters entered the Union lines to report that Wagner was being evacuated.

Shortly after midnight on September 7, five men from the Thirty-ninth Illinois slipped into Battery Wagner and saw the last Confederates leaving the work. Word of the evacuation was sent back to headquarters, and elements of the Thirty-ninth Illinois occupied Wagner. Though the Confederates were off the island, dangers remained. While the Federals rebuilt the captured batteries they came under constant enemy bombardments.

Fort Sumter had been rendered useless as an artillery position, yet the Confederates kept it as an infantry outpost and maintained the deadly line of obstructions and torpedoes that ran across the harbor's entrance. Unwilling to risk the loss of his monitors against the torpedoes, Dahlgren refused to attack and the campaign ended. While the navy stood down, the army also reduced its numbers off Charleston. For a few months, the Thirty-ninth Illinois garrisoned Morris and, later, Folly Island. In early December 1863, the regiment was ordered to Hilton Head Island.

With their terms of enlistment nearly expired, men of the Thirty-ninth were called upon to reenlist. The majority of the men, some 450, signed on for another three years. The regiment was the first in the department to reenlist and the first to be designated a veteran regiment. Each regiment that reenlisted as a body was granted a furlough, and on January 28, 1864, the regiment left Hilton Head for Illinois. Randolph and others who did not reenlist remained on Hilton Head and performed routine garrison duty.

The regiment never returned to Hilton Head. After reforming in Chicago, the men traveled by train to Washington, D.C., boarded transports, and sailed to Gloucester, Virginia. Arriving on April 26, 1864, they

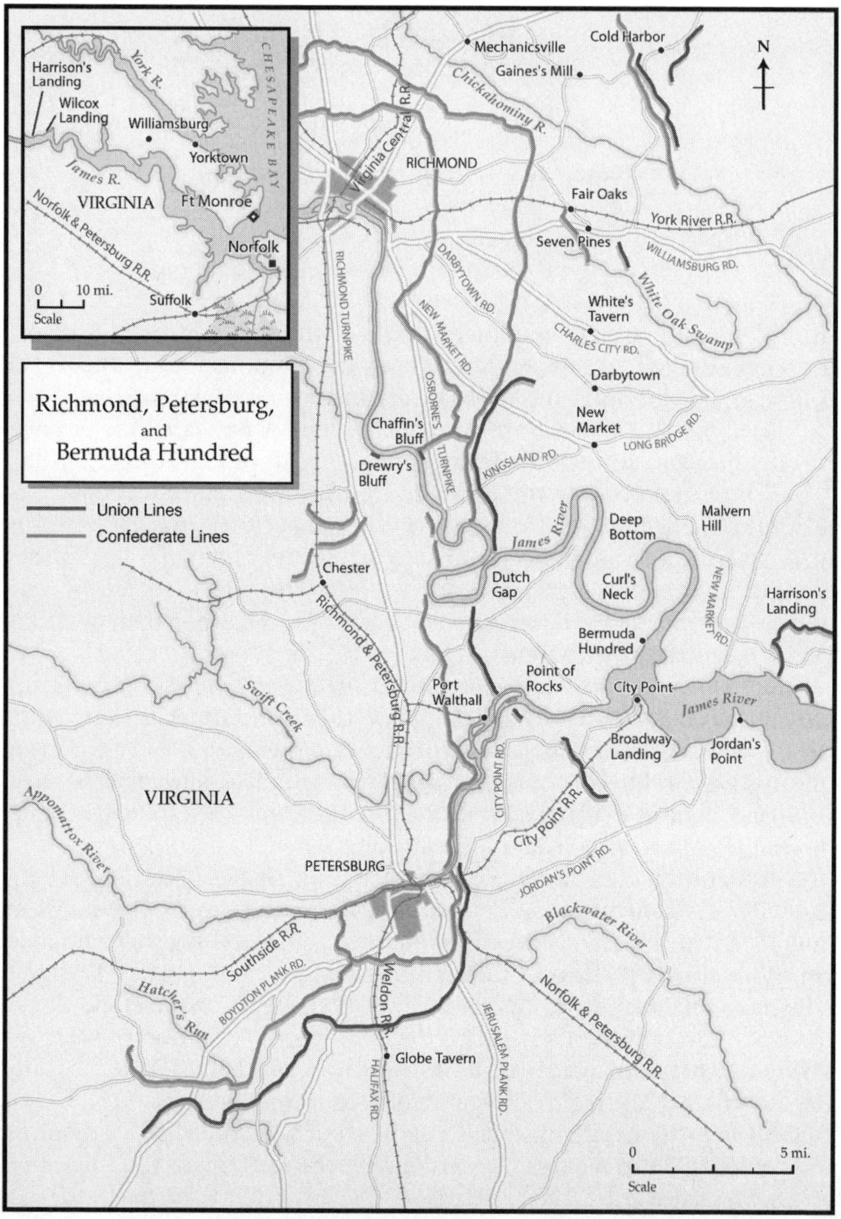

joined their comrades from Hilton Head who had come north with a large contingent of troops to unite in a new movement against Richmond. The Thirty-ninth was now part of the First Brigade (under Joshua B. Howell), First Division (under Alfred H. Terry), Tenth Army Corps (under Quincy A. Gillmore), Army of the James.

The Union called for the Army of the James, commanded by Major General Benjamin F. Butler, to move into the James River while General Grant advanced on Lee's army in northern Virginia. Butler was to capture City Point and other strategic sites to along the James River, then, after establishing a fortified base, to move against Richmond from the south. For the attack, Butler had nearly thirty-five thousand men in two army corps—the Tenth from South Carolina under General Gillmore and the Eighteenth commanded by General William F. Smith—as well as a cavalry division led by General August V. Kautz.

On the night of May 4, 1864, transports convoyed the army from the York River to the James. The next day, Union troops seized Fort Powhattan, City Point, and other positions along the James River while the bulk of the army landed at Bermuda Hundred, a neck of land between the James and Appomattox rivers. Also on May 5, Kautz's cavalry left Suffolk and headed for the Petersburg and Weldon Railroad in order to cut connections between Richmond and North Carolina.

At Bermuda Hundred, Butler dug in and cautiously probed Southern positions between Richmond and Petersburg. The Confederates, under General Pierre G. T. Beauregard, assembled reinforcements at Richmond and Petersburg. On May 12, to cover a second cavalry raid by Kautz against the Danville Railroad west of Richmond, Butler sent a portion of his army—some twenty thousand men—from Bermuda Hundred north toward Richmond. The Confederates pulled back to a strong defense line at Drewry's Bluff. Butler followed and took up a position opposite the Confederate defenses. On May 14 and 15, the two sides skirmished and exchanged artillery fire. Too weak to attack, Butler waited. On the morning of May 16, Beauregard with approximately eighteen thousand soldiers launched an attack, en echelon, from left to right on the Federal line. Commenced in the midst of a heavy fog, the assault was initially successful. But it soon stalled. The Federals, confused in the fog, managed to fend off the enemy and eventually retreated to Bermuda Hundred. Denied the conclusive victory he had wanted, Beauregard had nonetheless driven Butler away from Richmond. The battle cost the Confederates 2,184 casualties; Butler's command suffered 3,500 casualties.

During the fight, the Thirty-ninth Illinois was stationed on the Federal left on the western side of the Richmond–Petersburg Railroad. During the artillery exchange on May 14, Colonel Osborn was wounded, and since Lieutenant Colonel Mann was ill, Major Linton commanded the regiment. On May 15, the regiment dug in opposite the Confederate defenses. The next day, as the Confederates drove back the Federal right, orders reached the regiment to charge the enemy. Before the instructions could be carried out, however, Major Linton received an order to withdraw his men. Obediently Linton pulled back the regiment's left wing, but before he could reach the companies next to the railroad he fell wounded. The Confederates appeared on the regiment's right, driving them from the breastworks. A counterattack regained the works, but by now the order to retreat had reached the men on the right. The remaining soldiers managed to escape. In this, the Thirty-ninth's first full-scale engagement, the regiment suffered 127 casualties. With the rest of Butler's army, the Thirty-ninth Illinois returned to the entrenchments at Bermuda Hundred.

Beauregard followed. On May 20, he launched a probing attack on the right of Butler's Bermuda Hundred lines near Ware Bottom Church. Some of the Union rifle pits were overrun and a counterattack that included the Thirty-ninth Illinois was launched to recapture them. After a sharp fight, which cost 702 casualties, the Federals regained the works. The Confederates lost about 800 men as well as their brigade commander, Brigadier General William S. Walker, who was wounded and captured.

After the battle of Ware Bottom Church, the Confederates constructed their own entrenchments, known as the Howlett Line, across the neck of Bermuda Hundred, effectively bottling Butler and his command. In late May, realizing the futility of any movement by Butler against these fortifications, General Grant removed one-half of Butler's army and brought these troops into the Army of the Potomac for service against Lee's army east of Richmond. Remaining on Bermuda Hundred with the rest of Butler's forces, the Thirty-ninth Illinois settled into trench warfare and awaited further developments. —*S.R.W.*

★ ★ ★ ★ ★

—To refresh his memory in after years, should he be spared to survive the war, a few notes and observations are herein roughly sketched. This may be taken as an index of the mind of one who was intensely interested in the struggle in which he took a part as a private soldier, aspiring to nothing higher than to discharge his duty. It was his earnest wish that the Union cause might triumph and he considered no sacrifice too great to make for the country. Of ultimate success he never despaired.

September 1st, 1863—Autumn was ushered in without the day being particularly noted. The firing was rather heavier than has been for several days.

Sept. 2—Nothing of uncommon interest. Cannonading, from its frequency, attracts but little interest. Fatigue parties are sent to the front, at night, to work and all goes on well.

Sept. 3—The weather is quite pleasant.

Sept. 4—On guard and very unwell; not able for duty but do not like to have another to fill my place. The very breeze seems sickening.

Sept. 10—The above vacancy occurs on account of sickness, which for four days kept me prostrate on my couch, during which time not a single bite of food was tasted. Being able to scour my equipments, I resume duty again. I would not be unmindful of the Giver of blessings for the recovery of health and trust that it may be his will that I may be strong and hearty henceforth, while in the Army at least. During the period of my illness important events have transpired on this island. Fort Wagner and Battery Gregg have been possessed by our forces and there have been several severe attacks on Sullivans Island by the Ironclads. On the night of Sunday, the 6th, the enemy evacuated Fort Wagner and Battery Gregg. A deserter came into our lines, in the night, soon after the evacuation, or perhaps, while it was taking place, and informed Maj. Linton, 39th Illinois Regiment of the fact. Just before daylight volunteers were called for to go into the fort to test the truth of the deserter's report. But five men were wanted, more than this number instantly volunteered. Five men led by a noncommissioned officer entered the rebel stronghold just before the day and found it deserted as reported by the rebel. This party belonged to the 39th Regiment Illinois Volunteers. When they reported the fort was evacuated General Terry ordered the 3rd New Hampshire Regiment into the fort! Lieutenant Colonel Mann, of the 39th Illinois, very justly protested against this, contending that his own regiment should be the first to march into the fort. If the enemy had not evacuated an attempt would have been made to carry the fort by assault on the morning of the 7th. The plan for this was arranged; General Terry was to command in person. Company I was with the regiment for this duty.[1]

Sept. 11—Three companies have been doing provost guard duty Co. I 39th Illinois, Co. C 7th NH & Co. C 9th Maryland. These three companies were relieved today, by the 3rd NH Regiment, and sent back to their respective regiments.

Sept. 12—The firing has entirely ceased by our batteries since the occupation of all of Morris Island. The rebels fire occasionally from the batteries on James and Sullivans Islands.

Sept. 13, Sunday—Although on camp guard enjoyed something of the peace and quiet of mind which is needed by mortals. The regiment was sent on picket this evening; the camp guard was relieved and sent out too.

Sept. 14—Part of the men in the trenches were relieved this morning and permitted to return to camp, I was one of the lucky.

Sept. 15—This evening a flag was presented to the 67th Ohio Volunteers by Colonel Vorhees of the same regiment, on behalf of his wife. The Colonel made a patriotic speech. This oration having been had, a correspondent of the New York Tribune recited a poem, "The Northern Volunteers."[2]

Sept. 16—Inspection at 2 o'clock p.m. Heavy detail sent out to the front on fatigue at 6 o'clock p.m. At half past 11 o'clock in the night the rest of the regiment was sent out on fatigue, we marched up to Fort Wagner and marched back again. Thus two hours were consumed unnecessarily. The remainder of the night was very stormy; the rain poured down and the wind blew hard. Tents were blown down and bunks were wet. We were kept busy till daylight staking and holding our tent down to its place.

Sept. 17—The day was rainy. For a few minutes at a time the sun would shine and then a heavy shower of rain came pouring down. So the weather was changeable.

Sept. 18—A large detail on fatigue at the wharf, unloading boats. The day was clear and we had a chance to dry our blankets. A new wharf is being built at Lighthouse Inlet, Morris Island.

Sept. 19—Our forces have for some time past, (since the taking of Wagner and Gregg), been acting merely on the defensive; offensive operations ceased with the fall of the above mentioned rebel works. Large fatigue parties are at work day and night fortifying. Wagner and Gregg are being repaired and altered somewhat and other works are being thrown up. The rebels keep up a regular fire from Fort Johnson and batteries on James Island, Fort Moultrie and batteries on Sullivans Island. It is altogether a one-sided business, our batteries do not reply. Occasionally a man is killed or wounded but fortunately most of the missiles fall harmlessly around our men. The men are expert at dodging, yet once and awhile a poor fellow is called to his last account. The nights are rather cool and the days warm.

Sept. 20, Sunday—Rather dull day. In the evening went on picket, were on the left. The enemy did not annoy us from their batteries.

Sept. 21—The rebels do not have their own way quite so much as they did a few days ago. Our men now return their fire with interest. Relieved and got into camp at 8 o'clock in the night.

Sept. 22—Detailed for fatigue before breakfast this morning. Had to work on fort on Black Island. This is a small island on Lighthouse Inlet between Morris and James Islands; it is covered with woods, mostly pine and live oak. This position was occupied by our forces soon after the south end of Morris Island was taken. The rebels burst shells over our heads today while we were at work but fortunately no one was hurt. When we returned to camp at the close of the day we found that the rest of the regiment had gone on picket. Too heavy duty.[3]

Sept. 23—This evening when our pickets were being relieved a shell struck among them killing two men and wounding one all of the 39th Regiment Illinois Volunteers. Capt. Woodruff of Company K and a private of Company H were killed, the latter instantly; the Captain lived till the next morning. A sergeant of Company A was wounded. A sad record for today.[4]

Sept. 24—There was a grand review of all the troops on this island this morning. The regiments were formed in one line along the beach, the tide being low this was an excellent place for the review. The line was about one mile long. General Gillmore wore his newly won twin stars. A salute of 13 guns was fired.

Sept. 25—Nothing of special interest today.

Sept. 26—Paid two month's wages. Fatigue and picket duties are the order of the day.

Sept. 27, Sunday—On fatigue at Fort Gregg. The rebels fired on us from Fort Moultrie; the shells exploded close to us, but no one was hurt. The telegraph wire was cut by the fragment of a shell. We had a man stationed to watch the batteries of the enemy and when he saw the smoke of cannon his duty was to warn the men at work. Thus when the enemy fired from Fort Moultrie the watch man cried out, "Cover Moultrie," the men within get behind a bank of sand and lie close to the ground till the shell passed over. The rebels fired at Fort Wagner from their James Island batteries.

Sept. 28—On picket for the next twenty-four hours. Adieu to peace and comfort. Soldiers are abused. We will soon demand a truce to this in such a manner that our demands will be satisfied. Our heavy guns fired on Fort Sumpter today; what this was for we do not know. Sumpter is now merely a great pile of ruins, a ghost of its former self. The rebels still hold it as a mere matter of pride, it is of no use to them whatever.

Sept. 29—It is thought that the enemy has been trying to mount guns on the ruins of Sumpter, hence the firing on it.

Sept. 30—On fatigue at Black Island.

October 1—We were called up at 4 o'clock this morning and went to beach to drill! Shame on the commander who thus uses men! He is wanting in humanity and good common sense. The regiment was on picket in Fort Wagner this evening; we lay in the bombproofs till morning. This is a miserable place for men. It was so dark that we could not see anything at all. The air was very warm and impure. Rats, mice, "gray backs" and fleas disputed our possession of this, to us, miniature Pandemonium. How the rebels stood it in here during the bombardment in the hot days of July and August we cannot understand.

Oct. 2—At daylight we fell back to the trenches in the rear of Wagner, where we lay all day. There was nothing of special interest in the front today; firing was done on both sides.

Oct. 3—Nothing extraordinary today.

Oct. 4, Sunday—Regimental inspection in the forenoon and in the evening a heavy detail on picket in Forts Wagner and Gregg. The bombproofs of Wagner were as disagreeable as ever.

Oct. 5—Three companies remained in Wagner during the day. The rebels shelled our fatigue men on the fort; one man only was hurt and that but slightly. We were relieved after dark and returned to camp, where a detail for the morrow awaited some of us. We had scarcely returned tonight when we heard the report of musketry, apparently on the beach. The reports grew thicker and more continuous. This had been going on about twenty-five minutes when bugles were sounded and the long roll was beaten. The men soon fell into ranks and were formed in battle array on the beach but the fuss was all over and we had nothing to do but stand, and stomp around on the sand to keep warm, and "await further orders," which we did not with a very good grace. The "further orders" came at last, ordering the men to their quarters, it was past midnight before we were permitted again to recline upon our couches. The cause of this fracas we have been informed, was that the rebels attempted to board the Ironsides and at the same time to divert the attention of the fleet to enable two blockade runners to get out of the harbor to sea. The rebels went out in surf boats. The plan of the enemy failed; the two blockade runners and the boarding parties were captured. So says report but whether the above is anything more than a mere myth I can not yet say.[5]

Oct. 6—On fatigue in Fort Wagner from 6 o'clock a.m. till 5 p.m. The rebels shelled us vigorously all the time from the three batteries on James Island and from Fort Moultrie and one battery on Sullivans Island. The first shot fired was from Fort Johnson and two men of the 39th Illinois, one of Co. E seriously in the face, and one of Co. K leg slightly bruised; and the evening a man of the same regiment, Co. D, was wounded in the foot by a piece of shell from Fort Moultrie. This was all the damage the enemy did us although they kept up a constant and heavy fire; the shells were thrown into the fort and exploded all around. So much for the skill the men have acquired in covering.

Oct. 7—The nights are very cool, so that we need two woolen blankets to sleep under. The days are very warm for three or four hours, from about ten till two. On picket tonight in Fort Wagner. The rebels kept up a fire from James Island all night; one man of Co. K, 39th Regiment Illinois volunteers was wounded in the thigh.

Oct. 8—Most of the 39th Illinois came into camp at daylight this morning. During the past twenty-four hours 230 shots were fired at Fort Wagner. Three or four men were killed while on fatigue today, and 12 or 15 wounded.

Oct. 9—On fatigue at Fort Gregg, under fire as usual. Two men were wounded, one of Company C, in the fort by a shell from Moultrie, the other a sergeant of Company A, on the beach opposite Fort Wagner, whilst returning to camp in the evening, by a shell from Johnson; wounded in the leg—since amputated.

Oct. 10—Had a day's rest, which was badly needed. Duty has been too heavy for some time past. The effects of it are plainly visible and felt.

Oct. 11, Sunday—On camp guard and had to stay at the guard headquarters all day.

Oct. 12—A heavy detail of our regiment was on fatigue at Fort Wagner today; I was not relieved from guard in time to go out. So I had another day's rest. A man of Co. C, 39th Illinois was killed this evening between Forts Wagner and Gregg, when returning to camp from the latter. He was killed instantly.

Oct. 13—A detail was sent on picket this evening. Fortune favored me; I did not have to go out.

Oct. 14—Pickets returned to camp this morning.

Oct. 15—Rainy day. Regiment on fatigue at Wagner and Gregg. The rebels fired but little, no one was hurt.

Oct. 16—Brigade inspection at 1 o'clock p.m., and went on picket at 5 p.m.

Oct. 17—On duty in Fort Wagner today; firing rather light. Relieved at dark.

Oct. 18, Sunday—On fatigue in Fort Wagner. No one was hurt here. The rebels fired none till in the afternoon, when they opened on us with considerable vim. At Fort Gregg things were not so quiet; our men there were shelled all day. One man was wounded.

Oct. 19—In camp till 5 o'clock p.m., when we went on picket in Fort Wagner.

Oct. 20—Remained in the fort all day. Between 300 and 400 men are placed in the fort at night; at daylight all but about 50 men leave the fort, part go to camp and part fall back into the trenches.

Oct. 21—On fatigue in Fort Wagner; the rebels shelled us briskly, but no one was hurt.

Oct. 22—Up at 4 o'clock a.m. Lay on the beach till daylight. To satisfy the whims of Mr. Terry or some other shoulder strap ass we are deprived of the rest which nature demands. Mr. Terry (Gen.?) is not now in command on this (Morris) island, but it was under his tyrannical sway that the custom of working the men in the night and standing in line on the beach till daylight originated. In camp till evening when the greater part of the regiment went on picket; I was so fortunate as not to be on.

Oct. 23—On camp guard. Camp guards have to take their knapsacks packed, haversacks, canteens, etc., on guard; they have to stay at the guard house all day and night, not even being allowed to go to their meals. More of General Terry is this.

Oct. 24—Rainy day. Regiment on fatigue. Nothing of special interest to record today. All will not be so quiet on our side many days longer.

Oct. 25, Sunday—Cloudy, dismal and gloomy day. On picket in the evening. Sent to Fort Wagner. The rebels did not fire a single shot during the night.

Oct. 26—We returned to camp this morning. The day was cloudy and chilly; the sea rather rough. Our batteries are ready to open. In Wagner are mounted 14 guns and 2 mortars. Seven of these are Parrotts, six 100 pounders and one 200 pounder, two small brass pieces and five pieces captured when the fort was taken. The Parrotts are mounted on pivots and can be fired in any direction. All the morning we expected to hear these big guns commence thundering away at the rebel works. Our expectations were realized at 1 o'clock p.m. The first gun was fired from Gregg, Wagner and the new battery soon followed suit.[6] Fort Sumpter received the fire. A brisk cannonade on our side was kept up the rest of the day. The rebels made a feeble response from their batteries on James and Sullivans Islands. The enemy will have, during this contest, to receive the metal of 100, 200 & 300 pounder Parrott rifles from our land batteries.

Oct. 27—On fatigue, in the swamp near Fort Wagner, cutting sod. There was a heavy fire kept up all day at Fort Sumpter. The heavy missiles whistled terribly through the air and we could hear them strike against the battered walls of Sumpter with a tremendous crash; a cloud of dust could be seen to arise wherever the projectiles struck. At dark the fire slacked but was not entirely discontinued during the night. Two Monitors were engaged for a while. The rebels fired at Gregg and the new Battery, leaving Wagner unmolested.[7]

Oct. 28—Our guns kept firing away, making the ruins of Sumpter a still greater ruin. The 39th Illinois struck tents this morning and moved over to Folly Island; the rest of the brigade is to follow soon. We pitched our tents in an open field, for the night, without any regularity.

Oct. 29—Busy, today, clearing off the ground for a camp. The place selected is in the woods near the lower end of the island, midway between the ocean & Folly River.

Oct. 30—Formed camp today. The roar of the cannon on Morris Island was distinctly heard; the firing seemed to be unusually heavy.

Oct. 31—Mustered. At work on camp ground; there will be plenty to do for two weeks to come. We heard but little firing till late in the afternoon, when it became quite heavy.

November 1st, Sunday—The sullen roar of cannon was heard all day long, the Sabbath not being kept holy.

Nov. 2—We hear no news from the front although every gale that sweeps from the North brings to our ears the boom of cannon.

Nov. 3—Have been unwell for three months past, notwithstanding on duty all of time. It is the part of a soldier and a man to overcome and despise these little bodily infirmities, hence I have gone on in the regular routine of duty. Many of my comrades have, within a few days past, asked me if I were sick or if I had been sick. The answer was, invariably, no.

Nov. 4—We have to drill four hours in the day; two hours company drill in the forenoon and two Battalion drill in the afternoon. Firing still going on.

Nov. 5—Very little or no firing today.

Nov. 6—Nothing of special interest to record today.

Nov. 7—On camp guard. Whilst the lonely sentinel walked his beat, the sighing of the pines, the roar of the ocean, the doleful cry of the screech owl, interspersed with the boom of the distant cannon made music to his ears.

Nov. 8, Sunday—The day was quite warm. Soon after we retired the wind rose and the atmosphere turned so cool that we chilled and shivered in our tents till morning.

Nov. 9—Things seem to have lulled in the front; we have heard but little firing for three or four days. The day was unpleasantly cool. Mail was received per the Arago; it brought Northern papers of the 3rd instant.

Nov. 10—On guard at camp. Cool day and night. Considerable frost fell tonight, the first of this fall.

Nov. 11—The day was so cool that we shivered around with our overcoats on.

Nov. 12—Brigade inspection this afternoon on the beach. The day was so warm that we sought the shade to protect us from the heat of the sun.

Nov. 13—Firing is still going on at the front although we do not hear it so plainly as we did when we first came on the island.

Nov. 14—Mental activity completely crushed. Mind and body both prone to the ground. On grand guard tonight. Damp and cold on post. How long? Nine months for some and ten for others. Time, be swift in your flight and bring to us rest ere we perish.

Nov. 15, Sunday—The middle of the month. How time flies. We would rejoice at its flight were it not that it is too poorly improved. Each day brings us nearer to the end; what end? The end of life and, if life be rightly spent, the end of trouble. What is it that makes man cling with such tenacity to life? But few ever attain the acme of their ambition. Blighted hopes are strewn all along the path of life. The temple of Fame once ascended is a mere hollow shell, ready to tumble into ruins beneath one's feet.

Nov. 16—Long grand guard again! In the swamp, broke of another night's rest! Heaven protect us! The hand ____ Go, go forth.

Nov. 17—Nothing of interest to record today.

Nov. 18—Brigade drill in the forenoon. On grand guard at night. Grand guards are put out in the evening and relieved at daylight in the morning; none being on in the day time. The object of this guard, I suppose, is to prevent spies from sneaking around through camp.

Nov. 19—The regiment was inspected by the brigade inspector, in the forenoon, in the afternoon was battalion drill in the presence of the same officer.

Nov. 20—Nothing of special interest to record today.

Nov. 21—The usual drills are omitted on Saturday, so those who do not happen to be on duty have one day of comparative rest. It was my luck to be on grand guard again this evening.

Nov. 22, Sunday—A heavy cannonade was commenced before daylight in Charleston Harbor and kept up all day. Our comrade, John Cray, breathed his last at the regimental hospital this evening. It is only a few days since he was on duty with us in the company; he was stricken down with the bloody flux and fever. The short time before dark he said, "The tug of war has come" and then turned over and died.[8]

Nov. 23—We attended the obsequies of our departed comrade in the afternoon. The day was rainy and gloomy.

Nov. 24—There was nothing of special interest today. The regular routine of camp duty was decidedly monotonous.

Nov. 25—On grand guard tonight. The weather turned quite cool in the night.

Nov. 26—All the drills, inspection and dress parade were omitted today. So the national Thanksgiving was a day of quiet rest to us, the first we have had for a long time. There were no Divine Services in our part of the camp.

Nov. 27—The north breeze wafts to our ears the roar of the cannon on Morris Island, but we get but little reliable intelligence from there. Weather boisterous and cool.

Nov. 28—The day was rainy and in the night there was a thunderstorm.

Nov. 29, Sunday—Damp and cool day. Cleared off in the night and turned cold.

Nov. 30—Clear and cold day. Slight freeze at night. Farewell to our last Autumn in the army.

December 1—Today introduces us to our final Winter in the services of our country as soldiers. The introduction was with ice and chilling winds. At 1 o'clock p.m., today, a national salute was fired by the different batteries on the island, in honor of a great victory gained by General Grant over the rebels at Chattanooga. Then thrice welcome to this first day of Winter for our anxiety to get out of the army must not be taken for disloyalty. We are worn out and want to see the thousands of able bodied men in the North give some tangible evidence of their patriotism.[9]

Dec. 2—Drill and other tom foolery.

Dec. 3—Fine day. On camp guard.

Dec. 4—Pay day.

Dec. 5—Received orders to embark this afternoon. Destination to us unknown. With a firm trust in Providence we commit our frail bark to the tempestuous sea. We struck tents and were ready to start by the middle of the afternoon but the order to fall in was not given till 3 o'clock a.m., the next morning. So we bivouacked awaiting transportation. Sleep we had but little. Adieu to Folly Island.

Dec. 6, Sunday—We went aboard the steamer Monohanset at daylight and went to sea. I have only faint recollection of what passed on the voyage to Hilton Head, being buried in an oblivious sleep. When running into Port Royal Harbor, in the afternoon, my stomach became very badly deranged and I had to heave part of its contents into the ocean. The boat lay at anchor in the harbor till dark, she run up to the wharf at Hilton Head and the baggage was unloaded, the boat then dropped back and we lay on her till morning. Whilst lying in the harbor on the afternoon of Sunday I noticed several officers in the cabin of the boat playing cards. Villainous creatures to thus desecrate the Sabbath.[10]

Dec. 7—Disembarked early this morning and established a camp about 1 1/2 miles from the Hilton Head dock.

Dec. 8—Howells Brigade is constituted a separate command from the rest of the forces on the island. The Colonel commanding makes his reports and returns to Brig Gen. Seymour.[11]

Dec. 9—A system of target practice has been instituted for this brigade.

Dec. 10—Drills are again in full blast. Colonel Howell seems to be a rigid disciplinarian.

Dec. 11—Rainy and disagreeable day. Went to Hilton Head after commissary stores; for 75 cents had the semblance of a good meal.

Dec. 12—Rained all day.

Dec. 13, Sunday—Visited the soldier cemetery of Hilton Head. Each grave has a head board, with the name of the soldier, his rank, company, regiment and date of his death on it. There were 500 graves all made since 1861. This Necropolis is being enlarged almost daily.[12]

Dec. 14—Clear weather again. Nothing transpired beyond the usual routine of camp.

Dec. 15—On camp guard. Several rigid inspections and examinations.

Dec. 16—Nothing today to draw the pen of the Chronicler.

Dec. 17—Inspection of the 39th Illinois Regiment by the brigade inspector in the afternoon.

Dec. 18, Sunday—On guard.

Dec. 20—The regular routine.

Dec. 21—The same as above.

Dec. 22—Review of the forces pertaining to the post of Hilton Head, not including Howell's Brigade. Fine day.

Dec. 23—Grand review of all the forces on the island by General Gillmore.

Dec. 24—Drills omitted. Men busy ornamenting quarters and company parade grounds with evergreens. The regimental hospital was cleared of the sick and the officers had a festival in it tonight. They had a supper, toasts, speeches etc. The festivities were kept up till a late hour at night.

Dec. 25—Nothing to remind us of Christmas; there was some more yelling and hallooing in camp than common. We had for dinner wormy crackers, salt beef and coffee. No drills. Pleasant day.

Dec. 26—Recruiting for veteran volunteers was commenced this morning in the 39th Illinois. Lieutenant Knapp was appointed recruiting officer of the Regiment.[13]

Dec. 27, Sunday—Dull day.

Dec. 28—Enlisting veterans is all the stir we now have in camp. The excitement is high and is increasing. There was a "rally around the flag, boys" this evening. Colonel Osborn, Adjt Walker and others made speeches; patriotic songs were sung. Many re-enlisted tonight.[14]

Dec. 29—The "veteran fever," as the boys call it, runs high. Many strong men are suddenly stricken down with it and can find relief only in reenlisting.

Dec. 30—Cold and very disagreeable day. Reported to the Doctor; have had the diarrhea for four months. The suffering has been severe, especially when on guard of cold nights. The alternative was presented to me either to go under the sod or to go to the Doctor; the latter was more patriotic.

Dec. 31—Mustered for pay.

January 1st, 1864—A Happy New Year to the World. The Colonel, or somebody else, gave a dinner to the Regiment. The day was so unpleasant that I did not go out to the table. The boys brought me some pie & cake.

Jan. 2—Nothing of special interest to record.

Jan. 3, Sunday—Today, with three others, I was sent to the General Hospital at Hilton Head.[15] Alas my pride is humbled. I hoped not to have to go to a hospital while in the army. We went to the door of the hospital and then were conducted into a large room, labeled "Office." An officer here examined our descriptive lists and gave some directions to his "subs." We were next taken to a long ward with beds on each side; we were directed to lay our knapsack by the side of one of these beds in the far corner and become the occupant of it. The room was well warmed and we had been enjoying the luxury of a hot stove but a short time before it was announced that dinner was ready. The ward was evacuated instanter and there was a regular hotel scramble for the dining hall. Some were on crutches, they labored bravely but were left behind in the race. In obedience to orders we followed the rest. Seated at the table many of the patients began to supply their inward wants with avidity. Of some I might say they eat greedily. To one it was surprising to see patients of a hospital so eager to get to the table and so careful to improve the time while at it. I had scarcely straightened myself to leave the table when a man sitting on the opposite side snatched the bread which I left, his own ration not being enough to appease his voracious appetite. The dinner consisted of beef boiled, gravy, good soft bread enough of it for any man and water. Meals are brought into the wards for some of the worst cases. Next after dinner came the operation of bathing and changing clothes. There is no correspondence between the size of the clothes and the wearer; the drawers given me were much too large, the shirt reached almost to the ground. I suppose when I donned these robes of white that I resembled a priest. Nothing new transpired till supper; this consisted of bread, molasses and tea. Some of the boys had extra dishes in their side pockets, such as butter and preserves; these they went in on at the table.

Jan. 4—After breakfast this morning, the boys suddenly took off their hats and each went and set down by his own cot. I did not know the meaning of this and persisted in wearing my cap till I could get some light on the subject. The desired light shown forth thus; a fellow patient politely said to me, "Take off your cap, the Doctor is in." It was sufficient. "While in Rome do as the Romans do." It is the custom when the Doctor comes into the ward for all to take off their caps and keep silent till he retires.

Jan. 5—Health improving. Hospital life does not suit an active Campaigner. A man died in our ward (C) this morning of the diphtheria.

Jan. 6—Although I have a good bed and there is a warm stove to sit by I long for the pure air of camp.

Jan. 7—A man died in the ward (C) this morning; disease typhoid fever and diarrhea.

Jan. 8—Not so well today. Damp and cold all day.

Jan. 9—The first clear day since I have been in the hospital. Almost homesick sometimes; I must cheer up for a few months longer.

Jan. 10, Sunday—There was preaching in the dining hall this morning. Mrs. Major Dorman visited our ward at supper time this evening. She had some nice things to eat in a basket but by far the richest treat she gave us were some incidents of the war which she related to us. Her powers of narration are excellent. Mrs. Dorman is the wife of the chief paymaster of this Department. They are residents of St. Augustine Florida and being union people were, as she expressed it, "thrust out at the back door."[16]

Jan. 11—The day was warm and pleasant. The Arago arrived this morning; she brings no news of importance.[17]

Jan. 12—There was nothing today noteworthy. The day was cloudy and damp.

Jan. 13—Rainy day. One's best efforts are called into requisition to prevent his spirits from becoming dejected on a day like this.

Jan. 14—Time drags heavily. There is nothing to interest us; reading soon becomes dry, owing to mental health.

Jan. 15—Very fine day, like spring. Health not so good today. The diarrhea still lingers with me; it seems loathe to give up its prize.

Jan. 16—Nothing to record.

Jan. 17, Sunday—Services in the dining hall; preaching in the forenoon and prayer meeting in the evening.

Jan. 18—Rainy day.

Jan. 19—Health improving. Clear day and cool. The Fulton arrived from New York; no news of importance.

Jan. 20—Fine weather.

Jan. 21—Today a squad of patients were sent North. Lucky boys were they to get to breathe the pure air of the North.

Jan. 22—Had a restless night. Bowels broke loose with great fury. The Chronic Diarrhea is a bad disease.

Jan. 23—The weather is delightful. A warm stove is very comfortable in the morning and evening but as the sun rises the boys begin to draw back their chairs farther and farther from the fire and before noon they will be entirely deserted. In the heat of the day the sun is too warm to be pleasant; the shade is, therefore, sought. But this fair weather is liable to change in a few hours. Often the clear sky is obscured by dark clouds and instead of warm sunshine there is a chilly wind. These changes are frequent and sudden.

Jan. 24, Sunday—The usual services in the dining room.

Jan. 25—Things were considerably torn up today; they were whitewashing the ward.

Jan. 26—Finished whitewashing today; the ward looks much better.

Jan. 27—Scrubbing today; so things were through other three days. The improvement will well pay us for the trouble.

Jan. 28—One man died today in our ward (C), of the Diarrhea. The 39th Illinois Regiment embarked this evening on their way home on furlough. This is now a veteran regiment, four hundred (400) about of them having reenlisted. Those who did not reenlist were attached to the 62nd Ohio to serve their time out; a mistake and act of injustice in the War Department. My pride as a soldier has departed. The reputation of my own State is now in nowise dependent on Illinois Soldiers in an Ohio Regiment. The veterans only are going home on furlough; may they enjoy it.[18]

Jan. 29—There was a case of the small pox discovered this morning in Ward C. The patient was sent out immediately to a hospital for this disease outside the entrenchments. Got vaccinated today.

Jan. 30—Weather delightful. Sick at the stomach and dizzy headed.

Jan. 31, Sunday—The 62nd Ohio veterans, nearly all of the regiment, embarked today en route for home on furlough; also parts of the 47th & 48th NY Regiments. They were escorted to the pier by the brigade. A dark and strange looking fog hung over the harbor this afternoon and a pale rainbow was to be seen; the colors were not brilliant.

February 1—It seems to be my lot to suffer a variety of maladies; I now have a bad cold. Perhaps I will finish off with the small-pox. At any rate I hope to be fat and ready for the spring campaign.

Feb. 2—*"Yo no tengo nada que escribir hoy"* [I have nothing to write about today].

Feb. 3—Turned cool in the night; the day disagreeable with cold wind.

Feb. 4—Cool and clear day. Slight freeze in the night. Plenty of apples at the hospital; they were confiscated on account of the sutters selling them for too high a price.

Feb. 5—An expedition sailed from here today. I understand that it was composed of two brigades from this island and one from St. Helena.[19]

Feb. 6—Clear and rather cool.

Feb. 7, Sunday—An extra [sad] day. Attended services in the dining room this morning. A soldier died suddenly, in Ward C., of a disease of the throat. He was able to set up when I went to church but when I came back his bed was empty. He had been carried to the dead house!

Feb. 8—Health recovering entirely. Detailed to work at fencing a garden. A large garden is to be cultivated by the convalescents for the use of the hospital. The ground is now being fenced.

Feb. 9—Delightful day.

Feb. 10—Detailed to work again; not much to do. Time flies.

Feb. 11—Those of the 39th Regiment Illinois volunteers, who did not enlist as veterans, about 150 men, are in a separate detachment, doing picket duty at Braddock's Point, Hilton Head Island. The detachment is commanded by Capt. Pratt of the 62nd Ohio.[20]

Feb. 12—Murky day.

Feb. 13—Nothing of special interest.

Feb. 14, Sunday—St. Valentine's Day was with us decidedly void of interest.

Feb. 15—The small-pox is checked; there has not been a new case for about ten days.

Feb. 16—Celebrated my birthday piling brush in the clearing for the hospital garden. The weather turned quite cold in the night; the wind raised to such a gale that it almost made me sick to think of the billowy sea.

Feb. 17—The day was clear, cold and windy. There was a little ice this morning.

Feb. 18—At work in the garden. Cool day. Nothing of special interest to record.

Feb. 19—The day was very cold for us thin blooded South Carolinians. The wind whistled around, above and under the hospital building with great violence but the day would not be called cold in the North.

Feb. 20—There are at Hilton Head several families, refugees from Florida, living in tents. They are composed of men, women and little children. Being ragged and dirty they present a miserable appearance. The men intend to work for government. A few days ago in passing their camp these poor people presented a sad picture. The day was cool and very chilly. The women and children were huddling together, like chickens, on the sunny side of a stable. Some had blankets wrapped around themselves. Several of the women had infants in their arms. These are Union people. The children when very mad at anyone vent their spite on him by calling him "an old Rebel," or "a secesh."

Feb. 21, Sunday—Wealth, learning, luxury, fame and all that the world can give are unable to satisfy the cravings of the soul. From a higher fountain, from a purer spring must the immortal soul drink to be satisfied. Since true happiness pertaineth not to the vanities of the World, why is it that we are so careful to heap up around us the things of this life, why that we are so anxious to win the applause of our fellow men and so neglectful in fitting ourselves for the enjoyment of the good through the long cycles of eternity? Man seems to imagine every body mortal but himself. Too often alas too often as though to him this present life has no end he lives. The few moments that he would spend in communing with his heart are burst in upon by thoughts of the vile things of Earth. All our inclinations, our thoughts and feelings tend to drag us down to the lowest depths of degradation. We are drifting down a swift current, without any power to withstand the forces bearing us down to ruin. See we are nearing the cataract! Soon we will be hurled down the precipice of eternal destruction, unless we are aided by a more than human power. The danger is imminent. Hope at last arises. A Savior appears, first announced to the shepherds afterwards to all mankind. With raptures of joy we accept this free salvation.

Feb. 22—The shipping in the harbor was decorated with flags in commemoration of Washington's birthday.

Feb. 23—Fine weather again.

Feb. 24—About 80 men started home, from the hospital, on thirty days furlough, this morning. They went on the Fulton. Tonight about 150 wounded were brought to the hospital, from Florida. We were moved out to the convalescent camp to make room for the wounded. Our forces have been repulsed in Florida with heavy loss.[21]

Feb. 25—We are again living in a tent; it is better than in the ward with the sick.

Feb. 26—I have thought myself entirely well but it is a mistake. The weather is delightful. The sand blowing is the greatest discomfort.

Feb. 27—As I was walking on the beach this morning I saw a lot of prairie chickens, with the feathers on, drifted ashore. These were doubtless intended to grace some epicure's table but instead of this the sea cast them ashore to remind a soldier of his native prairies.

Feb. 28, Sunday—The usual services in the dining room.

Feb. 29—Nothing of special interest to record. Farewell to Winter. No more guard duty to do of cold frosty nights. How the blessings and comforts of home will be appreciated!

March 1st—The day was a fair promise of a delightful Spring, but we must not trust too much to fair promises. A beautiful exterior is often made to cover horrid deformities.

Mar. 2—Nothing noteworthy.

Mar. 3—The fair promise, on the 1st, of pleasant weather is broken; the day is stormy and rather cool.

Mar. 4—The weather is still stormy. The breakers beat against the shore with great fury. The sand blows so thickly that it almost blinds one.

Mar. 5—Fine weather today. Nothing transpired of special interest.

Mar. 6, Sunday—Regular Sabbath routine.

Mar. 7—"Marchemos voluntarios,
Al campo del honor,
Atacar a los Yankees,
Que vienen con Taylor."
[We are marching, willing volunteers,
to the field of honor,
to attack the Yankees,
who are coming with Taylor]
—Mexican War song

Mar. 8—Nothing noteworthy.

Mar. 9—Stormy weather.

Mar. 10—Storm at night. Wind, thunder, lightning and rain.

Mar. 11—Delightful Spring day.

Mar. 12—The everyday sameness becomes very wearisome. The opportunities for study are poor, not for the want of time but for the want of books and a place where one can be undisturbed by noise and foolish talking. Notwithstanding all these disadvantages I hope to accomplish something.

Mar. 13, Sunday—There was nothing to cause this Sabbath to be remembered more than others.

Mar. 14—The day, although clear, was rather chilly.

Mar. 15—*Hace mucho viento y frio. Una grande tempestad hizo en la noche* [It is very windy and cold; a big storm blew up in the night].

Mar. 16—Ice froze quarter of an inch thick tonight.

Mar. 17—Nothing to record today.

Mar. 18—Worked in the garden.

Mar. 19—Learned six pages of Spanish, read the "New South" and some anecdotes. Time shall not be altogether lost. I long for the day when I can resume my studies.[22]

Mar. 20, Sunday—How unavailing are external circumstances to satisfy the longings of the soul! There is an aching void the world can never fill. Wealth, ease and luxury cannot give true happiness, nor can poverty rob one of it. Happiness is not an offspring of Earth, it is of celestial birth and is vouch-safed only to those who give heed to the small voice, saying, "This is the way, walk ye in it."

Mar. 21—Nothing noteworthy.

Mar. 22—Cold stormy day. Ice half an inch thick at night.

Mar. 23—Two years today since the battle of Winchester, Virginia, and I am yet alive. The prospect of long life is better now than it was then but the future is unknown to us mortals. Let us be thankful for past blessings and trust the future to Providence. *"Carpe diem"* [seize the day].

Mar. 24—Reported for duty the second time. Nothing of interest to record.

Mar. 25—Returned to duty. Was ordered to the office of the surgeon in charge in the forenoon; he asked me if I were able for duty. I told him that I was and that I was ashamed to remain any longer at the hospital. The clerk took my name and told me to hold myself in readiness to go to the regiment in the afternoon. After a great deal of delay, I got underway at 4 o'clock p.m. By the dint of hard walking, I reached Braddock's Point at half past seven in the evening. The distance is 13 miles. This march was my introduction to the Spring campaign.

Mar. 26—Spent the day in reconnoitering the country. Very much pleased with the appearance of things.

Mar. 27, Sunday—Fine day, the birds sing gayly. Brigade inspector inspected the detachment in the afternoon.

Mar. 28—Went into the timber to cut wood. Time passes more pleasantly than at the hospital. Hope that I will not have to choose anymore while in the army.

Mar. 29—Signed the pay rolls. Stormy and disagreeable day.

Mar. 30—The detachment was paid today. On account of a mistake in the payrolls, I did not get my pay.

Mar. 31—On guard tonight. A bird in a bush would occasionally wake up in the night and sing a song and then drop off to sleep again.

April 1—The day was cloudy with occasional light sprinkles of rain.

Apr. 2—Nothing new to record. Time passes very pleasantly, although the duty is rather heavy, and it is our wish to remain here the rest of our time.

Apr. 3, Sunday—On picket. The day was very fine. All night we could hear firing, supposed to be in Charleston Harbor.

Apr. 4—The day was rainy and disagreeable.

Apr. 5—The nights are so cold that we need three blankets to sleep under.

Apr. 6—On picket tonight. There was a boat passed the post next to mine; three shots were fired at it and it went back to an island in the river. At about the same time there was quite heavy firing in the direction of Spanish Wells. We saw three rockets thrown up a few minutes after. The firing not more than ten minutes. This was about midnight.[23]

Apr. 7—Nothing to record today.

Apr. 8—Nothing of importance occurred.

Apr. 9—On guard. Rained till in the afternoon when it cleared off and we had a fine night. All quiet.

Apr. 10, Sunday—A feeling of sadness oppresses me. I know not what is the cause but it seems to me that there is something serious in the future.

Apr. 11—Nothing noteworthy.

Apr. 12—Visited a school for colored children, taught by a white lady from the North. The scholars were not far advanced; mental Arithmetic and Wilson's Third Reader were the highest branches. The scholars were mostly small. They were only moderately prompt in their recitations; I had seen classes of white children do no better. There was one very small boy, about as high as a table, recited well. He was quick and correct in his answers; he was reading in the first reader. The mistress said that the scholars were unusually dull today. Order was good.

Apr. 13—The order came, last night at 12 o'clock, for us to hold ourselves in readiness to march to Hilton Head to embark at a moment's notice. We send our pickets out as usual this morning; it was my time to go on guard. Everything remained quiet through the day. About dark a company of colored soldiers came to relieve us so we had to strike tents and march to the Head. It took nearly all night to reach this place, being ten o'clock when we started.

Apr. 14—Reached the Head at 3 o'clock this morning and bivouacked in the sand. Remained in bivouac all day awaiting transportation. Late in the afternoon it began to rain and the boys distributed themselves around in empty tents, wherever they could find them, for the night.

Apr. 15—The detachment occupied some tents, which were standing in the outskirts of town, this morning. Negro soldiers were placed on provost guard a few days since. The mounted patrol was also composed of colored soldiers. This was the occasion of a rather serious riot this evening. It appears that the patrol arrested one of the 100th NY

Regiment. His comrades not liking to see him taken by negroes began to throw brick bats at the guard. The officer in command of the negroes ordered the rioters of the 100th NY to disperse and they refusing to obey he ordered one man to fire. This shot was fired into the air. They yet refused to conform to law and order and in a few minutes about 25 shots were fired into the mob. The men of the 100th Regiment then ran for their arms but luckily they were well guarded and the men did not get them. The row was finally quelled without further shedding blood. This occurred just at dark. I learned that two men of the 100th New York Regiment were seriously wounded. I saw an ambulance driven from the field of action to the General Hospital but I could not ascertain how many were wounded. The 100th NY had come from Morris Island and was awaiting transportation.[24]

Apr. 16—The day was very disagreeable on account of the sand blowing.

Apr. 17, Sunday—This day was rendered memorable to the Soldiers of Hilton Head Island by the execution of two deserters which took place this afternoon. At 15 minutes past 1 o'clock p.m., the different regiments turned out with arms and equipments and marched outside of the entrenchments. On the ground where Colonel Howell used to drill his brigade the troops were formed in three sides of a hollow square. Here they stood at the *order arms* for a short time when fifes and drums were heard approaching playing a *dead march*. The unfortunate men were being driven to the scene of their execution. First in order was the provost marshal accompanied by another officer both on foot, next was a band playing a dead march, following was a guard of two platoons of 12 men each and the rear of these were the prisoners in a four horse army wagon, next was an ambulance with chaplains and surgeons in it, behind this marched an escort with arms reversed, last were the pall bearers. Each platoon of the guard was commanded by a sergeant and marched with arms shouldered. The prisoners sat on their coffins and were entirely loose. In the above order they were driven in front of the lines. When passing their own regiment they occasionally took off their hats perhaps nodding adieu to some friend and comrade whom they recognized. They were driven to the middle of the open side of the square and here the team was stopped and the parties took their positions. The prisoners jumped out of the wagons as though nothing was the matter. The coffins were placed on the ground with the ends towards each other and a few feet apart. The prisoners then sat down on them. Their sentence was read to them and to each regiment and detachment present, which was that they should be shot to death with musketry. After this was over a Catholic priest administered to the poor fellows the consolations of religion. We could not hear what he said so we can only report what we saw. The prisoners took off their hats and kneeled by one of the coffins and the priest kneeled between them with a book in his hand as if reading. They remained in this position for a few minutes when priest arose and stood facing them with his hands on their heads. This ceremony over he shook hands with them and stepped back to one side; the prisoners put on their hats and each resumed his seat on his coffin. An officer, whom I took for the provost marshall, tied their hands behind them, uncovered their heads and bound white fillets over their eyes. They kneeled on their coffins and the guard, already mentioned, took a position about ten paces in front of them. The commands were now given by signals. The pieces were brought to a *ready* and *aim,* not a second intervened till the fatal command *fire* was given and executed. The prisoners both fell dead, at the same instant, the one forward and the other backward. The one that fell forward did not struggle nor move, the other we could not see so well, the coffin being between us and him. The feet of the former lay upon the coffin the latter fell back clear of the coffin near one foot. As soon as they fell two officers, surgeons I suppose, went to them and examined and bared their breasts. The regiments and pieces of regiments then right wheeled and marched in columns by companies with arms at support, past the corpses, the left of the companies passing in a few feet of them. They lay just as they fell with the exception that their breasts were uncovered and the one that fell on face was slightly turned over. In the breast of one we saw six or eight bullet holes as we marched past. Thus perished two fine looking men of the 6th Connecticut Volunteers; their names I care not to perpetuate. They cooly stared death in the face and died bravely. If they had thus unflinchingly offered up their lives in a good cause they would merit the name *Heroes.* Alas that men will bring upon themselves an ignominious death! Behind the outward calm, which they manifested, there was evidently a fierce storm raging. They seemed to make a great effort to conceal their real feelings. The scene was very solemn and impressive. In marching in front of the lines when they came to the post band it struck up the same doleful tune which the band marching in front of the procession was playing. The wagon, which bore the culprits, was drawn by four horses and driven by one man who sat in the fore part of the wagon. The coffins were painted black; this added much to the mournfulness of the spectacle. There were present to witness the execution, besides the soldiers, a good many citizens and some women. A woman who would desire to see a human being shot to death, or put to death in any way, is utterly destitute of the fine feelings which should adorn the character of a lady. To be plain, although several females, I will not say women, witnessed the execution, I do not believe there was a single *true lady* present. Of the citizens present I have but a little better opinion. I saw a contemptible suttler sitting on his horse looking with a field glass, not content with all he could see with the naked eye. With the soldiers it was no matter of choice; they were ordered out and had either to go or disobey orders and suffer its consequences. The men detailed to shoot the deserters were of their own regiment (6th Connecticut). Let justice be done though the heavens fall. Justice could not save them. Mercy alone could avert their doom and there are times when the inopportunities of mercy cannot be heard. Although we pitied the unfortunate offenders of the law we said as above *"let justice be done."* The punishment was not from malice to the condemned but to prevent a repetition of the crime and as a warning to others. I hope that I may never be called on to witness another such a scene.[25]

Apr. 18—This morning was rainy but rain was not so disagreeable as the sand blowing so as almost to blind one. The persevering effort made this morning to rain succeeded in the afternoon finally and there was a heavy shower.

Apr. 19—At 3 o'clock p.m., we bid adieu to South Carolina. The detachment 39th Illinois embarked on the transport Baltimore in the afternoon; she got underway [and] started on her voyage to Fortress Monroe at 3 o'clock p.m. She is a miserable craft for transporting troops. We had either to stay on the upper deck or go below into a dark stinking "hole" so low that a tall man could scarcely stand erect. The vessel rolled like a log. The wind was blowing quite a stiff gale when we went out and as the vessel pitched and heaved I began to experience an unpleasant sensation about the stomach and went below there to lie prostrate with sea sickness for two days and two nights. I was not alone in my suffering.[26]

Apr. 20—Today was almost an entire blank in my life, old Neptune holding me with a strong grasp in his embrace.

Apr. 21—I was able to eat late this afternoon for the first time since going aboard. Went above in time to see Cape Hatteras. We could discern a low shore far away in the distance. The sea was very smooth. The transport Mississippi loaded with troops passed us, off the Cape, northward bound.[27]

Apr. 22—Land in sight on our starboard bow at day light; proved to be Virginia. Cape Henry Lighthouse soon hove in sight. This Cape is at the mouth of Chesapeake Bay, on the opposite side is Cape Charles; we passed in sight of it. The sand is drifted in great heaps on the extreme point of Cape Henry. Back a short distance is a heavy forest, the green trees being a pleasant relief from the glaring white sand. The lighthouse, a white tower, and a residence are all the buildings in sight. There were several wrecks near. We passed in a few rods of the Cape. We arrived at Fortress Monroe in the forenoon and anchored at Hampton Roads. The Capt. commanding detachment went ashore and received orders to proceed to York Town. We anchored at this place in the afternoon. Late in the night we disembarked landing in Gloucester Point VA, and bivouacked.

Apr. 23—We marched out about two miles from the Point and encamped. Ground was staked off for our veteran comrades when they join us; the 39th Illinois veteran part of it, are expected here in a few days. "Onward to Richmond," again.

Apr. 24, Sunday—We get our camp established yesterday in time to enjoy some rest today. May peace attend us on this day of rest.

Apr. 25—The weather here seems equally as warm as in South Carolina when we left there; vegetation is, however, not as forward by about one month.

Apr. 26—We received orders today to reduce our clothing to the following articles, viz: two shirts, two pairs of drawers, three pairs of socks, one woolen blanket, one gum blanket, one pair of pants, one blouse, one overcoat and two pairs of shoes. Shelter tents are to be issued and our wedge tents and clothing over the amount above specified is to be packed and sent to Norfolk for storage. This looks like active operations. Richmond is the prize at stake. The 39th Illinois veteran volunteers arrived here this afternoon, the regiment was recruited considerable while in Illinois.

Apr. 27—The detachment 39th Illinois volunteers was today turned over to the Regiment. Captain F. J. Platt, the commander of the detachment, is extremely popular; none of the boys find any fault with him and it is the regret of all that he is to leave us. He will not go without a token of respect from the men of the detachment. His rule was mild yet firm. The detachment was composed of two companies made up of all the companies of the regiment. It was feared that the companies containing these different remnants would not be agreeable among themselves. Such was not the case by far. A better feeling among men I never saw exist. Many of the men felt as if justice had not been done them by the Officers when the regiment left South Carolina. The boys, most of them at least, regret very much having to serve their time out in their own companies. A great consolation to them, however, it is that there are but few months longer.

Apr. 28—The 10th Army corps, that is the corps of South Carolina, is being concentrated on this side of the York River.

Apr. 29—Inspection this forenoon. Cool day and night. We received shelter tents today and are now living in our "dog houses." Things begin to look like active operations.

Apr. 30—Exit April. Mustered for pay. Activity prevails preparing for the coming campaign. Great is the confidence of all although heavy work is anticipated. The right kind of spirit pervades the ranks, but little murmuring and dissatisfaction exists. A cheerful and determined disposition is everywhere manifested. The troops here were reviewed by Major General Butler this afternoon. The General was saluted according to his rank when he arrived on the field. He looks so much like the pictures of him that he was at once recognized. We estimated the force present at 10,000 infantry and five batteries artillery. Brigadier Generals Ames, Foster and Terry were here on the field. Clouds of dust enveloped the men as they were marching. Tired, hungry and dirty we returned to camp in the grey dawn of twilight.[28]

May 1, Sunday—The day was rainy but not more disagreeable on this account. The pleasure derived from a sense of time well spent is not subject to such contingencies as the weather.

May 2—About sundown there was a heavy storm of hail and rain. The air became very cool and chilly. The hail lasted but a few minutes.

May 3—On brigade guard today. Colonel Howell relieved us at night that we might be ready for the duties of the morrow.

May 4—At 3 o'clock this morning the camp was aroused and began to get ready to move. We embarked at the pier on Gloucester Point early in the day and run up the river a short distance and anchored; here we lay all day with steam up ready to start at any moment. The right wing of our regiment went on the steamer Convoy and the left on the Iolas.[29] Troops were embarking all day at Gloucester and York Town. Against night there was a large fleet of transports and barges. The site was truly grand to see the vessels lying at anchor in the placid waters of the York River displaying their lights. We "turned in" regretting to take our eyes from so beautiful a scene but prospect of hard service soon to come admonished us to take all the rest we could get. Sometime in the night the fleet moved down to Fortress Monroe and anchored. Our sleep was so sound that we knew nothing of the move.

May 5—The vessels got under way early this morning and moved up to Newport News and after lying at anchor here about an hour began to move slowly up the river. Soon we passed the Roanoke, that huge three-turreted monitor. She resembles a monitor only in her turrets; she sits much higher out of water. Her color is a sort of a lead excepting her after turret which is painted red. Further up we passed another monitor (1 turret). Below Harrison's Landing, a few miles, we passed the Atlanta, of late the rebel ram Frugal.[30] Many places along the river looked quite familiar, especially James Town, the mouth of the Chickahominy and Harrison's Landing. A small force was landed at two places on the river; the one on the north bank and the other on the south at Fort Powhattan.[31] We passed City Point a little before sundown; our flag was there. We ran a few miles above this place and anchored for the night. Here a scene similar to that of last night was presented only on a larger scale. The transports that brought the 18th Army Corps were lying in the river; this embarked at Norfolk and Newport News.[32]

May 6—Early this morning the last of the 10th Corps debarked and a short time after took up the line of march in a southwest direction. The 18th Corps took a road to the left about two miles from the landing. The 39th Illinois was deployed as skirmishers and advanced in this order, the right approaching the James River. We advanced about seven miles and no opposition was encountered by the 10th Corps. Late in the afternoon we heard quite heavy firing to our left from which we supposed that the 18th Corps had met the enemy. We bivouacked in an old field and had a comfortable night's rest. The day was warm and the road dusty. General

Butler passed along the front about sundown. He was cheered vociferously. He went outside the pickets and, report says, came near being captured, one of his orderlies was taken. The road was strewn with stuff thrown away by the soldiers. There were blankets and overcoats enough thrown to carpet the road half the distance marched! Shoes, knapsacks, haversacks, soap, candles, blacking brushes, plates, knives, forks, spoons, ink, books, portfolios, etc., were scattered along in great profusion.

May 7—Fortifying was commenced last night and we were early this morning lying behind entrenchments. Axes are now busy felling trees. We were under arms at 3 o'clock a.m. In the middle of the afternoon there was a sharp engagement to the left of our position. The reports of the affair were so various and conflicting that we could learn but little about it. We could hear the musketry and artillery but did not see the fight. There were several cases of sun stroke today. The weather is very warm.

May 8, Sunday—Our regiment went on picket this morning to relieve the 85th Pennsylvania. The day was very warm and calm; scarcely a leaf moving. A storm of rebel fury may at any moment break upon us; let them come we are ready. The soldiers are in good spirits. I never felt more willing to go into battle than at the present time. We were relieved late in the evening and back to the rear and bivouacked for the night. There was some skirmishing on the left today.

May 9—We arose before daylight and girded ourselves for the conflict which seemed to be impending. Our brigade is the first of the First Division, 10th Army Corps. The 10th Corps is on the right and the 18th on the left; the right of the former rests on the James River and the left of the latter on the Appomattox. Soon after daylight we were on the move; the 85th Pennsylvania taking the lead and the 39th Illinois following next. When outside our pickets the 85th was deployed and advanced in line as skirmishers. About half a mile out some rebel cavalry was encountered and a slight skirmish ensued; the enemy falling back. Our first line of battle was formed on a ridge at a church; we occupied this position for about an hour and a half and then moved forward a quarter of a mile to an old graveyard and remained there all day. Firing had by this time entirely ceased. No one was hurt on our side. Companies of our regiment relieved the 85th Pennsylvania and let them fall back to rest. Five companies of our regiment were on picket at night, among them was Company I, and the rest lay in reserve at the graveyard. All was quiet along our lines during the night. The graveyard above mentioned is very ancient and deserves special notice. There are but two graves visible each marked by a flat stone lying on the ground and partially covered with soil. The epitaph of one is in a good state of preservation, it shows that he, who is buried beneath it, was of Liverpool and traded many years to this Province. He died in 1773. One corner of the other stone is broken off but we could make out that the deceased belonged to the ship John of Liverpool and died in 1772. They are both sandstones. Scattered around over a space of a few yards square are pieces of bricks. The ground is over grown with briars and strawberries, the latter were in bloom. Part of our Division went further to the left than we did and tore up, without any opposition, the Petersburg & Richmond railroad. The 18th Army Corps and all of the 10th excepting the first Division has been moving in the direction of Petersburg, this place is distant from where we are 9 miles. A regiment of colored cavalry when reconnoitering near Fort Darling got into an ambush and lost some men.

May 10—Colonel Vorhees, of the 67th Ohio, went with his own and 4 or 5 other regiments, and perhaps, a battery of artillery and seized a turnpike leading from Richmond to Petersburg yesterday when the advance was made. This he held today till forced back about noon by a superior force of the enemy. Early in the morning our artillery opened on the rebels and kept up a constant fire all the morning. At about 10 o'clock AM, musketry firing commenced, light at first but increased rapidly. Soon there was a continuous roll of musketry. We could hear tremendous yelling. Three or four of the musket balls came whistling past where we were stationed on picket. The engagement lasted an hour and a half. There were occasional lulls in the firing for a few seconds and it would then be resumed. From the information I can get it was a drawn battle. Our men fell back a short distance but were not followed up by the enemy. One piece of artillery was captured from our men and re-taken again. Major Butler of the 67th Ohio was over the field after the battle and says there were ten dead rebels to one union soldier.[33] Our men occupied the field in about three hours after the fighting ceased. I understand that the enemy asked permission to bury their dead under a flag of truce. Our men fought bravely, as usual. The line of skirmishers of the 67th Ohio repulsed the rebels advancing in line of battle three times; well done Buckeyes. The woods prevented us from seeing the engagement. If our right had not have gave way the enemy would perhaps have been handsomely repulsed. All was quiet during the night. Our forces fell back from the direction of Petersburg this afternoon. Our regiment was relieved from picket at sundown this evening; went to the rear and bivouacked for the night. We had a good night's sleep for the first time since landing on the banks of James River last Friday.

May 11—We lay in the woods today a few rods further back than last night's bivouac. The boys stretched their shelter tents, though not in much order; so things began to look something like a camp. A shelter tent is quite a luxury to a soldier after sleeping out under the canopy of heaven for several nights in succession. There was a heavy detail for fatigue at noon; I was one of the number. We had nothing to do on account of not finding the Officer to whom we were to report, nevertheless we were kept awaiting orders till night. A little before dark it began to rain. There was some firing in the front today. Our picket line was contracted; the reserve lying at the church previously mentioned. We had scarcely got to sleep tonight when we were informed that the rebels were masking a heavy force in the front on the right and were ordered to put our clothes on and be ready to fall in at any minute. The order came not till morning.

May 12—Early we were under arms and behind the entrenchments; no rebels came so we stacked arms and took shovels, picks and axes and in the use of these tools the 39th Illinois spent the day. It rained nearly all day. We hear so much and learn so little that we do not know what is going on around us; for an account of the battles that took place in our hearing we will have to depend on the future historian. There was fighting in the front today.

May 13—Things were so quiet during last night and this morning that we were permitted to sleep till after daylight. This was to us a day of rest.

May 14—At half past 2 o'clock this morning we were called up and started on the march.[34] We went out to the pike and from there to the Richmond & Petersburg Railroad; guarded an ammunition train. We came to the railroad at Chester Station; there we halted for about two hours awaiting some cars that were to have been there. Some men were sent down the Portwalthal railroad and brought up eight coal cars. These we pushed up to the front for wounded. Passed Clover Hill Junction and Halfway Station distant from Richmond 11 miles; from the Junction a branch railroad runs to Portwalthal on the Appomattox River; distant 4 miles. We learned that our forces had been fighting considerable during last night and found them in possession of the first line of rebel works. These our men passed to the right and attacked them in the rear. Fighting was still going on when we arrived. We went to work getting the wounded on the cars and sending them back to Chester. There were some horrible sights to be seen here but this was only a foretaste of what we were soon to witness. At 1 1/2 o'clock PM General Gillmore ordered us to the front. It took an hour more or less before our position was assigned us and during part of this time we were under a musketry and artillery fire and four men were wounded; three of Company I: George Lonebarger was the first man wounded, he was the only man wounded of our regiment at the battle of Winchester.[35] A position was assigned us in an open field on the left to support the 1st Connecticut battery. We lay down on the ground and were not engaged during the day excepting a few sharp shooters which were thrown forward. Occasionally rebel bullets struck the ground near us but the firing was not brisk; the shells of the enemy went over us mostly. Colonel Osborn was wounded in the arm severely; he remained on the field till night apparently disregarding the wound. Maj. Linton had a hole shot through the sleeve of his coat. The battery which we were supporting did splendidly; the loss was heavy. They made the heavens reverberate with the roar of their guns and covered the face of the Earth with smoke. About sundown the enemy made a demonstration to the right of us but they were driven into their entrenchments. At dark we moved to the right so as to connect with the next regiment. Our right rested on the railroad and our line of battle was at right angles with it. In this position we lay all night with arms in our hands. One-third of the men were allowed to sleep at a time. The regiment on our right was firing all the afternoon and they kept it up through the night. About midnight the enemy sallied forth and fired a few rounds. We were instantly on our feet and ready for them. We had scarcely got into line till two men of Company I were wounded by the same bullet. The storm soon blew over and things became comparatively quiet and so remained the rest of the night. The ground was muddy, the night was damp and chilly. Two men of Company I were killed and three wounded by a shell late in the evening.

May 15, Sunday—We fell back about 75 yards this morning at daylight; our position was in other respects just the same as that of last night. We threw up a line of rifle pits this morning so we could sit and listen to the bullets passing over our heads with impunity. At times during the day there was quite a heavy fire along some parts of the lines but not on the left. Yet we were not altogether quiet in our front. A fire was kept up all day between our pickets and those of the enemy and occasionally they would send a shell or a charge of shrapnel schrieking over our heads. A few of our men were wounded during the day. From the time that we were ordered to the support of the battery we were within musket shot of rebel batteries. The day was showery but when the sun came out for a few minutes at a time it was terribly hot. Firing was going on all night but in our front things were not very blustery. We availed ourselves of the cover of night to strengthen our works. During the day we could see the enemy parading a large force on a hill back of their batteries. Such were our observations today.

May 16—Terrible is the record of today and many are those who will remember it with sadness. Many brave men were shot down and left on the field in a helpless condition to fall into the hands of the rebels. The loss of the 39th Illinois Regiment was heavy. Our position has already been described. Back of us a few rods was a strip of woods; to our right the railroad passed through a deep cut, beyond this was woods. Early in the morning it was very foggy. The enemy made an attack on us about sunrise but he was repulsed and we enjoyed a season of quiet. At about 8 o'clock the fog cleared up and we could see the rebel works. The enemy seemed to be busy disposing of his troops. A regiment had been taken away from our left early in the morning so we had to extend our line to fill up the vacancy thus caused. We were therefore drawn up in the rifle pit in one rank and not very close together at that. There was no other line in the rear of us. It was perhaps 9 o'clock when the enemy made an assault in heavy force. They marched up in solid phalanx as steady as if they were on drill. We held our fire till they were within a few rods of us and then took deliberate aim giving them the contents of our muskets.

This first discharge no doubt caused many of the poor fellows much pain. Every man now pitched in with all his might. The rebels closed their ranks and continued to advance steadily. Several times were their colors brought down but almost instantly they were picked up again. One regiment, the 29th Virginia, drew our attention chiefly being on the front of the right of our regiment. The commander was on horseback and he was picked off by one of our men. By this time the rebel ranks were decimated so that they became very much disorientated and soon after they began to retreat. All was now favorable on the front and a tremendous yell went up along our line. Our exultation was of but short duration for our front was scarcely cleared of the enemy till it was discovered that we had no support on our right. The regiment (55th Penn) which was across the railroad from us either gave way or was ordered away. It is said that it was ordered to fall back before the attack was made.

Be that as it may our officers thought that there was a regiment at least on our right. Our critical situation was at once perceived; our right was turned. A retreat was at once ordered and we fell back into the woods, (it is true our line was not very well dressed) there we halted, about-faced and charged the enemy and retook our rifle pits. This was done under a hail storm of bullets and many of our men in this charge were laid *hor de combat* [out of action]. We succeeded in clearing our front the second time but it was of no avail; the enemy was in our rear in force. About one company of rebels were discovered coming along the railroad in our rear. Our men supposing that they wanted to give themselves up did not fire but called out to them to throw down their arms and surrender. Capt. Rudd who was then in command supposing that they were going to comply with the demand would not let our men fire. Their reply was a volley of musketry. Lead began now to rain down upon our rear and to remain longer in our position would have been annihilation. To retreat seemed impossible and none entertained the thought of surrendering. We made a desperate dash into the woods and run the gauntlet of a tremendous shower of bullets, the rebels crying to us "Halt, Halt, throw down your arms and surrender." We did not obey their demands but pushed on regardless of the storm of leaden iron and hail. All excepting our wounded escaped the clutches of the foe. The right got separated from the left. We fell back to the rear of the first line of battle, about three-quarters of a mile from the scene of conflict. There we halted and waited till the left of the regiment came up. Early in the engagement Major Linton was severely wounded so Captain Baker was left in command.[36] Colonel Mann came up at this place and took command; he was left in camp sick when we started out on Saturday. The entire column seemed now to be retreating and we were ordered to fall back. The column moved slowly back and in perfect order; not the confusion was to be observed. We took two positions and formed a line of battle and waited for wagons and ambulances to pass. We reached camp outside of our entrenchments at 9 o'clock in the night, worn out and hungry having been three days and two nights under arms and the greater part of the time under fire. The loss of our regiment, though heavy, was hardly so great as would have been expected under the circumstances. I have not yet learned the exact number killed, wounded and missing of the regiment; that of our Company was 26 men but one of whom was known to have been killed. L. Hurley was shot in the head in re-capturing our rifle pits. He did not speak; we left him in the agonies of death. Many of the men were slightly wounded. Most of those who could not walk were left on the field and fell into the hands of the enemy. Adjutant Walker was mortally wounded and died soon after he was taken to camp. Capt. Whiteman was mortally wounded. Captain Phillips missing.[37] Every man did his duty and no one flinched. Our company took three prisoners. Such was the day's work in which we participated. Lieutenants Lemmon and Fellows took guns and fought like tigers. General Butler complemented our regiment highly. Many more things might be written about this engagement but the above is enough of the horrible affair. It is the opinion of some of the Officers that we killed our number of rebels; that is one man for each that we had. On the right there was more fighting than on the left but it was so far off that we could not see it. The rebels forced our men back at first. But afterwards a heavy force was massed on the right and drove the enemy back into their entrenchments. The battle was 10 miles from Richmond. A cavalry force sent out by General Butler succeeded in cutting off the Richmond and Danville railroad. Our object was accomplished hence the reason why we returned to our entrenchments. It was our business to keep the enemy engaged till the cavalry expedition accomplished its mission of destruction. I understand that orders were given for us to fall back early in the morning but the order failed to reach us. War is an awful business and verifies the proverb *"Homo homini est"* [Man is (wolf) to man].

May 17—Captain Whiteman died this morning. Capt. Wheeler, Lieutenant Kidder and Lieutenant Kingsburry were wounded.[38] We were under arms at 3 o'clock this morning. In the afternoon there was an inspection. The day was pleasant and the rest we were permitted to enjoy was sweet. The thought of so many of our comrades who had fallen in battle alone embittered our comfort. The entire loss of our regiment in killed, wounded and missing was about 120 men; Company I suffered worse than any other company in the regiment. Companies F & H were not in the engagement. F had been sent out to the left early in the morning to reconnoiter and H was left at Chester Station.

May 18—At midnight the enemy made a demonstration in our front and we were called under arms and took our position in the trenches. About 3 o'clock AM we were permitted to go to our quarters and things were quiet till 8 o'clock AM when firing was resumed in front and we were called to the trenches. There we remained the rest of the day and all night. Quite heavy musketry firing was kept up till dark. This was about one mile in front of our entrenchments. A battery to the left of us shelled the woods very vigorously at times during the day but the enemy made little or no response. The gun boats in James River fired rapidly at intervals all day. There was nothing for us in the trenches to do but to be on the alert; our advance forces did not seem to give back any at all. Our losses were not very heavy; I saw only a few wounded brought in. The day was showery and when the sun shown out it was with great intensity. Meals were served to us in the trenches. All was quiet during the night and we slept soundly behind our breast works. The night was damp and chilly.

May 19—Early this morning the enemy opened a heavy fire on us with artillery. They continued to shell our works and camp for about one hour with great fierceness, then they abated somewhat but continued to fire a shot occasionally all day. Our batteries did not reply. The firing was at long range. The enemies guns almost completely enfiladed our position; for this reason we took shovels and went to work with a good will throwing up travises. None of our men were wounded in the trenches; three or four men in camp were struck by fragments of shells. The nature of their wounds I did not learn. There was but little musketry. The gun boats were busy all day belching forth thunder and lightning. All day in the trenches. There were three attacks made during the night, each of short duration but intense fierceness. The artillery in our works took a part in the fights. Our pickets were not driven into the entrenchments.

May 20—Still in the trenches, meals being brought to us. There was the usual amount of skirmishing today. At 2 o'clock p.m., our regiment marched out of the works to attack the enemy. We formed our line of battle in the woods near Ware Bottom Church; the right Company (I) was deployed as skirmishers and went into them pell mell. A heavy shower of bullets greeted us and we returned the complement. We kept our position for a few minutes loading and firing rapidly and then began to advance with a yell. The enemy returned firing as they fell back. Everything seemed to be going away before us when word was passed along that the left had been forced back and we were ordered to fall back. It was rather difficult to get the boys to obey. The retrograde movement was short both in time and space. We rallied on the colors and retook all our lost ground. After advancing as far as was contemplated we halted and exchanged our muskets for shovels, keeping the former close at hand, and in half an hour had a line of rifle pits. We were relieved at 9 o'clock in the night and spent the rest of the night in the trenches. There was but little to disturb the quiet of camp the remainder of the night. Lieutenant Colonel Mann was wounded early in the engagement so the command devolved on Captain Baker of Co. A. The rebels projected a great amount of lead at us but they shot too high. Our loss, that is of our regiment, was 68 men killed, wounded and missing. Co. I had two men wounded. The rebel Major General Walker was wounded and taken a prisoner.[39]

May 21—On fatigue at Battery No. 3. The rebel works in sight. Could see their flag in the parapets; it was cut down twice during the day by the gunners of No. 3. But little firing in front. Our regiment was on fatigue at night at Battery No. 1. At 11 o'clock in the night an attack was made all along our lines. The firing was very heavy. Our artillery opened from some of the batteries and there has been no cannonading equal to that of tonight since we have been here. The engagement lasted for about one hour. The enemy was repulsed. All quiet the rest of the night. We took our position in the trenches and there for the rest of the night remained.

May 22, Sunday—The morning was very quiet and so ought things to be on this day of rest. We went on picket in the evening. When we got to the front the enemy were burying their dead under flag of truce so we had to wait before we relieved the old picket. The 85th Pennsylvania was on our right. The night was very quiet but few musket shots were fired along the entire line. The stillness of the night was broken at regular intervals by the cannon of the gun boats in James River. We could hear the rebels chopping busily till midnight when it ceased and we could hear them digging. They seemed quite jovial, they whistled and sang merrily.

May 23—The day was equally as quiet as last night. We could see the rebels at work, perhaps three hundred yards from us, apparently erecting a battery. They were screened from view by the trees and bushes. The men moved lively, almost on the double quick; they were so large that they looked like giants. Our lines and those of the enemy were in a dense pine woods and each party had rifle pits; for this reason we could not tell exactly what each other were doing although we were in hailing distance. At noon a flag of truce was sent from our side to the enemy. It was met about midway between the lines by six rebel Officers. They carried a small dirty looking flag when they started to meet the Officers of our side but they seemed to be ashamed of it and before they met they furled their colors and we saw no more of the emblem of treason. There was a great difference between the appearance of the Union officers and the Rebels. The former looked neat and clean, the latter slouchy and dirty. The gray uniforms of the rebels were nearly the color of the soil where the coloquey took place. Would that our Officers had the earnestness of the enemy's and were less inclined to dress and make a show. In the afternoon the enemy sent an answer to the communications sent at noon. What the communications were concerning I did not learn. We were relieved and got to camp a short time after dark. The 39th Illinois and the 85th Pennsylvania did not fire a single shot while on picket this twenty-four hours; this was something remarkable.

May 24—About midnight firing commenced along the picket line opposite Battery No. 3. This caused us to have to get up and take our place in the trenches for the rest of the night. There was a heavy musketry along the most of the line; the artillery was not engaged. We were however too sleepy to take any note of firing which did not immediately concern us. At the place where the firing commenced the enemy was so near that the bullets came whistling through our camp, wounding one man, of Co. H., in bed. About all that we know about the affair, is that there was heavy firing and that our pickets were not driven in. At daylight we went back to camp. The day was quiet and so was the night. It is remarkable that there was no alarm at all in camp during the night and we were permitted to sleep till daylight.

May 25—There was a shower of rain last night and things look very much refreshed this morning, even the birds seem more gay. Still quiet. What does it mean? The regiment was on fatigue today. Having had twenty-four hours rest the boys feel much invigorated. A dispatch from Secretary Stanton was read to the various regiments here this afternoon and it was received with three cheers. The sum of it was that Grant had defeated Lee on the North Anna River and that the latter was in full retreat to Richmond with heavy loss. Our regiment was taken in off of fatigue to read this to it and was then sent back to work. It was considered a boar by the boys to have to march half a mile and back again, one mile, to hear this dispatch. At 10 o'clock in the night firing commenced in front of Battery No. 3. There was not much firing but enough to call us to the trenches. Occasionally stray bullets came through our camp and Lieutenant Burrell of Co. A was wounded seriously in the neck. So it is we know not what minute we will be shot down in our camp. Quiet was soon restored in front and the rest of the night passed without any further disturbance. We stayed in the trenches all night. A man of Co. B was drowned today, while bathing in James River.[40]

May 26—We came to camp at daylight. The morning was rainy. We moved our camp to Battery No. 2. In the evening we went on picket. The night was quiet.

May 27—Time passed rather slowly with us. The trees along the picket line showed evidences of the recent engagements. They are marked with bullets. The side next to the enemy show that many of them discharged their pieces at too great an elevation. There were bullet marks on the trees ten, twenty and forty feet high. The rebels were in sight all day but there was no firing along the lines. They seemed to have no care about concealing their position. A short time before sundown a band struck up and played several tunes. This we considered a nice treat from our enemies. After dark about one hour we were relieved and went to camp. We supposed that we would get to sleep in our tents tonight but in this we were mistaken for when we got our suppers we had to go to the trenches and stay the rest of the night. All was quiet.

May 28—"All is lovely and the goose hangs high." There was nothing of importance observable today. Everything was very quiet in front.

May 29, Sunday—There was a movement of troops from here today. Report says that the 18th Corps has gone to the Army of the Potomac.[41] Our camp is so situated and we are kept so busy that we have but little opportunity to observe what is going on out of our own brigade. The rebels have undoubtedly diminished their force in our front. There is no prospect of our forces assuming the offensive soon here. At 5 o'clock p.m., we went on picket. The night was calm and quiet. Company I being on the reserve we were permitted to sleep half of the night. The rebels were not disposed to disturb our rest. The night was rather chilly and an overcoat was quite comfortable. Such is the record of the last Sunday in May, 1864. As the time of our discharge draws nigh we begin to ask ourselves how many more Sundays thus to be spent? And take consolation from the fact that if ten or twelve will not be all there will not be many more added. We feel the need of rest for the body and food for the soul. These are scarce commodities in the army; hence our desire to doff the apparel of a soldier and don the habiliments of peace. Although the time, when this great change shall take place, is short, yet there are many dangers through which we may be called to pass and many of us, perhaps, will never realize our fond dreams of home and friends. Two weeks ago some of our comrades were so hopeful as we. Alas they were not permitted to return to their friends. Amidst the dreadful crash of musketry they fell bravely battling for our common country, for right and humanity. It may be our lot to share a similar fate and our prayer is that we may be prepared for what is in store for us whether it be prosperity or adversity. He who has brought us thus far safely through the perils and dangers of a soldier's life can yet protect us and believing that no harm can befall us unless He so wills it we will go forth fearlessly in the discharge of duty, flinching nothing that we may encounter in the path which we may be called to tread. We firmly believe that our cause is a righteous one and that the enemies against whom we contend are the enemies of humanity. At times when thinking of these things we are almost constrained to enlist for the war but then again we remember that there are many able bodied men in the North who have not evinced their patriotism in the field. To such I consider it right to give place. Three years is as long as a man ought to be exposed to the hardships and exposures of a soldier's life. Having done our whole duty as a soldier it remains for us to act the part of a good citizen. This done all will be done so far as our duty to our country is concerned.

May 30—Day in the trenches on picket. Weather very warm. All day we could hear cannonading, and that heavy, north of us. We supposed this to be General Baldy Smith fighting Lee's Army, part of it. Smith is reported to have crossed the James River a day or two since with 20,000 men and marched to reinforce the Army of the Potomac. This movement of troops from this place previously mentioned. Things were very quiet along our lines in front the greater part of the day. The pickets of the two opposing armies were quite sociable; this sociability has been increasing for several days. The pickets conversed with each other freely and exchanged papers. Things were going on in this style today; the rebels offered to exchange papers and to trade tobacco for coffee. The men on both sides had become very careless and left the ditches without any fear whatever. Suddenly a voice from the rebel lines warned us that hostilities were to commence in a few minutes. The words of warning were these: "Get into your pits, we are going to open fire." The boys took the warning, girded themselves for battle and set down into the ditches. This was about 5 1/2 o'clock p.m. About 10 minutes after notice was given the enemy opened to the left of us. They fired one gun and then cheered vociferously; the cheering was taken up along the lines and tremendous cheering went up from rebel throats. At this the 100th Regiment New York, which was on our right, ran like wild sheep. Where they stopped I have not yet learned, certainly not short of camp. The scamps by their cowardice left our right exposed and if the enemy had taken advantage of this they could have handled us roughly. As soon as the cheering had ceased the enemy opened a heavy artillery fire on us from different parts of their lines; one battery almost swept our ditch, fortunately the enemy fired but little from this. The cannonade raged with great fury for about half an hour, the rebels having it all their own way at first. The limbs of the trees were cut off around and over our heads. Camp was not neglected, the rebels sending many of their missiles into our fortifications. Most of the shells were too high to hurt the pickets. The enemy used no heavy artillery. Our artillery opened after the rebels had been at work about fifteen minutes and the pickets were in as much danger from the guns of their friends as those of their foes. The gun boats mingled in the latter part of the engagement. The 67th Ohio came to relieve us during the hottest of the firing but, according to orders, we did not fall back till quiet was restored. There was a great amount of noise but little damage done; nobody in our regiment was hurt. A little after sundown we fell back into a rifle pit near the outer edge of our slashing. Here we remained a short time and all being quiet went to camp. After supper we took our position in the trenches and slept till morning; the night was quiet. The night was cool. The boys at first had a great repugnance to sleeping in the trenches but now they care less for it. Duty is now much lighter than it was ten days ago. Rations are tolerably good for the time of the year. There is more of a disposition to complain than there was two weeks ago. There is not yet much grumbling but a disposition to be dissatisfied seems to be increasing. Nothing is really meant by this grumbling this only for the want of something better to talk about. Some are becoming slightly discouraged.

May 31—All was quiet till about the middle of the afternoon when the rebels opened a furious cannonade. Our batteries replied and the firing was very heavy. The shells of the enemy went crashing through the woods into the camps. The engagement lasted about half an hour. It was not much trouble to get the boys into the trenches. One man of Company G was wounded. The casualties of other regiments I did not learn. This storm over, we enjoyed quiet the rest of the day. Early in the morning we heard firing in the direction of Richmond but it was not kept up through the day. The rebels opened up on our gun boats in the Appomattox River from a masked battery, in the afternoon. This was the occasion of a sharp engagement in which the rebel battery was silenced. Some day since there was an affair at Wilson's Wharf, below us. So we have war on all sides, front, rear and both flanks. We stacked our arms behind the breast works and went to our quarters for the night with orders to take our places in the works as soon as firing commenced. We retired momentarily expecting to hear the signal of alarm. All was quiet till a short time before daylight when there was a great deal of noise and some little damage. The rebels opened their artillery with their accustomed fury. The scene was terrible to behold. The heavens seem to be a blaze of fire and full of all sorts of hissing sounds. The course of the shells could be traced through the air by a stream of fire; they would explode with great noise and flash. The pieces flying off in all directions cut the limbs of trees, buried themselves in the earth or knocked, whatever man or beast might be in their path, down either killing them or inflicting wounds. Behind our strong breast works we could look at the storm of iron, if not altogether with impunity, at least without much fear. The amount of firing was, perhaps, about as great on one side as on the other. The cannonade lasted about one hour when quiet was again restored. At this time the eastern horizon was tinted with the first dawn of morning. Thus began we the first day of June, 1864 and a noisy beginning was it. The casualties in our regiment were two men wounded, one of Company G and the other of Co. I. The wounds are not dangerous. It was my lot to be added to the list of the wounded of Co. I. A piece of a shell struck my right arm, knocking a hole in the skin and bruising the flesh considerably. I do not expect to miss an hour's duty on account of it. And now my record for the last nine months is closed. Tonight we go on picket. No one can tell what will there befall us. Our race may be almost run and if so all is well. The future of this world is dark and dangerous. For consolation we have to look beyond the clouds and fogs of Earth into that celestial atmosphere where all is serene and peaceful. There all is bright and joyful, there alone no sorrows are known. Here uproar and confusion reign supreme, allotting but little time to us poor mortals for rest and reflection. It would be ungrateful in us not to record our thankfulness to our Heavenly Father for past blessing. It is through His mercies that we are spared to make the record. Whatever may befall us in the future let no complaint escape our lips. We have enjoyed more good than we deserve. And shall we not taste the bitter of the cup? In prosperity or in adversity, in peace or in war, at home or amidst the terrible crash of battle we would be resigned to the Will of the Ruler of the Universe. Let us, therefore, be ready when Death comes knocking at the door. From the reports of deserters we understand that the rebels think that we are evacuating this place, hence their firing two days past. They are mistaken as they would find if they were to undertake to storm our works. There is not a very large force here but we believe ourselves able to repel any force which they may bring against us. Our fortifications have advanced to that state of completion that we can now work on them at our leisure. The line of fortifications extends from the James River on the right to the Appomattox on the left. The position strong by nature is rendered more so by engineering skill and hard work. We have gun boats on each flank, thus compelling the enemy, if they attack us, to come up in front of our works. From river to river, following the line of our works, is about three miles. Along this entire line are heavy breast works and at suitable distances are batteries, in all six, besides several cannons along the works. The batteries are constructed for defense in all directions. They are surrounded by stockades, palisades or abatis. So should the enemy, by hurling an overwhelming force on any one point, pierce our line they will yet have much to do before they get possession of the works. The timber is felled in front as far as a long range rifle will carry and the trees are lying so thick on the ground that it would be almost impossible for men to get through. Detailed from and in advance of the main works are two Redans. Along parts of the works are deep and impassable ravines. The batteries are numbered 1, 2, 3 and so on beginning at the right. About one mile in advance is a line of rifle pits which are occupied by our pickets. Great is our confidence in our ability to hold our position. The James River affords a convenient way for receiving our supplies. So perfect is our communication with Fortress Monroe that we get soft bread baked at that place and we get a daily mail. The New York and Philadelphia papers are received two days after date. This is the manner in which the Union army lives in the heart of Virginia and 15 miles from the rebel capital. All these things give us confidence. What better could we ask for so far in the enemy's Country? Chesterfield County is the scene of our present operations. The county bounded on the north by James River which separates it from Henrico County, in which Richmond is situated. The surface of the county is uneven and very much broken. The soil is of a grayish color and is poor. Coal is said to be abundant. There are no towns of importance excepting Manchester on the James opposite Richmond. We have not yet seen a school house in the county and only one church. We have been within 8 1/2 miles from Richmond and the same want of public spirit was manifest all along the route. Bermuda Hundred is the name by which we will hereafter know this place. There are springs of excellent water among the bluffs. The water used in most of the camps is not good, it is but four or five feet from the top of the ground. The climate is very warm, it seems to us warmer than on the coast of South Carolina. There is but little farming going on in this region of country. A large portion of the country is covered with dense pine forests. There are some fine county seats on the banks of the James River. I have noticed in the papers some severe censures on General Butler's conduct of the campaign. They are too simple to be worthy of notice. These critics will convince the soldiers here that they are utterly ignorant of what they pretend to write. I undertake here to say that General Butler has thus far accomplished all that he intended and that his army administered to the so-called Southern Confederacy such stunning blows that it has not yet recovered from the effects. Let no man pronounce the operations south of the James River a failure. With an army of about 25,000 or 30,000 men the rebels were driven into their inner line of fortifications and the railroads leading southward from Richmond, and in one instance in sight of the City, were torn up and otherwise destroyed. Reinforcements were prevented from going to Lee at a time when the rebel army was sorely pressed. When our forces moved up to Drury's Bluff it was not the intention to take Fort Darling, as seems to have been anticipated by some of the people in the North. The object was merely to create a diversion in favor of General Grant and also to enable General Kuntz to accomplish his mission of destruction on which General Butler had sent him and his brave cavaliers.[42] Previous to this a secure position had been secured on a peninsula between the James and Appomattox rivers. When the rebels on the morning of the 16th, taking advantage of a dense fog, came down on us with overwhelming numbers they were unable to drive us into our works in any hurry. The Army fell back leisurely and in good order. The men of course were much worn out having been under arms for three days and nights and much of the time under fire. Tell me, O ye wise men, what more would you have us do!

The End of Volume 6

Volume 7

BERMUDA HUNDRED, VIRGINIA, JUNE–SEPTEMBER 1864

For the first two weeks of June 1864, the Thirty-ninth Illinois stayed within the fortifications at Bermuda Hundred. On June 2, the Confederates, aware that part of Butler's army had departed, launched a dawn assault driving in the Federal pickets and seizing some rifle pits before a counterattack pushed them back. During the action, the Thirty-ninth sustained thirty-five casualties.

Despite a lull after the failed attack, duty in the trenches remained dangerous as the men came under occasional artillery bombardment and continuous fire from enemy sharpshooters. Whenever the soldiers were off duty, they would escape the stifling heat to rest and play cards in the shade. While Randolph and his comrades carried out routine duties, the Federal armies began a grand maneuver against Petersburg, Virginia. On June 9, a portion of Butler's command under General Gillmore moved from Bermuda Hundred, crossed the Appomattox River on a pontoon bridge, and advanced on the city. Finding Petersburg well defended, Gillmore made a few probing attacks, then returned to Bermuda Hundred. Meanwhile, north of the James River, General Grant was preparing to shift the bulk of his army south across the James and, in conjunction with Butler's forces, to capture Petersburg and march on the Confederate capital.

On the evening of June 12, Grant began moving his army from its position at Cold Harbor. General W. F. Smith's corps boarded transports and returned to Bermuda Hundred. Then, following Gillmore's route, the corps crossed the Appomattox and, on June 15, attacked the Petersburg defense line. By evening, the lead elements of the Army of the Potomac, after crossing the James River on a twenty-one-hundred-foot pontoon bridge, joined the assault. The Confederates under General Beauregard put up a desperate fight. In order to defend Petersburg, General Beauregard virtually abandoned the Howlett Line opposite Bermuda Hundred and called upon General Lee for assistance.

During the night of June 15, Union pickets at Bermuda Hundred discovered the empty enemy works, and early the next morning with the Thirty-ninth Illinois deployed as skirmishers General Terry advanced his division toward the Richmond–Petersburg Pike. The Federals occupied the Howlett Line and took a number of prisoners. That evening, however, divisions arrived from Lee's army, under Generals George E. Pickett and

Charles W. Field, and forced Terry back to the Bermuda Hundred line. From this position, the Federals held off Confederate attacks.

Back in their original camp, the Thirty-ninth Illinois remained at Bermuda Hundred for routine duties, the most important being to protect a pontoon bridge built across the James River at Deep Bottom near the northern tip of Jones Neck. During this time, General Philip Sheridan's cavalry corps returned from a raid against the Virginia Central Railroad northwest of Richmond. Stopped by Confederate cavalry, Sheridan brought his command around the Confederate capital, to a position east of the city. Initially hoping to cross the James River on the Deep Bottom pontoon bridge, Sheridan moved his cavalry toward Bermuda Hundred, but Confederate horsemen turned him back. In order to assist Sheridan and protect the cavalry's nine-hundred-vehicle supply train, the Thirty-ninth and other Union regiments were sent to various landings along the James River. Also during this time, Randolph and other men from the Thirty-ninth volunteered for fatigue duty. As a result he missed the regiment's engagement at the battle of Second Deep Bottom.

On August 13, the Thirty-ninth Illinois, now numbering barely two hundred men under Captain Leroy A. Baker, joined a movement north of the James River against the Richmond defense line. During this action, the regiment participated in an attack that overran Confederate fortifications along Darbytown Road near Fussell Millpond. A Confederate counterattack regained the position. The action cost the regiment ninety-seven men and seven officers. By August 20, the remains of the regiment had returned to their camp at Bermuda Hundred.

Four days later, with barely a hundred men fit for duty, the Thirty-ninth and a portion of the Tenth Corps were shifted to the Petersburg front where the soldiers continued to suffer through the hardships of trench warfare. On September 17, the regiment's rolls were further reduced when Randolph and others who had not reenlisted were mustered out. He and his companions were sent to Fort Monroe to complete their final separation from the army and begin their journey home. Ever the tourist, Randolph visited Washington, Baltimore, and Philadelphia, taking in the sights before he boarded the train for the final leg of his journey back to Illinois. —*S.R.W.*

★ ★ ★ ★ ★

June 1, 1864—The day and month was introduced in the noisy manner described in the closing pages of volume sixth. We went on picket at 5 o'clock p.m. Today was sultry. About ten o'clock in the night we could hear the enemy moving artillery, to our right. The rumbling of this had hardly ceased when the rebels opened a furious cannonade on us. Some of the missiles exploded near our pits but most of them went over, being intended for camp. The rebels got equally as much metal as they threw.

A shell struck a pine tree about one foot in diameter, a few feet from us, and cut it down. No damage was done to the picket line by the bombardment. This crazy spell lasted near three-quarters of an hour when the fury of the foe subsided and there was nothing to disturb the quiet of the night excepting an occasional sharp crack of the musket. Colonel Howell expected an attack tonight.

June 2—Early in the morning the crack of musketry on our left announced to us that the day's work had commenced and that it was not to be of a pacific nature. Every man instantly seized his musket and awaited the advance of the foe and we were not long kept waiting. The enemy appeared in our front in line of skirmishers. They were greeted with a shower of lead and in a few minutes found it too hot for their health. So our front was cleared excepting a few men who took cover behind trees and fired at us Indian style. It was my misfortune to be wounded in the lip early in the fight. The enemy having been repulsed I went back to the surgeon and when my wound was dressed started back to rejoin the company. Feeling weary I sat down, to rest, at the reserve of the 11th Maine. I had been here but a few minutes when I saw the left of the 39th Illinois falling back. Soon after the whole could be seen slowly falling back skirmishing with the enemy as they went. I followed along with a line, not having succeeded in reaching the company. When they got to an open field in front of our works the regiment formed in line of battle and gradually fell back to within a quarter of a mile of our entrenchments. Here I rejoined the company. There was a gun in the company which would not burst a cap so it was entirely useless; this I took when starting to the surgeon. Being the same as unarmed and unable to inflict any damage on the enemy, Lieutenant Lemmon ordered me to the camp. However reluctantly the order had to be obeyed. So my warfare was over for the day. Arriving at camp I got a musket, cleaned it up and replenished my cartridge box ready to meet the foe should they assault our works. The enemy did not appear in heavy force on the front of our regiment and we could have held our position had not the 7th Connecticut, which was on our left, been driven back. To our right was the 11th Maine. This and our regiment held their ground for some time after the 7th CT had given back. Our being exposed we were ordered to fall back which was done as already stated. The enemy advanced to our rifle pits. There was some sharp artillery practice during the day. In the afternoon the 3d NH charged and took some of the rifle pits, which the 7th CT had lost in the morning. Several prisoners were taken by them in this charge. The casualties on our side I have not learned; that of the 39th Illinois and 11th Maine was considerable. Lieutenant A. W. Fellows of Co. I was killed, he was shot through the head. He was in command of Co. A at the time. Three men of Co. I were wounded. Lieutenant Sweetser was severely wounded.[1] Night came on but it brought but little rest to us. The regiment was relieved and came into camp before dark.

We had not much more than got to bed when the pickets began to fire and kept it up at intervals all night. We had to take our places in the trenches and there remain till morning. This would not have been so bad had it not rained.

June 3—Able to face the foe. I am very thankful to come off so well. The loss of yesterday's engagement: killed, wounded and missing in the 39th Illinois was 38 men. After dark we heard awful cannonading north of here; it was the heaviest that we have yet heard. At midnight musketry began in our front and we had to get into the trenches where we slept comfortably till morning. A few rebel bullets came whistling over our works into camp. Capt. Snowden of Co. D was wounded.[2]

June 4—Went on picket at 5 o'clock p.m. Rained all night without a minute's intermission. My lip paining me added to the other discomforts made the night very uncomfortable. The enemy kept quiet, but three shots were fired during the night. So very dark was the night we could not see anything twenty feet from us.

June 5, Sunday—The rain ceased a little before noon. There was no firing along the line. We were relieved and had just gotten into camp when the enemy opened fire and a sharp artillery duel ensued. Some musketry in the night.

June 6—Sultry day. The rebels were unusually quiet; scarcely a shot was fired all day. The same quiet prevailed during the night and we enjoyed the rare luxury of a night's rest without once being disturbed. Thanks to the rebs for their good behavior. Their shelling annoys us a great deal but does us but little damage otherwise.

June 7—We commenced building a cover from hostile shells and bullets this morning. Our tents being placed behind these heavy banks of earth, our lives will not be so endangered, when in bed, as heretofore. We can sleep secure from all stray bullets. This evening was our time to go on picket. Tonight we enjoyed quiet along our lines.

June 8—In the afternoon the rebels shelled the picket line and camp, without doing any harm so far as I learned. We were relieved and returned to camp before sundown, where we found a movement of some kind on foot. Contrary to our expectations, the night was quiet and we were permitted to sleep soundly till the dawn of day.

June 9—There was quite heavy artillery firing by our men and the rebels the greater part of the forenoon. A little after noon there was tolerably heavy musketry which lasted about half an hour. It appears that the enemy were reconnoitering our position and running foul of our pickets. They were fired into and thus warned not to advance further, which warning they took. Having once established quiet again, we were not disturbed during the rest of the day and all night there was nothing to call us out of our beds.

June 10—We went on picket at the usual hour (5 p.m.). Nothing remarkable occurred during the day or night. Quiet prevailed along the lines.

June 11—There was nothing, today, of a hostile character excepting some artillery firing on the left, perhaps on the Appomattox River. We were relieved promptly and returned to camp, where cooks, as is their custom, had a warm supper prepared for us. A good night's rest was allotted to us.

June 12, Sunday—A cool, pleasant day. Sunday is to us the same as any other day of the week.

June 13—We have been reinforced by some regiments of hundred-days-men from Ohio. On picket again. The night was quiet, although General Gillmore expected an attack certain. Our duty is now reduced down to simply going on picket every third day; we are on twenty-four hours at a time, in the night we are not allowed to sleep. Besides picket we have to take our position in the entrenchments ready to repel the foe frequently and occasionally go on fatigue.

June 14—The day was chilly! All quiet. We were relieved in good time this evening. Some of the boys had gone to bed when that horrible sound "fall in" greeted their ears. We had to go out and sleep in the trenches. At 1 o'clock in the night we got up and moved further to the left. Here we again made our beds and slept till morning. The night was very damp.

June 15—The morning shone upon us in peace and quietude. At what moment the calm will be interrupted is a matter of extreme uncertainty.

June 16—This morning it was found that the enemy had left our front. They withdrew their forces during the night and our pickets had nothing to do but march forward and possess the rebel works. The movements of the Army of the Potomac in the direction of Petersburg, perhaps is the reason why the enemy evacuated. A few prisoners fell into our hands. Early in the morning we started on a reconnaissance to discover the position of the foe. When beyond the main line of rebel fortifications the 39th Regiment Illinois was deployed as skirmishers and with bayonets fixed advanced through the woods. We passed one line of rifle pits; in front of these the trees were cut down. Here the enemy could have given us a considerable trouble but they had left. We proceeded cautiously till about a quarter of a mile from the pike, where we met the enemy in considerable force. A brisk skirmish ensued without any important results further than to develop the position and strength of the enemy; he was found in too heavy force for us. We lost a few men in killed, wounded and missing; among the wounded was Capt. Rudd of Co. G, Co. I had two men wounded. It being no part of General Foster's plan to bring on an engagement he ordered us to fall back.[3] So we retreated slowly and in good order. The rebels followed us up but very cautiously. We would form a line of battle, throw out a line of skirmishers and wait till everything was ready and then move back a few hundred yards; the skirmishers would move back at the same time. Two pieces of artillery were brought to bear upon the enemy and did good service in checking his advance. Our men all back to the rebel fortifications, there we left a picket line. Our regiment went into camp which it reached about dark.

While we were in camp the enemy made a charge and retook their works. We went to the front and relieved a regiment on picket. The gun boats in James River were firing all night; we could see the explosion of some of the shells. We lay, tired as we were, awake expecting an attack. In the skirmish of the day some of us were in an open field and the rebels were in the woods beyond us. We could not see them only when they were firing and we were in plain view all the time. The bullets came whistling around us very close but by us lying close to the ground it was rather difficult to be hit. I did not discharge my piece for the simple reason that I did not see any rebels that I could hit. We had Longstreet's command pitted against us. Such was the day's work, not altogether dissimilar to the 16th of May last.[4]

June 17—There was a fire kept up all day between the pickets of the contending forces. The rebels came on our left, with their usual yell, in heavy force. They fired on our part of the line from their works. When the rebels retook their works yesterday our men occupied the line of rifle pits which we held previous to the 2nd instant. This was the position we held today when the enemy made the attack. The 24th Massachusetts was on our right and near Ware Bottom Church. The first assault was made just before day light, when it was quite dark. The enemy were repulsed in this attack. This dash of the rebels over, things were quiet with the exception of the picket firing already mentioned and some artillery which the enemy brought to bear on us till about 3 o'clock p.m., at which time a heavy force was hurled against our left and forced it back. We were only slightly engaged. We gave the rebels, for a time, quite a brisk fire by the left oblique. The order was passed along the line for us to fall back and when we got out of the pits to go back large quantities of lead was hurled at us. The line fell back about a quarter of a mile, to the rifle pits which the rebels occupied formerly. The 24th Massachusetts did not fall back and in order to protect the left flank of this gallant regiment some of the right companies of our regiment retook their pits. We then formed a line of skirmishers, touching the left of the 24th Massachusetts and at right angles with it, to connect with line held by the left. Just after dark there was a short and fierce attack; we held our own. We occupied the night in throwing up rifle pits; so morning found our skirmishers entrenched. There was random firing during the night. The 24th Massachusetts was relieved by the 11th Maine a little after dark; the 39th Illinois was able to stand picket two nights in succession.

June 18—Picket firing commenced at daylight and was kept up all day. Early in the afternoon the rebels opened on us with at least six pieces of artillery and shelled us furiously for about three-quarters of an hour. This ceased and there were a few minutes of profound stillness, when the familiar rebel yell was heard on our left which was succeeded by volleys of musketry. Soon after the order was given for us to fall back. We fell back to the line of pits held by the left. This made our line of pickets nearer in the right shape. The 11th Maine fell back in splendid order. After dark we were not relieved but sent back to the reserve. Here we lay buried in a profound sleep till morning. We had sentinels on the alert to give the alarm should anything occur. Three eventful days have the last been to us. I have not been able yet to ascertain our loss, although it was light. We have heard heavy firing in the direction of Petersburg for three days.

June 19, Sunday—At noon we went to camp. I am heartily tired of this petty skirmishing. In it nothing of importance is to be gained. All quiet in our front. Had a good night's sleep. A detail from our regiment was sent on picket this evening.

June 20—Our pickets were relieved about 2 o'clock p.m. and we received orders to be ready to march at 5 o'clock with two day's cooked rations and 100 rounds of cartridges to the man. So farewell to the poor comfort of camp. We are ready for the fiery ordeal through which we are to pass. The day was warm. We marched to the James River and slept on its banks till morning. During the night a pontoon was laid across the river and some regiments crossed over to the opposite side. There were two brigades of us commanded by General Foster. The pontoon was laid at a bend of the river above Bermuda Hundred, the name of the place I do not know.[5]

June 21—Early in the morning we crossed the river. Men were busy all day throwing up earth works. Our regiment stacked arms and lay in the shade till evening. The digging and slashing was mostly done by "Hundred Days men." Some rebel cavalry was seen scouting around. Wheat was ripe enough to harvest and oats were in the milk. The citizens have all left and the houses have recently been burnt along the river bank. Fruit of various kinds is plentiful. All night we went on picket; our company was on reserve. All was quiet. Cavalry were in advance of our infantry pickets. Our present operations are in Henrico County.

June 22—The morning was very warm. Work went on all night and there is no abatement. About noon the enemy appeared in our front and skirmishing with our pickets commenced. A few rebel cavalry and infantry got to a house in a field across which our picket line extended. A company of the 100th New York charged across the field to this house and the rebels got out in a hurry. At the same time our picket line was advanced and fired on the rebels. Each one of the pickets took a shovel and when he reached the place designated, which was the crest of a hill, dug a pit for his protection. The 100th New York Company took one prisoner; the rest were too fleet on foot. None of our men were hurt as I could learn. In the evening we were relieved from picket and marched to the river bank at the pontoon and bivouacked for the night. The gun boats shelled the woods back of us for half the night.

June 23—The regiment lay in the shade today. Details were on fatigue; it was my luck to have to slash. We slept in the Redan above the pontoon at night. A few rods below where we crossed James River, Four Mile Creek empties into it.

June 24—We were on fatigue today carrying brush for the abatis for the Redan. Late in the night we started for camp, leaving one brigade at Fourmile Creek. The road was very dusty. We reached camp about 1 o'clock in the night, tired and hungry.

June 25—Early this morning, before we were yet out of bed, we received orders to get ready to fall in immediately in light marching order. So we were under way and marching along the dusty road before breakfast. We marched to Point of Rocks on the Appomattox River and went aboard the steamer General Howard. We then run down to Wilcox's Landing on James River; there we disembarked and marched out two miles. The hardest of our day's work was now done; we lay in the shade till in the afternoon, when we embarked and went back to Point of Rocks; thence on foot to camp, distant about three miles, which we reached at 3 o'clock p.m. Wilcox's Landing, on the north bank of James River, is about 25 miles below Point of Rocks.[6] The object of us going down was to cooperate with General Sheridan in crossing James River. It seems that Sheridan encountered the enemy yesterday, near Charles City Courthouse, and found him too strong for cavalry alone to cope with. It was feared that the rebels might follow-up their slight advantage and capture the train while endeavoring to cross the river. For this reason three regiments of infantry were sent down from Bermuda Hundred. The trains were ferried across to the south bank of the river. Passed City Point the base of supplies for the Army of the Potomac. The river at this place was full of steamers, schooners and barges. There was a long train of cars on the railroad and a locomotive was puffing away.[7]

June 26, Sunday—The day was hot. A detail of the 39th Illinois was sent on picket this evening; I was one of the lucky number. Tonight, when I was a vedette, a rebel a few yards from me whistled "Home Again"; poor fellow! When will he be there? The night was quiet.

June 27—All quiet in our front. Heard heavy firing in the direction of Petersburg in the afternoon. The rest of the regiment went on picket at the usual hour.

June 28—Cool and pleasant morning. Heard firing in the direction of Petersburg all day and night.

June 29—On picket. Heard heavy musketry at Petersburg in the night.

June 30—There was occasional firing at Petersburg all day and at about 5 o'clock p.m., the cannonading became awful. There was nothing of special interest in our front. By some mishap we were not relieved till late in the night.

July 1—The day was exceedingly warm. Nothing transpired of note.

July 2—The day was hot. The sun rose and set without any thing of general interest to relieve the monotony of camp. Today the sword, which the Detachment of the 39th Illinois volunteers purchased for presentation to Capt. Platt arrived and was presented. It was a superb sword, and the sash and belt were very fine. Owing to circumstances we did not make a public presentation. We sent the sword to the Captain with a letter. It is intended to publish this letter and that of the Captain in reply, in the Chicago Tribune and the Captain's home paper. It fell to my lot to write the letter of presentation. There was a great delay in getting the sword on account of the express company receiving orders not to forward anything to the army; it was purchased in Philadelphia.

July 3, Sunday—Another Sabbath passed without any thing to endear it to memory. Went on picket in the evening. Almost in speaking distance of the enemy; heard them singing and preaching. Saw the flash of cannon and heard the noise in the direction of Petersburg.

July 4—A national salute was fired by our batteries at noon and while it was being done a band played the "Starspangled Banner." The firing was directed at the rebel works. Before firing the salute the flags of the various regiments were placed on the parapets. No sooner were the Stars and Stripes displayed than the rebels hoisted a flag on their works, a red flag with a blue cross.

July 5—Went on picket again this evening; what does it mean? All quiet in the night. Rebel vedettes about 50 yards from ours.

July 6—Deserters come into our lines daily; on an average perhaps three a day. Two came over last night and one today. The rebels fired three times at the one that came across today, we could hear them hollow [holler] "down him."

July 7—Warm day. Weather dry and dusty. Health of troops good. Most of the regiment went on picket this evening. There was a good harvest of deserters today, more than the average. So far as I can learn the deserters are mostly Virginians.

July 8—The rest of us went on picket at the usual hour. There was heavy musketry firing all night at Petersburg.

July 9—The enemy were reported, this morning, massing on our right, however, they showed no indications of making an attack and the day passed off without anything to disturb the quietude. An accident occurred, today, resulting in the death of two men and the wounding of one. Some of the 85th Pennsylvania picked up a shell, which had been fired by the rebels and did not explode, and were fooling with it when fire somehow or another got to the powder causing the shell to explode doing the damage above stated. Let this be a warning to others.

July 10—An occasional boom of distant cannon broke in upon the quiet of this Sabbath morning. How tired, very tired, one becomes of the continual roar of cannon and the sharp crack of musketry. The soul longs for something more peaceful, for something that does not cause such destruction to human life and limb. So must it be yet for a while. The longest and darkest night has an end, and when the sky is tinted with the first dawn of morning, in the abundance of our joy, we are apt to forget the dreariness contained in the sable curtains just lifted. O for faith to endure to the end! Said a good old Spaniard, "For every battle a crown." Went on picket this evening. Nothing new to report.

July 11—The day was dry and hot. In the afternoon a black cloud in the West gave promise of rain but this proved a delusive hope; there was only a very slight sprinkle, not enough to settle the dust.

July 12—Old Sol holds supreme sway and exercises his power with great intensity. The morning was unusually quiet. On picket this evening. The rule now is to go on picket every other day, going on every third day is the exception. We have to keep awake all night; to be found asleep, if reported, is *death* or such other punishment as the sentence of a general court martial may inflict. Heavy musketry in the direction of Petersburg the greater part of the night.

July 13—Nothing of special interest today. Papers from the North failed to reach us.

July 14—Inspection by brigade inspector at 9 o'clock a.m. Regular picket day. Mails and papers not received.

July 15—Died — Sgt. Spencer of Co. G, 39th Illinois on the 5th of the present month. Spencer was slightly wounded in the head June the first and was sent to Chestnut Hill Hospital near Philadelphia.[8] The gangrene soon after set in and reduced him very low; this was stopped finally and he wrote hopeful letters causing us to believe that his place in the company would not long be vacant. Our hopes were doomed to disappointment. The next intelligence that we received of our friend was that he died as above stated of inflammation of the brain. To our sorrow was added surprise. Sgt. Spencer was a law student of Michigan University. He anticipated with pleasure the time when he could resume his legal studies; his term of service was almost out, but oh vain, how vain are all human calculations! He proposed to me to read Caesar together, a short time before he left us, and we were thus engaged when his wound put an abrupt termination to our studies. We take consolation from the fact that he was a consistent Christian, one who took an active part in everything the object of which was the amelioration of mankind. In an eminent degree was Spencer a working man. His prospects for the future were bright but he did not suffer himself to be deceived by the alluring promises of this World. His hopes were stayed on a firmer foundation than Earth can afford and he is now gone to receive his reward. Truly "Death loves a shining mark." We deeply mourn the loss of our friend, but knowing that He, in whose hands we all are, doeth all things well, we meekly submit to His mysterious ways and say, "Thy Will be done."

July 16—Paymaster began to pay the regiment today. Nothing extraordinary occurred.

July 17, Sunday—Finished paying the regiment. Too much business for the Sabbath and the day was not so profitably spent as could be wished. Regiment on picket this evening. Heard the rebels holding prayer meeting. Firing at Petersburg in the night.

July 18—The day passed without anything of special interest. We were relieved at the usual hour.

July 19—Between 2 and 3 o'clock this morning we were called up and went to Battery No. 4. There we remained, behind the works, till 10 o'clock a.m., by order of General Terry. It began to rain at daylight with a fair promise to give us a copious supply of this, much-needed, element. The promise was well fulfilled; it rained all day and part of the night. The left wing of the regiment went on picket.

July 20—It cleared off today and the sun shone hot, warm would not express the temperature of the atmosphere. The right wing of the regiment went on picket. Time passes rather slowly.

July 21—We had a pleasant twenty-four hours' picket; the night being clear and quiet, the day cool.

July 22—Pleasant weather. Quiet prevails. Part of the 18th Army Corps went into camp near us. This is from New Orleans. On picket again this evening.[9]

July 23—"There is nothing new under the sun."

July 24, Sunday—The day was cloudy and cool; the weather, since the recent rains, has been very pleasant. General Terry is in command of the 10th Army Corps. For this reason we have to be under arms from 3 o'clock a.m. till sunup. Considering that we are on picket every other night the boys justly think the General tyrannical.

July 25—The rain set in before dark and continued all last night and being on picket we suffered severely. The night was the coldest that I ever saw in the month of July. The boys shivered with their blankets around them. At daylight fires were started up along the picket line and, strange as it may seem in this latitude, a warm fire was comfortable till 10 o'clock a.m. We were relieved in the evening and returned to camp; when we found the rest of the regiment had been sent on three days picket on the Appomattox River.

July 26—The day was pleasant, neither too warm nor too cold. Time passes and hastens us to the expiration of the term of our enlistment. General Birney has been assigned to the command of the 10th Army Corps. *Sic mutatur imperitor corporis decimi* [thus change the commandments of the body]. On picket and expecting an attack. The expectations not realized.[10]

July 27—All quiet and were relieved in good season.

July 28—All quiet with us today. It would be impossible for the enemy to surprise the army at this place so on the alert are we kept. We stack our arms every night at the breast works and at 3 o'clock in the morning we get up and are under arms till sunup.

July 29—For a few days past, active operations have been going on the north side of James River. The first installment of prisoners were sent here from the scene of operations this morning; about all that we can hear from the north side is the booming of cannon occasionally. The cars have been unusually busy on the Richmond and Petersburg Railroad and for three or four days past we have heard them at almost every hour of the twenty-four. The weather is sultry again. On picket this evening. General Butler offered any man a furlough who would take him "a live rebel," either a deserter or a prisoner; tonight the prize was not secured. Firing was heard all night at Petersburg also across the James River. All quiet in our front.

July 30—Marching orders were given this morning and two day's rations were brought out on the picket line to us. It was surmised that the enemy was evacuating in our front and we had orders to watch closely and if the rebels left to follow up. They did not leave so we made no forward movement. According to reports, and the movements here seemed to confirm them, all was going well at Petersburg; the enemy lost today one line of works. We hope that the day is not distant when they will not only lose Petersburg but their capital also.

July 31, Sunday—Companies I, C & G occupied a position along the breast works where there were no troops encamped. We had nothing to do but be ready to fight in case the enemy should make an attack. Things in our front remain *in status quo*. Everything seemed quiet in all directions.

August 1st—The news from Petersburg is discouraging. From the medley of rumors, current here today, we infer that our armies met with a sanguinary disaster on Saturday last. The heart sickens at the recital of the details of operations before the "Cockade City." But we will not despond of final success for temporary reverses will, at most, only prolong the struggle and "Right that day must win;" Then conquer we must, when our cause it is just, And this be our motto, "In God is our trust."[11]

Aug. 2—The morning was very sultry. Firing was heard at Petersburg this morning. We were reinforced here last Sunday by two brigades of the 10th Corps, temporarily attached to the 18th Corps and doing duty before Petersburg.

Aug. 3—Nothing of special interest to record.

Aug. 4—Military operations seem to have come to a dead stand. We are now acting strictly on the defensive. Parties are at work again today strengthening the fortifications.

Aug. 5—Two drills and dress parade is now a daily programme. Today we leveled down our "bombproofs" and put up our tents in regular order. About 6 o'clock p.m., the heaviest cannonading that we have yet heard in that direction commenced at Petersburg and continued for about one hour. The weather continues sultry. Almost diseased with the *ennui*.

Aug. 6—Put up shades over our tents. Not on picket so often.

Aug. 7, Sunday—Volunteered to dig for twenty days; six hundred men were called for out of the 10th Corps and the same number from the 18th Corps. The men are to work seven hours each day and receive eight cents extra pay per hour. Went on picket this afternoon. We now have division guard mounting before sending the pickets out.[12]

Aug. 8—The day passed off listlessly.

Aug. 9—Sultry.

Aug. 10—General Butler made other arrangements to get the digging done for which he asked volunteers. The job was let to the 16th New York heavy artillery. We offered our services in response to the General's call and were disappointed; he need not again ask us to volunteer for a special service. The weather is so warm and the boys are so lazy the daily routine is irksome.

Aug. 11—Nothing of interest to record.

Aug. 12—The diggers, General Butler wanted, are at work on the north side of James River and report says they are cutting a canal across a bend of the river.

Aug. 13—Early this morning some rebel rams run down the river and began to shell the camp of Butler's Navies.[13] Nine o'clock a.m., received orders to cook three day's rations and be ready to march at night. Brisk shelling still going on. In the evening I was detailed, as I was told, to guard the Corps medical supply train but it proved to be for a teamster. Drive a four horse team I could not and would not if I could. I claim to be a genuine son of Mars while in the army and no relation whatever to John. I finally agreed to feed a team till the next day but declaring that under no circumstances would I drive it. So I went to bed in the wagon but had not got to sleep till the team assigned me was ordered to be hitched up and go someplace; a driver was found and I moved my traps out of the wagon. For the rest of the night I slept comfortably on a bale of hay. Our Brigade struck tents and left during the night.

Aug. 14, Sunday—I got permission to return to the company this morning. The captain in command of the train and the wagon-master were very polite and were willing to act honorably. The task of "hunting" my regiment was now before me. Not knowing that it had left during the night I started back to camp but being informed of the fact on the way I was saved a useless walk. I could not learn where the regiment had gone so I was left in some doubt what was the best course to pursue. P. M. Holloway, of my own company, had charge of some hospital stores for which he expected transportation during the day when he intended to follow the regiment. After duly considering the matter, I concluded that it would be best to stop with him and go along with the hospital stores; I would by so doing be sure of traveling in the right direction. No team came today to take the baggage. During the day we heard artillery firing across the river and vague rumors came to us that our forces were engaged in fierce combat with the rebels; we could, however, learn nothing reliable.[14]

Aug. 15—A quiet morning dawned upon us; noon came, the evening followed and yet no transportation. There is a vacant place in the ranks of Co. I, which I would like to fill but my star seems to order otherwise for the present. The drum corps of the 39th Illinois was left in camp with orders to give all of calls of the brigade as usual. This is to deceive the enemy.

Aug. 16—Have not yet been successful in "hunting the regiment." This is the first solid rest that I have had since landing on the south side of James River on the sixth of May last. Two years ago from today we evacuated Harrison's Landing.

Aug. 17—Today I heard the first reliable news from the regiment since becoming separated from it. They have been fighting across the James River and the losses were heavy. Rest is no longer rest to me. I go this afternoon to try to find the regiment. My conscience acquits me; it was not my wish to be left behind. I am now ready for what awaits me. Soon I expect to be in battle. In God is my trust. At about 3 o'clock p.m., I started for the scene of operations on the north side of James River. Having to lug my knapsack and taking the wrong road, I did not reach Jones' Landing till almost dark; here I found some of the 39th Regiment on duty and I stayed all night. While on my way to the Landing there was a heavy cannonading going on in the vicinity of Dutch Gap; some of the shells exploded near the road where I was. This evening there was a terrific thunderstorm and the rain fell in torrents.

Aug. 18—Early this morning I started with a comrade in a cart, to the front, there to share with the regiment its perils and honors. After crossing the pontoon we drove in a northern direction. The way was mostly through dense woods and at places everything was so still that it seemed impossible that two hostile armies could be so near at hand. On first entering the timber we could see evidences that things had not always been so quiet as they were at that time. Trees had been cut down, their limbs shot away or their trunks shivered by cannon balls; and there were several heavy projectiles lying along the road. A drive of about six miles and one mile's walk brought us to the regiment. I took my place in the ranks and my comrade, after transacting his business, returned to Jones' Landing. I found the regiment strongly posted in the woods behind breast works which had been thrown up a few hours before; in front of these trees had been felled for a few rods thus making an excellent abatis. In front of us was a picket line. Within musket shot was the main rebel line and separated from us by the woods. There was picket firing during the day. In the evening made an attack along different parts of the line and for about one hour and a half there was heavy musketry and artillery firing. The enemy made the heaviest assault and gained a temporary advantage to the right of us. We were for a short time under an enfilading fire. Meanwhile skirmishing was going on in front of our brigade. We were at this time ordered to the right and by the withdrawal of part of our brigade the line was weakened to a mere skirmish line. When we got to General Terry's headquarters the firing on the right slackened and a heavy attack was made on the position which we had just left. We about-faced and marched back, under a hot fire, arriving just in the nick of time. The pickets were being driven in and it appeared that the enemy were coming in heavy force. A few well directed volleys sent them back to their breast works with fewer men than came out. The losses on our side were light; in our brigade there were but a few men killed and wounded. The picket line was reestablished at dark and a profound quiet brooded over the hostile armies. In the fore part of the night our men quietly withdrew to a position about two miles nearer the river. Here we halted for the night and made ourselves as comfortable as we could under the circumstances. The rain was the greatest hinderance to a good night's rest.

Aug. 19—We remained in the same position that we occupied last night all day. Fatigue parties were at work throwing up breast works and slashing. All quiet during the day. Raining. Details for picket and to work on entrenchments were made at night.

Aug. 20—Today we occupied the same position with one slight change in the afternoon. A short time after dark we began to move back towards the river and during the night the 2nd & 10th Army Corps crossed the river to Bermuda Hundred Peninsula. We marched back to our own camp which we reached just before daylight. The road was so muddy and slippery that the marching was very fatiguing and the men were well nigh give out when they got to camp.[15]

Aug. 21, Sunday—We re-fitted our old camp, which was torn up when we left, and enjoyed a season of rest. At dark we received orders to hold ourselves in readiness to march at a moment's notice, with one day's rations and our haversacks. Coffee in our canteens and in light marching order. At 11 o'clock in the night there was a detail sent for from our regiment of forty men to report to Capt. Lyons at Point of Rocks. I was one of the men detailed and after marching to the Point and countermarching till 2 o'clock a.m., we found the Captain. He wanted us to guard a pontoon bridge across the Appomattox River. We were not wanted till morning so we lay down on the wharf and slept until sunup.[16]

Aug. 22—Guards were posted this morning on the bridge from our detachment and we relieved a company which had been doing duty here for two months. We put on our guards this morning, one at each end of the bridge and one in the middle. Duty is light and there is a prospect of getting a season of rest of which we feel the need.

Aug. 23—Open the bridge at 5 1/2 o'clock this morning for gun boats to pass down the river. We put up our tents on a high hill and made comfortable camp.

Aug. 24—Our fond hopes of rest were dashed to the ground this evening. The regiment received marching orders and we were to be relieved. At half past 4 o'clock p.m., the first Division (Terry's) 10th Army Corps began to cross the Appomattox, on the bridge which we were guarding, and during the evening it all crossed over. Artillery was crossing in the night.

Aug. 25—We were relieved this morning with orders to report to the regiment before Petersburg. So we struck tents and started after breakfast. We met a part of the 18th Army Corps which had been relieved by Terry's

Division, going to Butler's front. We got to the regiment about 4 o'clock p.m. The camp which we were to occupy was covered with filth of nearly all sorts and the stench is truly sickening. Flies cover the ground and are so troublesome that a person can hardly eat or drink without swallowing them by the dozen. The camp is on the slope of a ridge in a pine grove and might, by cleanliness, have been made a delightful place for the weary soldier. I suppose that the men who encamped here had too much to do in the trenches to pay any attention to their camp. Yet this is hardly an apology for being so filthy. During the day and night there was a constant firing kept up, with musketry and artillery, in our front. Late in the afternoon there was very heavy firing on the left. We lay on reserve tonight.

Aug. 26—Before daylight this morning the rebels opened with mortars on our works and a lively bombardment ensued, both parties exhibiting great activity in the exercise of heaving iron.

Aug. 27—The bullets occasionally come whizzing through camp and sometimes killing or wounding some poor fellow. The bullets striking the trees with a crash make a disagreeable noise to the weary soldier who wishes to sleep. Went on picket tonight for forty-eight hours. There is a ditch for the pickets in which they are placed about as thick a line of skirmishers. This line is approached by a zigzag ditch. The usual picket firing was kept up during the night.

Aug. 28, Sunday—The day was rather quiet; there was but very little artillery firing and scarce the average amount of musketry. The casualties of the day in our regiment were one man killed and one wounded. Hardenburgh of G was killed; this man captured a stand of colors of the rebels on the 16th instant at Deep Run. He would have been promoted if he had lived. The same bullet that killed him wounded Corp'l Shinkle of Co. I. For a man to show his head above the works is almost sure death. The quiet of the day was made up for at night; the rebels kept up a constant firing, our men responded lightly. Ed Woodard of Co. I was wounded in the side during the night.[17]

Aug. 29—The 62nd Ohio, on our right, exchanged papers and traded coffee and pocket knives for tobacco with the rebels. The parties met each other halfway between the lines. John Rapp of Co. I 39th Illinois was trading with them this morning and at noon he was killed by them, shot through the head. He had his dinner in his hands and was going to a place to sit down to eat it when the fatal messenger came and he fell mortally wounded. His brains were spattered on a comrade who was nearby.[18] About the average amount of picket firing was done today. In the afternoon there was an awful artillery duel and with some slight intermissions it was kept up till late in the night. Mortars were mostly used and the two opposing sides seemed to be equally matched. Being between the hostile batteries the missiles passed over our heads. The air was vocal with hissing, screeching and all sorts of sounds terrible to hear.

The smoke hung over us. The constant sharp crack of muskets and the keen whistling of the bullets, the satanic noises of the shells passing over our heads and the villainous smell of powder all combined made our position seem like a veritable Pandemonium. At night the course of the shells could be traced through the air by the light which the burning fuses made. The sight far surpassed anything that we have seen since leaving Morris Island. In the night we were relieved and came to camp. After getting our suppers we went to bed and were soon oblivious to all danger, although we were not out of range of the enemies cannons and muskets as a frequent crashing through the trees attested. When we went to sleep heavy cannonading was going on; how long it continued I do not know. We had a good night's rest.

Aug. 30—We were under arms before daylight this morning and so remained for about half an hour. The day and night were unusually quiet. According to orders we made bullet proofs to protect our tents.

Aug. 31—Mustered for pay. The usual picket firing with an occasional discharge of a piece of artillery. The duty we now have to do is forty-eight hours in the trenches (that is on picket or on the skirmish line), and forty-eight hours in camp; sometimes there are other details for a few men. Tonight was our regular time to go into the trenches. The bullets come over the parapets so thick and near that it is not safe for a man to raise his head above the works even in the night. In the daytime if a man should expose himself to view he could scarcely live one minute.

September 1st—The rebels were discovered running a ditch parallel to our line and but a short distance in front of us. This gave rise to a sharp artillery duel in the afternoon. The line of rifle pits, which our regiment occupies when in the trenches, is in front of the rebel fort blown up some time ago. In the rear of our line is a deep ravine and in the bottom of this was commenced the mine.

Sept. 2—Musketry and artillery firing about as usual. One man wounded in the foot was all the damage the 39th Illinois sustained in the 48 hours duty which closed tonight. Our pickets are relieved after dark to prevent the enemy from seeing us. We were relieved as usual tonight.

Sept. 3—The days are very warm when the sun shines and the nights are cool. Before sunup a fire is quite comfortable but two hours after a shade is eagerly sought. The only noteworthy event today was the execution of a soldier of the 7th Connecticut Regiment for murdering a comrade. It seemed that he shot a comrade when in a skirmish line in Florida and recently acknowledged the crime. He was hung, this afternoon at 2 o'clock, till dead; he was suspended twenty-four minutes. The details of the execution I am in no mood to record at the present time.[19]

Sept. 4, Sunday—The time when we should go home, if spared, draws nigh. For some reason, I cannot tell why, it seems to me that I am never to see home again. A melancholy feeling pervades my soul. All around seems a dreary desert with not one oasis to welcome the weary traveler.

Perhaps the present is the black darkness which is said to precede the dawn of day. How long till the night shall have passed? Shall we not soon behold the day-star arise? Like a true soldier I will try to be of good cheer. We went on picket this evening at the usual time. At about midnight one of the heaviest cannonadings that we ever witnessed commenced and lasted for nearly one hour and a half. Along our batteries was one continual blaze of fire. The sky was filled with mortar shells, the burning fuses of which resembled meteors. The discharge of rifled cannons, smooth bores, columbiads and mortars of different calibers filled the air with a variety of sounds too terrible to describe. The rebel artillery men were but little less furious than our own. When the firing gradually ceased we could hear a brass band, in our camp, playing the "Red, White and Blue." The rebel picket hallooed across and told us that Sherman had taken Atlanta. We supposed that the reception of this good news was the cause of the heavy firing above mentioned.[20]

Sept. 5—At 2 o'clock this morning our main picket line was moved back of the batteries; three men from each company were left in the front trenches to watch the movements of the enemy. The reason for this disposition we could not learn. We lay all day in a ditch flanked on the right and left by batteries. Things were unusually quiet in front all day. The rebels opened on us in the afternoon with their artillery and landed in some shells uncomfortably near us; no one was hurt however. Soon, when our batteries opened on the enemy, the firing dried up. For the rest of our forty-eight hours we occupied the line taken when we fell back this morning. At 10 o'clock in the night there was a heavy shower of rain which added greatly to our misery. The [water] run through the trenches in streams. But the night with all its dreariness [ended] and the morning dawned.

Sept. 6—There was nothing unusual transpired today. Cloudy and rainy day. Relieved at the proper hour. The night was too cold to sleep comfortably under two blankets.

Sept. 7—Clear weather again. Nothing to record.

Sept. 8—Tonight was our time to go on picket. Heavy cannonading about noon, the occasion of it we did not learn.

Sept. 9—One man of Co. D. 39th Regiment Illinois was killed, this morning, on the skirmish line, by the premature explosion of one of our own shells. In the afternoon the rebels opened a heavy artillery on us and kept it up with great fierceness for near half an hour, our batteries keeping silent. I heard no one being hurt by the bombardment, although our camp was shelled with more than wanted vigor. News was received of another great victory by Sherman this evening and the troops cheered vociferousness, fifes and drums sounded and bands played. We were relieved from the trenches this evening and returned to camp. We now have to go on duty two days and are off one.

Sept. 10—Today the first installment of men who did not reenlist of our regiment were mustered out; there were about fifty of them. There was some difficulty about being discharged at the right time on account of the regiment not having been mustered into the United States service till the 11th of October 1861, three years from which date an effort was made to hold the men. An appeal was made to General Grant and he issued an order that the men of the 39th Illinois should be discharged three years from date of enlistment. The time of some of the men had been out two or three weeks. This afternoon a soldier was drummed out of camp for cowardice. What regiment he belonged to I did not learn; some said that it was the 6th Connecticut. His hair cut off close to the skin of his head. He marched between two guards, with bayonets fixed, commanded by a sergeant; following him was one drummer and one fifer playing a miserable tune. On his back was tied a board with the word *Coward* in large letters on it. He was bare-headed.[21] We went into the trenches this evening.

Sept. 11, Sunday—The rebels, as well as our own men, respected the Sabbath. The day was unusually quiet.

Sept. 12—Nothing of special importance today. We were relieved this evening and came to camp.

Sept. 13—There was a general inspection at 10 o'clock a.m. This will be my last. I was detailed for guard at the regimental commissary, so my warfare is virtually at an end, for the present.

Sept. 14—This forenoon there was an other of those furious cannonades, which have been so frequent an occurrence before Petersburg. About dark quite heavy musketry was commenced to the left of the 10th Army Corps and was kept up for nearly one hour when it was slackened; brisk firing was going on all night. In our front, things were unusually quiet.

Sept. 15—Today I should have been mustered out of the United States service but through the negligence of the Commissary of Musters I will probably have to stay here come next Monday, the 18th instant.

Sept. 16—By dint of perseverance and urging the matter we got our rolls made out and would have been mustered out if the Commissary of Musters had not been absent from his office; there are six of us. The trouble seems not to have been with the mustering officer but in our own regiment.

Sept. 17—Today we were mustered out of the United States services. So to trenches and to warfare generally farewell. We struck for City Point and there remained all night, sleeping on the ground and under the canopy of heaven.

Sept. 18, Sunday—At 10 o'clock a.m., we started for Fortress Monroe on the mail steamer Thomas A. Morgan. We reached the fort at 5 o'clock p.m. We went to Camp Distribution and got our suppers but the camp being full they could not furnish us quarters. So we had to look out for ourselves. We scattered. Corporal Riddle, of Co. I, Chief Musician Hallowell and myself slept on the floor of a colored man's eating saloon.[22]

Sept. 19—Fine morning. At Fortress Monroe we settle up with the government and go on our way rejoicing. We took our rolls to the paymaster this morning and in the afternoon received our pay. At 4 1/2 o'clock p.m., we took the mail steamer, two of us for Washington and the rest for Baltimore. Myself and friend wished to go to Washington to see that great City. We were aboard the boat all night and had for our bed a coil of wet rope. At Point Lookout we stopped and took on some passengers. The night was delightful.[23]

Sept. 20—We landed at Washington about 10 o'clock a.m.; the boat was behind time. We proposed traveling according to soldiers while we had on the uniform; therefore we inquired for the "soldiers' rest" but we found no place fit for men of our rank so we put up at a hotel (Made's House). After satisfying the stomach we started out to see the city. Washington, the capital of the United States, if it were not for the public works, would not be worth visiting. Everything seems to move along slow, even the people are in no hurry. The City covers a large area of ground but it is not densely populated. Pennsylvania Avenue is the principle thoroughfare, it runs north and south from the Capital and the streets crossing it are numbered 1st, 2d, 3d East or West etc., beginning at the Capital. The streets running parallel to Pennsylvania take the names of the letters of the alphabet. One is astonished at the great number of restaurants and from them it would seem that the people did nothing else but eat. Some of these are houses, to say the least of them, of doubtful character. Georgetown, separated from Washington by a creek, is a compactly built town. We took the general survey of the City, today, and formed a decidedly poor opinion of it. The citizens appear to be disloyal, that is the majority of them.

Sept. 21—Had a good night's rest, the first on a soft bed for a long time. Early this morning we visited the Capital and there spent the forenoon. To speak of the building is unnecessary. I was most interested in some historical paintings in the rotunda. The embarkation of the Pilgrim fathers and the baptism of Pocahontas held one spell bound till I was admonished that it was time to be going. The young Pocahontas was the embodiment of beauty. The Pilgrims could certainly either fight or pray which ever the occasion might demand. The Capital is not yet complete; men were busy at work on it. In the afternoon we went to the Navy yard. Two brass cannon captured by Captain Stephen Decatur from a gun boat at Tripoli attracted our attention; these are the most noted trophies in the yard. We saw them making cannon, shot, shell, bullets, conical and round and caps. The machinery by which these are made is very beautiful but we did not have much time to examine it. In the evening we took a walk to the President's mansion; nothing extraordinary from that source to record.[24]

Sept. 22—The patent office and Smithsonian Institute demanded our attention today. Of all the things that we saw there we can refer to but few and those which interested us most. At the Patent Office we spent the forenoon and were much interested; it was our only regret that we did not have more time. Franklin's printing press was the first object of interest that met our eyes. The personal effects of Washington are in the Office; among these are his sleeping tent and even the tent pins, dishes, looking glasses and two fine candelabras. New after these relics we were most interested in some articles from Asia and Africa. The presents of the Tycoon of Japan to President Buchanan was first among these in my estimation. Of the Japanese articles we noticed especially fine silks, beautifully flowered, tassels, silk robes, (15 presented to Mr. Harris, American Consul, on the occasion of his audience with the Emperor), and some very fine screens.[25] A gun from the emperor of Morocco to President VanBuren and a sword from Egypt, with hilt studded with diamonds and scabbard of gold, were curious articles. Two of the most precious relics of the past in the United States are to be seen in the patent office, these are the original draft of the declaration of Independence and Washington's commission as commander in chief of the American army. Our time was limited and after dinner we went to Smithsonian Institute. There we saw enough for a lifetime study. Birds, beasts, fishes, reptiles, minerals and skeletons are to be seen in great abundance. Manufactured articles are there from all parts of the World, even the remote Islands are represented. With many regrets we bid adieu to the public works of Washington, for the city we cared nothing. Late in the afternoon we took the cars for Baltimore where we arrived a little after dark. There is nothing remarkable about the country through which we passed. A good night's rest prepared us for seeing Baltimore.

Sept. 23—The day was rainy and therefore not favorable for sightseeing in the city. Baltimore is a very substantial looking city; the buildings are mostly of brick. The streets are regularly laid out and are kept very clean. On the whole the City presents a neat appearance. Battle monument is a beautiful piece of workmanship. The design is excellent; one might sit and gaze at it for hours and study the history and institutions of our country. Washington's monument, although much larger and taller is not so fine. It was erected by the State of Maryland to the memory of Washington and was 14 years in being built; it is 180 feet high. We paid 13 cents a piece and were given a lantern to ascend to the top. The ascent is by a flight of winding stairs. It requires a steady head not to become dizzy. From the top one has a splendid view of the City and surrounding country.[26] It was raining at the time of our visit, so part of the city was hid from our view by a mist. The shot tower is 255 feet high. At 1 1/2 o'clock p.m., we took the train for Philadelphia. We had a pleasant ride through a picturesque country. At Haverdegrace the cars cross the Susquehanna River in a ferry boat. Wilmington, Delaware is the largest town on the route. Next to it is Chester, Pennsylvania. From Wilmington to Philadelphia the cars run along the banks of the Delaware River. We arrived at the city about sundown. We stopped for the night in West Philadelphia.

Sept. 24—After breakfast this morning we went to Satterlee General U.S.A. Hospital to look for our friend Mr. Goltra whom we failed to find the previous evening.[27] He was just coming in from the city and we met at the gate of the hospital. We went with him into his quarters and after he had done some writing we started down into the city. The first thing on the programme was to purchase a suit of clothes. As for myself, I was quite ragged, having on the same uniform that I had worn since early in the spring. My shoes were bursted, socks full of holes, pants worn off at the bottom of the legs and rents sewed up roughly for the tenth time, blouse out at the elbows and forage cap gone to seed; so I cannot certainly be charged with extravagance for buying a new suit. We bought coat, pants and vest at one place, shoes at another, shirts, socks, neck tie and suspenders at a third place, hat at fourth and lastly a valise. We now repaired to a bathing saloon and washed off the last of Virginia's "sacred soil," thence we went to a barber shop and were shaved, had hair trimmed and shampooed. Here we doffed the last remnant of our military clothing and went forth, again after a space of three years, fully clad in citizens suit. It was now about 1 o'clock p.m. Our friend left us and returned to his quarters as soon as we had completed our purchases. We put up at the William Penn House during our sojourn in the city. This is a very common and plain sort of a house but everything is kept orderly and the table is splendid. Price of board per day $2.00. After dinner we started out to take a general survey of the city. From the first we were favorably impressed, afterwards we were almost delighted with the appearance of the city. The streets beginning at the Delaware River are numbered 1st, 2d, 3d, 4th and so on to the western limits of the city. The streets cross each other at right angles, dividing the City into squares. The streets are well paved with stone and are kept very clean. Sprinklers are kept running in dry weather to keep the dust settled. Neatness and cleaness are everywhere observable. The buildings are mostly substantial structures, being of brick and stone. Many of the business houses and residences are very fine being built of marble with highly finished fronts. The City is situated on a triangular shaped piece of land between the Delaware and Schuylkill Rivers at the junction of the latter with the Delaware. That part of the City Schuylkill is called West Philadelphia. On the opposite side of the Delaware is Camden, New Jersey and in the river are three or four islands occupied chiefly as coal yards. We employed the time industriously this afternoon perambulating the city and seeing what was to be seen. Large brick market houses are very numerous, from which one would infer that people lived well so far as edibles are concerned and my experience in the City testified to the truth of this inference. In the afternoon there was a demonstration by the Union party of the City; there was a long torch light procession, transparencies, banners, etc. Thus closed our first day in the City of Brotherly Love and our first, in reality, as citizens. We were quite tired when we retired but a good bed and sweet sleep soon made us forgetful of past fatigues.

Sept. 25, Sunday—We attended services at a Roman Catholic Church. We certainly derived but little profit from the ceremonies through which the priest went. In the afternoon we visited Fairmount water works and went to the Penitentiary and Girard College. The former of these is one of the most important public works of the City. It is on the Schuylkill River, in the western part of the city. The water is raised into a large reservoir, by ponderous machinery, from which it is distributed to all parts of the city, supplying every man, woman and child of this great Metropolis with an abundance of pure water. The reservoir is on a mound the base of which appears to be solid rock. The grounds around are nicely ornamented with shade trees and with statuary. Some of the statues are placed on cliffs of rocks. They are made of white marble and, standing in such wild places, looked like Fairies. The ascent to the top of the reservoir is by a winding path. A dam is constructed across the river, above which a small steamer, the "General Hooker," runs a few miles to carry excursion parties. Of the penitentiary we saw nothing but massive walls, enclosing several acres of ground. Girard College is surrounded by a stone wall and no visitors are allowed to enter on Sabbath, unless they have business with some of the Officers of the institution; we were therefore not admitted. Philadelphia is very quiet on the Sabbath. The street cars do not run and but few persons are to be seen moving about through the city. We frequently walked three or four blocks in the most business part of the city without meeting a single person. Twenty-four hours before one had to elbow his way to get along. The same streets which were so thronged on Saturday were today almost deserted. We noticed well dressed and respectable looking people wending their way to church. In Philadelphia order and neatness prevail.[28]

Sept. 26—Today we visited Independence Hall, the U. S. Mint, the Academy of Fine Arts and Laurel Hill Cemetery. Independence Hall is a plain brick building. It was on the ground floor that the old Continental Congress met and signed that immortal document which declared that all men were born equal. When it was signed, the bell in the wooden belfry was rung, proclaiming "Liberty throughout the land and to all the inhabitants thereof," thus rendering prophetic the inscription made upon it when it was cast fifteen years before. The bell is cracked and has been replaced by another. It is now in the hall placed on a frame and perched upon it is an American Eagle. There are in the hall several relics of the Revolution, among which are some cannon balls and shells. There is a thirteen inch shell found at Yorktown, supposed to be a mortar shell. The same chandelier that lighted the room when the United States were British Colonies still hangs there. There are several portraits, of men, configured in the early history of our country. An old man had charge of the hall. We procured a ticket of him to go up into the belfry. It was left to our own liberality how much we should give for the ticket; nothing is absolutely required but it is expected that everyone will give something.

The money goes to support the families of Soldiers. A little girl attends to the belfry. We gave her our ticket and she directed us how to go up. From this place one has a fine view of the city. The U.S. Mint next claimed our attention. It is a plain marble building, not very large. We were shown around through it by a man employed for that purpose. They were making two cent pieces, both men and women were at work. After we were shown the different process of *"Making Money"* we were requested to register our names; then we passed through the cabinet. There is an extensive collection of coins both Ancient and Modern of different nations. There are also some Roman antiquities; such as lamps and vessels used in sacrifices. From the Mint we went to the Academy of Fine Arts. Of all that we saw there a painting by West interested us most. It is so large that it covers one end of the room in which it is placed. The subject is "Christ Rejected." There are about one hundred different characters represented in it. So terrible do the Jews look that one can almost hear the rabble crying "Away with Him." The Roman characters are easily distinguished, they being more mild. Such deep sorrow was depicted on the faces of the women who sympathized with Jesus that my eyes became moist, I was actually shedding tears. But, remembering that it was only a picture and that I was a soldier just from the army, I wiped my eyes and passed on. In the afternoon we visited Laurel Hill Cemetery. This is a beautiful place. Everything that art can do has been done to render the place attractive. In the evening we took tea with friend, Mr. Goltra. Such was our sojourn in Philadelphia. It was far too short, but a desire to be at home caused us to be unwilling to tarry longer. We had a good night's rest, preparatory to our departure for our home in the West, which we have not seen for more than three years. Philadelphia is worthy of its name *"Brotherly Love."* If ever I should get into trouble among strangers let it be in Philadelphia.[29]

Sept. 27—Early this morning we took our departure for home via Pittsburg. The day being fine we had a pleasant ride through a picturesque and well improved country. We were interested in noticing what papers seemed to be in the greatest demand along the road. We were thus enabled to form an opinion how the people would vote next November. From close observation we were led to believe that Lincoln would get a majority of the votes along the line of the Pennsylvania Railroad. We were very glad to see such evidences of loyalty in the great State of Pennsylvania. It cheers the heart of a returning soldier to see good union men. We want no conditional unionists, we want no apologists for the rebellion and rebels; such persons are an abomination to one who has stood in the breach for three years, to one who has been exposed to perils by land and by sea. We are in no mood to philosophically debate the doctrine of secession disguised under garb of "State Rights." The most important town on the road between Philadelphia and Harrisburg is Lancaster. The train, on which we started, stopped so often and made such slow speed that we had to wait for the express train, accordingly we got off the train at Lancaster. This town is situated in the midst of the best improved country in the United States. It is rather a pleasant looking place. Here we heard, for the last time on our journey home, the, "Boot shine sir, Boot black sir," of the little boot blacks. These boys are decidedly an improvement to a town. After a good dinner we got aboard the express, which soon came thundering along, and were again tending homeward. Over the rest of this road the speed was good and the stops short. We jostled along swiftly and dark found us well in the mountains. This being our third trip through this region the scenery presented nothing new. At Altoona my comrade Mr. Halloway stopped as he would have had to wait at Pittsburg for the train on which we started, his trunk being on it. At Huntington, I believe though I am not certain, a young lady got on the train; the car was crowded but I happened to be occupying a seat alone so she shared it with me and thus I had company the rest of the night and till in the next day. She proved to be a rural school miss going to Ohio. She was social, (as Pennsylvanians usually are), and was interesting. Her mountaineer graces did much to make this night ride on a rail pleasant. Soon after she took her seat she opened a basket and gave me some nice cake; this very acceptable as it now is in the night and I had not yet my supper. The school mistress had never traveled much and I made myself [useful] to her in procuring a ticket for her and getting her trunk re-checked at Pittsburg. At the last named city we arrived late in the night. After about half an hour's delay we got on the Pittsburg, Fort Wayne and Chicago train and were again hastening to the regions towards sunset. My eye lids now became heavy. I had a seat visavis to two ladies and they too were sleepy. I dropped off to sleep and after a short nap, awoke and my head was so badly mixt up with the ladies' that at first I could hardly tell mine from their heads. During the rest of the night I was oblivious to all that was going on around. Occasionally being aroused I found myself enveloped in crinoline, we were tumbled together promiscuously. After making a few frantic efforts to extricate myself I would again be seized by sleep and become senseless to my situation; thus I passed the night worse wrapt up in petticoats than it was my will to be.

End of Volume 7

End of Diary of a Soldier
Of the 39th Regiment Illinois Volunteers

Epilogue

For those who remained with the Thirty-ninth Illinois, hard fighting lay ahead. The regiment continued to serve in the trenches at Petersburg until the latter part of September when it was shifted north of the James River. The regiment participated in battles along the New Market and Darbytown roads on October 7 and 13, 1864. Again the Thirty-ninth suffered heavy casualties, and by the end of the engagements, First Lieutenant James Hannum commanded its remaining members. A few skirmishes followed, but at the end of October the regiment, still north of the James, settled back into the routine of trench warfare. During the rest of the winter, the Thirty-ninth received new equipment and replacements, and sick and wounded soldiers, now recovered, also returned to fortify the ranks. In the spring of 1865, now part of the First Brigade, First Division, Twenty-fourth Corps, the regiment stood positioned south of the James River. On April 2, 1865, the men led the attack against Fort Gregg during the final assault on the Petersburg defenses. In a desperate struggle in which seven of nine color guards fell, the Thirty-ninth Illinois entered the fort. After a thirty-minute hand-to-hand fight, Fort Gregg and its garrison were captured.

In the lead of the Army of the James, the Thirty-ninth now joined the pursuit of Lee's army and reached Appomattox Court House in time to cut off the Confederate retreat. After Lee's surrender, the regiment remained to serve in the occupying forces in Richmond and later in Norfolk, Virginia. The regiment was mustered out on December 7, 1865. The soldiers returned to their home state. On December 16, at Camp Butler, Springfield, Illinois, the regimental flags were turned over to state authorities and the men received their final pay.

Despite the pride he took in his service, Randolph apparently did not participate in postwar reunions, nor did he publish his personal reminiscences. The author of the classic regimental history on the Thirty-ninth Illinois published in 1889, Surgeon Charles Clark makes no mention of Randolph save in the roster listing for the privates of Company I. The simple entry reads: "Randolph, Valentine C. Enlisted from Lincoln September 16th, 1861. Mustered out September 17th, 1864, at expiration of service. Is living, but address not known." With the publication of his journals, Randolph will now be known, as will the campaigns and travails of his regiment and comrades. —*S.R.W.*

Appendix

A BRIEF BIOGRAPHY OF VALENTINE C. RANDOLPH

Charles Stanley

Valentine Cartright Randolph was born on February 16, 1838. He was the seventh of the fourteen children of James and Nancy Randolph, who had moved in 1831 from Virginia to central Illinois, settling in Aetna Township in Logan County. "He was reared on a farm, and in early life was taught the important lessons of industry, so essential to success in life," according to a memoir written after Randolph's death by Jarvice G. Evans, a Methodist clergyman. Evans met Randolph around 1878 and played a reoccurring role in his life.

In 1857, Randolph attended a preparatory school at Illinois College in Jacksonville and then in the fall of 1860 began studies at Dickinson College in Carlisle, Pennsylvania. When the war broke out in early 1861, Randolph withdrew from college and returned home.

In September of 1861, a company of volunteer infantry was organized by Hiram M. Phillips, a combat veteran of the Mexican-American War who became its captain. "It was a magnificent body of men—the majority of them were large in form, robust in muscle, young and spirited," according to a profile of the unit, soon to be designated as Company I, that was published in the 1889 history of the 39th Illinois Volunteer Infantry.

Randolph enlisted from the town of Lincoln, in Logan County, on September 16. The company muster roll shows him as one of the shorter members of the unit, standing 5 feet 4 3/4 inches and described as having sandy hair, black eyes, and a light complexion. His occupation was listed as "student."

There were eighty-five original members of Company I who enlisted for three-year terms. As the war progressed, that number decreased, chiefly by disability discharges. In January of 1864, the regiment's soldiers were offered a month's furlough and a bonus if they reenlisted. In Company I, forty-one soldiers took the offer. But dozens of others throughout the regiment declined. Randolph was among them.

Randolph, apparently having contracted malaria, had been sick at his quarters since November of 1863 and was transferred to the military hospital at Hilton Head, South Carolina, in January. He was not released for duty until spring of 1864. On June 1 and 2 Randolph sustained two slight wounds, one to the right wrist and one to his upper lip.

On September 16, 1864, with his three-year term of enlistment up, Randolph was discharged and made his way back to Illinois.

In the fall of 1865 Randolph entered Ohio Wesleyan University, from which he graduated in 1868. He went on to the Garrett Biblical Institute, from which he received a Bachelor of Divinity degree in 1869.

He began his career as a Methodist minister at the church in the central Illinois village of San Jose and typically switched assignments within the Illinois Conference after one to three years.

On June 23, 1870, Randolph married Angela H. Houghton, whom he had met while both were students at Ohio Wesleyan. Their home, said Evans, "was a model one, where we always found a warm welcome and a hospitable entertainment. It was a Christian home whose elevating influences were felt by all who entered as its guests."

In 1881, Randolph was transferred to the Central Tennessee Conference and was stationed in Nashville. But after two years he was back in Illinois, again accepting assignments to small-town Methodist churches. He was twice offered church-related educational positions but always preferred to remain in the pastorate. However, in March of 1892, when a position opened up at Hedding College, a Methodist College founded in 1855 in Abington, Illinois, Evans, then the college's president, was able to convince him to take it. Randolph served as vice president and taught Greek and Latin.

Absorbed into Illinois Wesleyan University in the 1930s, Hedding College in Randolph's day offered daily prayer meetings but banned dancing, alcohol, tobacco, football, and secret fraternities. Randolph fit in well. "He was scholarly, industrious, painstaking," said Evans. "He constantly grew in the confidence and affection of his students. He was not only scholarly and faithful in his work, but as a member of the faculty he was considerate and prudent, and his council was uniformly wise."

Over the years, Randolph's health declined. He developed kidney problems, which likely were a result of the malaria he had contracted while in the army. Bit by bit, his physical vitality slipped away to the point where even attempts at gardening tired him out. On January 1, 1895, Randolph's kidney trouble overtook him, and he died from acute albuminuria.

At Randolph's funeral service at the Methodist church in Lincoln, his casket was draped with the U.S. flag and covered by many floral arrangements. The choir opened with the hymn "Nearer My God to Thee," and the congregation finished with "Rock of Ages."

Randolph's college roommate, the Reverend A. M. Danely, a Methodist minister then located in Decatur, spoke of their friendship, and Evans wept as he gave the funeral discourse.

With an escort from the local Grand Army of the Republic union army veterans organization, Randolph's remains were taken to what is now called the Old Union Cemetery in Lincoln for burial in a plot purchased by his wife.

Valentine and Angela Randolph had no children. Angela moved in with her brother, Albert Houghton, who had served in the Civil War as a major in the 2nd Ohio cavalry. She died at his home in Florida in 1925, never having remarried. Her sustenance at the time included a twelve-dollar-a-month pension for her husband's war service.

Records at the Old Union Cemetery in Lincoln indicate that Angela was buried at Greenwood Cemetery in her hometown of Wellington, Ohio. But the large marker at Old Union Cemetery shows both of their names.

Notes

Volume 1

1. Charles M. Clark, *The History of the Thirty-ninth Illinois Volunteer Veteran Infantry (Yates phalanx) in the War of the Rebellion,* 24–25.

2. The full quotation for the epigraph is *Dulce et decorum est pro patria mori* (To die for the fatherland is a sweet thing and becoming; Horace *Odes* III.ii.13).

3. Lieutenant Waller was Emory L. Waller of Company I, Thirty-ninth Illinois. Two-headed Janus was the Roman god of gates and war. During time of war the gates to his temple were open; during periods of peace the gates were closed.

4. Henry Poff was Henry M. Poff of Company I, Thirty-ninth Illinois.

5. Camp Mather was a camp of instruction named for Thomas S. Mather, the Illinois adjutant general from 1858 to 1861. It was located on Indiana Avenue near Twenty-sixth Street in Chicago.

6. William B. Slaughter of Company G, Thirty-ninth Illinois, before the war had been a pastor at Bule Island, Illinois, where he recruited part of his company. The full quotation is *Sed fugit interea, fugit inreparabile tempus* (Meanwhile, Time is flying—flying, never to return; Virgil *Georgics* ii.284).

7. Stephen Arnold Douglas, born in Vermont, came to Illinois in 1833. He became a prominent legislator in Chicago, best known for his Popular Sovereignty theory, his debates with Abraham Lincoln, and his appearance as the 1860 presidential candidate for the northern wing of the Democratic party. After the firing on Fort Sumter, he enthusiastically backed Lincoln and the war but died of typhoid fever on June 3, 1861. He was buried on his estate, Oakenwald, located between Thirty-first and Thirty-fifth streets on Chicago's South Side, along Lake Michigan. Before his death Douglas had donated ten acres for the establishment of a university. Sometimes referred to as Douglas University or the University of Chicago, the school suffered financial difficulties and was closed in 1885. During the war a portion of his estate, termed Camp Douglas, was used as a training camp and later a prisoner of war camp.

8. Charles G. Finney established the businessmen's prayer meeting in Boston during the great revival that swept the United States in the late 1850s. The meetings, held at noon and usually led by lay ministers, soon became popular across the Northern states.

9. Benton Barracks was located about four miles from St. Louis. General John C. Fremont established the camp on the state fairground and nearby property and named it for his father-in-law, Senator Thomas Hart Benton.

10. The eagle referred to was Old Abe, a golden eagle, the mascot of Company C, Eighth Wisconsin, who served with the regiment for nearly four years before being retired to the state capital in September 1864. Austin Light was the colonel of the Thirty-ninth Illinois from July 22 to November 25, 1861, when he was dismissed from service. John C. Fremont was commander of the Western Department from July 25 to November 2, 1861. Sterling Price was commander of the Missouri State Guard.

11. Thomas O. Osborn, one of the principal organizers of the Thirty-ninth Illinois, served as the regiment's lieutenant colonel and colonel. General Samuel R.

Curtis was commander of the Army of Southwest Missouri, Department of Missouri. Merriwether Jeff Thompson was initially commander of pro-Confederate Missouri irregulars and later a general in the Missouri State Guard. Hiram M. Phillips was captain and Albert W. Fellows was second lieutenant, both of Company I, Thirty-ninth Illinois.

12. Located on the southern approach to St. Louis at Ironton Gap, Pilot Knob was the southern terminus of the St. Louis & Iron Mountain Railroad.

13. Mr. Parkhurst remains unidentified.

14. William H. Seward was U.S. secretary of state.

15. Franz Sigel was a German revolutionary and military officer who commanded a brigade in the Army of Southwest Missouri from November 1861 to February 1862.

16. Colonel Burgess remains unidentified.

17. Ward Hill Lamon was Lincoln's former law partner and U.S. marshal for the District of Columbia. Early in the war Lamon helped recruit loyal Virginians for the U.S. Army. He was never commissioned as a general.

18. Rev. McReading was Chaplain Charles S. McReading of the Thirty-ninth Illinois. Amos Savage was lieutenant and later captain of Company G, Thirty-ninth Illinois. Homer A. Plimpton (Plinton) was in Company G, Thirty-ninth Illinois. Sylvester W. Munn, captain of Company A, Thirty-ninth Illinois, was promoted to major in January 1862.

19. Dr. Post remains unidentified.

20. The reference is to Abraham and Isaac in Genesis 22. Randolph makes a reference to families fighting against each other and his belief that his Southern relatives were fighting against God.

21. "The Sucker State" was a nickname given to Illinois; its citizens were sometimes referred to as "suckers." There are a number of theories about the origin of the nickname, including a comparison between miners going and coming at the lead mines at Galena and the sucker fish that go upriver to spawn in the spring and return downriver in the fall. Another theory claims that the people of southern Illinois who came to the state from Kentucky were compared to the sprouts termed "suckers" on the tobacco plant that were stripped away to keep them from sapping the growth of the tobacco leaves. In this comparison, the poor people who left Kentucky to settle Illinois were seen as suckers, or a burden to the citizens of standing in Kentucky.

22. Dickinson College, located in Carlisle, Pennsylvania, was chartered in 1783 and named for John Dickinson.

23. The Irvine Female College, located in Mechanicsburg, Pennsylvania, was chartered in 1857 and named for Washington Irving, who served as a trustee.

24. A native of Maryland, General Otho H. Williams was a Continental officer in the American Revolution who distinguished himself during the Southern campaigns. In 1787 he sponsored the town of Williamsport, Maryland, as a possible site for the nation's new capital.

25. William Gesford of Company I, Thirty-ninth Illinois.

26. "Hank Gott" was probably Henry Poff.

27. Julian M. Sturtevant was president of Illinois College. Sturtevant and the college were noted for their connections to the reform movement and abolitionism. Governor Yates of Illinois, for whom the Thirty-ninth Illinois received its nickname "Yates Phalanx," was the college's first graduate.

28. This refers to the naval victory at Port Royal Sound, South Carolina, on November 7, 1861, that resulted in the seizure of the sound and the surrounding Sea Islands.

29. Joseph W. Richardson of Company A, Thirty-ninth Illinois, died of typhoid fever at Williamsport, Maryland, on November 17, 1861, and was buried there.

30. Confederate diplomats James M. Mason and John Slidell were captured onboard the British mail ship *Trent.*

31. John B. Floyd was a former Virginia governor, secretary of war in the Buchanan administration, and Confederate general. While secretary of war he was an avid proponent of secession, and he directed military arms and artillery to be sent to Southern arsenals and forts before the war began.

32. For the dismissal of Colonel Light, see entry for December 3, 1861. Frank B. Marshall was adjutant of the Thirty-ninth Illinois from August 1861 to July 1862.

33. The Hampton Battery was a Federal artillery company from Maryland.

34. Orrin L. Mann was commissioned major of the Thirty-ninth Illinois in December 1861.

35. *Paradise Lost,* an epic poem written by John Milton, was first published in 1667.

36. Benjamin Franklin Kelly, a Union general, spent most of his career commanding forces in West Virginia and Maryland, guarding the Baltimore and Ohio Railroad.

37. Mr. and Mrs. Boyd of Clear Spring remain unidentified.

38. Reference is being made to the locks and dams of the Chesapeake and Ohio Canal.

39. Thomas J. "Stonewall" Jackson's brigade organized in the spring of 1861 and was made up of the Second, Fourth, Fifth, Twenty-seventh, and Thirty-third Virginia Infantry regiments and the Rockbridge Artillery Battery.

Volume 2

1. Quotation is from Clark, *History,* 30.

2. Ibid., 58.

3. Adjutant Buck remains unidentified.

4. Sergeants W. C. McMurry and O. P. Nelson, Corporal Thomas Johnson, and privates B. Johnson (either Abiram B. Johnson or Joel B. Johnson) and George Riddle were all members of Company I, Thirty-ninth Illinois.

5. Word of the Confederate advance was brought to Major Mann at Bath on January 3, 1862. Mann took sixty men and engaged Jackson's cavalry some five miles south of Bath. He was cut off as the outnumbered Federals began to retreat but, thanks to his swift and agile stallion, managed to escape his pursuers.

6. This was Company F, Fourth U.S. Artillery.

7. This was Colonel William G. Murray of the Eighty-fourth Pennsylvania.

8. Turner Ashby, a Virginia planter and politician from the Shenandoah Valley, organized a cavalry command early in the war, served as colonel of the Seventh Virginia cavalry, and became Jackson's cavalry commander in the valley. He was promoted to brigadier general on May 23, 1862.

9. Nathaniel P. Banks was a Massachusetts politician, a former speaker of the house and governor of Massachusetts, and president of the Illinois Central Railroad, whom Abraham Lincoln had appointed as a major general in May 1861. Alpheus S. Williams was commander of the First Division, Fifth Army Corps, under

Banks. Frederick West Lander, engineer and railroad surveyor of transcontinental routes, was commissioned brigadier general on May 17, 1861, and commanded a division in western Virginia.

10. M. V. Lyan was Martin V. Lyon, Company I, Thirty-ninth Illinois.

11. Joseph Young remains unidentified.

12. Mr. Weber remains unidentified.

13. The British built Fort Cumberland around a fortified trading post in 1754–1755. The post served as the starting point for George Washington's expedition to the forks of the Ohio River and General Edward Braddock's expedition against the French at Fort Duquesne. At various times Washington served as the fort's commanding officer.

14. The First Virginia Cavalry and Fifth Virginia Infantry were raised by the government that was formed at Wheeling, Virginia, in June 1861 and that was initially accepted as the "loyal" state government. Later, after the western counties organized themselves as the new state of West Virginia, the regiments were designated West Virginia regiments.

15. The Boa Constrictor (sometimes called the Anaconda Plan) was the Union strategy of surrounding the South and squeezing it into submission by capturing key cities and industrial centers. George B. McClellan was commanding general of the Federal armies.

16. Francis H. Pierpont and John Letcher were the two governors of Virginia during the Civil War. Pierpont was the leader of the loyal, or restored, state government that first organized in Wheeling and later moved to Norfolk. Letcher was the governor of Virginia from 1860 to 1864, serving both as governor before secession and as governor of Confederate Virginia.

17. Fort Donelson was the Confederate fortification on the Cumberland River guarding the water approach to Nashville, Tennessee. It was captured by Federal forces on February 16, 1862.

18. Generals Simon B. Buckner and Bushrod R. Johnson were Confederate commanders captured at Fort Donelson. There was no General West in the garrison.

19. Lieutenant Rudd was Oscar F. Rudd, Company G, Thirty-ninth Illinois.

20. General Carson was Brigadier General James H. Carson, commander of the Frederick County militia, Sixteenth Brigade, Third Division, Virginia Militia.

21. Captain Woodruff was Joseph Woodruff, Company K, Thirty-ninth Illinois.

22. "Ultima Thule" is a term for the northernmost part of the inhabitable world, a very distant, mysterious, or mythical region.

23. General Lander died on March 2, 1862. Rumored causes of death included pneumonia, apoplectic seizure, and drunkenness, but most likely he succumbed to an infection from a wound received at Edwards Ferry, Virginia.

24. James Shields was an Irish-born Illinois politician who had served as a general in the Mexican War. Shields later became governor of Oregon and served as a U.S. senator for both Oregon and Minnesota. Commissioned a brigadier general on August 19, 1861, he took command of Lander's division, the Second Division, Fifth Corps, on March 13, 1862.

25. J. W. Weedman was Jacob F. Weedman of Company I, Thirty-ninth Illinois.

26. After General Shields was given command of Lander's division, Lieutenant Simon Brucker of Company C, Thirty-ninth Illinois, was detailed to establish a headquarters for Shields in a large residence near Cherry Run. One

evening, for a joke, Brucker sent word to Colonel Osborn that General Shields was at the house. Osborn, his staff, and the band of the Thirty-ninth Illinois immediately went to the house, where Brucker told Osborn the general was in the parlor. With the band playing outside, Osborn entered the room and found a history book on the Mexican War that Brucker had opened to a picture of General Shields. In order to keep the joke going, Colonel Osborn allowed Major Munn to go out on the porch and imitate Shields. In a thick Irish brogue, Munn addressed the men, who believed they were listening to General Shields.

27. Fort Frederick was a stone fort built on North Mountain by the colony of Maryland in 1756.

28. The Valley Female Institute was a Methodist school located in Winchester from 1854 to 1860. The Eastern Lunatic Asylum was located in Williamsburg, Virginia. Opened in 1773, it was the oldest publicly supported mental hospital in North America. The Western Lunatic Asylum, founded in 1825, was located in Staunton, Virginia.

29. Traitor Mason was James Murray Mason, born in Fairfax County, Analostan Island, Virginia, who studied law and settled at Winchester, Virginia, in 1820. Active in politics, he served as a U.S. congressman and senator and authored the 1850 Fugitive Slave Act. After Lincoln's election, he helped lead Virginia's secession movement. Mason was named the Confederacy's commissioner to Great Britain but was captured onboard the British steamer *Trent* and briefly imprisoned until Great Britain demanded his release. He was unable to gain European recognition of the Confederacy but remained in Europe until after the war. His home at Winchester, located west of the town, was known as Selma. Mason's family remained at Selma until the approach of Federal troops in March 1862 when they fled to Richmond. During the war, the house was demolished by Federal troops who used the wood for firewood and the stone foundations for nearby fortifications.

Volume 3

1. Clark, *History,* 84.

2. Colonel Sullivan was Colonel Jeremiah Cutler Sullivan of the Thirteenth Indiana.

3. Lieutenant Colonel Daum was Lieutenant Colonel Philip Daum, the artillery commander in Shields's Division.

4. The Battle of Kernstown is sometimes referred to as the Battle of Winchester. General Shields instructed the men of the Thirty-ninth Illinois to place the name Winchester on their battle flag for this engagement.

5. This was the battery of Captain Joseph C. Clark, Jr., commander of Company E, Fourth U.S. Artillery.

6. Colonel Nathan Kimble was commander of the Fourteenth Indiana, and later commander of the First Brigade, Second Division (under Shields), in Banks's Command.

7. Colonel William G. Murray of the Eighty-fourth Pennsylvania was killed at Kernstown.

8. Island Number 10 and Pittsburg Landing were Union victories to the west. Island Number 10 in the Mississippi River near New Madrid, Missouri, was captured on April 7, 1862. The battle of Pittsburg Landing, also known as Shiloh, was fought on the Tennessee River on April 6–7, 1862.

9. Sol was the Roman god of the sun. The USS *Merrimack* was a U.S. steam frigate that was converted into the Confederate ironclad *Virginia* in the spring of 1861. On March 8, 1862, the *Virginia* destroyed the sloop *Cumberland* and frigate *Congress* in Hampton Roads, Virginia. The next day it fought the Union ironclad *Monitor* to a draw. The presence of the *Virginia* greatly handicapped Union moves against Richmond on the peninsula. Randolph is wrong in reporting it sunk on April 9. It was in service until the Confederates evacuated Norfolk. Unable to reach Richmond due to its deep draft, the *Virginia* was destroyed on May 11, 1862.

10. On April 13, 1861, at Fort Sumter, Charleston, South Carolina, Major Robert Anderson, commander of the fort, agreed to surrender the fort. The actual lowering of the flag and evacuation occurred on April 14.

11. Camp Douglas was an area of Stephen Douglas's estate in Chicago that was initially used as a training camp. After the capture of Fort Donelson it was converted into a prisoner of war camp.

12. "Watchman what of the night" is found in Isaiah 21:17. Randolph uses the reference to comment on the prospect of peace.

13. From April 5 through May 4, 1862, Confederate forces in a defense line running from the York River to the James River and taking in the old town of Yorktown kept McClellan's army from moving on Richmond. The line and town were evacuated on the night of May 3, 1862.

14. Richard Taylor commanded a brigade in Richard Ewell's division in Jackson's command in the Shenandoah Valley.

15. Chief Justice of the U.S. Supreme Court from 1801 to 1835, John Marshall was born in Fauquier County, Virginia, in 1755 and moved to Richmond, Virginia, after his marriage in 1783. "F. F. V.'s" refers to the phrase "First Families of Virginia," meaning the families descending from the initial European Virginia settlers and sometimes applied to any aristocratic Virginia families. General Abram Duryee was a brigade commander in McDowell's Army of the Rappahannock.

16. General Irvin McDowell, Northern commander at First Bull Run, later commanded the First Corps, Army of the Potomac, the Army of the Rappahannock, and the Second Corps, Army of Virginia. Edwin McMaster Stanton, Union secretary of war, was appointed on January 13, 1862.

17. General Banks was not surrounded, but after defeating the Federals at Front Royal, Jackson threatened Banks's line of retreat, forcing the Federals to flee up the valley toward Winchester.

18. Company members who had been left in Strasburg for health reasons and listed as being taken prisoner include L. E. W. Craig, Richard C. Charleston, and John W. Grooms.

19. Oris Sanford Ferry, colonel of the Fifth Connecticut, became brigadier general on March 17, 1862.

20. This was Samuel Sprigg Carroll, colonel of the Eighteenth Ohio, commander of the Fourth Brigade, Shields's Division.

21. J. D. Lemon was James D. Lemon, who later became first lieutenant; E. S. Waller was Emory L. Waller; Samuel Gilmore later became captain; and J. B. Craiger was James B. Creager, all of them Company I, Thirty-ninth Illinois.

22. Shields's division was broken up on June 26, 1862. Ferry's and Kimball's brigades were sent to the Peninsula while Carroll's and Tyler's brigades joined the

Army of Virginia. Shields was nominated for the rank of major general, but the Senate did not confirm. He was not given a new command, and on March 28, 1863, he resigned from the army.

23. The Virginia Protestant Episcopal Seminary, originally established in Fairfax, Virginia, moved to Alexandria in 1823. The Marshall House Tavern was where Colonel Ephraim Elmer Ellsworth, commander of the Fire Zouaves (Eleventh New York), was killed by James T. Jackson, proprietor of the Marshall House, after he removed a Confederate flag that had been flying over the building. Jackson was then killed by Private Francis E. Brownell.

24. The SS *North America* was a 499-ton paddlewheel steamer. The SS *Georgia,* a 551-ton paddlewheel steamer, and the SS *Louisiana,* a 1,126-ton paddlewheel steamer, were chartered by the U.S. Army to serve as transports. SS *Metamora* was a 282-ton sidewheel army transport.

25. SS *John Tucker* was a 352-ton sidewheel army transport, the *Young America* a 138-ton sidewheel army transport. Fort Washington was a masonry fort built to guard the water approach to Washington, D.C., completed in 1824 on the eastern bank of the Potomac River nearly opposite Mount Vernon. The fort is currently a national park. During the Civil War, Mount Vernon was watched over by the Mount Vernon Ladies Association under the direction of Sarah Tracy and Upton Herbert, who stayed at the estate. The house was unharmed by either side, and tours of the home were given to Union soldiers throughout the war.

26. Fortress Monroe, built between 1819 and 1834 on Point Comfort, Virginia, was one of the largest fortifications ever built by the United States. It guarded the entrance to Hampton Road, an important naval anchorage and the approach to Norfolk and Richmond. Garrisoned at the start of the Civil War, the fort was not captured by the Confederates and served throughout the war as a vital Union base. It still serves as an army post.

27. Artillery pieces were often given nicknames. In this case the "Lincoln" gun was the prototype fifteen-inch Rodman, a massive cannon weighing 49,099 pounds. It had a fifteen-inch smooth bore and was capable of firing a 440-pound round shot. The cannon had been cast at Fort Pitt Foundry and brought to Fort Monroe for testing. The "Union" gun was cast in the same manner as a fifteen-inch Rodman but had a twelve-inch rifled bore. It was also manufactured at Fort Pitt Foundry and was capable of firing a bullet-shaped projectile weighing up to 670 pounds. The gun was sent to Fort Monroe and mounted next to the "Lincoln" gun, which can still be seen at Fort Monroe today.

28. Rips Raps is a shoal about one mile off Fort Monroe where the United States started a fortification in 1826 known as Fort Calhoun. Together, Forts Monroe and Calhoun (sometimes called Castle Calhoun) were to create a cross fire across the ship channel leading to Hampton Roads. Fort Calhoun was unfinished at the start of the Civil War but did remain in Union hands and was garrisoned and armed. The fort was renamed, from Calhoun after the South Carolina senator John C. Calhoun, to Fort Wool for John E. Wool, the Union general who had secured Forts Monroe and Calhoun for the North at the start of the war.

29. The Seven Days' Battle lasted from June 25 to July 1, 1862, and saw General Robert E. Lee attacking and driving General George B. McClellan's army away from Richmond. The battle cost the Confederates over twenty thousand casualties while the Federals suffered nearly sixteen thousand casualties.

30. Berkeley Plantation was the birthplace of William Henry Harrison, the ninth president of the United States, and headquarters for General McClellan at Harrison's Landing. Nearby was Sherwood Forrest Plantation, home of John Tyler, Harrison's vice president, who upon Harrison's death became the tenth president of the United States. Both homes are still standing.

Volume 4

1. Professor Thaddeus Sobieski Lowe, an aeronautic scientist, was appointed chief of the U.S. Army aeronautics in the summer of 1861. As part of the Bureau of Topographical Engineers, he operated a squadron that eventually contained seven balloons for use in aerial reconnaissance. Lowe used his balloons at Yorktown and during the Seven Days' Battle with McClellan's army.

2. Chaplain Samuel Day was the chaplain of the Eighth Illinois.

3. General George B. McClellan was nicknamed the American Napoleon. At this time, Erasmus D. Keyes commanded the Fourth Corps in the Army of the Potomac, John J. Peck commanded the Second Division in Keyes's Fourth Corps, and Orris S. Ferry commanded the Third Brigade in Peck's Second Division. The balloon *Intrepid* was one of Lowe's balloons used during the Seven Days' Battle.

4. For Berkeley Plantation, see vol. 3, n. 30 above.

5. Tophet is a place referred to in 2 Kings 23:10, a hilled site outside the walls of Jerusalem where people would burn their children as a sacrifice to their god Moloch, sometimes referred to as Baal.

6. In using the term "Magnus Apollo," Randolph is referring to General Keyes as leader or person of authority.

7. The Thirty-ninth Illinois had been organized one company short, Company H. In April 1862, soldiers from the regiment had returned to Illinois to find recruits for existing companies. At this time a group of men were recruited and sent to Camp Butler, Illinois, where they were grouped with other recruits into a temporary company termed Company H, Thirty-ninth Illinois, and used to guard Confederate prisoners at the Camp Butler. In June, Chauncey Williams of Company I, Thirty-ninth Illinois, arrived with some men he had recruited and combined them with the men at Camp Butler to form Company H. Williams was elected captain, and the company was mustered into service on July 11, 1862, and joined the regiment at Harrison's Landing on July 24.

8. Major Patton remains unidentified.

9. Randolph is referring to the ironclad CSN *Richmond,* which was started at the Gosport Navy Yard near Norfolk and then taken to Richmond for completion when the Confederates evacuated Norfolk. Though referred to as a second *Merrimack,* the *Richmond* was much smaller and built to a different plan.

10. The *Galena* and *Monitor* were the first ironclads to be completed by the United States. The *Monitor,* a raftlike vessel with a flat bottom and a single revolving turret, was finished in time to fight the Confederate ironclad *Virginia* at Hampton Roads on March 9, 1862. In late April 1862, the *Monitor* was joined by the recently completed *Galena,* an ironclad screw steamer. After the destruction of the *Virginia* on May 11, 1862, the *Galena* and *Monitor* led a flotilla of warships up the James in an attempt to capture Richmond but were turned back by obstructions and Fort Darling located at Drewry's Bluff.

11. Randolph is referring to Ambrose E. Burnside, commander of the amphibious expedition that seized most of eastern North Carolina from February to July 1862. On July 3, 1862, Burnside and seventy-five hundred men were ordered to Fort Monroe to reinforce General McClellan, but instead of joining McClellan at Harrison's Landing the soldiers were sent to reinforce General Pope in northeastern Virginia. Later, after the Battle of Antietam, Burnside took over the Army of the Potomac from McClellan.

12. By Fort Drewry, Randolph means Fort Darling, a Confederate fortification eight miles below Richmond on the James River at Drewry's Bluff. On May 18, 1862, the fort high on a bluff overlooking obstructions had stopped the *Monitor, Galena,* and other warships from reaching Richmond.

13. The Battle of Cedar Mountain on August 9, 1862, saw General Banks attacking forces under General Jackson near Cedar Mountain outside of Culpeper, Virginia. Though initially successful, Banks was defeated by a Confederate counterattack and was forced to withdraw. The battle was the opening of the Second Bull Run Campaign.

14. The College of William and Mary was chartered in 1693 and is the second oldest institution of higher learning in the United States. In 1781 it became the nation's first university. It was closed in 1781 during the Yorktown Campaign in the Revolution and again in 1862. At this time its principal structure, the Wren Building, was burned down. The Eastern Lunatic Asylum was also located in Williamsburg.

15. Cyrus the Younger, the younger son of King Darius II of the Persian Archaemenid Dynasty, attempted to overthrow his brother Artaxerxes using Greek mercenaries. The two met at the battle of Cunaxa north of Babylon on the Euphrates River in 401 BC, and Cyrus sought out his brother and wounded him but was himself killed.

16. Yorktown, Virginia, was the site of the surrender of the British army under Lord Charles the Earl Cornwallis to George Washington. It was also the site of a siege between John Bankhead Magruder's Confederate forces and George McClellan's Union army.

17. It was common for artillerymen to name their cannon after famous individuals, in this case John Bankhead Magruder, Confederate commander of the Army of the Peninsula who held off McClellan's army at Yorktown from April to early May 1862. The other cannon was probably named for Daniel Harvey Hill who served in the Peninsula and at the Battle of Big Bethel.

18. SS *Merrimac* was a screw-propelled, iron-hulled steamer of nearly two thousand tons chartered by the Quartermaster Department.

19. Reference is to Aesop's fable, "The Crab and His Mother," in which the mother told her son that he should walk straight. The son replied that he would follow her example. Since she could not walk straight, she realized how foolish it was to find fault with her child.

20. Hampton, Virginia, located three miles from Fort Monroe, was occupied by Federal forces in July 1861. When Union troops were withdrawn from the area, Confederate forces under General Magruder entered the town and then set fire to it to keep it from being used by the Federals. Refugee slaves who established their own community known as the Grand Contraband Camp later occupied its ruins.

21. Camp Hamilton was an encampment established on the Segar Farm at the north end of the bridge over Mill Creek, near Fort Monroe, where Northern missionaries early in the war established a school for refugee slaves.

22. Carolus Clara Aqua was Corporal Charles W. Clearwater of Company I, Thirty-ninth Illinois.

23. The USS *Stepping Stones* was a paddlewheel ferryboat of 226 tons purchased by the U.S. Navy in September 1861 and outfitted as a gunboat.

24. Joseph King Fenno Mansfield, commander of the Union forces at Suffolk from July 22 to September 8, 1862, when he was given command of the Twelfth Corps, was subsequently killed at Antietam.

25. In early September 1862, Robert E. Lee directed his army to Maryland. Among his officers were Ambrose Powell Hill, Daniel Harvey Hill, James Longstreet, and Stonewall Jackson.

26. The Isthmian games were athletic events similar to the Olympic Games though on a smaller scale. Held at Corinth, they occurred each year before and after the Olympic Games. The biblical reference is probably 1 Corinthians 19.

27. John Adams Dix commanded the Department of Virginia from June 17, 1862, to July 15, 1863.

28. The Sea Board and Roanoke Railroad ran from Washington, Virginia, near Norfolk to the Roanoke River at Weldon, North Carolina.

29. Henry Alexander Wise, former governor of Virginia, commanded forces in the defense of Richmond and southeastern Virginia after the Peninsula Campaign.

30. There is a Lieutenant James identified as serving as an engineer on the Suffolk defenses. See *War of the Rebellion: Official Records of the Union and Confederate Armies,* vol. 18, p. 651.

31. Francis B. Spinola, a New York politician, raised the Empire Brigade made up of New York regiments. He and his command were at Suffolk, Virginia, from October 1 to December 28, 1862. The brigade was made up of the 132nd, 158th, 163rd, and 164th New York Infantry regiments.

32. The Natural Bridge is a limestone arch, 215 feet high, 90 feet long, varying in width from 50 to 150 feet over Cedar Creek, south of Lexington, Virginia. The Dismal Swamp covers about 223,000 acres in southeastern Virginia. In the center of the swamp is the 3,000-acre Lake Drummond. The color of the lake's water comes from the tannic acid from the bark of the cypress, juniper, and gum trees. George Washington explored the region in 1763 and later organized a company to drain and timber the area and build canals. The Jericho Canal connected Suffolk to Lake Drummond.

33. A Mr. Duke is reported in *War of the Rebellion,* vol. 18, p. 651, as assisting Federal forces in the Dismal Swamp area.

34. The Battle of Perryville on October 8, 1862, was an engagement between Union forces under General Don C. Buell and Confederates commanded by Braxton Bragg. Although it was a draw, Bragg withdrew from Kentucky after the battle.

35. Major General John James Peck's division at Suffolk, part of the Seventh Corps, consisted of brigades commanded by Henry W. Wessells, Francis B. Spinola, Robert S. Foster, and Orris S. Ferry.

36. Morpheus is the Greek god of dreams.

37. The HMS *Cadmus* and *Peterel* were British warships that carried dispatches to and from British consuls in the Confederacy and Lord Lyons, the British minister to the United States. The vessels were often stationed at Hampton Roads. November 9 was the birthday of Prince Albert Edward, the Prince of Wales and heir to the British throne. He succeeded to the throne as Edward VII in 1901.

38. In 1862 the Federal government authorized bounties to volunteers in order to encourage enlistment. Nine-month volunteers received twenty-five dollars, twelve-month volunteers fifty dollars, and three-year volunteers one hundred dollars.

39. Samuel Perkins Spear was colonel of the Eleventh Pennsylvania Cavalry Regiment.

40. General Ferry was a radical Republican. General Peck was a War Democrat who backed the war effort.

41. On December 13, 1862, General Burnside launched a series of unsuccessful attacks against Confederate positions outside Fredericksburg, Virginia. Burnside's command was badly defeated.

42. Michael Corcoran, an Irish immigrant, commanded the Sixty-ninth New York at the First Bull Run, where he was captured. Exchanged, he raised the Corcoran Legion, which was composed of the 155th, 164th, 170th, and 182nd New York Infantry regiments.

43. William Woodward was second assistant surgeon of the Thirty-ninth Illinois. Commissioned in December 9, 1862, he joined the regiment at Suffolk.

44. The issuing of the Emancipation Proclamation caused some Union soldiers to question if the war was being fought to save the Union or to free and uplift the slaves, who might then become competition for land and jobs. This was true with the Illinois units, since the state had close connections to the slave states of Kentucky and Missouri.

45. In May 1862, after the occupation of eastern North Carolina by Burnside's expedition, the Federals began forming North Carolina regiments with white North Carolinians.

46. SS *Eastern City* was a 616-ton paddlewheel steamer also known as the *Cossack* that was purchased by the Quartermaster Bureau at the start of the war.

47. Hallowell was Robert Hallowell, chief musician in the Thirty-ninth Illinois's band.

48. The *New Bern Progress* was a prewar weekly newspaper in New Bern that was continued after Union occupation both on a weekly and a semi-weekly basis.

49. Cedar Grove Cemetery was established by Christ Church. The cemetery became the city cemetery in 1853. Confederate dead from the Battle of New Bern were interred there. The wall around the cemetery was built of coquina, a whitish limestone made up of seashells.

50. John Gray Foster was commander of the Department of North Carolina and the Eighteenth Corps, from December 24, 1862, to July 18, 1863. Joshua B. Howell was colonel of the Eighty-fifth Pennsylvania and later commander of the Second Brigade, Third Division, Eighteenth Corps.

51. While at New Bern, the Thirty-ninth Illinois received from Illinois governor Richard Yates a flag that bore his portrait.

52. The New Bern Battleground was located six miles below New Bern. It consisted of a defense line running from the Neuse River west across the Atlantic and North Carolina Railroad to Brice's Creek. On March 14, 1862, the Confederate defenses were overrun by Union forces under General Burnside. The Confederates retreated from New Bern, which was occupied by the Federals for the remainder of the war.

53. The SS *Sentinel,* the former *Mayo,* was a 311-ton screw-propelled vessel owned by the Quartermaster Bureau. Fort Macon was a masonry fortification completed before the Civil War to guard Beaufort Harbor and the approaches to the towns of Beaufort and Morehead City. The fort was captured by Burnside's expedition on April 26, 1862, after a brief siege.

54. Bull's Bay, a bay just north of Charleston, was used as an anchorage for Union vessels and was often suggested as a landing point for attacks against Charleston. Benjamin Franklin Butler, Union general and prominent politician, had been recalled from commanding New Orleans in December 1862, and his name was often mentioned for other commands including that of the Department of the South.

55. The SS *Mary Sanford* was a 757-ton screw-propelled steamer that was later purchased by the navy for use as a gunboat.

56. Neptune is the Roman god of the waters.

57. The Black Hole of Calcutta was a one-room, eighteen-foot-square military jail at Fort William, Calcutta, India. On June 21, 1756, 146 prisoners from the East India Company were forced into this room by their Indian captors, and in the morning only 23 prisoners were still alive.

58. Port Royal Sound, the deepest natural harbor south of New York, was captured by the U.S. Navy on November 7, 1861, and became the home of the South Atlantic Blockading Squadron. The *General Meigs* was a 329-ton iron-hull screw steamer hired by, and later purchased by, the Quartermaster Bureau. Jonathon F. Linton was first lieutenant, Company D, Thirty-ninth Illinois, and later the regiment's quartermaster.

59. Hilton Head Island, a sea island at the mouth of Port Royal Sound, was occupied by the Federals on November 7, 1861. It was the site of the headquarters of the Department of the South and home to extensive military camps, depots, slave refugee camps, and other support facilities including a town.

60. The basic field ration for a Union soldier was one sixteen-ounce biscuit known as hardtack and a quarter pound of salt meat or bacon.

61. St. Helena Island is a sea island on Port Royal Sound. During the Civil War the island was home to extensive campgrounds, a quartermaster depot, and naval repair shops. Dr. William Jenkins owned a number of plantations on St. Helena Island. Randolph could have walked through the 615-acre Dr. Jenkins Plantation that was intersected by Seaside Road and fronted Station Creek, or he may have walked on the boundary between the Dr. Jenkins Plantation and the 570-acre "Scott Place," also owned by Jenkins. A Mr. Bryant was originally a superintendent on Edisto Island, but when that island was evacuated by the Federals in July 1862, he was reassigned to the Dr. Jenkins Plantation on St. Helena Island. This was probably Mr. Oliver Bryant. "Miss Lucy" could possibly have been Miss Lucy McKim of Philadelphia, who worked with the former slaves on the St. Helena Island.

62. Federal troops were authorized on May 25, 1861, a clothing allowance of \$3.50 a month. A soldier was allowed to turn in worn-out clothing for new ones. If he overdrew the yearly \$42.00 allowance, the difference was deducted from his pay.

63. Beaufort was the principal community in the Port Royal area. Located on Port Royal Island, it was occupied by Federal forces in early December 1861 and was home to camps, hospitals, slave refugee camps, and military depots and support facilities. During the war many Northerners came to Beaufort to work with the slaves and establish businesses.

64. The Port Royal Experiment was a term given to the operations run initially by the Treasury Department and later the War Department to assist and educate the area's slave population.

65. The Sea Island African slaves spoke a Creole blend of English and various African languages, which resulted in a language known today as Gullah.

66. Randolph is referring to Spanish moss *(Tillandsia usneoides),* which is not actually a moss but, rather, a flowering plant that grows hanging from tree branches in full sun or partial shade in the southeastern United States. Spanish moss is not a parasite but an epiphyte, which absorbs nutrients and water from the air and rainfall.

67. The first church would have been the Chapel of Ease, an Episcopal chapel built of tabby, an early form of concrete. It was painted white, which may have caused Randolph to think it was wooden. The brick church was the St. Helena Baptist Church. Both churches had an adjoining graveyard.

68. Although popular legend reports that only one white man was left in Beaufort when it was occupied by the Federals, there were at least two businessmen in the town, and a few white, non-planter families living on the Sea Islands. The *Free South* was a newspaper started by James M. Latta; its first issue was published on January 17, 1863. The H. S. Gibbs House, used as boardinghouse and a hotel, was named Stevens Hotel in honor of General Isaac Stevens, onetime commander of Beaufort and Port Royal Island.

69. The SS *Wyoming* was a sidewheel steamer of 383 tons chartered by the Quartermaster Department.

70. General Hunter resented the presence of General Foster in his department, and eventually Foster, on February 18, 1863, returned to North Carolina. Control of the men from the Eighteenth Corps was given over to General Hunter, and they were eventually merged into Hunter's Tenth Corps (see introduction).

71. The artillery fire heard by Randolph came from monitors testing their guns in the Broad River just south of his campsite on St. Helena Island. Fort Jackson was a masonry fortification completed in 1809 and rebuilt in 1842 on the south bank of the Savannah River opposite Five Fathom Hole, a deep anchorage three miles east of Savannah. Fort Jackson was located on the inner ring of Savannah's defenses and did not come under attack by the Federals.

72. Randolph may be referring to the feuding between the "Copperhead" Democrat Illinois legislature in office in the first part of 1863 and the state's Republican Governor Yates.

73. The *Milton* was a 597-ton sailing ship, the *George C. Collins* a 234-ton sidewheel steamer, and the *Convoy* a screw steamer, all chartered by the Quartermaster Department.

74. Captain Hedley Vicars was a British officer in the Ninety-seventh Regiment during the Crimean War. He was killed during the siege of Sebastopol on March 24, 1855. Hedley was a devout Christian. Catherine Marsh published a biography of his life, including his letters and diary, and an abridged version was published to inspire Confederate soldiers.

75. The United States Christian Commission was an organization established in November 1861 from the YMCA. The organization often established office near army camps where they distributed Bibles and religious tracts, promoted temperance, and provided food and coffee. Dr. Charles H. Brown of the Education Commission of Boston and Mr. John H. Brown of the Port Royal Relief Committee were both at Port Royal working with the former slaves.

76. This was Jean Margaret Davenport Lander, a British native, child prodigy, and noted Shakespearian actress. In 1860 she married the noted frontier explorer Frederick West Lander who later commanded Union forces, including the Thirty-ninth Illinois, in Virginia.

77. Dr. Croshers was James Crozier, first assistant surgeon, Thirty-ninth Illinois.

78. The U.S. Navy ran a repair facility on Land's End and in Station Creek, where the navy located floating machine shops. The *Montauk* was a *Passaic* class monitor, one of seven sent to Port Royal for the attack on Charleston (the *Passaic* class was an improvement over the original *Monitor,* being larger and more seaworthy and carrying heavier guns). Fort McAllister was a Confederate earthen fortification that had been started in 1861 near the mouth of the Ogeechee River at Genesis Point, fifteen miles south of Savannah. The fort came under attack by Union warships seven times in 1862 and 1863, including bombardments on January 27, February 1, February 28, and March 3, 1863.

79. Cole's Island was a strategic island located at the mouth of the Stono River, a river that provided an avenue of attack against Charleston.

80. A tower ironclad, the *Keokuk* had two fixed towers at its bow and stern with one heavy gun in each tower. General Steven's brigade would have been Brigadier General Thomas G. Stevenson's brigade, which occupied Seabrook Island, south of Charleston Harbor.

Volume 5

1. Howell's brigade consisted of the Fifty-sixth New York and the Eighty-fifth Pennsylvania.

2. The SS *New England* was an 852-ton paddlewheel steamer hired by the army.

3. The *Thomas F. Secor* and the *Harriet A. Weed* were 210-ton paddlewheel steamers hired by the army.

4. The village was Legareville, a small summer village located on the eastern side of John's Island overlooking the Stono River. Folly Island, a barrier island located south of Charleston Harbor, was occupied by the Federals on April 5, 1863, and became the staging point for the attack on Charleston that was launched in early July 1863.

5. The Marine artillery consisted of a battery of three twelve-pound howitzers commanded by Lieutenant C. J. Sands.

6. Tantalus was the son of Zeus who dined with mortals, but he abused his guests and was punished by being "tantalized" with water that he could not drink and food he could not eat. The bird that Randolph identified as an albatross is most likely a brown pelican, a common sight along the South Carolina coast.

7. The *New Ironsides* was a 4,120-ton ironclad screw frigate. Fort Sumter was a three-tiered masonry fortification built in the center of Charleston Harbor. Sometimes referred to as Sumpter, it was named for Thomas Sumter, a South Carolina Revolutionary War leader. Along with Fort Moultrie and other Confederate batteries on Sullivan's Island, Fort Sumter controlled the entrance to Charleston Harbor. Between Fort Sumter and Sullivan's Island ran a line of obstructions that included explosive devices known as torpedoes that were designed to explode on contact with a ship's hull.

8. The term should be "en barbette," meaning guns located on the fort's top tier, in the open, positioned to fire over the parapet.

9. The tower ironclad *Keokuk* was struck ninety times during the April 7, 1863, engagement, with nineteen shots piercing it at or below the waterline. It remained afloat throughout the night but sank the following morning off the south-

ern end of Morris Island. Norman Wiard, who served as the U.S. superintendent of ordnance stores during the Civil War, developed Wiard guns, which were made of semi-steel and were produced in two calibers, 2.6 inch and 4.62 inch, the latter being the bore of both a twelve-pound howitzer and a rifled gun while the former was the bore of a six-pound rifle.

10. Morrison Island was a name once applied to Morris Island before the Civil War.

11. Captain Bazell Rodgers of the Sixty-second Ohio was killed on April 13, 1863.

12. Randolph is referring to sand flies *(Culicoides),* small, biting midges that breed primarily in salt marshes. Also called sand fleas, adult sand flies are able to pass through mosquito netting, and like the mosquito only the female bites, as they require blood to mature their eggs. They are attracted to animals with high body temperatures. The sand flies tormented Civil War soldiers serving on the coast of South Carolina.

13. Major Mason was the paymaster. Major Moore and Major Mason, army paymasters, paid the soldiers of the Thirty-ninth Illinois in greenbacks.

14. Israel Vodges was brigadier general and commander of U.S. Forces at Folly Island, Tenth Corps, Department of the South, from April 8 to July 19, 1863.

15. This was John E. W. Hallowell of Company I, Thirty-ninth Illinois.

16. The Federal forces on Folly Island constructed a battery on the southwestern tip of the island overlooking the entrance of the Stono River.

17. Randolph is referring to reports on the Battle of Chancellorsville on May 1–4, 1863, which started well for the Union army but ended in defeat. The chaplain was John C. Gregg of the Sixty-second Ohio.

18. Up until the summer of 1863, Charleston was the South's principal blockade running port.

19. Stonewall Jackson was mortally wounded, accidentally, by fire from his own troops just after routing the Federal right wing at Chancellorsville in early May 1863.

20. Israel S. Baker of Company I, Thirty-ninth Illinois.

21. The vessel was the blockade runner *Ruby,* a 177-foot-long iron sidewheel steamer that ran aground in Lighthouse Inlet on June 11, 1863.

22. Quincy A. Gillmore, brigadier general, was named commander of the Tenth Corps and the Department of the South on June 12, 1863.

23. The USS *Pawnee* was a 1,289-ton screw steam warship. The USS *Commodore McDonough* was a sidewheel New York ferryboat bought by the navy and converted into a warship.

24. On July 9 the gunboats *Pawnee* and *Commodore McDonough,* the monitor *Nantucket,* and the mortar schooner *C. P. Williams* escorted army transports into the Stono River where the soldiers were landed on James Island. The movement was a diversion to pull Confederate attention and troops away from Morris Island.

25. The two regiments were the Fifty-fourth Massachusetts, a regiment of black soldiers raised primarily in the North, and the Second South Carolina, a regiment raised at Port Royal, South Carolina, made up of former slaves from South Carolina, Georgia, and Florida. Colonel James Montgomery, commander of the Second South Carolina, was in charge of a brigade that consisted of both regiments.

26. Gehenna is a reference to the valley of the son of Hinnom, south of Jerusalem, a place of torment or suffering.

27. On the morning of July 11, 1863, the Federals tried to overrun Battery Wagner. The attacking force consisted of the Seventh Connecticut followed by the Seventy-sixth Pennsylvania and Ninth Maine. The assault failed and cost the attackers 400 casualties of which 241 were suffered by the Seventy-sixth Pennsylvania. After this failure, the Federals began building batteries to fire on Battery Wagner in preparation for a second assault. Confederate batteries and forts—including Battery Bee, located on Sullivan's Island across the harbor from Morris Island—fired on the Union lines.

28. On July 12, Federal artillery disabled the steamer *Manigault,* which was operating near Morris Island, and the next night shells set the vessel on fire.

29. Secessionville was a summer resort town located on the eastern side of James Island overlooking the marsh that separates Morris and Folly islands from James Island. The Confederates heavily fortified the area around the village, and batteries were built nearby to fire on the Union positions.

30. George C. Strong, brigadier general, commanded the forces that landed on Morris Island on July 10, as well as the July 11 attack on Battery Wagner, and also the brigade that spearheaded the July 18 assault on Battery Wagner, in which he was mortally wounded. While on Morris Island, the Federals received word of the crucial Union victories at Gettysburg (which Randolph calls Emmitsburg, Pennsylvania) and Vicksburg, Mississippi.

31. Clemens F. Steele was lieutenant colonel of the Sixty-second Ohio. On the night of July 18, 1863, the Federals, after an all-day bombardment, launched a massive assault against Battery Wagner. Spearheaded by the Fifty-fourth Massachusetts, the attackers managed to enter the fort but were driven out by the Confederates and forced to retreat. The attack cost the Federals 1,515 casualties out of 5,000 men engaged.

32. USS *Paul Jones* was an 863-ton sidewheel gunboat. Fort Johnson was a Confederate harbor fortification located on the northeastern tip of James Island.

33. After the failure of the July 18 attack on Battery Wagner, the Federals started siege lines toward Battery Wagner and began erecting breaching batteries in the center of Morris Island. Two of these works, Battery Brown and the Naval Battery, contained two eight-inch Parrotts, rifled cannons capable of firing shots that weighed two hundred pounds. Randolph is probably referring to Battery Brown.

34. In early August, reinforcements for the Federal army began to arrive from North Carolina including Brigadier General Robert S. Foster's brigade of the 13th Indiana, 112th New York, and 169th New York.

35. On August 17, 1863, at 5:00 a.m., the Federals opened a bombardment on Fort Sumter, which lasted from August 17 until August 23, 1863. Some five thousand shot and shell were fired into Fort Sumter.

36. On August 17, fleet captain for the Federal squadron Captain George W. Rodgers received permission to leave the monitor *Weehawken,* which was serving as the squadron's flagship, to take command of a vessel he formerly captained, the monitor *Catskill.* During a bombardment of Battery Wagner, Rodgers was in the ship's pilothouse when a Confederate artillery bolt struck the pilothouse, causing iron plates to break off and striking and killing Rodgers.

37. Just before the bombardment of Fort Sumter, the Federals began the construction of a unique battery in the marsh between Morris and James islands. Termed the Marsh Battery, it was designed to fire shells seventy-nine hundred yards into Charleston. Soldiers from the Thirty-ninth Illinois helped construct the bat-

tery and mount its cannon, an eight-inch Parrott that a member of the regiment called the Swamp Angel, referring to the fact that he had helped build a pulpit from which a swamp angel could preach. Randolph is comparing the quick construction of the Marsh Battery to the miraculous appearance of a gourd, placed by God over Jonah to give him shade, in the book of Jonah 4:6.

38. The Confederate battery at Cumming's Point was named Battery Gregg.

39. On the night of August 26, a Union attack overran Confederate rifle pits two hundred yards from Battery Wagner.

40. This was Henry A. Purviance, lieutenant colonel of the Eighty-fifth Pennsylvania.

41. Throughout the campaign the Confederates made extensive use of explosive devices known as torpedoes. They were used as land mines around Charleston and were also placed in the water throughout the harbor. They could be detonated by electric current or by striking an ignition point on the exterior of the torpedo. On occasion the Confederates would float torpedoes down the Stono River hoping to sink Union vessels. They were also mounted on spars and placed on the bow of vessels ranging from rowboats to blockade runners, ironclads, and submarines.

Volume 6

1. On the evening of September 6, 1863, five companies of the Thirty-ninth Illinois were serving as the grand guard, protecting the sappers in the trenches before Battery Wagner. A deserter came into the lines and told Lieutenant Colonel Mann that the fort was being evacuated. Word was sent back to General Gillmore, who directed Mann to send in five "resolute" men to ascertain if Wagner was evacuated (Clark, *History,* 146). The men entered the work just as the last Confederates were leaving. The fuses lit to blow up Wagner's magazines were put out and the men reported Wagner abandoned. The rest of the men from Thirty-ninth Illinois occupied the fort. For their actions the five soldiers received a thirty-day furlough from General Gillmore. General Terry was Alfred Howe Terry, brigadier general commanding U.S. forces on Morris Island.

2. Colonel Vorhees was Alvin C. Voris, colonel, Sixty-seventh Ohio.

3. Black Island was a marsh island located between Morris and James islands. The Federals established a battery on Black Island to fire on Confederate works located on James Island.

4. Joseph Woodruff, captain of Company K, Thirty-ninth Illinois, was mortally wounded by a shell fragment on the night of September 23, 1863. He died two hours later. Woodruff was well respected within the regiment, and after his death the regimental officers passed a resolution honoring the captain.

5. On the night of October 5, 1863, the ironclad frigate *New Ironsides* was attacked by the Confederate torpedo boat *David,* which detonated a spar torpedo against the ironclad, but, although the attack caused considerable excitement, no great damage was done to the *New Ironsides*. The *David* managed to escape and return to Charleston.

6. After its capture, Battery Wagner was rebuilt by the Federals, with artillery directed toward Charleston Harbor and James Island, and was renamed Fort Strong in honor of Brigadier General George C. Strong, who was mortally wounded during the July 18, 1863, attack. Battery Gregg was also rebuilt and oriented to fire on Fort Sumter, Charleston, and other Confederate positions. It was renamed Fort Putnam

in honor of Colonel Haldiman S. Putnam, who was killed during the July 18, 1863, assault on Battery Wagner.

7. On October 26, 1863, the Federals opened their second great bombardment of Fort Sumter. The shelling, primarily from Morris Island with support from the navy, lasted for forty-one days and nights. The Federals fired 18,677 projectiles into the fort, reducing it to a pile of rubble.

8. John Craig, Company I, Thirty-ninth Illinois, died of disease on Folly Island, on November 23, 1863.

9. The salute celebrated General Grant's victory in the Chattanooga Campaign, which culminated with the November 25, 1863, victory at Missionary Ridge.

10. SS *Monohausett* was a 465-ton paddlewheel steamer chartered by the army.

11. Brigadier General Truman Seymour commanded the July 18, 1863, attack on Battery Wagner. Wounded in the attack, he later returned and took command of the U.S. forces on Morris Island from October 18 to November 10, 1863. He then commanded the district of Hilton Head from December 6, 1863, to February 5, 1864.

12. The soldiers' cemetery on Hilton Head was located in the north central part of the island just outside the entrenchments that surrounded the army's headquarters complex. The graves were later moved to the National Cemetery in Beaufort, S.C. Today the site of the graveyard is located along Union Cemetery Road.

13. This was Cyrus F. Knapp, lieutenant, Company D, Thirty-ninth Illinois.

14. Joseph D. Walker was former sergeant major and later adjutant of the Thirty-ninth Illinois.

15. The hospital on Hilton Head was known as the Hospital Quadrangle. It was 320 feet square, with an interior courtyard, and was the largest structure on the island, containing 60,000 square feet of floor space and 300 beds.

16. Mrs. Major Dorman, a nurse, and her husband, a paymaster, both remain unidentified.

17. The SS *Arago* was a 2,240-ton paddlewheel steamer chartered by the army.

18. On January 28, 1864, the Thirty-ninth Illinois left Hilton Head to begin their leave.

19. In early February 1864, the Federals sent an expedition under General Truman Seymour to Jacksonville, Florida, to establish a sanctuary for Unionists, disrupt Confederate supplies, and possibly establish a loyal government. Jacksonville was occupied on February 7, 1864.

20. Capt. Pratt was Captain Thomas J. Platt of the Sixty-second Ohio. Braddock's Point is the southwestern tip of Hilton Head Island.

21. The SS *Fulton* was a 2,307-ton paddlewheel steamer chartered by the army. After the occupation of Jacksonville, Florida, the Federals began a movement toward Tallahassee. On February 20, 1864, at Olustee, a Federal column numbering fifty-five hundred encountered Confederates numbering fifty-two hundred. In an all-day battle the Federals were defeated and forced back to Jacksonville.

22. The *New South* was a newspaper published at the town of Port Royal on Hilton Head Island beginning in March 1862. The founding editor was H. J. Windsor, who was later succeeded by Joseph H. Sears.

23. Spanish Wells was a plantation and Union picket-post site on Hilton Head overlooking Calibogue Sound.

24. In April 1864, black soldiers were serving as the provost guard on Hilton Head Island. Difficulties occurred in the Department of the South when black soldiers tried to arrest white soldiers.

25. In October 1863, the Sixth Connecticut received two hundred replacements. Three of these men, German-born Henry Schumaker of Company C, Henry Stark of Company E, and Gustav Hoofan of Company B, deserted their post. They were captured and placed in the provost guardhouse on Hilton Head. The three escaped, stole a boat, and were caught in Ossabaw Sound south of Hilton Head. They were court-martialed and sentenced to be shot. Though in shackles they managed to escape again in a boat and reached Wassaw Sound before a naval picket boat discovered them. A review of the trial records revealed that Hoofan's name had been put down as Huffman by the judge advocate. The commander of the Sixth Connecticut used this error to get Hoofan spared and returned to duty. Schumaker and Stark were executed on April 17 by a firing party from the Sixth Connecticut in the presence of all available troops present for duty on Hilton Head Island.

26. The SS *Baltimore* was a 252-ton screw steamer chartered by the army.

27. The SS *Mississippi* was a 2,008-ton iron-hulled screw steamer chartered by the army.

28. Major General Benjamin Butler commanded the Army of the James. Of the Tenth Corps, Army of the James, Brigadier General Adelbert Ames commanded the Third Division, Brigadier General Robert S. Foster commanded the Second Division, and Brigadier General Alfred H. Terry commanded the First Division.

29. The SS *Convoy* was a 410-ton screw steamer owned by the Quartermaster Bureau. The *Iolas* was a 180-ton paddlewheel steamer chartered by the Quartermaster Bureau.

30. The USS *Roanoke* was built as a wooden steam frigate. During the war it was cut down and converted into a triple-turreted monitor, though unlike the other monitor-class vessels, it had a high freeboard. The USS *Atlanta* was a former 1,006-ton Confederate ironclad ram that was captured by the U.S. Navy near Savannah, Georgia, on June 17, 1863, and taken into the U.S. Navy. The *Atlanta* had been originally the blockade runner *Fingal* before being converted by the Confederates into an ironclad ram.

31. Fort Powhattan was the site of a fort built on the James River before the War of 1812 to defend the water approaches to Richmond. After the War of 1812, the work was superseded by Fort Monroe and Fort Calhoun, which guarded the entrance into Hampton Roads and the James River. Fort Powhattan fell into disrepair, though the Confederates used it for a time as a battery site. Since Fort Powhattan was too exposed to enemy attack, the Confederates placed their main defensive works on the James River at Drewry's Bluff.

32. On July 15, 1864, the Eighteenth Corps, which was made from the Departments of North Carolina and Virginia, became part of Butler's Army of the James. Major General William F. "Baldy" Smith commanded the corps.

33. This was Major Lewis Butler, Sixty-seventh Ohio.

34. Randolph is describing the movements leading up to and events of the Battle of Drewry's Bluff, Virginia. See the introduction to volume 6.

35. George Lonebarger, Company I, Thirty-ninth Illinois.

36. Leroy A. Baker, captain, Company A, Thirty-ninth Illinois.

37. On May 16, 1864, of the Thirty-ninth Illinois, Lewis Hurley, Company I, was killed; James W. Wightman, captain, Company C, was mortally wounded; and Hiram M. Phillips, captain, Company I, was wounded and captured.

38. Andrew W. Wheeler was captain, Company K, Thirty-ninth Illinois. Lesmore D. Kidder, first lieutenant, Company B, Thirty-ninth Illinois, was wounded. Elisha Kingsburg, second lieutenant, Company E, Thirty-ninth Illinois, was wounded and had an arm amputated.

39. This was the Battle of Ware Bottom Church, on May 20, 1864. Lieutenant Colonel Mann was wounded in the left leg, and Captain Baker of Company A, the senior officer left on the field, took command of the regiment. The Confederate brigadier general William Walker became separated from his command and appeared in front of the Union line. He tried to pretend he was a Union officer, but the bluff did not work and a volley from the Federals killed his horse and wounded him in the arm, side, and leg. He was taken prisoner. The wound to his left leg was so severe that the leg had to be amputated.

40. From May 23 to May 27, General Lee and General Grant fought an engagement along the North Anna River, where Grant narrowly missed being defeated in detail by the Confederates. James Burrill, second lieutenant, Company A, Thirty-ninth Illinois, was wounded on May 25, 1864.

41. During the night of May 28 and the morning of May 29, General Smith was sent by transport with the First Division, Eighteenth Corps, and the Second and Third divisions, Tenth Corps, to join General Grant's forces moving against Richmond from the northeast.

42. Brigadier August Valentine Kautz's raids destroyed, on the Richmond and Danville Railroad, the stations at Coalfield, Powhattan, and Chula; on the Southside Railroad—a line that ran from Petersburg to Lynchburg—the stations at Black's and White's, Wilson's, and Wellsville; and track, rolling stock, and supplies.

Volume 7

1. This was Al C. Sweetser, first lieutenant, Company B, Thirty-ninth Illinois.

2. George O. Snowden, captain, Company D, Thirty-ninth Illinois.

3. Oscar F. Rudd, Company G, Thirty-ninth Illinois, died July 11, 1864, at Fort Monroe Hospital. General Robert S. Foster commanded at this time the First Division, Tenth Corps, Army of the James.

4. The forces that attacked the Federals were General George Pickett's and General Charles W. Field's divisions from General James Longstreet's First Corps, Army of Northern Virginia. At this time Longstreet, who had been badly wounded in the Battle of the Wilderness on May 6, 1864, was not in command of the corps, which was being led by Lieutenant General Richard Heron Anderson.

5. The pontoon bridge crossed the James River at Deep Bottom at the northern end of Jones Neck, a peninsula that pushed out into the James River northeast of Butler's lines at Bermuda Hundred. The Federals fortified the northern end of the pontoon bridge, giving them a position from which they could easily move troops from Bermuda Hundred to positions north of the James and back again. Soon a second pontoon bridge was added at Deep Bottom.

6. Point of Rocks, also referred to as Broadway Landing, was a site on the Appomattox River, about two and a half miles from its junction with the James River, where pontoon bridges crossed the Appomattox and gave the Federals the ability to shift men between Bermuda Hundred, City Point, and the Petersburg front. The SS *General Howard* was a 158-ton paddlewheel steamer hired by the army.

Wilcox Landing was the site of the pontoon bridge used by Grant's army to cross the James River and advance on Petersburg.

7. In late July, General Philip Sheridan's cavalry corps returned from a raid against the Virginia Central Railroad. Sheridan was initially ordered to cross the James River with his nine-hundred-vehicle supply train at Bermuda Hundred, but Confederate cavalry turned him back. Union troops were sent to protect various crossings along the James River. Sheridan's command eventually crossed at Douthard's Landing and was ferried across the James on July 25 and 26. City Point, after its occupation by General Butler's forces in early May 1864, became General Grant's headquarters during the siege of Petersburg. The town also became the Federals' logistical and supply center for the campaign.

8. W. W. Spencer, sergeant of Company G, Thirty-ninth Illinois, was wounded on July 2 and died on July 5, 1864. The Mower General Army Hospital was located at Chestnut Hill, Philadelphia, and was one of the largest U.S. Army hospitals used in the Civil War. It covered twenty-seven acres and contained thirty-six hundred hospital beds.

9. Randolph is referring to the Nineteenth Corps. A portion of the Nineteenth Corps, which arrived from New Orleans in mid-July, was briefly camped at Bermuda Hundred and Petersburg before being transferred to Washington, D.C.

10. Major General David B. Birney was made commander of the Tenth Corps on July 23, 1864.

11. Petersburg received the nickname "Cockade City" during the War of 1812 because of the bravery of the Petersburg Volunteers who wore a rosette in their hats.

12. Randolph volunteered to assist in the digging of Dutch Gap Canal, a 174-yard passage through a neck of land called Dutch Gap that would allow Union warships to pass around enemy obstructions and batteries at Trent's Reach, a narrow point in the James River at the northern end of Butler's Bermuda Hundred lines. The work was supervised by Captain Peter S. Michie and continued from August 10 to December 30, 1864, when the bulkhead at the northern end was opened by an explosion of twelve thousand pounds of powder. Final completion did not occur until April 1865, however, which was too late for military use. After the war the canal was improved and became the standard shipping route for vessels on the James River.

13. On August 12, Confederate ironclads from the Richmond Squadron shelled Dutch Gap in an unsuccessful attempt to disrupt the Federals ("Butler's Navies," or "navigators") there. The Confederate vessels were also in a position to fire on Union vessels in the James River east of Dutch Gap.

14. P. M. Holloway would have been Philip M. Halloway, Company I, Thirty-ninth Illinois.

15. The movement of the Second and Tenth corps occurred at the conclusion of the Battle of Second Deep Bottom, August 13–20, 1864.

16. Captain James W. Lyon of the Fourth Rhode Island served on detached duty as an assistant engineer, Department of Virginia.

17. Henry M. Hardenburgh of Company G, Thirty-ninth Illinois, captured the regimental colors of the Eighth Alabama on August 8, 1864, at the Battle of Deep Bottom. For his bravery he was promoted in the field to lieutenant in the U.S. colored troops, but before he could receive his commission and assignment he was killed on August 28 in front of Petersburg. Thomas W. Shinkle, corporal, Company I, Thirty-ninth Illinois, was wounded on August 28, 1864, in front of Petersburg and later killed on April 2, 1865, during the attack on Fort Gregg, Petersburg, Virginia.

18. John W. Rapp was killed on August 29, 1864, in front of Petersburg.

19. The man executed was Private John Rowley of Company D, Seventh Connecticut, who had shot Jerome Dupoy during the Battle of Olustee, Florida. The two men, German substitutes, could speak little English. They served in the same company and had quarreled before the battle. Dupoy had cut Rowley and Rowley swore vengeance. During the confusion of battle, Rowley shot Dupoy in the head, thinking his deed would go unseen in the midst of the battle. The incident was reported, but the company commander had no proof that the shooting was intentional. However, unrest among other members of the company caused Rowley to be confined in the guardhouse. While imprisoned he suffered from visions of ghosts and eventually confessed to the murder. He was tried, found guilty, and sentenced to death.

20. The Confederates evacuated Atlanta on September 1, 1864, and the city was occupied the next day by elements of Sherman's army.

21. An unnamed member of Company I, Sixth Connecticut, was marched through the brigade with the drum corps playing the Rogue's March.

22. The SS *Thomas Morgan* was a 480-ton iron-hulled paddlewheel steamer. Randolph's companions were George Riddle and Philip M. Halloway, Company I, Thirty-ninth Illinois.

23. Point Lookout, Maryland, is located where the Potomac River meets the Chesapeake Bay. It was the location of a large Federal prisoner of war camp.

24. At the Capitol rotunda, the *Embarkation of the Pilgrims* by Antonio Capellano was added in 1844, and the *Baptism of Pocahontas* by John Chapman was added in 1840. At the Navy Yard, the two bronze guns were Spanish twenty-seven-pounders cast in Barcelona, Spain, in 1788, which had armed two gunboats captured by Stephen Decatur at Tripoli on August 3, 1804. They are still on display at Leutze Park at the Washington Navy Yard.

25. In 1860, during James Buchanan's term as president of the United States, the first diplomatic delegation from Japan arrived and presented the president with gifts. Buchanan had the presents deposited in the Patent Office. Mr. Townsend Harris was the first U.S. envoy to Japan, serving from 1856 to 1861.

26. The Battle Monument, completed in 1825, commemorates the men who died in the defense of Baltimore during the 1814 Battle of North Point. The Washington Monument, a 160-foot column topped by a statue of George Washington, was completed in 1829.

27. The Satterlee General Hospital in Philadelphia was one of the largest military hospitals in the world. Covering sixteen acres, it had twenty-one wards and forty-five hundred hospital beds. Mr. Goltra remains unidentified.

28. The Fairmount Water Works located on the Schuylkill River was designed by Frederick Graff and completed in 1815. The neoclassical-style complex was a popular tourist attraction throughout the nineteenth century. The Eastern State Penitentiary was designed by John Haviland and opened in 1829. The massive stone structure covered eleven acres. It was completed in 1836 with 450 individual cells designed to place each inmate into solitary confinement so they would become regretful and seek repentance for their criminal habits. Like the Fairmount Water Works, the Penitentiary was a popular tourist site. Founded in 1848, Girard College was established by a bequest from Stephen Girard to serve as a school for poor, orphaned boys. The SS *General Hooker* was a fifty-one-ton screw steamer.

29. Independence Hall, the U.S. Mint, the Academy of Fine Arts, and Laurel Hill Cemetery were all popular tourist attractions before, during, and after the Civil War. Independence Hall was completed in 1753 to serve as the Pennsylvania State House. Both the Continental Congress and the Constitutional Convention met in the building. In 1830 the Greek revival architect John Haviland had altered the building Randolph visited. The U.S. Mint was the second to be built in Philadelphia and was completed in 1833. It was replaced by a larger mint in 1901. The Pennsylvania Academy of Fine Arts was established in Philadelphia in 1805 and is America's first art museum and school of fine arts. The work *Christ Rejected,* painted in 1814, can still be seen at the academy. The artist Benjamin West was elected the first honorary member of the Pennsylvania Fine Arts Academy in 1805. Laurel Hill Cemetery was established in 1836 along the Schuylkill River.

Notes on Sources

A number of sources were used in compiling the notes for the journal. The most vital resource was Charles M. Clark's *The History of the Thirty-ninth Illinois Volunteer Veteran Infantry (Yates phalanx) in the War of the Rebellion.* Clark was the regiment's surgeon and as such gives an interesting perspective to the regiment's history, often emphasizing medical care, the treatment of wounds, and the soldiers' overall health. The book contains a roster of the regiment's officers and soldiers as well as antidotal information. Other useful sources for Illinois units and soldiers can be found on the Web pages for the Illinois GenWeb Project and the National Park Service's Civil War Soldiers and Sailors System. Also a great deal of information can be gleaned from the standard *War of the Rebellion: Official Records of the Union and Confederate Armies,* especially from the regimental reports of the Thirty-ninth Illinois and its companion units.

Information used in the notes was also found in general reference works, including Stewart Sifakis, *Who Was Who in the Civil War;* Patricia L. Faust, editor, *Historical Times Illustrated Encyclopedia of the Civil War;* Mark Mayo Boatner III, *The Civil War Dictionary;* Richard N. Current, editor in chief, *Encyclopedia of the Confederacy;* and David C. Roller and Robert W. Twyman, *The Encyclopedia of Southern History.* Frances H. Kennedy, editor, *The Civil War Battlefield Guide,* provides a succinct and comprehensive overview of campaigns and battles. A solid overview of armies and their organization can be found in Francis A. Lord's *They Fought for the Union.*

For specific engagements and regional studies, see Robert W. Johannsen, *Stephen A. Douglas;* Alexander S. Webb, *The Peninsula: McClellan's Campaign of 1862;* Gary L. Ecelbarger, *Frederick W. Lander: The Great Natural American Soldiers;* Brian S. Wills, *The War Hits Home: The Civil War in Southeastern Virginia;* Stephen R. Wise, *Gate of Hell: The Campaign for Charleston Harbor, 1863;* and Andrew A. Humphreys, *The Virginia Campaign of '64 and '65: The Army of the Potomac and the Army of the James.* The editor was allowed to use the manuscript "The New South's First City: Occupied Beaufort, South Carolina, 1861 to 1865," by John Martin Davis, which covers activity in the Department of the South. Useful for the South Carolina entries are Theodore Rosengarten, *Tombee: Portrait of a Cotton Planter; Letters from Port Royal,* edited by Elizabeth Ware Pearson; and *Letters and Diary of Laura M. Towne,* edited by Rupert Sargent Holland. Also quite helpful were the pertinent sections from the classic compilation found in *Battles and Leaders of the Civil War.*

Information on vessels was found in *Civil War Naval Chronology;* William Lytle and Forrest Holdcamper, *Merchant Steam Vessels of the United States 1790–1868;* Charles Dana Gibson and E. Kay Gibson, compilers, *Dictionary of Transports and Combatant Vessels, Steam and Sail, Employed by the Union Army, 1861–1868;* and Stephen R. Wise, *Lifeline of the Confederacy: Blockade Running during the Civil War.*

Helpful were regimental studies or works that related to units serving in close proximity with the Thirty-ninth Illinois. This included W. W. H. Davis, *History of the 104th Pennsylvania;* Daniel Eldridge, *The Third New Hampshire Regiment;* Henry F. Little, *The Seventh Regiment;* George H. Stowits, *History of the One-Hundredth Regiment of New York State Volunteers;* Stephen W. Walkley, Jr., *History of the Seventh*

Connecticut Volunteer Infantry: Hawley's Brigade, Terry's Division, Tenth Army Corps, 1861–1865; Charles K. Caldwell, *The Old Sixth Regiment: Its War Record, 1861–65;* and *A Citizen-Soldier's Civil War: The Letters of Brevet Major General Alvin C. Voris,* edited by Jerome Mushkat.

★ ★ ★

Battles and Leaders of the Civil War, 4 vols. South Brunswick, New York: Thomas Yoseloff, 1956.

Boatner, Mark Mayo, III. *The Civil War Dictionary.* New York: David McKay, 1973.

Caldwell, Charles K. *The Old Sixth Regiment: Its War Record, 1861–65.* New Haven: Tittle, Morehouse & Taylor, 1875.

Civil War Naval Chronology, 1861–1865. Washington, D.C.: Naval History Division, 1971.

Clark, Charles M. *The History of the Thirty-ninth Illinois Volunteer Veteran Infantry (Yates phalanx) in the War of the Rebellion.* Chicago: Veteran Association of the Regiment, 1889.

Current, Richard N., ed. *Encyclopedia of the Confederacy.* New York: Simon and Schuster, 1993.

Davis, W. W. H. *History of the 104th Pennsylvania.* Philadelphia: Rogers, 1886.

Denison, Frederick. *Shot and Shell: The Third Rhode Island Heavy Artillery Regiment in the Rebellion 1861–1865.* Providence: J. A. & R. A. Reid, 1879.

Ecelbarger, Gary L. *Frederick W. Lander: The Great Natural American Soldiers.* Baton Rouge: Louisiana State University Press, 2000.

Eldridge, Daniel. *The Third New Hampshire Regiment.* Boston: E. B. Stillings, 1893.

Faust, Patricia L., ed. *Historical Times Illustrated Encyclopedia of the Civil War.* New York: Harper and Row, 1986.

Gibson, Charles Dana, and E. Kay Gibson, comps. *Dictionary of Transports and Combatant Vessels, Steam and Sail, Employed by the Union Army, 1861–1868.* Camden, Maine: Ensign Press, 1995.

Holland, Rupert Sargent, ed. *Letters and Diary of Laura M. Towne.* New York: Negro Universities Press, 1969.

Humphreys, Andrew A. *The Virginia Campaign of '64 and '65: The Army of the Potomac and the Army of the James.* New York: Charles Scribner's Sons, 1885.

Illinois Genealogy and History. *Illinois in the Civil War.* www.rootsweb.com/%7Eilcivilw/

Johannsen, Robert W. *Stephen A. Douglas.* Champaign: University of Illinois Press, 1997.

Kennedy, Frances H., ed. *The Civil War Battlefield Guide.* New York: Houghton Mifflin, 1998.

Little, Henry F. *The Seventh Regiment.* Concord: J. Evan, 1896.

Lord, Francis A. *They Fought for the Union.* New York: Bonanza Books, 1960.

Lytle, William M., and Forrest R. Holdcamper, comps. *Merchant Steam Vessels of the United States, 1790–1868.* Staten Island: The Steamship Historical Society of New York, 1975.

Mushkat, Jerome, ed. *A Citizen-Soldier's Civil War: The Letters of Brevet Major General Alvin C. Voris.* DeKalb: Northern Illinois University Press, 2002.

National Park System. *Civil War Soldiers and Sailors System.* www.itd.nps.gov/cwss/index.html.

Official Records of the Union and Confederate Navies in the War of the Rebellion. 32 vols. Washington, D.C.: Government Printing Office, 1901.

Pearson, Elizabeth Ware, ed. *Letters from Port Royal.* New York: Arno Press, 1969.

Roller, David C., and Robert W. Twyman. *The Encyclopedia of Southern History.* Baton Rouge: Louisiana State University, 1979.

Rosengarten, Theodore. *Tombee: Portrait of a Cotton Planter.* New York: William Morrow, 1986.

Sifakis, Stewart. *Who Was Who in the Civil War.* New York: Facts on File, 1988.

Stowits, George H. *History of the One-Hundredth Regiment of New York State Volunteers.* Buffalo: Matthews and Warren, 1870.

Walkley, Stephen W., Jr. *History of the Seventh Connecticut Volunteer Infantry: Hawley's Brigade, Terry's Division, Tenth Army Corps, 1861–1865.* Hartford: N.p., 1905.

War of the Rebellion: Official Records of the Union and Confederate Armies. 128 vols. Washington, D.C.: Government Printing Office, 1889–1901.

Webb, Alexander S. *The Peninsula: McClellan's Campaign of 1862.* New York: Charles Scribner's Sons, 1885.

Wills, Brian S. *The War Hits Home: The Civil War in Southeastern Virginia.* Charlottesville: University Press of Virginia, 2001.

Wise, Stephen R. *Gate of Hell: Campaign for Charleston Harbor, 1863.* Columbia: University of South Carolina Press, 1994.

———. *Lifeline of the Confederacy: Blockade Running during the Civil War.* Columbia: University of South Carolina Press, 1988.

Index

Military Unit Index

Subject Index